G000112455

The Right to Self

The Sri Lankan Tamil National Question

Helena J Whall

Tamil Information Centre

The right to self-determination:
The Sri Lankan Tamil National Question

Published by:
Tamil Information Centre
Thamil House
720 Romford Road
London E12 6BT

© Tamil Information Centre, 1995

ISBN 1 85201 005 3

Design and layout by Vasi Krishna
Cover design by Graham Gaunt and Krishnarajah

Printed by:
Set Line Data Ltd.
61 Ewer Street
London SE1 0NR

The march toward self-determination can be done only by a people with democratic aspirations and goals, or it is not worth the effort.

Edward W Said, *The Politics of Dispossession*

Contents

Preface

This scholarly study by Helena J Whall examines the dynamics of self-determination as an international legal norm and the dilemmas of its application in specific situations. This comprehensive research provides useful insights into the interplay of countervailing forces which compete in either broadening or limiting the meaning and scope of this universally accepted principle of Internationa Law. It highlights the fact that international covenants and conventions do not guarantee implementation of such principles and norms. As a matter of fact, shifting regional and global alliances and changing perceptions of national interests, either promote the ideals embodied in such norms or impede and obstruct their implememtation.

Though this study is focused on the Tamil minority's quest for self-determination in Sri Lanka, its significance spans across the national, regional and global landscape. Indeed, the Tamils' struggle has some historical and geo-political nexus with other similar aspirations in South Asia, e.g., the Christians in Nagaland, the Sikhs in the Punjab, and the Muslims in Kashmir. Especially valuable is Helena's indepth historical perspective on the origin, infancy and steady growth of this dynamic principle, which has come to baffle its most enthusiastic champions in the South-East (like India and former Soviet Union), as well as its lukewarm supporters in the North-West (like Great Britain and Canada).

While the era of Western colonialism has almost come to an end the principle of self-determination has not lost its talismatic appeal. As it were, on the demise of the old colonial empires, many polyethnic super-states have emerged, particularly in Asia and Africa. In many of these newly independent countries of Asia and Africa - as well as in some old countries like Great Britain, Spain and Canada - there is a *prima facie* inherent conflict between preponderant majorities' claim to territorial integrity of the existing polyethnic states (unwittingly called nation-states) and national minorities' quest for self-determination in the form of autonomous or independent homelands. To be sure, these "nations within nations" and "maps within maps", are occupying the national agenda of many countries.

It is imperative that the prevailing paradigms of national unity and territorial integrity evolve a *modus vivendi* with the dyanmics of distant ethno-cultural entities through some form of, what Helena calls, internal self-determination. These competing forces of distinct ethno-cultural identities refuse to accept the status of marginalisation within the existing polyethnic superstates. As pointed out by Hurst Hannum, the concept of self-determination has been virtually ignored "as former colonies have accepted without question the boundaries drawn by the colonial powers, despite the fact that those boudaries often bear no relevance to ethnic, religious, or linguistic realities."[1]

The ruling elites in many newly independent countries believe that cosmetic federalism and economic development would eventually result in the assimilation of ethno-cultural minorities or reduce them to virtual redundancy. However, the empirical evidence leads to a different direction. To be sure, there are many determined ethno-cultural minorities who refuse to be wished away or bombed out of existence. For instance, the "Basques, Samis, Tamils, Sikhs, Kurds, Maoris, Miskitos, Corsicans, Quebecois, Karens, and scores of other ethnic, religious, or national groups have rejected absorption into the majority political culture."[2]

The modern territorial state extracts, regulates and allocates more resources than any other political entity in recorded history. By the same token, its power to distribute patronage and benefits and inflict deprivations and punishments has increased enormously. Hence, the competition for access to these resources and opportunities among preponderant majorities and national minorities has been intensified. In addition, there is an enormous growth in the lethal power of the modern territorial state. This brute force is frequently used to crush any demand of a national minority for sharing power, regional autonomy, or independence.

Even some numerical majorities, like the native Africans in South Africa and the Bengalis in East Pakistan (now Bangladesh) encountered state oppression when they demanded a fair share in political power. Bangladesh is a classic example, where a peaceful movement for a genuine autonomy met the brutal military response from the ruling regime in Islamabad (Pakistan). It culminated in a colossal refugee problem, India's military intervention, dismemberment of Pakistan, and the birth of a bleeding new nation of Bangladesh. The human and economic cost of this tragedy was staggering for Pakistan, India, and Bangladesh. Helena's concept of internal self-determination would have saved not only the contesting parties from this tragic experience, but also the international community which had to share the cost of this political insanity. One would have expected India and Sri Lanka to learn some lessons from the experince of Bangladesh in dealing with the aspirations of the Tamils, and the Sikhs repectively. However, the evidence thus far indicates no qualitiative difference in Pakistan's handling of the Bangladesh crisis, Sri Lanka'a dealing with the Tamil aspirations, or India's response to similar situations in Punjab, Kashmir and Nagaland. Both Sri Lanka and India have mishandled relatively manageable political and ethno-cultural problems and pushed them to a full-scale insurgency.

The bloody conflict in the Balkans is another unfortunate case in point. The leadership of the Supra-Serbian Empire (popularly known as Yugoslavia), which is the product of an imperial political culture, could not handle the challenge of ethno-cultural aspirations for self-determination. They have missed the opportunity of transforming this empire into a commonwealth of free nations, with open frontiers and free trade. They could have saved themselves from this mutual suicide and spared the rest of the world from pain and anguish of this ongoing genocide. In this context, the Western countries have exhibited the bankruptcy of leadership. They have not even paid a conceptual lip-service to the principle of self-determination enshrined in the UN Charter and reaffirmed in subsequent covenants and conventions.

On the other hand, the civility and political sophistication demonstrated by the Czechs and the Slovaks provide some hope tht a peaceful transformation is in the realm of possibility. Back in the 1960's, Malaysia and Singapore had shown a similar political maturity when they parted company without a shooting war. If two ethno-cultural communities cannot live together, instead of bledding each other to death, they can try to live as neighbours. It involves the transformation of a political culture of dominance to a political arrangement of sharing and co-operation. By transforming the hegemonic state structure, the *prima facie* conflict between the principle of self-determination and the notion of territorial integrity can be resolved. Political entities can enjoy independence at ther vertical level and maintain and develop horizontal co-operation for regional economic development with open frontiers and free trade.

In South Asia, in particular, the way out of this tragic situation lies in the transformation of the existing imperial systems, inherited from the British, into a South Asian Commonwealth of free nations, with closer economic and cultural ties - somewhat like the European Community. The South Asian Commonwealth will improve the human rights environment in the region. It would save Sri Lanka, India, Pakistan, and Bangladesh significant resources presently consumed by the gigantic paramilitary and security establishments for protecting the imperial fortresses. In this new political and ethno-cultural landscape the sanctity of human life would take precedence over the sanctity of existing and somewhat arbitrary boundaries; and the politics of compassion would put a human face on the politics of cynicism.

Finally, Helena's imaginative approach greatly facilitates an objective understanding of the status of self-determination as an essential norm of International Law. Her judicious application of this norm in the case of the Tamils in Sri Lanka has far-reaching ramifications not only for South Asia's ethno-cultural mosaic, but also for the rest of the world.

Gurcharan Singh, Ph.D.
Director, International Studies Department
Marymount Manhattan College, New York
January 1995

Notes

1 Hurst Hannum, "The Limits of Sovereignty and Majority Rule: Minorities, Indigenous Peoples, and the Right to Autonomy," in: New Directions in Human Rights, edited by Ellen Lutz, et. al. (Philadelphia: University of Pennsylvania Press), 1989, p.14.

2 Ibid.

Acknowledgements

This study is the result of a request made on behalf of the Tamil Information Centre (TIC), London, to amend and up-date (and in the event, entirely re-write), a dissertation that I submitted for the MA (Area Studies: South Asia), SOAS, London University, in the summer of 1991.

I wish to express my thanks to Mr. V. Varadakumar (Director of TIC) and Mr Mayan Vije (Director of TIC) for supporting me throughout the entire preparation, and without whom this study would never have seen the light of day. I want to thank all those members of staff at TIC and at the Tamil Refugee Action Group (TRAG), London, for making my research possible and moreover enjoyable. My appreciation goes to Vasi Krishna for design and layout of the book. My gratitude also extends to those members of staff at SOAS, who encouraged me in this academic endeavour, namely, Mr. M. Lau, Dr. V. Menski and Dr. D. Taylor. I also wish to acknowledge Rohit Barot and Mr V. Hewitt at Bristol University, who were responsible for initiating my interest in the Indian sub-continent.

My warm-hearted thanks must also go to my family and friends who have shown the greatest of patience and no end of encouragement. Lastly, but by no means least, I wish to thank all of those who have shared with me their experiences in Sri Lanka, and without whom I would not have begun to understand the hopes and fears of the Tamil-speaking people, for whom this book is dedicated.

Helena J Whall
August 1994
London

List of tables

List of maps

Abbreviations

ACTC	All Ceylon Tamil Congress
APC	All Party Conference
CNC	Ceylon National Congress
CWC	Ceylon Workers Congress
CSCE	Conference on Security and Co-operation in Europe
DPLF	Democratic Peoples Liberation Front
DUNF	Democratic United National Front
DDC	District Development Councils
DMK	Dravida Munnetra Kazhagham
ENDLF	Eelam National Democratic Liberation Front
EPRLF	Eelam People's Revolutionary Liberation Front
EDF	Eelavar Democratic Front
FP	Federal Party
ICCPR	International Covenant on Civil and Political Rights
IGO	International Governmental Organisation
IPKF	Indian Peace Keeping Force
JVP	Janata Vimukti Peramuna
LSSP	Lanka Sama Samaja Party
LTTE	Liberation Tigers of Tamil Eelam
MEP	Mahajana Eksath Peramuna
NAM	Non-Aligned Movement
NEP	North-East Province
NGO	Non-Governmental Organisation
NSSP	Nava Sama Samaja Party
PSC	Parliamentary Select Committee
PA	People's Alliance
EROS	Eelam Revolutionary Organisation of Students
PLOTE	Peoples Liberation Organisation of Tamil Eelam
PPC	Political Parties Conference
PTA	Prevention of Terrorism Act
Rs	Rupees

SAARC	South Asian Association for Regional Co-operation
SLFP	Sri Lanka Freedom Party
SLMC	Sri Lanka Muslim Congress
TELO	Tamil Eelam Liberation Organisation
TNA	Tamil National Army
TULF	Tamil United Liberation Front
UF	United Front
UN	United Nations
UNCHR	United Nations Commission on Human Rights
UNESCO	UN Economic, Social and Cultural Organisation
UNHCR	United Nations High Commissioner for Refugees
UNHRC	United Nations Human Rights Committee
UNP	United National Party

The right to self-determination: The Sri Lankan Tamil national question

On 22 November, 1988, the United Nations General Assembly declared the 1990's to be the "International Decade for the Eradication of Colonialism". The Assembly reaffirmed that colonialism "in all its forms and manifestations" was incompatible with the UN Charter and posed a serious threat to international peace and security. A consensus resolution commemorating the thirtieth anniversary of the Declaration on the Granting of Independence to Colonial Countries and Peoples (1960), G.A. Res. 1514 (XV) was adopted at the General Assembly's Special Committee on Decolonisation, 22 January - 20 August, 1990. The twenty-four member body, which oversaw the decolonisation process for a large number of countries that are now member-states of the UN, reaffirmed the inalienable right of all peoples under colonial rule to self-determination and independence, in accordance with the 1960 Declaration.

Restricting the right to self-determination solely to colonial territories, however, now seems to be obsolete, because in the context of the few colonial territories left, it does not impose any obligations for the rest of the states parties to the 1960 Declaration. Indeed, the early 1990s have witnessed the eradication of some of the worst forms of colonialism in the world today. For example, the drafting of the interim constitution in South Africa on November, 18, 1993, signified the end of apartheid in South Africa. Elections have since held and Nelson Mandela has been sworn in as the country's first President of a democratic South Afica. Similarly, the PLO-Israel Peace Accord signed in Washington on September 13, 1993, had as its point of departure a clear recognition of the Palestinian peoples' right to self-determination. Israeli troops have since left the occupied territories, leaving the Palestinians to police their own autonomous territory. Despite the virtual demise of traditional Western colonialism, however, the principle of self-determination shows no sign of disappearing from the language of international relations. Instead, the principle of the right of peoples to self-determination contin-

1

ues to retain its vigor.

The right to self-determination can be considered an established principle of international law today. It is eminently a democratic right or principle, having its historic roots in the works of Locke and Rousseau, and in the doctrine of popular sovereignty purported during the revolutionary years in seventeenth and eighteenth century Europe. Government should be based on the will of the people, not on that of the monarch; and people living in a geographically distinct part of an existing state who are not content with the government of the country to which they belong should be able to secede and organise themselves as they wish.

The concept of self-determination has had five main manifestations, these are; national self-determination, manifested in the French Revolution; class self-determination, based on the theories of Lenin and Marx; minorities' self-determination, as expounded by President Woodrow Wilson; racial self-determination, which gave rise to the decolonisation period, and ethnic self-determination, its most contemporary manifestation.[1] Part One of this study will focus predominantly on the last variation of the right to self-determination.

The principle of self-determination is increasingly finding prime of place in the rhetoric used by ethnic groups living within independent states to legitimise their demands for greater regional autonomy, territorial separation and independence. Indeed, few modern states today can claim to be free from the demands of an ethnic group to the right to self-determination. For the purposes of this study, an "ethnic" group is defined as:

"...a group within a larger society that displays a common set of cultural traits, a sense of community among its members based on a presumed common heritage, a feeling of ethnocentrism on the part of group members, ascribed group membership, and in some cases, a distinct territory. Each of these characteristics is a variable, differing from group to group and among members of the same group".[2]

Ethnic claims to the right to self-determination occur in three main types of situations. The first instance can be found in the democratic West, often labelled as the "First World", where an "ethnic revival" has taken place: a development characterised by a newly discovered assertiveness among various minority ethnic groups. These include amongst others, the Basques and Catalans in Spain, the Welsh and the Scots in the United Kingdom, and the Quebecans in Canada. The second instance can be located in the "Third World", where states that inherited artificial frontiers that did not reflect pre-existing ethnic divisions are increasingly experiencing claims of ethnic self-determination and serious inter-ethnic violence as they struggle to adjust to a post-colonial political process. Such inter-ethnic conflicts seem to have proliferated since the start of the 1960s when the process of decolonisation was at its peak. There have been bloody and protracted ethnic conflicts in the Congo, Nigeria, Bangladesh, Sudan, India, Sri Lanka, Iraq, Ethiopia, Uganda, Lebanon and Cyprus, to name but a few. Very few of these ethnic conflicts have been resolved. The last instance of ethnic claims to self-determination can be found in the "Second World". With the collapse of the former USSR and its "satellite socialist states" in Eastern Europe, the Second World has experienced a proliferation of ethnic claims to self-determination and an attendant period of renewed ethnic conflict, (Eastern Europe having been the main area of concern regarding the damaging impact of ethnic conflict on interstate politics during the inter-war years).

However, whilst ethnic nationalism and the use of force, human rights abuse and protracted and violent inter-ethnic conflict, are often the result of denials of ethnic claims to self-determination, there have been few attempts to determine the scope and content of the right to self-determination outside of the colonial context and its relevance to ethnic groups living within independent states. Part One of this study attempts to rise to this challenge.

The application of the principle of self-determination outside the colonial context is complicated, with two dimensions to the problem, the "external" and the "internal". The "external" aspect concerns the right of a people not to be governed by an alien, external policy. But the scope and consequences are uncertain. The right belongs to "all peoples" - but who are these peoples? Some cases are clear. Colonial and dependent peoples are the subject of the right to external self-determination and the exercise of that right relates to the liberation from external dependence (from another state) and the establishment of their own separate states. Also, states which are subjected to military occupation are entitled to restore their self-determination, and become independent, if they so wish. This certainly applies to all peoples which have have been occupied by military forces since the end of World War Two. It is more complicated in regard to more long-standing occupations, however, since these may also have led to gradual integration. It is doubtful that the right to independence can be applied to occupations so longstanding that they existed before the emergence of the United Nations. A broader application of the right to external self-determination suggests that the subjects of this right are also peoples living in racist systems and under the regime of

3

apartheid.

Except for clear cases of colonialism, apartheid and recent occupations, certain minimum requirements must be fulfilled in order to give grounds for a claim of self-determination. The people who are claiming the right to self-determination must be clearly different in at least some key respects from the dominant population in the country concerned. Ethnic, cultural, linguistic differences will be required, but will not as such be enough. There must also be a clear territorial division. When members of the group demanding self-determination are geographically dispersed among the dominant population, there will rarely be a valid claim for self-determination. In the majority of cases, the claim of self-determination is unlikely to be accepted by the majority of the international community. Since 1945, the secession of Bangladesh from Pakistan in 1971, has been the only case of a successful claim to self-determination, and this was largely due to the military intervention of India on behalf of East Pakistan.

Whilst it has been contended that "the principle of self-determination may soon be widened to permit some form of secession...given the rapid pace at which the USSR, Czechoslovakia and Yugoslavia are disintegrating",[3] the right of peoples to external self-determination continues to provide little succour for ethnic groups living in sovereign states. The voluntary dissolution of the Soviet Union, and the recognition by the international community of those republics which no longer wished to belong to Yugoslavia, confirmed instead, the unconditional right of self-determination of peoples of federated republics.[4]

Outside of the colonial context, the "peoples" to whom the external right of self-determination applies continues to be the peoples of a state in their entirety. There remains a strong insistence on the "illegitimacy" of secession. The principle of territorial integrity is part of the principle of sovereignty and normally overrides the claim of self-determination. Thus, the external right to self-determination accords primary respect to the inter-state order.

Amongst the euphoria that greeted South Africa's recent adoption of majority-rule, there was a resonant voice of dissent, the white far right demanded the right to self-determination for the Afrikaans. Whilst it is certainly ironic, that yesterday's perpetators of oppression in South Africa are fearful that they might become tommorrow's oppressed, the South African case demonstrates that at the heart of the Afrikaans' fear, lies a more universal phenomenon, the "minority complex", the fear of being a minority in a majority-ruled state. It is precisely because of the international community's concern with the phenomenon of "post-modern tribalism", the transfer of defined parts of the populations and territories of existing multinational or multicultural states in order to constitute different uninational and unicultural states, and the fear of the disintegrative tendancies of the principle of self-determination, that positive international law currently supports the position that only anti-colonial, anti-occupation and anti-racist movements, can invoke the right to self-determination.

The fear of burgeoning secessionist movements was expressed by UN Secretary-General Boutros-Boutros Ghali in his *An Agenda for Peace*:

"Yet if every ethnic, religious or linguistic group claimed statehood, there would be no limit to fragmentation, and peace, security and economic well-being for all would become ever more difficult to achieve."[5]

Accordingly, the rights that minority groups are entitled to, are the rights provided in Article 27 of the International Covenant on Civil and Political Rights (ICCPR), 1966.

The fact remains however, that ethnic groups who are victims of internal oppression, who face marked discrimination, who have a highly developed sense of their own distinctiveness, and who in many cases occupy a contiguous territory, have nonetheless relied on the United Nation's clear recognition of the right of peoples to self-determination in making their secessionist claims, while disregarding the accompanying caveats, that the principle does not supersede the principle of territorial integrity.

What purpose then, if any, does the right of peoples to self-determination have for ethnic groups outside the colonial era? Any study of the contemporary application and appropriation of the principle of self-determination, by sovereign state governments and separatist movements alike, necessarily results in the unearthing of divergent and opposing perceptions of the substance and scope of the principle. Contemporary international law provides no simple answer to the problem of separatist movements. On the contrary, two inconsistent themes pervade the discourse surrounding the right of peoples to self-determination, one supporting a right of separatism, and the other denying it. On the one hand, the principle of self-determination of peoples, implies that every people has a right to its own nation-state. On the other hand, however, lies an equally venerable principle of international law, which upholds the territorial integrity of existing states. In separatist struggles, it seems that one principle or the other must give way. Where a separatist movement establishes that its people do not currently possess a nation-state of their own, the first principle would require that the existing territorial boundaries be re-demarcated, but this redrawing would violate the territorial integrity of the existing state. If, conversely, territorial integrity takes priority, then ethnic groups within the existing state will forfeit their claims to independence, irrespective of their "legitimacy". In reality, however, the incumbent government and the separatist movement, will more often than not find themselves at loggerheads with each other, each stalwartly maintaining its respective rhetorical stance on the principle of self-determination.

The use of such exclusive and uncompromising rhetoric by state governments and ethnic groups claiming nationality rights, inevitably results in the abuse of human rights and in the use of force, and often ends in armed conflict. The persistence of conflicting interpretations of the right, deems any attempt at understanding or resolving the issues underpinning ethnic conflicts, virtually impossible. A solution to an ethnic conflict, will rarely be found in a resolution based upon separation, nor in a resolution based upon forced assimilation, forced expulsion, genocide, or simple military might. Nor are either of these approaches to the resolution of ethnic conflicts viable options in the present international order.

It is increasingly being recognised that there is a synthesis between the question of group rights as a human rights matter and the principle of self-determination. Precisely because the human rights norms are constitutive, other norms have had to be reinterpreted in their light, lest anachronisms are produced. Accordingly, the principle of self-determination has been "updated" or "actualised". The question of group rights, more especially when it is related to territorial rights and regional autonomy, represents the practical and "internal" working out of the concept of self-determination. Such recognition is therefore the "internal" application of the concept of self-determination.

In the discourse surrounding the right of peoples to self-determination outside the colonial context, it is becoming increasingly popular to speak of the concept as having an internal aspect. Internal self-determination concerns the right of a people to govern itself. This means having its own representative government, responsive to the interests and needs of the people rather than to the will of some external, hegemonial power. Internal self-determination is denied through the existence of client regimes which base their power not on internal consensus but on the threat of external intervention if the government is removed by internal democratic processes.

However, the principle of internal self-determination can also be understood in a different way, as the right of a people to control significant aspects of internal matters (culture, education, property relations, social matters and welfare), while external matters (defence against armed attack from third parties, international trade relations, diplomatic intercourse) are left in the hands of a larger political entity, e.g., a federal state. Internal self-determination therefore becomes almost synonomous with local autonomy. International law, however, is still very vague with regard to the degree to which a homogenous or ethnic group living within an independent state is entitled to internal autonomy.

Part One of this study attempts to determine the content and scope of the internal right to self-determination, by examining both its "political" aspect and its "economic, social and cultural" aspect. In this way, it aims to reveal, firstly; to what extent the internal right to self-determination constitutes *more* than "the synthesis and summa of human rights", and secondly, to what degree the most recent version of the principle of self-determination, as a standard for the democratic legitimation of the governments of sovereign states, has served to emasculate the meaning and relevance of the right to internal self-determination, by presenting democracy under the banner of the internal aspect to self-determination as a pacifier and as a means of avoiding the external form of the principle, thereby removing from the right any resemblance to its former usage as an anti-imperialist force.

It is clearly no longer arguable that a state's denial of a group's claim to the right to self-determination is an internal affair, based upon the assumption that as a "sovereign" state it can determine its *domaine reserve*, thereby ruling out the possibility of international mediation. Indeed, the international community can exert pressure against states that oppress their own peoples by denials of the right to self-determination. Whilst the term "sovereignty" continues to be used in international legal practice, its referent in modern international law is quite different.[6] International law still protects sovereignty, but it is the sovereignty of the people, popular sovereignty, rather than the sovereign's sovereignty. Largely as a result of the international human rights programme, the international law's object of protection is no longer the power base of the tyrant who rules directly by naked power or through the apparatus of a totalitarian political order, but the continuing capacity of a population freely to express and effect choices about the identities and the policies of its governors. This contemporary change in the content of sovereignty has necessarily changed the cast of characters who can violate that sovereignty. In other words, it has become possible for the person who wields the authority of the government against the wishes of the people by naked power, by putsch or by coup, or by the usurpation of an election, to be guilty of violating the popular sovereignty. Such a person is not entitled to invoke its national sovereignty to establish or reinforce his/her own position in international politics. Sovereignty can no longer be used to shield the actual suppression of popular sovereignty from external rebuke and remedy.

It is becoming increasingly apparent that in many states national guarantees of minority and human rights are not sufficient to protect the peoples' sovereign rights. In the light of this, the principle of non-interference in the affairs of other governments is duly undergoing review. At the recent Human Rights Conference held in Vienna, June, 1993 in response to the furore between the "North" and the "South" over the "universality" of human rights, Ms Sidney Jones of the human rights body "Asia Watch" stressed that human rights must be seen as an international issue.

"If governments and their security forces are primarily responsible for human rights abuses, it is illusory to think that the same governments are best equipped to protect human rights...the only possible way...is to acknowledge from the outset that responsibility for protection transcends national boundaries".[7]

Not long ago, international efforts to implement the right of self-determination were met with fierce opposition from governments who wished to administer their colonies without outside interference. In a similar fashion, many independent post-colonial states have not taken kindly to increased international interference into the intimate political process by which governments are empowered by the people. Many Third World states are beginning to resent the proliferation of international monitoring of their human rights records and its subsequent linkage with foreign aid, recognising in such policies a form of "neo-colonialism". Similar criticism has been levelled at the new "Right to Development" by those who maintain that the development that the dominant Western powers continue to impose upon the Third World is in reality no more than "development for servitude".

Part One concludes by tracing how the linkage of human rights standards and practises of democracy with questions of development aid, trade agreements, security and environment in international relations since the end of the Cold War, has in effect, led there to be "no debate of difference between 'intervention', whatever its semantic mask, and imperialism; a non-word in today's Orwellian lexicon of control."[8]

Part One therefore, reveals that by making the right to democracy, development and human rights virtually synonomous with the right to internal self-determination, the international community is making it possible to intervene in a group's claim to the right to self-determination, thereby denying the principle its fundamental defining characteristic, that of self-definition, whereby a group of people who choose to determine their own future, qualify as peoples and are consequently entitled to self-determination.

Part Two of this study provides an empirical case study of Sri Lanka, a country which is suffering from one of the world's most violent and intransigent inter-ethnic conflicts. This study questions the validity of the established rationale for seeking to deny ethnic groups the right of self-determination in all its attributes, based upon the two-fold fear of "ethno-nationalism"; an ideology that requires that a nation shall be defined ethnically, that the state should as far as possible be congruent with the nation so defined, and that loyalty to the nation shall be superior to all other loyalties, and the fear of the disintegrating tendancies of the proliferation of secessionist movements. In Sri Lanka, as in many other countries of Asia and Africa that have been smothered by centuries of colonialism, ethno-nationalism is seen as an emancipatory, progressive force. Ethno-nationalism is recognised to be an instrument that will enable the Tamil-speaking people to retrieve, nourish and develop their distinct cultural identities.

Part Two demonstrates that due to the consistent failure of the various Sinhalese-dominated Sri Lankan governments to accord to the Tamil-speaking people their internal right to self-determination, the Tamil community have demanded the right to external self-determination, thereby catapulting the Island into a state of civil war. It is hoped that this empirical study will amply illustrate that if ethno-nationalism sometimes degenerates into "ethnic-cleansing" or "ethnic anarchy", it is because an impenetrable, unjust order fails to respond to legitimate aspirations in the first instance. It ultimately attempts to reveal that the Tamil secessionist movement owes its origin to the failure of the Sri Lankan state to acknowledge the growth of Tamil sub-nationalism as a legitimate manifestation of the participatory ethos of democracy.

Too often, inter-ethnic conflicts are analysed within the boundaries of a single sovereign state, in other words, individual states are regarded as "closed" systems which are then studied in isolation, whilst the wider inter-state setting of facts and values, within which individual states have to function are disregarded. An understanding of the issues involved any modern inter-ethnic conflict, which implements one of the most significant features of the inter-state environment, namely, the right of peoples to self-determination, can only be gained by placing the discourse firmly within an international framework of analysis.

The denial of the right of peoples to self-determination in a sovereign state usually generates friction with neighbouring states, where separatist movements habitually seek sanctuary and succour, often precipitating both the internal and external migration of tens of thousands of refugees, which ultimately places great economic, social and political strains on both the state concerned, and in neighbouring or overseas states of refuge. In a climate where the majority of civil unrest in the world is currently due to ethnic tensions, and where the "developed" world is fast becoming intolerant of the stream of refugees escaping ethnic war-zones, any form of conflict resolution undertaken in these areas must take into consideration not only the intra-state dimension, but also the inter-state dimension of the conflict.

The underlying assumption of many separatist claims is that the concept of self-determination provides a unilateral right. The assumption is that a viable "self" can unilaterally proclaim its own independence. However, the response of sovereign states who have been faced by such claims, reveals the problems inherent in such a belief. The rhetoric which asserts the principle of self-determination by both sovereign states and separatist movements, often ignores the multilateral character of claims to self-determination. The multilateral nature of such claims must be taken into consideration in the actual implementation of the right to self-determination, if a lasting solution is to be found to the many competing claims for national recognition that exist today.

"In those instances in the past where the principle of self-determination has been more or less openly (even successfully) applied and has gained wide international acceptance, it has been in a context not of unilateral declarations, but rather in contexts such as that following World War I, or in the decolonisation process following World War II. Here the concept of self-determination was a principle accepted by the major powers and international organisations as a basis for negotiating the details of competing claims for new political arrangements and new patterns of sovereignty...The concept of self-determination must be understood, not as a principle for unilateral implementation, but as a principle guiding the adjustment of competing claims for national recognition in a system of international order".[9]

In order to understand those instances where the right to self-determination has been successfully applied and accepted by the international community, it is important to acknowledge that inter-state relations take place in a decentralised power structure, which necessarily endorses a competitive self-help mentality. It is becoming increasingly apparent that the major powers at the top of the power structure, will only dirty their hands in a regional war-zone, if intervention is sure to offer strategic benefits, resources or dividends. Whilst at the bottom of the power structure, in a system in which no state trusts its neighbouring state, where each state's immediate national interest is power, and where violence is an ever present danger or possibility, minorities are often regarded as a threat to the minor state's security. Not only do states fear that the group may act as a Trojan horse serving the interests of outside powers, but states also fear internal dissension because a divided state will necessarily be weaker than a united rival. When ethnic groups are regarded as a source of internal weakness, they are therefore often likely to be persecuted than accommodated.

There are two doctrines, both largely mythological, which often hinder open examinations of the multilateral nature of claims to the right of self-determination. The first is the doctrine that ethnic conflicts are domestic affairs and are therefore not the concern of the international community. A group's claim to the right of self-determination has traditionally been viewed as an internal affair, whilst the state has been deemed capable of satisfying the claim by promoting minority rights and human rights protection, and by according to the group greater political autonomy through the devolution of state power. This doctrine is maintained despite the occurrence of both informal and formal outside state involvement in inter-ethnic conflicts. The doctrine of an internal affair is useful to the incumbent government for it permits the government an open role in international discussions, whilst forcing the separatist movement into a covert role. The second is the doctrine that ethnic conflicts are "regional" affairs and are therefore not the concern of the international community. The assumption of the international community in many cases is that the conflict should be dealt with by the appropriate major regional organisation.

Part Three of this study, attempts to place the discourse surrounding the intra-state ethnic conflict in Sri Lanka firmly within an international framework of analysis. It is hoped that by providing a comprehensive account of the international dimension of the conflict, it will demonstrate that the determination of claims to the right to self-determination should not be left in the hands of the concerned government or self-interested third-party states. In other words, it illustrates that a group's claim to the right to self-determination should be recognised as a supra-national and supra-regional affair, the denial of which, inevitably bars an open discussion of the nature of the responsibilities of various governments and as a result, not only hinders any comprehensive understanding of the issues involved, but also prohibits opportunities for the resolution of inter-ethnic conflicts.

For many in the West, the nature of peace and war have, to a large extent, been redefined by the ethnic conflicts that have marked the post-Cold War era.[10] The status of the idea of national liberation, which has been suffering from decline since its high point in the 1960s, hit new depths in the early 1990s. The bloody intra-ethnic fighting in the former Yugoslavia in particular, seems to have brought to a definitive end a long period in which national liberation was widely regarded as one of the highest values, justifying violence and providing a rationale for war. Whilst in the past, there were always those who condemned terrorism and who acknowledged the murder and the massacre in national liberation wars, there were also those who commended the ends but tolerated the means. Today, however, the national fight is more often than not against one's own neighbour, and is therefore deemed to be a manifestation of the "narcissism of minor difference",[11] rather than as a struggle against a neo-imperial oppressor, and is therefore popularly portrayed as senseless and destructive. The portrayal of societies which are suffering from ethnic conflict as endemically violent and barbaric, is to camouflage the anti-imperialist imperative of many ethnic nationalist struggles.

Such conflicts are accordingly triggering not concern and help, but abandonment by the international community. It is an abandonment of the victims as well as the aggressors, but it is characteristic of the new attitude that it does not attempt to clearly distinguish between the two. The announcement by the French and the British government that 1993 was to be the last winter that their troops will spend in Bosnia, was done not only to put pressure on those who are fighting to reach a settlement, but to make the preparations to simply walk out on the former Yugoslavia in the near future.

However, whilst many Western states are keen to distinguish themselves from the "other", i.e., those states which are embroiled in a fight over nationality rights, these same states are often actively involved in not only providing unmonitored aid to such countries (which is then used directly for military purposes within its borders), but also in providing arms, training, and refuge to extra-parliamentary groups. The "double-standards" of the international community, further compound the problems entailed in resolving intra-state ethnic conflicts. Indeed, the "internationalisation" of an intra-state ethnic conflict, more often than not, complicates the already difficult task of bringing the warring parties to the negotiating table.

What impact will the combination of the "war-weariness", so easily manufactured in the West's popular consciousness, and the international community's fortuitous diplomatic duplicity have on the nature and future of protracted and violent intra-state ethnic conflicts? What is the future prognosis for those ethnic groups whose struggles, not against the external oppressor but the internal oppressor, were conveniently shelved during the Cold War and which have been largely forgotten since the Cold War?

Part Three is divided into two sections. The first section examines the role of the United Nations in protracted and violent intra-state ethnic conflicts, and the effectiveness of the range of measures open to the UN for preventing, managing and resolving such disputes, such as preventative diplomacy, peace-making, peace-keeping and post-conflict peace-building. It focuses particularly on the UN's current involvement in the ethnic conflict in Sri Lanka. It attempts to illustrate that the United Nations not only lacks the appropriate mechanisms with which to deal with violent and protracted ethnic conflicts, particularly those arising from denials of the claim to the right to self-determination, but that it is inherently partisan and political.

The "internationalisation" of the ethnic conflict in Sri Lanka after the July, 1983 massacre, evoked international concern not only among "state-actors" such as India, Western donors of aid to Sri Lanka, and "host" countries to tens of thousands of Tamil asylum-seekers, but it also created links with "non-state" actors such as the UN Human Rights Commission and its Sub-Commission on Prevention of Discrimination and Protection of Minorities, and with non-governmental organisations (NGOs) concerned with minority and human rights.

In the absence of a formal UN mechanism which could entertain complaints about self-determination from the parties concerned, as well as from sympathetic governments, non-governmental organisations, and concerned individuals, the UN Human Rights Commission and its Sub-Commission continue to function as the major lobbies for the international recognition of a group's claim to the right to self-determination. The second section of Part Three therefore examines the concerns that have been raised before the UN Human Rights Commission and its Sub-Commission by sympathetic governments, NGOs and individuals with regard to the ethnic conflict in Sri Lanka. It focuses particularly on the forty-ninth UN Commission on Human Rights held in February,

1993, at which fifteen NGOs raised the issue of the Tamils' right to self-determination. It also examines the recommendations that have been raised before the UN Human Rights Commission and its Sub-Commission on ways in which the conflict might be resolved.

There is a clearly stated duty on all UN member states to promote the realisation of self-determination in conformity with the principles and purposes of the UN Charter. It is apparent that failure to do so, often results in violent ethnic conflict, which in turn, can result in human rights abuse and threats to international peace and security. Certainly, the time has come for the United Nations and its member states to give serious consideration to the progressive development of the concept of self-determination in the post-Cold War era. An examination of the scope and substance of the right to self-determination and the identification of the relevant criteria for determining the legitimacy of a claim is well overdue. This study concludes by recommending ways in which the UN could more effectively deal with claims to the right to self-determination, such as identifying or creating a mechanism, which could consider claims to self-determination from the "peoples" concerned, where there is a risk of disturbance of the peace or violations of fundamental human rights.

Notes

1 Ronen. V., "The quest for self-determination", (1979).

2 M. N. Marger., "Race and ethnic relations: American and global perspectives", (1991), p.35.

3 Cohen. D., "Quebec's sovereignty option: A look at practical and legal problems", in: The Oxford International Review, Vol.IV No.3 September (1993), pp.19-22, p.22.

4 Jayawickrama. N., "The right of self-determination", report of the Martin Ennals Memorial Symposium on Self-Determination, University of Saskatoon and International Alert, p.5.

5 United Nations Security Council, *An Agenda for Peace: Preventative Diplomacy, Peacemaking and Peacekeeping*, Report of the Secretary-General pursuant to the statement adopted by the Summit Meeting of the Security Council on 31 January, 1992, UN Document A/47/227 (S/24111), United Nations: New York, 17 June, (1992).

6 See W. M. Reisman., "Sovereignty and human rights in contemporary international law", in: The American Journal of International Law, Vol.84, (1990), pp.866-876.

7 Ms. Sidney Jones of "Asia Watch" at the Human Rights Conference in Vienna, June, 1993, reported in the *Financial Times*, Friday 11, June, 1993.

8 John Pilger, "The US fraud in Africa: Operation Restore Hope is part of a new age imperialism", in: NewStatesman Society, 8 January, (1993), pp.10-11.

9 Nixon. C. R., "Self-determination: The Nigerian/Biafra case", in: World Politics, Vol.24, (1971/2), pp.473-497, p.494.

10 See Martin Woolacott., "Wars that no longer seem justified", in: *The Guardian*, December, 22, 1993.

11 Ignatieff. M., "Blood and belonging: Journeys into the new nationalism", p 14.

Part 1

The Right to self-determination

The right to self-determination: The Sri Lankan Tamil national question

Part One analyses the evolution of the principle of self-determination, from its origins in seventeenth and eighteenth century Europe, in an attempt to determine its contemporary international status. It traces the genesis of the principle from its "selective" implementation during the nineteenth century, to its "universal" application in the mid-twentieth century. It charts the development of the right, from incoherence to coherence, as it has been "updated" or "actualised", and has been gradually synthesised with the human rights norms and the modern aspects of the "democratic entitlement".

Part One focuses primarily on the application of the right to self-determination to peoples living within existing independent states outside of the colonial context. While much of the discourse surrounding the question of the consequences of the principle outside of the colonial context, and by implication, the attempt to identify the "peoples" to whom the principle applies, has assumed that the subject of the right is the whole people of the state, and that the principle of territorial integrity makes any secessionist claim illegitimate, Part One asks, does this insistence exclude the principle of self-determination entirely, in so far as groups or peoples constituting less than the whole people of the state are concerned?

In an attempt to answer this question, Part One explores the scope and content of the "internal" right to self-determination, one of the two component parts of the birfucated principle, and its implications for groups or peoples living within independent states in the post-decolonisation era. Whilst colonial and dependent peoples are the subject of the "external" right to self-determination, the exercise of which relates to the liberation from external dependence (from another state), peoples living within an independent state are the subjects of the "internal" right to self-determination, the exercise of which entitles peoples to determine their own political, economic, social and cultural destiny. The "internal" right to self-determination means that full guarantees are provided for a democratic process in which every citizen can participate under conditions of full equality.

Whilst the international community continues to deny ethnic groups the right to external self-determination, ethnic groups continue to appropriate the principle to legitimise their demands for greater regional autonomy, territorial separation, and in the final instance for independence. Moreover, denials of the claim, invariably lead to human rights abuse, the use of force, and in some cases to civil war, thus constituting one of the major contemporary threats to international peace and security. Certainly, the "internal" right to self-determination can only be successfully applied and consistently maintained in a liberal democratic consitutional framework. Moreover, the concept of self-determination has been both universalised and internationalised, and can now be said to portend, not only a duty owed by all governments to their peoples, but also by each government to all members of the international community.

Part One examines whether the application of the "internal" right to self-determination is a "domestic" affair or whether the international community can impose an obligation on a foreign state to respect its subjects' right to "internal" self-determination. In turn, it examines the controversy that currently surrounds the international community's increasing intervention in the affairs of what it considers to be non-representative, oppressive regimes, in order to guarantee a peoples' right to "internal" self-determination.

In this way, Part One examines to what extent the most recent version of the principle of self-determination, as a standard for the democratic legitimation of the governance of sovereign states, and as a measure by which to gauge a state's human rights standards and economic development, has served to emasculate the meaning and relevance of the right to "internal" self-determination. In other words, Part one illustrates how the principle of self-determination has been "domesticated" in the post-Cold War era, making it devoid of all anti-imperialist sentiment.

CHAPTER 1

(i) The evolution of the right of peoples to self-determination

The right to self-determination has its genesis in the "social contract" theory first promulgated by political theorists in seventeenth and eighteenth century Europe. The social contract theorists, elaborating upon the "natural law" theme which had hitherto preoccupied political philosophers, reiterated that there are certain inalienable rights belonging to individuals which are retained upon entrance into society, such as the right of resistance in the face of oppression, whilst further regarding as legitimate, only those governments that are based upon the consent of the governed.

These ideas were developed in the writings of John Locke whose ideas were influential in the drafting of the American Declaration of Independence. Locke maintained that individual men and women upon their birth into this world retain an inherent right to resist oppressive civil authority. He asserted that legislative power has certain absolute limitations. Legislative power, he wrote, is "in the utmost Bounds of it...*limited to the publick good* of the Society. It is the Power, that hath no other end but preservation, and therefore can never have a right to destroy, enslave, or designedly to impoverish the Subjects."[1] Where the legislative power adopts a policy of tyranny, he wrote, then by virtue of "a Law antecedent and paramount to all positive Laws of men" the "Body of the People, or any single Man" has the liberty to "appeal to Heaven."[2] In other words, Locke recognised man's natural right of resistance. However, he did stress that resistance is only justified in the face of "a long train of Abuses, Prevarications, and Artifices."[3]

The concept of popular sovereignty encompasses the right to rebel against one's own government. It rejects the theory that a monarch or a government has power over its citizens by virtue of where they are situated rather than by virtue of their consent. The right to rebel against a non-representative government was derived from the rejection of the feudal, territorial sovereignty principle. The territorial principle was supplanted by a principle of government by the consent of the governed.

"The history of self-determination is bound up with the history of the doctrine of popular sovereignty proclaimed by the French Revolution: government should be based on the will of the people, not on that of the monarch, and people not content with the government of the country to which they belong should be able to secede and organise themselves as they wish. This meant that the territorial element in a political unit lost its feudal predominance in favour of the personal element: people were not to be any more a mere appurtenance of the land."[4]

In 1776 the seeds of the concept of the sovereignty of the people were first sown in the United States Declaration of Independence. It was predominantly the theories of John Locke that Thomas Jefferson based the Declaration upon. In what is undoubtedly the most famous formulation of the natural rights doctrine of resistance to civil authority, the Declaration clearly assumes that the right of resistance appertaining to individual men and women may not be exercised in the absence of some degree of oppression.

"We hold these truths to be self-evident, that all men...are endowed by their Creator with certain inalienable Rights...That whenever any Form of Government becomes destructive of these ends, it is the Right of the People to alter or abolish it, and to institute new Government...Prudence, indeed, will dictate that Governments long established should not be changed for light and transient causes;...that mankind are more disposed to suffer, while evils are sufferable, than to right themselves by abolishing the forms to which they are accustomed. But when a long train of abuses and usurpations...evinces a design to reduce them under absolute Despotism, it is their right, it is their duty, to throw off such Government."[5]

Writing in a pre-nationalist era, John Locke and his fellow social contract theorists were guilty of assuming that the only units of analysis in their hypothesis were the individual and the state, with whom the individual was deemed to have signed the contract. Minority and ethnic groups or communities were disregarded.

The international community's concern with the social and political conditions that give rise to ethnic tensions, and to the demands of minority groups for some degree of political, social, economic or cultural autonomy, or in the last resort to secession, whereby a segment of a state's population attempts to withdraw both itself and the territory it inhabits from the ambit of the governing state's political authority, has over the years assumed many different titles. International concern for the plight of ethnic, religious, or linguistic minorities contained within a state's boundaries arose long before the establishment of any formal international apparatus to deal with the problem.

The earliest attempts by the international community to secure certain fundamental rights for minorities can be found in various seventeenth and eighteenth century treaties involving the cession of territory and the conference of protection to religious minorities in the ceded province. During the early nineteenth century the international community extended its concern to securing fundamental civil rights in areas subject to a transfer of sovereignty. In 1815 the first formal recognition of "national" rights was made during the Congress of Vienna, with special reference to Poland. The parties to the treaty agreed that "the Poles, who are respective subjects of Russia, Austria and Prussia, shall obtain a Representation and National Institutions, regulated according to the degree of political consideration, that each of the Governments to which they belong shall judge expedient and proper to grant them."[6]

At the close of the First World War the seeds containing the concept of the "nation" as the legitimate political unit developed into a principle of nationality demanding international attention. Whilst the idea of "national" self-determination had a long history during the revolutionary years of the late eighteenth and early nineteenth centuries in Europe, it was not until the present century that it became a widely accepted principle in international relations, finding mention in various international legal documents.

(ii) The juridical status of the right to self-determination before 1945- The League of Nations

The right to national self-determination was first promulgated at an international level by the USSR in 1917. It was intended to apply both to nationalities in Europe (chiefly those under the Austro-Hungarian monarchy) and to colonial peoples. It was first proclaimed in Lenin's *Theses on the Socialist Revolution and the Right of Nations to Self-Determination* (January-February 1916) in which he advocated self-determination not only for "Austria, the Balkans, and particularly Russia", but also for colonial peoples ("Socialists must...demand the unconditional and immediate liberation of the colonies without compensation") This proclamation was reiterated in several other documents, among which was Lenin's *Fourth Letter from Afar* (25 March 1917), in which he listed "the liberation of all colonies; the liberation of all dependent, oppressed, and non-sovereign peoples among the conditions for peace."[7]

In his thesis *Decree on peace*, Lenin gives a definition of annexation which serves well as an inverse definition of the right to self-determination, the right to self-determination of a nation being eminently anti-expansionist and opposed to state aggrandisement. Lenin characterised annexation as:

"...any incorporation of a small or weak nation into a large or powerful state without the precisely, clearly and voluntarily expressed consent and wish of that nation, irrespective of the time when such forcible incorporation took place, irrespective also of the degree of development or backwardness of the nation forcibly annexed to the given state, or forcibly retained within its borders, and irrespective, finally, of whether this nation is in Europe or in distant overseas countries."[8]

Lenin implicitly suggests that the principle of self-determination be applicable not only to colonial nations "in distant overseas countries" but also to nations in independent states, such as in Europe, thereby giving express legitimacy to secession. It is also clear in Lenin's writings, that he rejected many of the assumptions that were later entrenched in the United Nations Charter, i.e., that the right of national self-determination can be exercised only once, as part of an anti-colonial or anti-racist struggle, and that all other peoples constituting less than the whole population of the state then forfeit the right and must accept the post-colonial boundaries, no matter how arbitrary they might be. Lenin deemed the principle of self-determination to be of continuing applicability, to be invoked at any time by an oppressed nation, even in a sovereign state.

During this period, in a different part of the world, the right to self-determination was also proclaimed as a valid principle by the American President Woodrow Wilson. However, Wilson's view of the principle differed markedly from Lenin's. Whilst they both meant to apply self-determination to Europe and to colonies, the American conception of how it should be extended to colonial countries was greatly qualified by the need to take account of the interests of colonial powers. The fifth of the famous fourteen points proclaimed by Wilson in his address delivered before a Joint Session of Congress, on 8 January 1918, requested:

"A free, open-minded, and absolutely impartial adjustment of all colonial claims, based upon a strict observance of the principle that in determining all such questions of sovereignty the interests of the populations concerned must have equal weight with the equitable claims of the government whose title is to be determined."[9]

The discrepancy between the two conceptions of the principle of self-determination was also apparent in the criticisms of the Soviet views voiced by the American Secretary of State R. Lansing. He wrote that Lenin's programme menaced "the stability of the future world by applying the self-determination principle to the colonial world", and went on to note that:

"...however justified may be the principle of local self-government, the necessities of preserving an orderly world require that there should be a national authority with sovereign rights to defend and control the communities within the national boundaries."[10]

In the inter-War years the principle was to a large extent implemented in Europe, whereas the staunch opposition of colonial powers prevented its application to colonies. In the years immediately prior to the formation of the League of Nations, it was assumed by President W. Wilson that the employment of national self-determination as an operative political principle would allow an orderly geographical realignment of peoples on the basis of national affinities. It was thought that this would have the desired effect of bringing the more artificial institution of statehood into line with the more natural phenomenon of nationhood, and would thereby satisfy the demands of nationalism and irredentism, which had blossomed so insistently during the nineteenth century.

Several years before the inauguration of the League of Nations, Lord Acton warned about the dangers of nationalist doctrines in a world where pure nation-states were an anomaly. He stated:

"The greatest adversary of the rights of nationality is the modern theory of nationality. By making the state and the nation commensurate with each other in theory, it reduces practically to a subject condition all other nationalities that may be within the boundary. It cannot admit them to equality with the ruling nation which constitutes the state because the state would then cease to be national, which would be a contradiction of the principle of its existence. According, therefore, to the degree of humanity and civilisation in that dominant body which claims all the rights of the community, the inferior races are exterminated, or reduced to servitude, or outlawed, or put in a condition of dependence."[11]

The Paris Peace Conference of 1919 quickly showed the unworkable nature of national self-determination as an operative principle. Thereafter, a shift of emphasis was evident. Rather than speak about national self-determination as a touch-stone for testing the legitimacy of any future realignment of the political allegiances of national groups, a solution was sought in the expansion of the already existing doctrine of "minority rights". Under this approach the international concern for national or ethnic minorities contained within multinational states could be demonstrated without seeming to authorise self-determination for all such groups, which still carried a dangerous implication of political independence.

The actual solution to the problem of disaffected minorities adopted at the Peace Conference had two elements. First, those territorial readjustments made by the Conference, the dismemberment of some states and the creation of others, were performed where practicable, with an eye to the demands of national self-determination and were decided by the extensive use of plebiscites to determine the political desires of the inhabitants. Secondly, where territorial realignment did not result in an adequate solution to the minority problems, the Conference sought to protect minority groups through treaty guarantees, in the hope that these minority treaties would in the future suppress those special conditions which give rise to minority grievances and which can arguably legitimate a claim to self-determination. In the event, the League of Nations chose to employ the external pressure of international commitments and world opinion as an inducement for states to moderate their minority policies, instead of relying on whatever internal pressure would result from an international endorsement of self-help measures on the part of such minorities where a state's policies were manifestly immoderate.

Traditionally, claims to secede are based upon the right of peoples to self-determination, according to which all peoples have the right to determine their own destiny. A liberal interpretation of the right to self-determination suggests that the right to secede flows naturally from principles of self-government, such as those embodied in the American Declaration of Independence and the French Declaration of the Rights of Man and of the Citizen. One year after the Treaty of Versailles, the League of Nations made a formal statement of its understanding of the status of secession within the framework of self-determination and minority rights.

At the Paris Peace Conference, representatives of the Aaland Islands made a request for annexation to Sweden based on the right of peoples to self-determination. An International Commission of Jurists, entrusted with the task of giving an advisory opinion upon the legal aspects of the Aaland Islands question, pointed out that the principle was not mentioned in the Covenant of the League, and that the principle had not yet attained the status of a positive rule of international law, although it had been recognised in several international treaties:

"...in the absence of express provisions in international treaties, the right of disposing of national territory is essentially an attribute of the sovereignty of every State. Positive International Law does not recognise the right of national groups, as such, to separate themselves from the State of which they form a part by the simple expression of a wish, any more than it recognises the right of other States to claim such a separation".[12]

In a subsequent report on the Aaland Islands question, the Commission was even more explicit in its rejection of a legal right to secessionist self-determination:

"To concede to minorities either of language or religion, or to any fractions of a population, the right of withdrawing from the community to which they belong, because it is their wish or their good pleasure, would be to destroy order and stability within States and to inaugurate anarchy in international life: it would be to uphold a theory incompatible with the very idea of the State as a territorial and political entity".[13]

The Commission of Jurists noted that it did not give an opinion "as to whether a manifest and continued abuse of sovereign power, to the detriment of a section of the population of a State, would...give to an international dispute...such a character that its object should be considered as one which is not confined to the domestic jurisdiction of the State concerned".[14] However, the Commission of Rapporteurs did go so far as to say that the separation of a minority from a state and its attachment to another state could be considered as a "last resort when the State lacks either the will or the power to enact and apply just and effective guarantees" of religious, linguistic, and social freedom.[15]

The Leagues of Nation's decision to employ international guarantees of minority rights, demonstrated the world community's reluctance to accept secession as a method for vindicating minority or ethnic group rights. However, there seemed to be an implicit recognition in the Aaland Islands case, that a minority retains a right of reversion to self-determination where treaty protections and the pressure of international opinion fail to obtain the desired results. In other words, the recognition of the right to self-determination as a remedy for manifest and continued abuse of basic minority rights was suggested but not authoritatively endorsed during the League period.

(iii) The juridical status of the right to self-determination post 1945- The United Nations

Redrawing the map of Europe after the First World War, the victors had attempted to respect ethnic boundaries at least with regard to the empires of the defeated nations, but the right to self-determination had virtually no impact upon the colonial empires of the great powers. However, an increasing moral hostility to colonialism coupled with a renewed surge of world-wide nationalistic fervour during the inter-War years, thrust the right to self-determination onto the agenda of what came to be known as the United Nations.

When the United Nations superseded the League of Nations, discussions inevitably arose over whether a similar regime to protect minorities should be re-created. The decision not to re-establish such a regime was made for several reasons. Firstly, the experiences of the inter-war years had revealed how a state, notably Hitler's Germany, was able to abuse the minority issue for its own territorial aggrandisement. After World War Two, this increased the fears of certain states that the preservation of a minority identity within their boundaries would increase their own insecurity. As well as the threat of external intervention, it was felt that the granting of minority rights would merely freeze a situation of majority/minority antagonism.

Another reason for opposing a system of international minority protection was the argument that the situations in the various multi-ethnic states varied so much that it was not possible to provide a well-defined, universal system that would suit all occasions. Rather, it was felt that dealing with each case on an *ad hoc* basis was to be preferred. Also, in the minds of many delegates at the UN drafting committees, was the hope that the population movements that had accompanied the end of the Second World War would finally end the "national question" in Eastern Europe and so remove the need for a system of international group protection. Events in Eastern Europe in the early 1990s have shown just how wrong they were.

By 1945, the American stance on the minority issue had changed considerably, especially since Wilson had championed minority rights and national self-determination at Versailles. After the Second World War, the US advocated a policy of assimilation for different ethnic groups on the basis of equal treatment before the law. At the close of World War Two, the US experience of dealing with minority issues was markedly different from the Soviet experience, where minorities had been given *de jure* rights by the Constitution of the USSR. However, many other governments were prepared to accept the US position on assimilation and this international preference for a shift away from the protection of minority rights to the safe-guarding of individual rights was eventually to find expression in the United Nations Charter, 1945 and in the Universal Declaration of Human Rights, 1948.

The principle of individual rights and non-discrimination eased out an approach based on group rights and minority protection within the United Nations. Among the UN Member States at the drafting of the Charter, the hope was that a system of individual human rights protection on the basis of non-discrimination would be sufficient to guarantee the protection of minority rights. Despite the fact that in its infant years many of the most serious problems that the UN faced actually came from minority groups, it adopted a policy which deliberately de-emphasised the minority protection issue. Today, adherents of an international system of minority protection continue to argue that the minority issue will not disappear simply because the UN refuses to deal with it, insisting that a system of human rights protection alone, is not sufficient to protect minority groups.

However, the principle of self-determination was finally accepted in the UN Charter. The first reference to the right of self-determination appears in article 1(2), which provides that one of the purposes of the United Nations is "To develop friendly relations among nations based on respect for the principles of equal rights and self-determination of peoples". The second reference appears in article 55, concerning Economic and Social Cooperation, in which it instructs the UN to promote higher standards of living, solutions to health and cultural problems, and universal respect for human rights "with a view to the creation of conditions of stability and well-being which are necessary for peaceful and friendly relations among nations based on respect for the principle of equal rights and self-determination of peoples". Through these provisions the principle had made great strides, for it was now embodied in an internationally binding treaty.

"The embodiment of that principle in the Charter marks not only the recognition of the concept as a legal principle and a principle of contemporary international law, but also the point of departure of a new process -the increasingly dynamic development of the principle and its legal content, its implementation, and its application to the most varied situations of international life".16

However, it had a number of weaknesses. Firstly, it did not lay down a legally binding obligation to be fulfilled immediately, but merely set forth a goal for the Organisation and propounded a policy that member states pledged to pursue by taking joint and separate action in cooperation with the UN (Article 56). Secondly, self-determination was taken to mean "self-government" only and not independence. Independence was set as one of the possible goals for trust territories solely (Article 76b), while mere self-government was envisaged for non self-governing territories (Article 73b).

Indeed, the term "self-determination" briefly referred to in the state-centred and very specific context of articles 1(2) and 55, is nowhere to be found in those parts of the UN Charter that deal with dependent territories. Chapter XI, which concerns Non Self-Governing Territories, refers in Article 73b to the duty of the governing state to:

"develop self-government, to take due account of the political aspirations of the peoples, and to assist them in the progressive development of their free political institutions, according to the particular circumstances of each territory and its peoples and the varying stages of advancement".

In Chapter XII, entitled International Trusteeship System, Article 76 provides that:

"The basic objectives of Trusteeship shall be: (b) to promote the political, economic, social and educational advancement of the inhabitants...and their progressive development towards self-government or independence as may be appropriate to the particular circumstances of each territory and its peoples and the freely expressed wishes of the peoples concerned".

Thirdly, in actual practice, colonial empires were allowed to survive, albeit in the guise of the trusteeship system, or subject to the general commitments set out in Article 73. Fourthly, self-determination was conceived of as a means for ensuring peace and friendly relations, it was not considered an independent value, with the obvious consequence that it was to be set aside whenever its fulfilment gave rise to tension and conflict between states. Lastly, the principle was upheld only in so far as it did not bring about or authorise secession. In other words, the territorial integrity of states was held to be paramount.

When the Charter of the United Nations was drafted, almost all of its members were independent. Thus, the focus was on the rights and obligations of the sovereign member-states. It was still not popular to consider the rights of those nations that remained dependent. There were, however, recognised duties that colonial powers had towards the peoples they governed, but they did not at that time clearly include any duty to grant independence.

In this context, the right to self-determination mentioned in article 1(2), clearly relates to the rights of the peoples of one state to be protected from interference by other states or governments. The coupling of "self-determination" with "equal rights", cannot be regarded as incidental. It was clearly the equal rights of states that was being provided for, not the equal rights of individuals, or for that matter of groups. The concept of self-determination as referred to in the UN Charter, did not refer to a right of dependent peoples to be granted independence, or indeed to vote.[17] Thus, the phrase "self-determination of peoples" in article 1(2) should be interpreted to mean the sovereignty of states.

"Self-determination of peoples usually designates a principle of internal policy, the principle of democratic government. However, Article 1, para. 2, refers to relations among States. Therefore, the term "peoples", too - in connection with "equal rights" - means probably States, since only States have "equal rights" according to general international law."[18]

However, regardless of the cautious way in which the right to self-determination was referred to in the UN Charter, the General Assembly began in the 1950s to adopt a moral stance on the issue of colonialism, and with the increase in Afro-Asian membership of the UN in the 1960s, the right to self-determination was increasingly invoked as a right of dependent peoples to independence.

Notes

1 J. Locke., "Two treatises of government", *The second treatise*, p.135.
2 Ibid., p.168.
3 Ibid., p.225.
4 A. Sureda., "The evolution of the right of self-determination", 17, (1973), cited in: L. Brillmayer., "Secession and self-determination: A territorial interpretation", in: <u>Yale Journal of International Law</u>, Vol.16, (1991), pp.177-202, p.180.
5 United States Declaration of Independence (1776), quoted in: Buchheit. L.C., "Secession. The legitimacy of self-determination", (1978), p.55.
6 Ibid., p.61.
7 Lenin's essays are in Collected Works, xix, (1916-17; repr., New York, 1930), 192.
8 V. I. Lenin, "Selected works", (1977), Vol.2, p.475, cited in: I. G. Shivji, "The right of peoples to self-determination: An African perspective", in: Twining. W., (ed.), "Issues of self-determination", p.34.
9 Wilson. W., "Public Papers: Wars and Peace", i, (Washington, DC, 1927), pp.155-62, quoted in: Cassese. A., "International Law in a divided world" (1990), p.132.
10 Lansing. R., "Papers Relating to the Foreign Relations of the US", ii, (1939-40), pp.247-8, quoted in: Casesse. A., p.132.
11 Lord Acton, (1907), pp.297-298, quoted in: Ryan. S., "Ethnic conflict and international relations", (1990), p.30.
12 League of Nations Off. J., Spec. Supp. 3, at 5 (1920), cited in: Buchheit. L.C., p.71.
13 The Aaland Islands Question; Report Submitted to the Council of the League of Nations by the Commission of Rapporteurs, League Doc. B. 7.21/68/106, (1921), ibid., p.71.
14 Ibid.
15 Ibid.
16 Aureliu Cristescu, Special Rapporteur of the Sub-Commission on Prevention of Discrimination and Protection of Minorities, of the Commission on Human Rights, "The right to self-determination: Historical and current development on the basis of United Nations instruments", United Nations Department of Public Information, (1978), p.1.
17 Ibid., p.2.
18 H. Kelsen, "The Law of the United Nations", (1951), pp.51-52, cited in: Buchheit, L.C., p.131.

CHAPTER 2

Declaration on the Granting of Independence to Colonial Countries and Peoples, (1960)

During the late 1950s and the 1960s, the action of socialist states, vigorously supported by an increasing number of Third World countries, succeeded in gradually transforming the narrow and selective provisions of the UN Charter into a universal principle having a direct impact on international reality. While colonial empires were gradually being dismantled, the principle of self-determination was given a normative value which upgraded it to the highest standards of the international community. It was first and most notably sanctioned in the Declaration on the Granting of Independence to Colonial Countries and Peoples, Resolution 1514 (XV), which the General Assembly adopted unanimously on December 14, 1960.

The Declaration "solemnly proclaimed the necessity of bringing to a speedy and unconditional end colonialism in all its forms and manifestations." Article 2 reads: "All peoples have the right to self-determination; by virtue of that right they freely determine their political status and freely pursue their economic, social and cultural development." In addition to this forceful statement of the right to self-determination, a conditional clause in the form of Article 6 reads: "Any attempt aimed at the partial or the total disruption of the national unity and the territorial integrity of a country is incompatible with the Purposes and Principles of the Charter of the United Nations."

Thus by 1960, the application of the principle of self-determination to "colonial countries and peoples" had been well established in international law. However, a great deal of debate has since centred on the issue of whether the principle of self-determination is not, or at least not necessarily, an exceptional rule, limited to colonial territories. The idea that self-determination is a general principle, capable of having practical consequences outside of the colonial context is controversial and has given rise to an abundance of discourse on the subject. If a broader view is taken, the question arises as to what consequences the principle of self-determination has outside the colonial context and by implication, what is the status of secession as an aspect of self-determination in the post-decolonisation era?

Questions relating to the status of secession within the wider UN's campaign for decolonisation involve the extent to which an unqualified endorsement of self-determination in a UN document drafted under the impetus of the decolonisation sentiment, may legitimately be invoked to support a secessionist claim, particularly where the secessionists allege domination by an "alien" people. The uncertainty surrounding the status of secession, is clearly instanced in the Declaration on the Granting of Independence to Colonial Countries and Peoples.

The inter-relationship of articles 2 and 6 of the Declaration was never made clear during the discussion of the draft. Articles 2 and 6, have instead been open to subjective interpretation and the member states and their organisation, the UN, prejudiced by their unqualified conviction that the national unity and territorial integrity of their states are non-nego-tiable, have greatly influenced the exposition of the paragraphs, and therefore the declaration's overall utility to minority or ethnic groups within sovereign states who claim some form of autonomy, separation or secession. Delegates at the drafting of the Declaration discussed at great length whether the practical implication of the general principle articulat-ed in article 2, justified a people in claiming a right to separate from a member state or whether the "territorial integrity" provision in article 6 would apply to such situations.

The 1960 Declaration clearly adopts a functional definition of colo-nialism, speaking of colonialism in "all its forms and manifestations". Thus, it does not limit itself by its express terms, to the subjugation of non-European peoples by Europeans. Rather, it undertakes a more practi-cal approach in which the emphasis is upon the *fact of subjugation* by a racially or ethnically distinct group, which need not be European.[1]

This crucial point was clarified in Resolution 1541 (XV),[2] and may be viewed as an authentic interpretation thereof. It was concerned *inter alia*, with identifying the features of a non-self-governing territory's status which would under Charter obligations require the annual submission of information by the administering state. The criteria to decide whether a given territory falls into the colonial category in contemporary practice has been enumerated in Principle IV and V of the Annex as follows:

"*Prima facie* there is an obligation to transmit information in respect of a territory which is geographically separate and is distinct ethnically and/or culturally from the country administering it.

Once it has been established that such a *prima facie* case of geographical and ethnical or cultural distinctness of a territory exists, other elements may then be brought into consideration. These additional elements may be, *inter alia*, of an administrative, political, juridical, economic or historical nature. If they affect the relationship between the metropolitan State and the territory concerned in a manner which arbitrarily places the latter in a position of status of subordination, they support the presumption that there is an obligation to transmit information under Article 73(e) of the Charter."

A territory accordingly, is *prima facie* non-self governing if it is both geographically separate and ethnically distinct from the "country administering it". The UN found it expedient to adopt a "salt water" theory of colonisation, i.e., the inclusion of unwilling nationalities was deemed to be illegitimate, only if the state and its colony were geographically separated by land or sea. However, although geographical separateness has usually been taken to require separation across land or sea (this was arguably the case in the successful secession of East Bengal from Pakistan in 1971), there is no good reason why other defining characteristics, including historical boundaries or *de facto* boundaries, established through the hostile action of the government in question, might not also be relevant.[3]

However, geographic and ethnic separation or distinctiveness in itself is not adequate, it is also necessary that the relationship between the state as a whole and the territory concerned be one which arbitrarily places the latter in a position or status of subordination. Measures discriminating against the people of a region on grounds of their ethnic origin or cultural distinctiveness, may thus define the territory concerned as non-self governing, according to these criteria, thus reinforcing or even constituting the case for self-determination by the subjected people.

So far as distinct groups inhabiting a specified territory within an independent state are concerned, it might be possible that they may be treated in such a way by the central government that they become, in effect, non self-governing territories with respect to the rest of the state. However, cases of internal colonialism, or neo-colonialism are rarely recognised by the international community and remain very much the exception.

It is clear that the 1960 Declaration was aimed at facilitating the process of decolonisation and that Paragraph 6 was designed to be one of the instruments to achieve that end. The intention was clearly to facilitate the smooth progress of nation-building. However, the process of decolonisation was far from smooth and was regularly contested, as many colonial powers were keen to keep hold of their colonies.

At first, several of the colonial powers resisted the idea that there was a legal right of self-determination, it was, in their view, merely a political aspiration. But gradually their resistance to the idea of a legal obligation to grant the right to self-determination became more muted. The colonial powers accepted broader interpretations of their duties under Article 73(e), in Chapter XI of the UN Charter, especially in terms of the provision of information by member states to the United Nations on the political progress of Non Self-Governing Territories and Trust Territories. The evolution of the concept of self-determination was historically bound up with the decolonisation process and with the acceptance that it was obligatory to bring forward dependent peoples to independence, despite the fact that Article 73 of the UN Charter had spoken only of self-government.

As a result, those who formulated the Declaration found it essential to prevent the ex-colonial powers from intervening in the process of decolonisation.[4] To that end, they incorporated the provision that when independence is granted to post-colonial countries and peoples, any attempt to disrupt the national unity and territorial integrity of these newly independent states is incompatible with the UN Charter.

Hence, a broad interpretation of the Declaration, suggests that the prohibition of interference in the territorial unit and political independence of newly born states by outside powers, especially by the ex-colonial powers, was the primary concern of Paragraph 6. In view of this, it would be unreasonable to take it for granted that this paragraph militates against the right of self-determination by territorial separation. Instead, the paragraph seems to prohibit the expansionist aspirations of incumbent governments of UN member states. Such a prohibition as that incorporated in Paragraph 6, may therefore not be applicable in respect of a separatist attempt within an existing state by an aggrieved group.[5]

Concomitantly, even if it is accepted that paragraph 6 of the 1960 Declaration was designed to categorically protect the territorial integrity of existing states, a liberal interpretation of the Declaration suggests that it cannot be understood and applied in a socio-political and legal vacuum. The International Court of Justice in its *Advisory Opinion on the Namibia Case* held that:

"The court must take into consideration the changes which have occurred in the supervening [period], and its interpretation cannot remain unaffected by the subsequent development of law, through the Charter of the United Nations and by way of customary law. Moreover, an international instrument has to be interpreted and applied within the framework of the entire legal system prevailing at the time of interpretation".[6]

Concern for the need to protect and promote human rights and dignity is now high on the international community's agenda. The 1960 Declaration itself was the outcome of international humanitarian concern for the plight of colonial peoples. As such, Paragraph 6 must be construed in a manner which best serves the protection and promotion of fundamental human rights, one of the main purposes of the UN The infringement of human rights is clearly contradictory to the purposes of the UN, therefore, a state which does not comply with the purposes of the UN should not legitimately be entitled to UN remedies.

The world community is currently witnessing the massive violation of human rights by many UN member states within their territories under the cloak of territorial integrity. The UN, however, is often reduced to a passive role because of the diverse political interests of its members. From this perspective, a plain and literal reading of Paragraph 6 of the 1960 Declaration, protecting the territorial integrity of the state, is tenable whenever member states ensure the realization of fundamental human rights within their borders or whenever the UN acts as an enforcer and protector of those rights in the event of violation. However, when a member state infringes human rights within its territory and the UN cannot or does not respond to prevent the violation of human rights, the deprived people may not be barred by Paragraph 6 from resorting to any self-help remedy to realize their rights, even if that action infringes the territorial integrity and political unity of the existing state. The illegality of the violation of human rights in turn, must serve as a basis to justify any such action.[7]

"The foundation of decolonisation is the recognition and indeed the acceptance of the principle that the consequences of colonial conquest need to be reversed. This recognition includes the correlative principle that the process of reversal must be upon a just basis and that justice should be a manifest consequence in the new order brought about by decolonisation...The fact that the conquered people continue to suffer the same ills and consequences - and sometimes even more - as those that they have experienced under the burden of colonialism, means that decolonisation has not ushered in self-determination. If this latter means authentic, independent and free self-expression as well as the pursuit of self-realisation with due regard for the interests of the other on the basis of justice, then this has not yet become the experience of the decolonised".[8]

Clearly, as long as peoples living within independent sovereign states continue to suffer "the same ills and consequences" under their new rulers, that they suffered under traditional colonialism, then the principle of self-determination retains its applicability.

Realistically, however, both the context of the Declaration on the Granting of Independence to Colonial Countries and Peoples and the plain terms of Paragraph 6, outweigh any broad secessionist interpretations of the right to self-determination in article 2. It seems inescapable that the use of the phrase self-determination in the Declaration means colonial self-determination. The history of UN practice lends substantial support to the doctrine that the principle of self-determination, as interpreted by that body, is primarily an instrument for decolonisation, not an authorisation of secession. The reactions of the UN to separatist claims evidence a lack of sympathy for separatist demands that conflict with the principle of the territorial integrity of established states.

Notes

1 Reisman. W. M., "Somali self-determination in the Horn: Legal perspectives and implications for social and political engineering", in: Lewis. I. M., (ed.), "Nationalism and self-determination", (1983), pp.159-173, p.161.

2 G.A. Res. 1541 (XV), Principles Which Should Guide Members in Determining Whether or not an Obligation Exists to Transmit the Information Called for under Article 73(e) of the Charter, 15 Dec., (1960).

3 Crawford. J., "Outside the colonial context", in: Macartney. W. J. Allan., (ed.), "Self-determination in the Commonwealth", (1988), p.13.

4 Islam. M. R., "Bangladesh Liberation Movement", (1987), p.275.

5 Ibid., p.276.

6 ICJ Report. 31 (1971), cited in: Islam. M. R., p.276.

7 Ibid., p.277.

8 M. B. Ramose, "Self-determination in decolonisation", in: Twining. W., (ed.), "Issues of self-determination", (1991), pp.25-28.

CHAPTER 3

Self-determination as a human right: International Covenants on Human Rights, (1966)

The late 1960's witnessed the further evolution of the right to self-determination. Despite its collective overtones the right to self-determination was increasingly referred to as a "human right" and was incorporated in international human rights instruments. The most significant instance is article 1 of the International Covenant on Civil and Political Rights, (ICCPR), 1966,[1] which has become the basic universal human rights instrument.

During the early years of the United Nations, the major arenas for debates concerning the scope of the principle of self-determination were the drafting committees of the various international documents dealing with human rights. The first of these documents promulgated under the auspices of the United Nations, The Universal Declaration of Human Rights (1948), contained in article 21(3) language that was reminiscent of that used by President Wilson, proclaiming that "The will of the people shall be the basis of the authority of the government"[2]

The General Assembly noted in this same resolution that the fate of minorities was a "complex and delicate question" and rather than including a specific provision in the Declaration on the question of minorities decided to request the Commission on Human Rights to make a thorough study of the issue. In 1950 the General Assembly also called upon the Commission on Human Rights "to study ways and means which would ensure the right of peoples and nations to self-determination and to prepare recommendations for its consideration by the General Assembly..."[3]

As early as 1952, the UN General Assembly declared its decision to include:

"...in the International Covenant or Covenants on Human Rights an article on the right of all peoples and nations to self-determination in reaffirmation of the principles enunciated in the Charter of the United Nations. This article shall be drafted in the following terms: "All peoples shall have the right of self-determination", and shall stipulate that all

States, including those having responsibility for the administration of Non Self-Governing Territories, should promote the realisation of that right, in conformity with the Purposes and Principles of the United Nations, and that States having responsibility for the administration of Non Self-Governing Territories should promote the realisation of that right in relation to the peoples of such Territories".[4]

In the final draft, the International Covenant on Civil and Political Rights, ratified or acceded to by 113 states as of November 1991, but also binding on other states as customary law, states categorically in Part 1, in identical language to its counterpart in the International Covenant of Economic, Social and Cultural Rights:

1. All peoples have the right of self-determination. By virtue of that right they freely determine their political status and freely pursue their economic, social and cultural development.

2. All peoples may, for their own ends, freely dispose of their natural wealth and resources without prejudice to any obligations arising out of international economic co-operation, based upon the principle of mutual benefit, and international law. In no case may a people be deprived of its own means of subsistence.

3. The States Parties to the present Covenant, including those having responsibility for the administration of Non-Self-Governing and Trust Territories, shall promote the realization of the right of self-determination, and shall respect that right, in conformity with the provisions of the Charter of the United Nations.[5]

Thus the right to self-determination was transformed from a legal obligation imposed upon the colonial Powers in the process of decolonisation, to a universal human right, a right of "all peoples". In the Declaration on the Granting of Independence to Colonial Countries and Peoples, Resolution 1514, 1960, the reference to "peoples" was conditioned by allusions to colonialism. By 1966, the right of peoples to self-determination had made its appearance in the two International Covenants on Human Rights as a free standing maxim, beyond the confines of normative practices on decolonisation. The provision in article 1 of both Covenants was significant, because for the first time, the right of self-determination had been formulated within a universal document concerning human rights, which recognised the legal obligations of the states parties to it.

The Commission on Human Rights subsequently turned its attention to the problem of the implementation of the instrument. The result was the establishment of a Human Rights Committee to deal with alleged violations of the ICCPR. The process of implementation naturally began with a system of monitoring, similar to that practised under article 73e of the UN Charter. In a similar fashion, the 113 states parties to the ICCPR are legally obliged to "undertake to submit reports on the measures they have adopted which give effect to the rights recognised herein and on the progress made in the enjoyment of those rights".[6] These reports are scrutinised by the Human Rights Committee which is made up of eighteen members elected by states parties to the Covenant who serve in their personal capacities[7] for a term of four years.[8] While the Committee is not a court it does have the right to question the reports submitted by members. It transmits its reviews and appropriate comments to the states parties to the Covenant and the UN Economic and Social Council (ECOSOC). An Optional Protocol permits individuals to lodge complaints against accepting states.[9]

Two distinct issues arise with respect to article 1 of the ICCPR. The first relates to its status as a "human right" in the Covenant, having regard to its location in Part 1 of the Covenant, whilst the second concerns its scope, and in particular, whether the term "peoples" is to be limited only to peoples under colonial rule.

The inclusion of article 1 in a separate untitled Part of the ICCPR raises questions concerning the relationship between the Parts of the Covenant, in particular between Part I (self-determination) and Part II (Articles 2-5), which sets out certain equality rights, and makes provision for derogation from certain rights in times of public emergency, and Part III (Articles 6-27), which contains all the other substantive human rights. By placing the right to self-determination at the beginning of both Covenants (and not within the list of the other human rights), it indicates that this right is considered a pre-requisite for the realisation of all other human rights.

"The right to self-determination is a fundamental right, without which other rights cannot be fully enjoyed. Consequently, the enjoyment of that right is essential to the exercise of all individual rights and freedoms. That is why it is accorded pride of place in the International Covenant on Human Rights".[10]

The Human Rights Committee not only considers reports and complaints, but periodically makes more general findings on the state of civil and political rights and prepares summaries of the developing normative expectations arising from the ICCPR. In its general commentary on article 1, however, the Committee has been rather cautious. Nevertheless, it has acknowledged the primacy of the right to self-determination among the other fundamental human rights enumerated in the Covenant.

"In accordance with the purposes and principles of the Charter of the United Nations...article 1 recognises that all peoples have the right of self-determination. The right...is of particular importance because its realisation is an essential condition for the effective guarantee and observance of individual human rights and for the promotion and strengthening of those rights".[11]

The inference that the right of self-determination is a pre-requisite to all other human rights, is further substantiated by General Assembly Resolution 637/VII, which declares that "the right of peoples and nations to self-determination is a pre-requisite to the full enjoyment of all fundamental human rights" and recommends that UN member states:

"...uphold the principle of self-determination of all peoples and nations and called for information under Article 73(c) of the Charter on the extent to which the right of peoples and nations to self-determination is exercised by the peoples of Non Self-Governing Territories, and in particular regarding their political progress".[12]

However, the inclusion of article 1 in a separate part of the Covenant has made its relationship with the rest of the Covenant obscure. In particular, it begs the question as to whether or not the complaints procedures established by article 41 of the ICCPR and by the Optional Protocol to that Covenant, extend to complaints of violations against article 1 and by implication, to complaints of violations against the right to self-determination. Whilst it is often maintained that those complaint procedures apply only to violations of individual rights under Parts II and III,[13] there is no textual basis for such a limitation. Article 41 refers to "violations of any of the rights set forth in the Covenant" and the Optional Protocol also refers to "violations of any of the rights set forth in the Covenant" (Preamble, article 1, 2), and to "any provision of the Covenant" (article 4). Similarly, article 7 of the Optional Protocol states that:

"Pending the achievement of the objective of resolution 1514 (XV) adopted by the General Assembly of the United Nations on 14 December 1960 concerning the Declaration on the Granting of Independence to Colonial Countries and Peoples, the provisions of the present Protocol shall in no way limit the right of petition granted to these peoples by the Charter of the United Nations and other international conventions and instruments under the United Nations and its specialised agencies".[14]

Although the rights of petition referred to in article 7 include rights to petition about violations of individual rights, their primary focus is clearly on the right to self-determination. If the Optional Protocol had intended to categorically exclude communications relating to article 1 of the Covenant, it is difficult to see why article 7 of the Protocol was necessary.

There are, accordingly, no grounds for excluding article 1 in principle from the complaints procedures established by article 41 of the Covenant and by the Protocol, or for treating that provision as merely preambular or incidental in its effect. But difficulties of a procedural kind will be encountered in bringing communications to the Human Rights Committee under the Optional Protocol (as distinct from under article 41), in respect of article 1. Under the Optional Protocol individuals may bring complaints against states party to the ICCPR, accepting that procedure. The principle difficulty is that articles 1 and 2 of the Protocol, deliberately refer only to "communications from individuals...who claim to be victims of a violation of any of the rights set forth in the Covenant". In accordance with this, article 90b of the Human Rights Committee's rules of procedure provides that:

"Normally, the communication should be submitted by the individual himself or by his representative; the Committee may however, accept to consider a communication on behalf of an alleged victim when it appears that he is unable to submit the communication himself".[15]

The implication, is that there is no possibility for minority or group actions under the ICCPR procedure. The Human Rights Committee has consequently been faced with a dilemma. The right to self-determination is a right in the Covenant, albeit a right of a different kind from the rest and standing alone in Part 1, but it is a right of peoples not of any individual, and only individuals may bring communications. The difficulties these requirements present for persons or groups claiming a violation of article 1 are well illustrated in the few cases which have been presented to the Committee.

So far, the Human Rights Committee has not had much occasion to explain the content of the right to self-determination. However, in the petition-based case of the Mikmaq Tribal Society, it was presented with an opportunity for comment.[16] In this case, the Grand Captain of the Mikmaq Tribal Society (a band of Canadian Indians) claimed on his own behalf and on behalf of "the Mikmaq people", that Canada was continuing to deny that people the right of self-determination contrary to article 1 of the ICCPR. While it rejected the communication as "inadmissible", the Committee based its rejection on the applicant's inability to demonstrate that he was authorised to represent the tribe or that he personally, had been deprived of a right protected by the Covenant. The Committee concluded that:

"...the author has not proven that he is authorized to act as a representative on behalf of the Mikmaq tribal society. In addition, the author has failed to advance any pertinent facts supporting his claim that he is personally a victim of a violation of any rights contained in the Covenant".[17]

The second sentence in this passage is ambiguous, since it could have been based merely on the onus of proof and on the facts adduced, or more fundamentally on the ground that self-determination can never be a right of individuals as distinct from groups, so that an individual communication relating to article 1 of the ICCPR could never satisfy the Protocol's admissibility requirements. If, as it seems likely, the latter view were taken, it would follow that the Protocol, while apparently allowing communications under article 1 of the Covenant, had directly excluded them. But even if the former interpretation is adopted, the result will be that individual communications in relation to article 1 will hardly ever be admissible, since it will rarely be the case that all members of the people in question are either themselves individual applicants under the Protocol or are clearly identified and represented by persons sufficiently connected to them.

However, the ICCPR also validates free and equal political participation, as well as the cultural rights of minorities. The Committee's finding in the above related case leaves open the possibility that another individual might succeed in bringing a comparable petition, if he or she can demonstrate having the *bona fides* to act in a representative capacity and alleges a denial of cultural autonomy or free and equal political participation.

The Committee on Human Rights has not determined who the "peoples" are to whom the right to self-determination applies. Its view of self-determination has in fact precluded the necessity of such a finding. But it has had to make certain findings of a jurisdictional nature on the right to self-determination. Dealing with a series of cases in which groups have claimed that they were indeed "peoples" for purposes of article 1 of the Covenant namely, the Mikmaq Indians, the Lubicon Lake Band Indians of Canada and the Samis of Sweden the Committee has determined as follows:

"While all peoples have the right of self-determination and the right freely to determine their political status, pursue their economic, social and cultural development and dispose of their natural wealth and resources, as stipulated in Article 1 of the Covenant, the question whether the Lubicon Lake Band constitutes a "people" is not an issue for the

Committee to address under the Optional Protocol to the Covenant. The Optional Protocol provides a procedure under which individuals can claim that their individual rights have been violated. These rights are set out in Part III of the Covenant, articles 6-27, inclusive. There is however, no objection to a group of individuals, who claim to be similarly affected, collectively to submit a communication about alleged breaches of their rights".[18]

Although initially couched in terms of alleged breaches of the provisions of article 1 of the ICCPR, the Committee stated that there was no doubt that many of the claims presented by the Lubicon Lake Band raised issues under article 27 of the Covenant, which reads:

"In those States in which ethnic, religious or linguistic minorities exist, persons belonging to such minorities shall not be denied the right, in common with other members of their group, to enjoy their own culture, to profess and practice their own religion, and to use their own language."

Accordingly, the Committee concluded that historical inequities and other more recent developments did threaten the way of life and culture of the Lubicon Lake Band, thereby constituting a violation of article 27 of the Covenant, so long as they continued.

The right to self-determination is guaranteed to the peoples of a state in their entirety. Clearly, all members of distinct minority groups are part of the peoples of the whole territory, in this sense they too are the holders of the right to self-determination. But in article 27, minorities as such are not accorded the right to self-determination. They are provided with the right to enjoy their own culture, religion and language. The Covenant gives entirely discrete rights to minorities on the one hand (minority rights, as elaborated in article 27), and to peoples (self-determination rights, as provided in article 1) on the other. Moreover, article 27 is couched in terms of the rights of the individual as a member of a minority, clearly enabling individuals to join in bringing a claim in which they have each had an individual right infringed.

"The right to self-determination is a collective right, a fundamental human right forming part of the legal system established by the Charter, the beneficiaries of which are peoples - whether or not constituted as independent States - nations and States. National minorities exercise this right through the enjoyment of the rights granted to them by article 27 of the International Covenant on Civil and Political Rights and of other individual human rights, whether civil, political, economic, social or cultural."[19]

To conclude, it seems that the inclusion of article 1 in both Human Rights Covenants, representing as it does a victory for those states advocating recognition of a legal right of self-determination, appears in spite of its possible secessionist interpretation, rather than as a confirmation of that interpretation. It was instead, an indication of the strong desire for a sweeping statement of the right to self-determination as a weapon against colonialism. A close examination of the debates at the Human Rights Commission suggest:

"...that the principle of self-determination would be invoked only for the liberation of colonial peoples and territories. It was not to be construed as implying the right of individuals within nations to express their special ethnic, cultural or religious characteristics or the exercise of the democratic method in internal affairs."[20]

However, UN member states have in subsequent years expressed views to the General Assembly which in part at least, defend a wider interpretation of article 1 of the ICCPR.

"It is no accident that the first article of each of the International Covenants proclaims the right of self-determination. We should always remember that under the Covenants, self-determination is a right of peoples and not of governments. Moreover, it is not only peoples suffering occupation by a foreign power which are deprived of their right of self-determination, accompanied by equally appalling violations of many other fundamental rights, perpetrated against peoples by their own countrymen. Amin's atrocities in Uganda and Pol Pot's in Cambodia are perhaps the most glaring contemporary examples. But they are by no means the only ones. Self-determination is not a single event, but a continuous process."[21]

Notes

1 General Assembly Resolution, 2200 A (XXI) December, 16, (1966).

2 Article 21(3), G.A. Res. 217, UN Doc. A/810, at 71, 75 (1948), cited in: Buchheit. L.C., "Secession: The legitimacy of self-determination", (1978), p.76.

3 G.A. Res. 421, 5 UN GAOR, Supp, 20, pp.42-43, UN Doc. A/1775 (1952).

4 G.A. Res. 545, VI UN GAOR, Supp 20, at 36, UN Doc. A/2119 (1952), cited in: Crawford. J., "Outside the colonial context" in: Macartney, W. J. Allan., (ed.), "Self-determination in the Commonwealth", (1988), p.3.

5 G.A. Res., 2200 A (XXI) December, 16, (1966).

6 International Covenant on Civil and Political Rights, Article 40(1).

7 ICCPR, Articles 28 and 30.

8 ICCPR, Article 32.

9 The Optional Protocol was opened for signature on December 19, (1966).

10 Aureliu Cristescu, Special Rapporteur of the Sub-Commission on Prevention of Discrimination and Protection of Minorities of the Commission on Human Rights. "The right to self-determination: Historical and current development on the basis of United Nations instruments", UN Department of Public Information, (1978), p.2.

11 General Comments of the Human Rights Committee, UN Doc. CCPR/C/21.Rev.1, at pp. 10-11 (1989), cited in: Franck. T. M., "The emerging right to democratic governance", in: AJIL, 86, (1992), pp.46-91, p.60.

12 G.A. Res. 637/VII, cited in: Anna Michalska, "Rights of peoples to self-determination in international law", in: Twining. W., (ed.), "Issues of self-determination", p.79.

13 This issue was raised before the Human Rights Committee by Communication No. 78/1980, AD on behalf of the Mikmaq Tribal Society v. Canada, GAOR A/39/40 (1984), 200.

14 Optional Protocol, December 19, 1966, Article 7, cited in: Crawford. J., p.4.

15 Text cited in: Tardu, M. E., "Human rights: The international petition system", (1985), cited in: Crawford. J., p.4.

16 Communication No. 78/1980, AD on behalf of Mikmaq Tribal Society v. Canada, GAOR A/39/40 (1984), 200.

17 GAOR A/39/40, (1984) 203, cited in: Crawford. J., p.5.

18 Communication No. 167/1984, Bernard Ominayak, Chief of the Lubicon Lake Band v. Canada.
19 Aureliu Cristescu, p.2.
20 Moskowitz. M., "The politics and dynamics of human rights", (1968), pp. 160-161, cited in: Buchheit. L.C., p.84.
21 Marston, G., (ed.), "United Kingdom materials in international law", in: British Journal of International Law, 56, (1985), p.460, quoted in: Crawford. J., p.6.

CHAPTER 4

Declaration on Principles of International Law concerning Friendly Relations and Co-operation among States, (1970)

Of crucial importance to an understanding of the present status of the right to self-determination outside of the decolonisation era is the General Assembly's 1970 Declaration on Friendly Relations.[1] The Declaration was the outcome of a study of the fundamental principles of the United Nations Charter and the duties stemming therefrom, including "the principle of equal rights and self-determination of peoples". A Special Committee was established by the General Assembly in 1963 to study these principles and member states were invited to submit in writing to the Secretary General any views or suggestions they might have regarding these principles. The Declaration that emerged out of the extensive debates in the Special Committee on Friendly Relations,[2] although a product of extensive compromise, is a forceful and significant document. Although as a General Assembly resolution, the Declaration is not a binding document, having no specific legal authority, it is nonetheless indicative of widely held views on the subject of self-determination. The Declaration states:

"By virtue of the principle of equal rights and self-determination of peoples enshrined in the Charter of the United Nations, all peoples have the right freely to determine, without external interference, their political status and to pursue their economic, social and cultural development, and every State has the duty to respect this right in accordance with the provisions of the Charter.

Nothing in the foregoing paragraphs shall be construed as authorising or encouraging any action which would dismember or impair, totally or in part, the territorial integrity or political unity of sovereign and independent States conducting themselves in compliance with the principle of equal rights and self-determination of peoples as described above and thus possessed of a government representing the whole people belonging to the territory without distinction as to race, creed or colour.

Every State shall refrain from any action aimed at the partial or total disruption of the national unity and territorial integrity of any other State or country".[3]

That portion of the Declaration which deals with the principle of equal rights and self-determination attempts to reconcile many of the conflicting viewpoints regarding the status of self-determination, its scope, and means for implementation. The debate over the legal significance of the Charter's recognition of self-determination, (for example, whether it is a legal right or a political principle), was once again revived in the preparatory discussions of the Declaration by the General Assembly. The phraseology finally adopted in the Declaration in Paragraph 1 clearly favours the view that self-determination is in fact a right, and not merely a political principle.

The scope of the right to self-determination was also clarified in the Declaration. The final draft of the Declaration rejected the polar views expressed during the debate, on the one hand, the desire to limit the principle to cases of colonialism, and on the other, to broaden the principle to encompass a right of secession, in favour of a description which states that by virtue of the principle "all peoples have the right freely to determine, without external interference, their political status and to pursue their economic, social and cultural development".

The Declaration also attempted a classification of the relationship between human rights and self-determination. Paragraph 2 implies that the concepts are separable by saying that the subjection of peoples to alien subjugation, domination and exploitation constitutes a violation of the principle of equal rights and self-determination of peoples *as well* as a denial of human rights. Paragraph 3 reaffirms the duty of every state to promote the respect for and observance of human rights and fundamental freedoms.

The provision of the Declaration concerning the means of implementing the principle of self-determination demands special attention. As adopted, paragraph 4 of the Declaration suggests that the achievement of self-government may take the form of "[T]he establishment of a sovereign and independent State, the free association or integration with an independent State". However, it also contains a suggestive but obscure addition to this list, by appending the language "or the emergence into any other political status freely determined by a people". Of equal significance here, is the fact that the implementing provision is addressed to the peoples themselves rather than to states, thus implying a right of self-implementation.

Finally, and most importantly, paragraph 7 which deals with the maintenance of territorial integrity, has been interpreted to recognise for the first time in an international document of this kind, the legitimacy of secession under certain circumstances.[4] Much of the discourse concerning the status of the right to self-determination in the post-decolonisation era has centred around paragraph 7 of General Assembly Resolution 2625 (XXV). The first part of paragraph 7 warns that nothing in the foregoing text should be construed as authorising or encouraging the dismemberment or impairment of the territorial integrity or political unity of sovereign and independent states. Paragraph 7, however, implies that not all states will enjoy this inviolability of their territorial integrity, but only those states "conducting themselves in compliance with the principles of equal rights and self-determination of peoples as described above." In a telling final clause, paragraph 7 offers a partial definition of the meaning of the compliance provision, by stating "and thus possessed of a government representing the whole people belonging to the territory without distinction as to race, creed or colour."

The notion embodied in this final clause, is clearly a direct descendant of the belief repeatedly expressed in the writings of Locke, Jefferson, and Wilson, that the legitimacy of government derives from the consent of the governed and that consent cannot be forthcoming without the enfranchisement of all segments of the population. By placing the language at the end of paragraph 7 in the form of a saving clause, the drafters apparently affirmed a corollary to the "consent of the governed" concept. If a government does not represent the whole people it is illegitimate and thus in violation of the principle of self-determination, and this illegitimate character serves in turn to legitimate "action which would dismember or impair, totally or in part, the territorial integrity or political unity" of the sovereign and independent state.

Traditionally, the self-determination norm on which secessionists base their claim is thought to turn on democratic principles of consent and popular sovereignty. According to this argument, self-determination represents a liberal democratic value (with secession as the liberal democratic alternative), while the principle of territorial integrity remains feudal, undemocratic and oppressive. The idea that government must stem from the consent of the governed seems to allow a dissafected group the right to opt out of an existing state. If consent is the keystone of legitimacy, then a non-consenting individual must be allowed to leave. In this way, principles of democratic government translate into a right of secession.

The only countervailing principle, that of territorial integrity of existing states, suffers from a suspect historical association with monarchy and feudalism. Therefore, so the argument goes, territoriality must give way to liberal democratic principles and the right of self-determination.

However, the apparent simplicity of this position is misleading, for it places too much weight upon consent as the cornerstone of state legitimacy.[5] Despite the rhetoric of liberal democracy, actual consent is not necessary to political legitimacy. A refusal to consent has never exempted an individual from state authority. Thus, "[S]eparatists cannot base their arguments upon a right to opt out because no such right exists in democratic theory".[6] Government by the consent of the governed, does not necessarily encompass a right to opt out, it only requires that within the existing political unit, a right to participate through electoral processes is available. Moreover, participatory rights do not entail a right to secede. On the contrary, they suggest that the appropriate solution for dissatisfied groups, rests in their full inclusion in the polity, with full participation in its decision-making processes.[7]

It is important to note what the Declaration does *not* say. The Declaration does not give unlimited recognition to separatism. On the contrary, the opening lines of paragraph 7 reaffirming the territorial integrity and political unity of independent and sovereign states, suggests that the drafters elected to start from the conservative position of giving *prima facie* respect to the present state-centred order. The innovation of the Declaration rests in its implicit acceptance of limitations upon the deference to be accorded to the territorial integrity of states, limitations arising from the state's duty to provide a democratic government and protection for basic human rights.

Additionally, the question concerning whether the presence of a representative democracy vitiates any claims to separatist self-determination seems to be answered by the Declaration. What appears to be required, is a denial of political freedom and/or human rights as a *sine qua non* for a legitimate separatist claim. It suggests that states are under no obligation imposed by international law to recognise separatist demands beyond providing protection for human rights and a representative government that does not discriminate on the basis of race, creed or colour. If these conditions are satisfied, the instrument apparently consigns discussions regarding the political status of such groups within their states to the level of internal constitutional law.

The right to self-determination applies only to those peoples living under racist regimes and forbids self-determination where there is a non-racist, representative government. However, this view assumes that self-determination means only independence, and that in turn, independence in a post-colonial situation can only mean secession, violating the territorial unity of the whole. The starting point is not the correct one. It is certainly not the approach taken by the Committee on Human Rights, whose practice on this matter and the concurrence of states as evidenced in the dialogues upon the examination of state reports, bears examination.

It has been clear from the outset, that self-determination was not tied only to independence. The peoples of an independent territory have always had the right to choose the form of their political and economic future. While independence has been the most frequently chosen path, other possibilities have always existed. General Assembly Resolution 1541 (XV) spoke of self-determination being exercised "through independence, free association, integration with an independent state, or emergence into any other political status freely determined by a people". Thus, self-determination has never simply meant independence. It has meant the free choice of peoples. During the era of colonialism, that choice was focused on the possibility of independence or other post-colonial status. That is the aspect of colonialism that reflects the entitlement referred to in article 1 of the International Covenant on Civil and Political Rights, that all peoples may "freely determine their political status". But the entitlement goes beyond that. The entitlement is also to "freely pursue their economic, social and cultural development". How can that be done if self-determination does not also provide for free choice not only as to *status* but as to *government*?

The right to self-determination remains an ongoing one. It is not only at the moment of independence from colonial rule that peoples are entitled freely to pursue their economic, social and cultural development. It is a constant entitlement, and that in turn means people are entitled to choose their own government. The Human Rights Committee has consistently told states appearing before it for the examining of their periodic reports, that a free choice be afforded to the people on a continuing basis, as to their system of government, in order that they can determine their economic, social and cultural development.

Clearly, this is virtually impossible to achieve in a one-party state. At the Copenhagen meeting in 1990, the representatives of the Conference on Security and Co-operation in Europe (CSCE) unanimously proclaimed "their conviction that...pluralistic democracy" is a prerequisite "for progress in setting up the lasting order of peace, security, justice and co-operation that they seek to establish in Europe".[8] Pluralism can take many forms, but self-determination requires the ongoing choice of the people as to their political governance, and in turn, their economic, social and cultural development. Self-determination can be exercised in many ways, including an open and pluralistic political process, without being incompatible with the clauses in relevant instruments that call for the protection of territorial integrity.

The first instance of the legal impact of the Declaration on separatist claims was given by the International Commission of Jurists (I.C.J.) in its 1972 study, entitled The Events in East Pakistan, 1971.[9] In the jurists report, the Commission whilst characterising the 1970 Declaration as "the most authoritative statement of the principles of international law relevant to the questions of self-determination and territorial integrity.",[10] perceived the principle of self-determination as essentially conflicting with that of territorial integrity, and it chose to interpret paragraph 7 of the Declaration in the light of the maxim *pacta sunt servanda* namely, that self-determination is a right that can be exercised only once. "According to this view," they said, "if a people or their representatives have once chosen to join with others within either a unitary or a federal state, that choice is a final exercise of their right to self-determination; they cannot afterwards claim the right to secede under the principle of the right to self-determination."[11]

In a crucial passage the report concludes:

"It is submitted, however, that this principle is subject to the requirement that the government does comply with the principle of equal rights and does represent the whole people without distinction. If one of the constituent peoples of a state is denied equal rights and is discriminated against, it is submitted that their full right of self-determination will revive."[12]

In rebutting the *pacta sunt servanda* argument, namely, the maxim, *rebus sic standibus* can be used, provided the situation has not changed substantially. This principle would seem to allow the renewal of a group's right to self-determination should their political situation radically change.

Any proposals for the international recognition of the continuing applicability of the right to self-determination to peoples living within independent states, will obviously encounter forceful objections. The objections can be divided into arguments purely legal in character and fears of a psycho-political nature.[13] Many of those objections based on arguments more purely legal in character, have been mentioned above. The non-legal arguments against secession are more numerous. They include: (i) the fear of Balkanisation, or the fear of a precipitation of secessionist claims, *ad absurdum;* (ii) the fear of infinite divisibility, indeed very few states are ethnically homogeneous; (iii) the fear of the effect that such a right could have on the democratic system, by allowing a disaffected minority to threaten dismemberment if state policies do not reflect their wishes; (iv) the danger of giving birth to non-viable and small entities which would in turn rely on international aid; (v) the fear of "trapped minorities" within the seceding state, who may be exposed to discrimination; and (vi) the fear of "stranded majorities" in cases where the seceding territory is economically or strategically crucial to the parent state.

To conclude, the Declaration on Principles of International Law concerning Friendly Relations and Co-operation among States, 1970, clarified and reconciled the different approaches to the right to self-determination, as espoused over the preceding years in the various UN resolutions and international instruments. It borrowed from the League of Nations's approach, i.e., the primacy of seeking an improvement of the condition of individuals and minority groups within multi-ethnic states, by subjecting those states to external international pressure. It inverted the movement to establish self-determination as a human right, by demanding a protection of human rights as an element (along with others, such as the establishment of a representative government), to be observed when acting in compliance with the principle of self-determination. Lastly, it reinforced the external pressure to respect the principle of self-determination, by brandishing a legitimisation of secession where the coercive force of international opinion was insufficient to moderate a state's internal policies.

Notes

1 Declaration on Principles of International Law concerning Friendly Relations and Co-operation among States in accordance with the Charter of the United Nations, G.A. Res. 2625, Annex, 25 UN GAOR, Supp. 28, at 121, UN Doc. A/5217 (1970).

2 See Buchheit. L.C., "Secession. The legitimacy of self-determination", (1978), for an extensive account of the debates in the Special Committee, pp.88-97.

3 General Assembly Resolution. 2625, (XXV), (1970).

4 Buchheit. L.C., p.92.

5 Brillmayer, L., "Secession and self-determination: A territorial interpretation", in: Yale Journal of International Law, Vol.16, (1991), pp.177-202.

6 Ibid., p.184.

7 Ibid., p.185.

8 Conference on Security and Co-operation in Europe(CSCE), Document of the Copenhagen Meeting of the Conference on the Human Dimension, June 29, (1990), Preamble, at 1307.

9 Secretariat of the International Commission of Jurists, The Events in East Pakistan, 1971 (1972).

10 Ibid., p.67.

11 Ibid., p.69.

12 Ibid.

13 See Buchheit. L. C., for a comprehensive list of these objections, pp. 21-27.

CHAPTER 5

Self-determination and intervention

International law embraces certain behaviourial norms, which by virtue of their fundamental nature, are intended to be the first principles of civilised international conduct. These principles are acknowledged to be the starting points in the formulation of a state's external conduct and they operate as a yardstick against which the international community can measure the legal acceptability of the behaviour of its members. Certain overriding principles of international law exist, forming a body of *jus cogens*. The major distinguishing feature of such rules is their relative indelibility. They are rules of customary law, the operation of which voids any treaty, international or national instrument, law or act that violates one of its norms. Such rules can only be set aside by treaty or acquiescence in the formation of a subsequent customary rule of contrary effect. Examples of this class of rules are; the principle of self-determination, the prohibition of the use of force, the principle of permanent sovereignty over natural resources, the law of genocide, the principle of racial non-discrimination, crimes against humanity, and the rules prohibiting trade in slaves and piracy.[1]

The importance of the right to self-determination in international relations is reinforced by its consideration as a peremptory or *jus cogens* norm,[2] i.e., it has a binding mandatory nature, and cannot be denied under any circumstances.

"The principle is the most important of the principles of international law concerning friendly relations and co-operation among States, and constitutes the basis for the other principles. It has as its corollary sovereign equality. Non-intervention, another such principle, should not be used as a cover for violations of self-determination; it should protect States and peoples struggling for their independence, since acts of intervention are violations of the principle of equal rights and self-determination of peoples".[3]

The United Nations Charter reiterated the pre-eminence of these principles of international law. The prohibition against the threat or use of force in international relations embodied in article 2(4) of the UN Charter, has been called the "principle norm of international law of our time."[4] It is complemented by another of the cardinal principles of international law, that which upholds the age-old principle of state sovereignty, the non-intervention by states in the internal affairs of sister states. Article 2(7) of the UN Charter, provides that nothing in the Charter "shall authorize the United Nations to intervene in matters which are essentially within the domestic jurisdiction of any State." The non-intervention norm has been further recognised by the General Assembly in the Declaration on the Inadmissibility of Intervention in the Domestic Affairs of States and the Protection of Their Independence and Sovereignty, 1965.[5] These principles are intended to have general applicability, deviation from which can only be justified in exceptional circumstances, such as defence, peace and security (in which case there is collective intervention by an International Governmental Organisation or by its members following a specific resolution), and in rare cases for humanitarian considerations, in particular, in flagrant cases of institutionalised racism and violence against a majority, and in classical colonialism.[6]

The UN General Assembly Declaration on Friendly Relations, 1970, attempts a fairly explicit elaboration of the primary norms of international conduct expressly stated or implicit in the UN Charter, including, *inter alia*, the principle prohibiting the use of force, the principle of non-intervention, and the principle of equal rights and self-determination of peoples. Yet in the absence of an hierarchical ordering of the above principles, when translated into the reality of modern state practice, these principles often come into stark conflict with one another. The relationship between the principle of self-determination and the norms of non-intervention and the proscription of the use of force provides an interesting example of this tension.

According to Professor Brownlie, the principle of self-determination "informs and complements other general principles of international law, viz., of State sovereignty, the equality of States and the equality of peoples within a State. Thus self-determination is employed in conjunction with the principle of non-intervention in relation to the use of force and otherwise."[7]

Nevertheless, whilst "[T]he present position is that self-determination is a legal principle, and that United Nations organs do not permit Article 2, paragraph 7, to impede discussion and decision when the principle is in issue",[8] a residual conflict of principles still troubles many states.

Whilst the relationship between these principles remains obscure, it raises several problematic questions. Firstly, is it possible to assume that one aspect of *jus cogens* is more important than another. Secondly, do

denials of self-determination fall "essentially" within the domestic jurisdiction of states, or has it become a recognised exception to the principle
of non-interference in a state's domestic jurisdiction. Lastly, does a state
that supports (politically, economically, or militarily) a movement for
self-determination violate the norms against the use of force and
non-intervention, or can it legitimate its actions by claiming that it
responds to the demands of the alternative principle of self-determination.
A related question, is whether a state that aids a sister state in the suppression of a group under its control, who is claiming a right to self-determination, violates the principle of self-determination and/or the principle
of non-intervention, despite an invitation for intervention from the governing state.

Much of the conflict between these interrelated and complimentary
principles, rests on whether a broad interpretation is given to statements
that mention self-determination in a context suggesting its applicability to
non-colonial circumstances and thus suggesting a possible right of intervention in separatist/secessionist movements. The General Assembly for
example, has clearly expressed its conviction that in circumstances
involving colonial and alien domination and racist regimes, peoples have
an "inherent right to struggle by all necessary means at their disposal
against colonial powers and alien domination in exercise of their right of
self-determination."[9] Similarly, paragraph 6 of the 1970 Declaration of
Friendly Relations provides that "[I]n their actions against, and resistance
to, such forcible action [which deprives peoples of their right to
self-determination] in pursuit of the exercise of their right to self-determination, such peoples are entitled to seek and to receive support in accordance with the purposes and principles of the Charter of the United
Nations."[10]

In addition, General Assembly Resolution, 2625 states:
"Every State has the duty to refrain from any forcible action which
deprives peoples referred to in the elaboration of the principle of equal
rights and self-determination of their right to self-determination and freedom and independence".[11]

Today, it is still the orthodox view for international law to recognise as
its subjects only sovereign states, to which individuals or groups have no
direct access. Accordingly, the right of peoples to self-determination can
at best place an obligation upon a state to accord its citizens a measure of
self-determination, assuming that it has subscribed to treaties or international agreements requiring that it do so. It does not bestow a right to peoples to demand that their governing state comply with their self-govern-

ing wishes.

However, this doctrine is no longer an accurate description of contemporary international law. There is evidence of a shift towards the recognition of individuals as subjects of international law. The assault on the state-centred prejudice of international law has been pursued on a number of fronts. For example, individuals are now widely considered to be proper subjects of the international law concerned with human rights. More importantly, the United Nations General Assembly has curtailed to a certain extent its previous practice of addressing its resolutions to states, asking them to respect the right of their citizens to self-determination, and has begun to affirm directly the right of the peoples themselves to compel the compliance of their governors. General Assembly pronouncements, like the 1970 Declaration, which requested that states offer aid directly to the group struggling for self-determination, thereby compelling the compliance of their governors, are becoming more common.[12]

On the strength of such General Assembly pronouncements, a state wishing to relegate non-intervention and the prohibition against the non-use of force to a secondary normative status and to intervene, even forcibly, on behalf of a people struggling for self-determination, would appear to have a colourable claim for the legality of its action. This certainly seems to be the case in circumstances of a colonial struggle for self-determination. But does this right to intervene extend beyond the colonial situation. Can norms of non-intervention and non-use of force be overridden by the principle of self-determination. Clearly, it is not advocated that interventionary force may legally be used to aid a group illegitimately claiming a right to self-determination. However, under the present legal order, there is no well-defined basis in law for chastising an intervenor's subjective decision regarding the legitimacy of a group's claim to self-determination or for criticising its judgement in giving prime of place, in its normative hierarchy to the prohibition of the use of force.

Secessionist movements are traditionally excluded from such a right, to seek and be given support, regardless of their frequent claim, that in substance their situation differs very little from institutionalised domination and exploitation by "aliens". Traditionally, non-intervention means non-interference against a state and not non-intervention in its support. A sovereign, independent state is entitled to request from any third state the aid that it deems necessary. The notion of intervention excludes action taken with the consent or permission of the government of the state in question. At the same time, third-party states cannot assist secessionists, for they would in effect be using force against the territorial integrity of an independent state. Accordingly:

"...self-determination, considered as the right to non-intervention, means the right that foreign States shall not interfere in the life of the community against the will of the government. It does not include the right that a foreign state shall not interfere in the life of the community against the interests of the population but at the request or at any rate with the tacit approval of the government".[13]

The legal basis for refraining from supporting secessionists is the sovereign equality, independence and territorial integrity of states. From the point of view of inter-state relations the basis is practical, it is "designed to discourage states from becoming involved in unstable and ambiguous situations".[14]

In the context of normative political theory, the foundation of non-intervention is that intervention is unlikely to serve the interests of a people. The people concerned should be left "to work out their own salvation", for it is only then that they can develop the special virtues necessary for maintaining freedom and justice. Only freedom and justice that have been earned can ever hope to attain permanence.[15]

In the absence of an hierarchical ordering of the above principles of international law, a state's preference for one norm over another at a given time will often be dictated by pure political expediency and self-interest. Such a relativist tendency often results in inconsistent pronouncements by the same state.

India and Pakistan's adoption of various positions during the protracted dispute over the fate of Kashmir, provides an interesting example. Pakistan argued that the principle of self-determination should be applied to the people of Kashmir, thereby allowing them to decide for themselves their future political affiliation. For its part, India vehemently denied that the principle of self-determination had any relevance when the putative "self" was a constituent part of a country. The Indian representative at the Security Council, 1964, unreservedly declared that "the principle of self-determination cannot and must not be applied to bring about the fragmentation of a country or its people".[16] The Indian spokesman went on to point out the dangers of a wide interpretation of the principle for the "innumerable countries in Africa and Asia with dissident minorities".[17]

In 1971, however, the position of the two parties was effectively reversed under the stimulus of the secession of Bangladesh from Pakistan. In response to the Security Council's attack on India's armed invasion of Bangladesh as a defiance of world opinion, the Indian delegate stated that the recognition of Bangladesh, apart from being an acknowledgment of an "inevitable political reality",[18] was also an imperative requirement for the restoration of peace and stability in the area. Furthermore, he argued that as a matter of international law, conditions are suitable for the emergence of a separate state when a "mother State has irrevocably lost the allegiance of such a large section of its people as represented by Bangla Desh and cannot bring them under its sway".[19]

Pakistan inveighed against India's support for the secession, and the language used by the Pakistan representative to the Security Council bore a distinctly menacing aspect:

"[T]here will not be a Bangla Desh only in Pakistan. There will be a Bangla Desh everywhere. We will see to it that it is not only in Pakistan. There will be Bangla Desh everywhere!"[20]

It does seem, that by and large, "the whole regime of non-intervention is in urgent need of a new set of rules".[21] There is a rising tendency towards covert intervention and other subtle forms of involvement in today's highly interdependent and inter-penetrable world. It is generally recognised that the non-intervention norm is a "lop-sided legal regime",[22] favouring the established authority (the government), regardless of the nature of that authority, and that third-party intervention is far from uncommon in secessionist wars, and is unlikely to diminish. The non-intervention norm is riddled with exceptions, leaving the highly controversial humanitarian-style intervention increasingly condoned.

Whilst the UN specifically forbids any violation of national sovereignty, the UN in recent years has increasingly begun to doubt the absolute need for consent to intervene from the concerned parties.

"The dynamics and priorities of a new era, along with the difficulties in working with local authorities, have raised profound questions about the absolute need for consent from the parties in the first place. In Somalia and former Yugoslavia, the Security Council has taken the view that desperately needed humanitarian intervention should not necessarily be held up indefinitely by the intransigence of local authorities".[23]

Accordingly, the term "humanitarian intervention" has come to represent "merely the latest preferred euphemism for foreign intervention, with or without the consent of the invaded country".[24]

However, the validity of the non-intervention norm is increasingly being questioned in cases where the incumbent government is illegitimate by virtue of being based on racial supremacy or colonial subordination. Similarly, intervention in support of the insurgents, is increasingly being regarded as permissible, so long as the target (the government), is neither just, nor likely to become just if left to its own devices, i.e., if intervention promotes justice and provided that the intervening party is not self-serving.[25] Accordingly, under certain circumstances "intervention against a liberation movement may be unlawful and assistance to the movement may be lawful".[26]

A justification for intervention in cases where external intervention results in popular self-determination, that is, in the replacement of despotic or unrepresentative governments by popularly elected ones, has been articulated as follows:

"Article 2(4), like so many in the Charter and in contemporary international politics, rests on and must be interpreted in terms of this key postulate of political legitimacy in the 20th century. Each application of Article 2(4) must enhance opportunities for ongoing self-determination. Though all interventions are lamentable, the fact that some may serve, in terms of aggregate consequences, to increase the probability of the free choice of peoples about their government and political structure. Others have the manifest objective and consequence of doing exactly the opposite....Here, as in all other areas of law, it is important to remember that norms are instruments devised by human beings to precipitate desired social consequences".[27]

Clearly, for those who adhere to self-determination as the "key postulate of political legitimacy in the 20th century", the moral evaluation of intervention in any situation is obviously affected by whether the intervention promotes or impedes the self-determination of the people concerned.

One difficulty with Reisman's argument as a legal justification for intervention (a difficulty that it shares with the analogous excuse of humanitarian intervention), is that often an intervention carried out for other reasons has been excused by a fictional or forced reliance on local invitation or on self-determination. States have been very reluctant to condone, let alone justify, intervention on grounds such as these, (India's invasion of Pakistan on behalf of Bangladesh, is such an example.)

"Even the democratic governments in the United Nations have not claimed a right to intervene forcibly to bring about the free choice of peoples in other countries. The United States, despite occasional 'rollback' oratory, has never justified its military interventions elsewhere on the ground suggested by Reisman. In Vietnam and currently in Central America, the legal justification for intervention has rested on the claim that foreign intervention had taken place and that U.S. action in response to the request of the government was justified on the basis of the collective self-defense provisions of the Charter. It is true the Grenada intervention was considered by many in the United States as politically desirable because it would lead to democratic rule in place of a repressive regime. However, significantly, the US Government did not assert that as a legal ground...The difficulty with Reisman's argument is not merely that it lacks support in the text of the Charter or in the interpretation that States have given Article 2(4) in the past decades. It would introduce a new normative basis for recourse to war that would give powerful states an almost unlimited right to overthrow governments alleged to be unresponsive to the popular will or to the goal of self-determination. The implications of this for interstate violence in a period of superpower confrontation and obscurantist rhetoric are ominous. That invasions may at times serve democratic values must be weighed against the dangerous consequences of legitimising armed attacks against peaceful governments".[28]

Similarly, western juristic opinion remains strongly against justifying third-party intervention on behalf of a people seeking self-determination. In its judgement in the *Nicaragua case*, the International Court went out of its way to reject the argument that self-determination justifies intervention. The Court said:

"There have been in recent years a number of instances of foreign intervention for the benefit of forces opposed to the government of another State....It has to consider whether there might be indications of a practice illustrative of belief in a kind of general right for States to intervene, directly or indirectly, with or without armed force, in support of an internal opposition in another State, whose cause appeared particularly worthy by reason of the political and moral values with which it was identified. For such a general right to come into existence would involve a fundamental modification of the customary law principle of non-intervention...In fact, however, the Court finds that States have not justified their conduct by reference to a new right of intervention or a new exception to the principle of its prohibition....The Court therefore finds that no such general right of intervention, in support of an opposition within another State, exists in contemporary international law".[29]

It has generally been concluded by international jurists, that the argument that self-determination justifies intervention must be rejected. However, it does not follow that the principle of self-determination is irrelevant. After all, the international community is interested not only in the validity or invalidity of justifications for the use of force, but also in responding to the situations thereby created. The degree of international responsibility flowing from an intervention may well depend on its consequences. Within this paradigm, long-term military occupation of another state, would be a more serious violation of international law than a short-term intervention resulting in genuine local self-determination. More significantly, the link that would normally exist between illegal intervention and non-recognition of a new government formed as a result, would perhaps be avoided if the new government were to result from a genuine act of local self-determination or is otherwise clearly supported by the local population. This, it is argued, is the best interpretation of the creation of Bangladesh.

To conclude, it is apparent that the relationship of the principle of self-determination to other crucial norms of international behaviour remains terribly obscure. Norms such as non-intervention and the proscription of the non-use of force, are of such a fundamental character that questions of their applicability cannot be left to the mercy of outside states interested in a civil conflict to decide when a legitimate assertion of a right to self-determination justifies forceful intervention. The open-ended subjectivity involved in unilateral determinations of "legitimacy" has to be removed. The scope of legitimate self-determination has to be delimited so that the number of instances of permissable deviation from the former two principles can be reduced.

In an attempt to avoid the dangers of subjectivity, attempts to determine which side is legitimate have often demanded a strict neutrality on the part of outside states. In other words, states have maintained that "if a people wishes strongly enough to form a separate political community, the matter is one to be resolved between them and the larger unit of which they form a part".[30]

This sentiment was expressed with unmistakable clarity in the Separate Opinion of Judge Ammoun in the *Western Sahara* case, (1975) in which it was stated that:

"Nothing could show more clearly the will for emancipation than the struggle (for liberation from foreign domination) undertaken in common with the risks and immense sacrifice it entails. That struggle is more decisive than a referendum, being absolutely sincere and authentic. Many are the peoples who have had recourse to it to make their right prevail."[31]

If, as the present legal order suggests, the proper model for secessionist conflicts is a gladiatorial one, in which the rivals demonstrate their respective desire for separation or union by the intensity of their struggle, then any external support for either side must constitute an interference with the supremely Darwinian character of the struggle. In an order that only perceives legal legitimacy in success, as if it were assured that "right" could become "might" and assert itself at the end, outside inter-vention must destroy the atmosphere that the system relies on to reveal this legitimacy.[32]

"[O]ne could paint a rather demonic picture of international opinion demanding sanguinary evidence of a people's suffering - greater than that endured by the Biafrans, but perhaps less than that inflicted upon the East Pakistanis - before a claim to separation from their tormentors will be considered legitimate".[33]

Secessionist movements are more often than not the weaker party and can hardly ever win militarily. At best they can raise the costs and create a stalemate for a while. The success or failure of a secessionist movement should not depend on third-party state involvement. In its present inability to distinguish legitimate from illegitimate claims to secessionist self-determination, the international community is seriously handicapped in its attempt to minimise instances of unwarranted third-party interven-tion in secessionist conflicts. Similarly, the danger of unrestrained inter-vention inevitably brings in its wake the possibility of escalation and the confrontation of major power-blocs.

Notes

1 Brownlie. I., "Principles of public international law", (1979), p.513.

2 In the International Court of Justice's case on Nambia, Judge Ammoun called the right to self-determination a norm of the nature of the *jus cogens*, derogation from which is not possible under any circumstance. Judge Ammoun, Barcelona Traction case, ICJ Rep. (1970), 304.

3 Aureliu Cristescu, (Special Rapporteur of the Sub-Commission on Prevention of Discrimination and Protection of Minorities, of the Commission on Human Rights), "The right to self-determination: Historical and current development on the basis of United Nations instruments", (1978), p.1.

4 Henkin, "The reports of the death of article 2(4) are greatly exaggerated", in: 65, AJIL, p.544, (1971), cited in: Buchheit. L. C., "Secession: The legitimacy of self-determination", (1978), p.33.

5 G.A. Resolution 2131.

6 There is also, in theory at least, the case of "belligerency", see Heraclides. A., "The self-determination of minorities in international politics", (1991), p.27.

7 Brownlie. I., p.597.

8 Ibid.

9 Basic Principles of the Legal Status of the Combatants Struggling against Colonial and Alien Domination and Racists Regimes, G.A. REs. 3103, Dec. 12, (1973), reprinted in 68, AJIL, (1974), cited in: Buchheit. L. C., p.34.

10 G.A. Res. 2625 (XXV), (1970), Paragraph 6.

11 G.A. Res. 2625 (XXV) Annex.

12 Buchheit. L. C., pp.22-23.

13 Cassese. A., (ed.), "UN Law/Fundamental Rights: Two Topics in International Law", p.140.

14 Little. R., "Intervention: External involvement in civil wars", (1975) p.33, cited in: Heraclides. A., p.26.

15 Ibid.

16 19 UN SCOR, 1088th meeting at 27, para.70 (1964), cited in: Buchheit. L. C., p.106.

17 Ibid., paragraph 71.

18 26 UN SCOR, 1611th meeting at 21, para.192 (1971), cited in: Buchheit. L. C., p.210.

19 Ibid., 13, para.124.

20 27 UN SCOR, 1611th meeting at 21, para.192 (1971), cited in:

Buchheit. L. C., 106.

21 Heraclides. A., p.30.

22 Ibid.

23 Boutros-Boutros Ghali, "UN peace-keeping in a new era: A new chance for peace", in: The World Today, Vol.49, No.4, April (1993), pp.66-69, p.68.

24 John Pilger, "The US fraud in Africa: Operation Restore Hope is part of a new age imperialism", in: New Statesman Society, 8 January, (1993), pp.10-11.

25 Heraclides. A., p.31.

26 Brownlie. I., p.598.

27 Reisman. W. M., "Coercion and self-determination: Construing Charter Article 2(4)" in: AJIL 642, (1984), cited in: Crawford. J., in: Macartney. W. M. Allan., (ed.), "Self-determination in the Commonwealth", (1988), p.9-10.

28 O. Schachter, "The legality of pro-democractic invasion", 78 AJIL, 645, (1984), cited in: Crawford. J., p.11.

29 ICJ Report (1986) p.14, 108-9.

30 Higgins. R., "International Law and Civil Conflict", in: Luard, E., (ed.), "The International Regulation of Civil Wars", (1972), cited in: Buchheit. L. C., p.41.

31 The Separate Opinion of Judge Ammoun in the Western Sahara case (1975) ICJ 12, 100, cited: in Buchheit. L. C., p.213.

32 Buchheit. L. C., p.40.

33 Ibid., p.213.

CHAPTER 6

The right to self-determination of "peoples" living in independent states in the post-decolonisation era

Much of the discourse surrounding the question of the consequences of the right to self-determination outside the colonial context, has been focused on the attempt to identify the "peoples" to whom the principle applies. The preceding chapters have revealed that the concept of peoples has been liberally invoked in international law in dealing with the right to self-determination. For example, the Charter of the United Nations recognised in Article 1(2) the principle of "self-determination of peoples". Article 2 of the 1960 Declaration read "all peoples have the right to self-determination". Common Article 1 of the 1966 International Human Rights Covenants declared that "all peoples have the right of self-determination", and paragraph 1 of the 1970 Declaration referred to the "self-determination of peoples".

However, the term "peoples" has not been authoritatively defined in any of the instruments that employ it. Furthermore, it is not used to convey identical meanings in any of these instruments. The Human Rights Committee has so far declined to define the term, arguing that the right of self-determination is not an individual right but a collective right, and that it is, for that reason, beyond the competence of that institution to examine any complaint of the violation of that right. If UN resolutions and state practice are adopted as a guide, an international consensus exists only to the extent that the inhabitants of non self-governing colonial territories and those living under alien and racist regimes are unquestionably "peoples" who may choose for themselves one of the several options that constitute self-determination. By contrast, the principle does not apply to the population of a sovereign state with a government, which however oppressive and authoritarian, does not practice systematic racial or religious discrimination. This exclusion has greatly limited the scope of the principle and confined its application to three types of situations only, all of which are becoming increasingly rare.

Freezing the concept of self-determination at the point of decolonisation, however, perpetuates a system that denies the benefit of international law to those peoples who need its protection now. There is, therefore, an urgent need to clarify the scope and content of the right of self-determination and its application, in particular, the position of cohesive groups of ethnic, religious and linguistic minorities and indigenous peoples in relation to the exercise of this right.

Whilst it has often been felt that the lack of a precise definition of the term "peoples" has presented an obstacle to legal and political development, it is now widely argued that no dominant group or groups should have the monopoly in defining the "others". The more plausible thesis today, is that of self-definition, whereby groups of people who choose to determine their own future qualify as "peoples" and are consequently entitled to self-determination. A common language, culture and religion may play a determining role in such a process of self-definition, but the collective desire to live together is what finally constitutes a definition of a "people".

"No doubt there has been continuing doubt over the definition of what is a "people" for the purpose of applying the principle of self-determination. Nonetheless, the principle appears to have a core of reasonable certainty. This core consists in the right of a community which has a distinct character to have this character reflected in the insitutions of government under which it lives. The concept of distinct character depends on a number of criteria which may appear in combination. Race (or nationality) is one of the more important of the relevant criteria, but the concept of race can only be expressed scientifically in terms of more specific features, in which matters of culture, language, religion and group psychology predominate. The physical indicia of race and nationality may evidence the cultural distinctiveness of a group but they certainly do not inevitably condition it. Indeed, if the purely ethnic criteria are applied exclusively many long existing national identities would be negated on academic grounds as, for example, the United States."[1]

Whether a group is a "people" for the purposes of self-determination, depends on the extent to which the group making a claim shares ethnic, linguistic, religious or cultural bonds, although the absence or weakness of one of these bonds or elements does not necessarily invalidate the claim. The subjective standard should weigh the extent to which members within a group perceive the group's identity as distinct from the identities of other groups. Any attempt to define the nature and characteristics of the "people" who are the subject of the right to self-determination, however, should not constitute an excercise in labelling or classification, for the right to self-determination is eminently concerned with the right to self-definition. However, in order to avoid either a minimalist or maximalist approach to this question, it has been necessary to engage in an effort to spell out the universal, rigorous criteria by which the defining characteristics of the claimants to self-determination would be accepted as widely as possible.

In this connection, reference can be made to the conclusions of the UNESCO meeting of Experts on Further Study of the Rights of Peoples (Paris, February, 1990) which identified the following criteria as being commonly taken into account in deciding that a group of individuals is a people:

"A people for the rights of peoples in international law, including the right of self-determination, has the following characteristics:

1. a group of individual human beings who enjoy some or all of the following common features:

(a) a common historical tradition

(b) racial or ethnic identity

(c) cultural homogeneity

(d) linguistic unity

(e) religious or ideological affinity

(f) territorial connection

(g) common economic life

2. the group must be of a certain number who need not be large (e.g. the people of micro-states) but must be more than a mere association of individuals within a state;

3. the group as a whole must have the will to be identified as a people or the consciousness of being a people - allowing that groups or some members of such groups, though sharing the foregoing characteristics, may not have the will or consciousness; and

4. possibly, the group must have institutions or other means of expressing its common characteristics and will for identity."[2]

Thus the main attributes of peoplehood as generally recognised, are commonality of interests, group identity, distinctiveness and a territorial link. It is apparent therefore, that the term "peoples", must also refer to a group of persons within a specific geographical entity, as well as to all the persons within that entity. However, in a report written for the UN, Aureliu Cristescu stated:

"A people should not be confused with ethnic, religious or linguistic minorities, whose existence and rights are recognised in article 27 of the International Covenant on Civil and Political Rights."[3]

If minorities are not "peoples" under international law, what are they? The issue of minority protection has become one of the main challenges facing the UN today. One of the UN's tasks has been to work out an acceptable definition of who constitutes a minority. The most satisfactory and acceptable definition was the one proferred by Francesco Capotorti in a report commissioned by the UN Sub-Commission on Prevention of Discrimination and Protection of Minorities. He suggested that a:

"...minority is a group numerically inferior to the rest of the population of a State, in a non-dominant position whose members - being nationals of the State - possess ethnic, religious or linguistic characteristics differing from those of the rest of the population and show, if only implicitly, a sense of solidarity, directed towards preserving their culture, traditions, religion or language."[4]

The pertinent question for present purposes, is whether or not a minority thus defined, can be referred to as a "people" entitled to enjoy the right to self-determination. It is often argued that minorities do not enjoy an unconditional right of self-determination in view of the principle of political unity and territorial integrity of sovereign states. This principle dictates that in the exercise of the right of self-determination "any action which would dismember or impair in whole or in part, the territorial integrity or political unity of sovereign and independent states" is neither authorised nor encouraged. This qualification suggests that the exercise of self-determination by a people living within a sovereign and independent state, e.g., an ethnic, religious or linguistic minority, may only take the form of secession if two conditions exist, namely, that the state is pursuing a policy of gross discrimination against such a people on the basis of their race, creed or colour, and that such a people are excluded from participation in the electoral process.

Aureliu Cristescu's exclusion of minorities as "peoples" entitled to the right to self-determination, is clearly an extension of the attempts within the UN to confine the right to self-determination to peoples living under colonial, alien or racist regimes, based upon the assumption that the emergence into a sovereign nation is the logical conclusion of the pursuit of the right to self-determination. If, however, we do not confine ourselves to assuming that peoplehood and the right to self-determination automatically leads to independent statehood, it is not difficult to appreciate that a minority can fulfill all the requirements of a "people".

"Unless the United Nations has not developed clear-cut ideas about the holder of the right to self-determination my opinion is that minorities can also be considered holders of the right to self-determination. Minorities must be considered as people. They must live also in a territory or they must have been living in a territory which is now occupied; they must have cultural or religious characteristics; they must be politically organised so that they can be represented; and they must be capable of economic independence. It does not depend on governments as to how they are describing an entity as a people; it depends on objective and subjective criteria of a group. It depends also on the self-consciousness of identity. I think therefore, that national and racial, perhaps also religious, minorities could be considered peoples in the sense of an autonomous concept of the United Nations instruments. For them self-determination is inalienable."[5]

A close study of the ethnic conflicts in the contemporary world discloses that many are actually motivated by factors unrelated to self-determination. One factor is a lack of democracy, which is most commonly evidenced by authoritarian rule from the centre and the denial of real participation in the political process. The central authorities may be of a different ethnic, linguistic or religious group, but the primary complaint of minorities is often lack of political power.

Another factor which motivates ethnic conflict, is the existence of discrimination against, or persecution of minorities by the state and its majority population. This often leads minorities to fear not only for their physical safety, but also for the survival of their culture. However, the extent to which international law currently goes beyond the recognition that measures of this kind are necessary or legitimate and actually requires them to be taken is doubtful.

Article 2(2) of the Racial Discrimination Convention, 1966, imposes an obligation on states parties to it to take "special measures" to protect disadvantaged groups and to ensure real equality for them. However, it seems to envisage primarily individual measures (e.g., in employment or education) rather than collective measures of a public law kind. Similarly, article 27 of the International Covenant on Civil and Political Rights 1966, in its negative formulation, seems to leave the protection of minorities as a matter for discretion rather than obligation. Article 27 is concerned only to ensure that individual rights can be exercised in community with other members of the group. It confers on minority groups "the possibility of cultivating their own religious, educational or linguistic values as a recognition of their fundamental human rights and freedoms".[6] Finding itself elaborated upon in an international human rights instrument, the rights conferred on minority groups under article 27, are individual human rights, not collective or group rights.

"In the case of the protection of minorities, what is protected is not the religious or linguistic group as a whole but the individuals belonging to this group, the former being nothing but a name and not a group."[7]

Critics of the insufficiency of the UN reliance on a human rights and non-discrimination approach to the issue of minority protection, have long been adhering to the necessity of establishing an international system of minority protection.

"Prohibition against discrimination is nonetheless not good enough. National minorities should receive positive safeguards. They should be given the opportunity to continue their existence as nationalities...It is not enough that minority members should have protection as individuals for their linguistic and cultural rights. A national minority is a collective and its interests in education and other establishments of its own serving groups of minority members are the interests of a group and not of an individual. Minority protection should therefore be directed towards the collective population."[8]

In December 1992, the General Assembly made a landmark decision when it adopted the Declaration on the Rights of Persons Belonging to National and Ethnic, Religious and Linguistic Minorities. The Declaration clearly has norm-creating determinacy and will play a natural part in any discussions held on the right of self-determination in the future. In the Saskatoon Statement on Self-Determination adopted by substantial majority at the Martin Ennals Memorial Symposium on Self-Determination, 1993, it was stated that:

"National, ethnic, religious, linguistic, and other minorities are entitled to respect and the fullest opportunity to maintain and develop their distinctive characteristics. Minorities lacking adequate resources to do so should be accorded a fair share of public funds, sufficient to enable the preservation of their distinctive characteristics. States should, at a minimum, conform to the principles set forth in the Declaration on the Rights of Persons Belonging to National and Ethnic, Religious and Linguistic Minorities, which was adopted by the UN General Assembly in December 1992. The legitimate rights of the majority in a state should be exercised in the context of effective participation by members of minorities in the larger society".[9]

Furthermore, the Martin Ennals Memorial Symposium on Self-Determination recommended that the United Nations should immediately establish a High Commissioner, Working Group or Special Rapporteur with appropriate resources to monitor the implementation of the Declaration on the Rights of Persons Belonging to National and Ethnic, Religious and Linguistic Minorities.

Minority groups, however, do not have the monopoly on the appropriation of the principle of self-determination. Indigenous peoples are also beginning to legitimise their demands and grievances through the principle of self-determination. Having determined to some extent the content and scope of the term "peoples" in international law, can it be said that indigenous groups are also "peoples" for the purposes of the excercise of the right to self-determination?[10] With regards to indigenous peoples, Professor Erica-Irene Daes has observed that they are unquestionably "peoples" in every social, cultural and ethnological sense of the term:

"They have their own specific languages, laws, values and traditions; their own long histories as distinct societies and nations; and a unique economic, religious and spritual relationship with the territories in which they have so long lived. It is neither logical nor scientific to treat them as the same "peoples" as their neighbours, who obviously have different languages, histories and cultures, and who often have been their oppressors. The United Nations should not pretend, for the sake of a convenient legal fiction, that those differences do not exist".[11]

While indigenous peoples enjoy no special status today, it is increasingly being felt that colonialism, which resulted in the marginalisation, if not the annihilation of substantial sections of many indigenous peoples, also made such local populations colonised peoples. The Working Group of the Sub-Commission on the Prevention of Discrimination and Protection of Minorities is currently drafting the Declaration on the Rights of Indigenous Peoples, in which indigenous peoples may be granted the right to self-government, in other words, a limited right to self-determination. This would mean that the existing state would have a duty to accommodate the aspirations of indigenous peoples through constitutional reforms designed to share power democratically. It would also mean that indigenous peoples would share the duty to reach an agreement, in good faith, or share power within the existing state. With regard to indigenous peoples then, the right to self-determination seems to have been interpreted to mean the right to negotiate freely their political status and representation in the states in which they live, i.e., a kind of belated state-building, through which, after many years of isolation and exclusion, they could join with other peoples that make up the state on mutually agreed and just terms.

While many indigenous peoples may in fact opt for power-sharing, there is general support for the view that the draft Declaration on the Rights of Indigenous Peoples should contain a clear and explicit recognition of the right of self-determination without qualifications, limitations or discrimination. Indeed resorting:

"...to 'acceptable compromises' or duplicitous and ambiguous phrases designed to preserve the status quo, or the entrenchment of the 1970 UN Declaration on Friendly Relations Among States within the operative paragraphs of the draft Declaration, would constitute discrimination. It would perpetuate the history of denial and discrimination that has faced indigenous peoples since the time of first contact."[12]

Indeed, the fundamental problem facing indigenous peoples, is their lack of control over their own lives and their own destiny. Without such control, the land dispossession, cultural genocide and other human rights abuses faced by indigenous peoples will continue.

In October 1993, Australian Prime Minister Paul Keating, promised the Aborigines in Australia a "new deal" which effectively overturned the legal basis for Captain Cook's seizure of the Continent, and set an important new international precedent for Aboriginal or indigenous peoples' land claims and demands for greater social justice.

The new deal constitutes a compromise package aimed at developing a new system of land ownership in Australia which recognises native title. The agreement was a historic piece of legislation which supported a controversial decision made in 1992 in the Australian High Court. The Mabo ruling, named after one of the plaintiffs, rejected Britain's justification for settling Australia, finding that its doctrine of *terra nullius*, land belonging to no one, ignored prior Aboriginal occupation. "As Mabo was an historic judgment," Prime Minister Keating said "this is historic legislation, recognising in law the fiction of *terra nullius* and the fact of native title. With that alone the foundation of reconciliation is laid, because after 200 years we will at last be building on the truth."[13]

There clearly remains a sharp difference of opinion on whether the concept of self-determination is an "umbrella" encompassing a wide range of possible meanings in different contexts, or whether it has one meaning at all times and in all circumstances, namely, the right of peoples to secede, to form a new state or to join another state.

If self-determination were interpreted in its most demanding sense, i.e., as an unconditional right to secede, to form a new state, or to join another state, the term 'peoples' would be understood narrowly to mean very special groups and contexts. In other words, if self-determination includes an actual or potential right to secession, the beneficiaries would be; the whole population of a colonial territory; the whole population of an independent country which has been illegally occupied in violation of article 2(4) of the UN Charter; and the population of a distinct territory within a sovereign state whose government violates the principle of equal rights and self-determination of people by excluding from representation in government on the basis of equality (one person, one vote), the members of the ethnic or minority group forming the vast majority in that distinct territory.

A liberal interpretation of the term "peoples", to include indigenous peoples and certain ethnic, linguistic and religious groups in independent states would, on the other hand, attract a narrow construction of the concept of self-determination, conferring in most cases only the right to self-government or greater autonomy within sovereign states. For national or ethnic, linguistic and religious minorities, self-determination would mean only the right to preserve group identity. To transform and expand the right of self-determination into an umbrella which would shield everybody, however, would only serve to water down the meaning and relevance of the right and draw attention away from the application of other political, economic and cultural rights which might be capable of addressing many of the issues at stake. If, for example, "autonomy" is presented under the banner of self-determination as a mere pacifier and as a way of avoiding its secessionist implications, it may not only be misleading, but may also create false expectations. Similarly, political rights, political participation and elections (respect for which is likely to reduce the demand for secessionist self-determination) should also be called by their proper names, based on the relevant provisions in international instruments, rather than placing them under the banner of autonomy. If several recognised rights were placed under a self-determination umbrella, the latter would necessarily be overextended and would no longer provide the shelter sought. Moreover, when different meanings are gathered under supposedly the same right, people will understand that right in the way they want to and in the way that suits their own interests, thereby creating not only confusion but also conflict.

"The heterogenous terminology which has been used over the years - the references to 'nationalities', 'peoples', 'minorities', and 'indigenous populations' - involves essentially the same idea...In fact, there is a sort of synthesis between the question of group rights as a human rights matter and the principle of self-determination. The question of group rights, more especially when it is related to territorial rights and regional autonomy, represents the practical and *internal* working out of the concept of self-determination. Such recognition is therefore the *internal* application of the concept of self-determination."[14]

In the discourse surrounding the right of peoples to self-determination outside of the decolonisation era, it is becoming increasingly popular to speak of the concept of self-determination as having two component parts, an "internal" and an "external" aspect.[15] Principally, the external aspect involves the right to independence of the colonised or non-self-governing countries and the establishment of their own separate states. Colonial and dependent peoples are the subject of the right to external self-determination and the exercise of that right relates to the liberation from external dependence (from another state).

The principle of internal self-determination, on the other hand, rests ultimately upon the doctrine of liberal democracy, and is therefore anti-imperialist in intent. Other elements, which are often an expression of the principle of self-determination, such as the principle of state sovereignty, territorial integrity and non-intervention, are deemed to be derivative.[16] In other words, state practice has isolated only one element in the principle, the element of anti-colonialism and absolutised it.[17] It has also raised the derivative elements, state sovereignty, territorial integrity and non-intervention to the level of the main principle and made it the overriding element.[18] This practice has robbed the right of self-determination of its fundamental defining characteristic, anti-imperialism.[19]

"This is so because national oppression; which...is often an expression of unequal and uneven national (regional) development, is derived from colonial history and perpetrated by independent States in alliance with imperialism whose local manifestation is the neo-colonial political economy".[20]

In the early 1900's, V. I. Lenin had already warned of the dangers of trampling on national rights and severely criticised the practice of Great Russian chauvinism. His critique and warning are of even greater relevance today, in an era of escalating nationalist sentiment:

"It would be unpardonable opportunism if, on the eve of the *debut* of the East, just as it is awakening, we undermined our prestige with its peoples, even if only by the slightest crudity or injustice towards our own non-Russian nationalities. The need to rally against the imperialists of the West, who are defending the capitalist world, is one thing...It is another thing when we ourselves lapse, even if only in trifles, into imperialist attitudes towards oppressed nationalities, thus undermining all our principled sincerity, all our principled defence of the struggle against imperialism".[21]

As early as 1949, a reference was made to the internal and external components of the right to self-determination in the Special Report of the

United Nations Commission for Indonesia,[22] which "may indicate that a greater latitude for the exercise of minority self-determination may be expected in the formation of a new State than in a forced dismemberment of an existing State".[23]

The report summarises the results of a United Nations Round Table Conference with Netherlands and Indonesian representatives, undertaken for the purpose of facilitating the transfer of sovereignty of the Dutch colonies to the Republic of the United States of Indonesia. During the negotiations, it transpired that the Provisional Constitution of the Republic of the United States of Indonesia referred only to an "internal right of self-determination", providing for "the right of populations to determine, by democratic procedure, the status which their respective territories shall occupy within the federal structure of the Republic of the United States of Indonesia." The Netherlands representative, on the other hand, claimed to attach particular significance to an "external right of self-determination, providing for the right of populations to disassociate their respective territories from the Republic of the United States of Indonesia."

"When used in this manner, the right of 'external' self-determination involved in the formation of a State seems to be the equivalent of what, in an already existing State, would be called a right of secession."[24]

The delegates at the Conference elaborated on their interpretation of the actual substance of external self-determination. Plebiscites were to be held in certain territories under the auspices of the United Nations Commission for Indonesia, to determine whether such territories would form component states of the republic. Each component state would then be given an opportunity to ratify the final constitution of the republic and, in the event that a component state decided not to ratify it would be allowed "to negotiate a special relationship with the Republic of the United States of Indonesia and the Kingdom of the Netherlands." The Indonesian situation illustrates the problem that arises when a part of an independent state wishes to secede.

"As can be seen in the Indonesian situation, the problem of a segment of a State wishing to disassociate itself from the unified country falls neatly into an interstice between internal and external self-determination. The seceding province obviously wishes to readjust its political status vis-a-vis the remaining State (which seems to be an aspect of internal self-determination); yet by proclaiming itself an independent entity it may apparently resist any attempt at forced reunification under the principle of external self-determination (the parent State having become an 'outside party')."[25]

The concept of the internal right to self-determination was brought to the forefront and significantly elaborated upon in the International Covenant on Civil and Political Rights, 1966.[26] This aspect of the right is endorsed in article 1, paragraph 2, which reads:

"By virtue of that right [the right to self-determination] they [all peoples] freely determine their political status and freely pursue their economic, social and cultural development".

"The Covenants clearly endorse not only the right of *external* self-determination, but also the right of *internal* self-determination: the right of a people to establish its own political institutions, to develop its own economic resources, and to direct its own social and cultural evolution...A people should be free both from interference by other peoples or states and from deprivation of its rights to self-determination by a tyrant or dictator."[27]

The right of self-determination that the "peoples" of an independent country are entitled to, is the right to determine their own political and economic, social and cultural destiny. Such a right has in fact long been championed by the Human Rights Committee. The Committee on Human Rights, acting under the ICCPR, has continually fostered the idea that self-determination is of continuing applicability outside of the colonial context. The Committee addresses the matter of the continued application of self-determination to post-colonial situations in virtually every single examination of a state upon the report that it is required periodically to submit. In its earliest form this was developed as the dual doctrines of external and internal self-determination. The external aspect of self-determination requires a state to take action in its foreign policy consistent with the attainment of self-determination in the remaining areas of colonial or racist occupation, and ultimately entitles a group of people to pursue their political, cultural, and economic wishes without interference or coercion by outside states. But the right to internal self-determination is directed to their own peoples.[28] The Committee on Human Rights, when examining the report of states parties to the ICCPR, asks not only about any dependent territories that such states may be responsible for (external self-determination), but also about the opportunities that its own population has to determine its own political and economic system (internal self-determination).

In spite of India's recent denunciation of post-colonial self-determination,[29] the Committee's view of the matter finds widespread acceptance among states appearing before it. The very recent third periodic report of

Colombia affords a graphic example. Under the heading of "Self-determination under Article 1 of the Covenant", Colombia reported at great length on its subject's opportunities to participate in the social and political structures of the country, to change the government through elections, to contribute to the formation of policy and to determine events. Virtually no states refuse to respond to probing comments and questions on internal self-determination and the Committee is not told that no such right exists. Rather, it is accepted that the right exists and the debate is most frequently is about the forms that it can take.

When the Covenant came into force, the right of self-determination entered its third phase of enunciation. It ceased to be a rule applicable only to specific territories (at first, the defeated European powers; later the overseas Trust Territories and colonies) and became a universal right. It also stopped being a principle of exclusion (secession), and became one of inclusion, the right to participate fully in the life of the society in which one lives. The internal right to self-determination entitles peoples in all states to free, fair and open participation in the democratic process of governance freely chosen by each state.

The second instrument that is recognised to fully stipulate the internal aspect of the principle of self-determination is the Helsinki Declaration, 1975. Whilst the Helsinki Declaration is only a regional and not an international instrument, it does reveal the present status of the principle of self-determination, as expressed by some of the major developed powers in the West.

The Final Act of the Conference on Security and Co-operation (CSCE) in Europe, interestingly builds on the old UN Charter language, while at the same time making it clear that self-determination is a general right and applies to all peoples. In the form of a non-binding Declaration rather than a treaty, its significance is as a statement of views rather than a formal commitment. Principle VIII in the Decalogue in the First Basket, deals with "Equal rights and self-determination of peoples". For present purposes, the inclusion of the principle of "Equal rights and self-determination of peoples" is important, because the Final Act was concerned primarily with Europe which contains virtually no Chapter XI territories. The argument that the principle of self-determination is irrelevant outside of the colonial context, was therefore expressly rejected at the Helsinki Conference. The Final Act provides that:

"The participating States will respect the equal rights of peoples and their right to self-determination, acting at all times in conformity with the purposes and principles of the Charter of the United Nations and with the relevant norms of international law, including those relating to territorial integrity of States.

By virtue of the principle of equal rights and self-determination of peoples, all peoples always have the right, in full freedom, to determine, when and as they wish, their *internal* and *external* political status, without external interference, and to pursue as they wish their political, economic, social and cultural development".[30]

This has been interpreted to mean that all peoples, always have the right to choose a new social or political regime free from opposition from an authoritarian government. Principle VIII, however, is supplemented by another principle in the Decalogue, Principle III, "Inviolability of Frontiers" which reads:

"The participating States regard as inviolable all one another's frontiers as well as the frontiers of all States in Europe and therefore they will refrain now and in the future from assaulting these frontiers.

Accordingly, they will also refrain from any demand for, or act of, seizure and usurpation of part or all of the territory of any participating state".[31]

The sentiment expressed within the CSCE at the time of drafting therefore, was more or less the same as that reflected in the United Nations at the drafting of the Charter, and like that expressed in the League of Nations before that, i.e., a strong scepticism against any efforts to promote secession by minorities within independent states. It is clear that states in their common interest will continue to "be reluctant to provoke or to encourage secessionist movements based purely on minority criteria."[32]

The Final Act of the Helsinki Conference clearly adopted a statist approach. The right of peoples to self-determination is set alongside the principle of the inviolability of frontiers, the territorial integrity of states and the principle of non-intervention in the domestic affairs of a state. However, the internal aspect of the principle of self-determination was expressly stated in the Helsinki Declaration, albeit subsumed by the principle of territorial integrity, and therefore demands analysis.

The internal aspect of the principle of self-determination is of particular relevance to groups of people living in independent states outside of the colonial context. Since ethnic groups are increasingly using the principle to air their grievances and governments are correspondingly denying the principle, resulting in the abuse of human rights, the use of force and civil war, a greater understanding of the scope and content of the internal application of self-determination to the question of group rights, more especially when it is related to territorial claims and demands for greater regional autonomy is becoming increasingly necessary.

Although the era of decolonisation is drawing to an end, self-determination does not appear to have lost its relevance. In nearly fifty countries, conflicts related to self-determination are currently taking place.[33] However, "the violence we see around us is not generated by the drive for self-determination, but by its negation. The denial of self-determination, not its pursuit, is what leads to upheavals and conflicts."[34] The violence, the xenophobia and racism, "ethnic cleansings", genocide and assassinations that often accompany those conflicts and the internal displacements and external refugee flows that invariably occur, are clear evidence that the drive for self-determination remains a powerful mobilising force.

The internal right to self-determination, is generally recognised to have two aspects which are interdependent and complementary. A "political" aspect and an "economic, social and cultural" aspect. Both aspects are referred to directly in paragraph 2, article 1 of the ICCPR, 1966. Let us examine firstly the "political" aspect of the internal right to self-determination.

The political aspect of the internal right to self-determination is endorsed in point 1, paragraph 2, article 1, which states that the right of peoples to self-determination includes the right to "freely determine their *political* status" (emphasis added). The political aspect of the internal right to self-determination, is based upon the principle of internal democracy, i.e., all people should be allowed to decide upon their own institutions. The internal right to political self-determination was first formulated in the Universal Declaration of Human Rights, 1948. While it does not refer *expressis verbis* to the right to self-determination, it does declare that "the will of the people shall be the basis of authority of government." (Article 21, para.3.) The political aspect of the right to internal self-determination in domestic law is safeguarded by the constitutional principle that "people are the source of authority" or the principle of "sovereignty of the people".

Peoples living within independent states are the subjects of the political aspect of the internal right to self-determination. This right is exercised in relation to state authority. The internal aspect of self-determination, like the external aspect of self-determination, has its roots in the liberal democratic principle that a government should rest on the consent of the governed. Indeed, the entire anti-colonial movement was based on this premise. The imposition from outside of colonial governments that had no roots in the desire of colonial peoples was outlawed. The idea of self-determination as the right to determine one's own destiny, and not to have it imposed from above or by an alien power, continues to find expression outside of the colonial context, in the political aspect of the internal right to self-determination.

The political aspect of the internal right to self-determination, is directed against authoritarian regimes and is therefore directed not only against external interference, but also and mainly against internal interference. Those peoples in newly formed independent states are entitled to exercise the political aspect of the internal aspect of self-determination, in the form of electing and keeping the government of their choice and having the right not to be oppressed by the government. The choice of domestic political institutions and authorities "must not be conditioned, manipulated or tampered with by the domestic authorities themselves".[35] If a government systematically and grossly violates human rights, the aggrieved group or people can invoke the political aspect of the internal right of self-determination, which constitutes the core element of a right of resistance against a dictatorship.

A broad interpretation of the political aspect of the internal right of self-determination therefore, acknowledges the right of oppressed peoples within sovereign states to self-determination, which ranges from some form of autonomy up to and including secession.

"If an identified group of peoples in an existing state is deliberately discriminated against by the government in power, it is difficult to explain why that group must remain in that state without any right to redress. In the event of an inability to realize "internal" self-determination within that state, secession by the aggrieved people as an ultimate remedy cannot be gainsaid."[36]

The second aspect of the internal right to self-determination, the right of peoples to "economic, social and cultural" self-determination, is endorsed in point 1, paragraph 2, article 1, of the International Covenant on Civil and Political Rights, 1966, which states that the right of peoples to self-determination includes the right to "freely pursue their *economic, social and cultural development*" (emphasis added). Both practically and politically, the full recognition and realisation of economic, social and cultural rights are extremely crucial to the democratisation process in those states where the principle of non-discrimination and equality, central to the right of self-determination, is thrown overboard as some cultures, languages and religions are accorded superior, while others, inferior status within the same state boundaries.

"The recognition by the International Covenants and other important

United Nations instruments of the economic, social and cultural aspects of the right to self-determination, represented a milestone in the development of the content of that right. The interdependence of the various aspects of development, based on the right to self-determination, is now commonly recognised throughout the world and has led to the formulation of the concept of balanced and integrated development, which is playing an increasingly important part in the efforts to establish a new international economic order. At the same time, the elaboration of the various economic, social and cultural aspects of the right to self-determination has resulted in the adoption of new rules forming a veritable international law of development".[37]

Economic self-determination, integral to the second aspect of the right to self-determination, has its historical roots in the Bolshevik Revolution of 1917.

" Hitherto what had reigned and exercised hegemony both in international law and practice was the right to private property. It was the Soviet state which for the first time in any significant way breached the hegemony by nationalising private property."[38]

The UN Resolution of Permanent Sovereignty over Natural Resources, 1962, illustrated the erosion of the hegemony of the right to private property.[39] The original concept of private property in Marxist-Leninist theory referred to and embraced the relations of exploitation between classes. Soviet state theory and ideology, however, gradually couterpoised private property with state property, not social property. In other words, the concept of private property was reduced to the legal ownership of the means of production.

"It is in this restricted and distorted form that the concept of private property/state property has found its way in much of the debate so far as the right to or freedom of private property is concerned."[40]

The African state in particular, has interpreted the principle of economic self-determination almost exclusively in terms of their "trade union" demands for the so-called New International Economic Order (NIEO), and against some of the grossly inequitable practices of the multi-national corporations, other economic institutions (e.g., World Bank, IMF, etc.) and the world capitalist market. These demands, which are made under the rubric of economic self-determination (the term often used is economic independence), are a *fortiori* seen as the right of "states" rather than "people".

"This conception too results in a truncated form of anti-imperialism rather than a comprehensive conceptualisation where imperialism is seen as manifesting itself in dominant/exploitative relations of production and exploitation on the economic level while socially and politically maintained by compradorial alliances which find concrete expression in authoritarian, undemocratic states."[41]

The evolution of the right to development, from its original conception to its inauguration in the General Assembly Declaration, has been fast. The right to development is considered a specifically African contribution to the international human rights discourse. Keba M'Baye, a Senegalese jurist, is credited with having first propounded this right in 1972 and later getting it formally recognised in Resolution 4 (XXXIII) of the UN Commission of Human Rights, in 1977. Finally, the UN General Assembly adopted a Declaration on the Right to Development in its Resolution 41/128 of 4 December, 1986.

"Development provides a vital contribution to the observance and promotion of human rights and fundamental freedoms. Since the right of peoples to self-determination forms the basis for the enjoyment and development of individual human rights and also has major implications for the political, economic, social and cultural advancement of every nation, it remains a corner-stone of the new international economic order. Promotion by the United Nations of the right of peoples to self-determination and the progressive development of this right will be an essential means of achieving a new international order and a better, more just and equitable world".[42]

Rights falling under the category of economic self-determination, are set forth in Article 1(2) of the ICCPR, which states:

"All peoples may, for their own ends, freely dispose of their natural wealth and resources without prejudice to any obligations arising out of international economic co-operation, based upon the principle of mutual benefit, and international law. In no case may a people be deprived of its own means of subsistence".

Whilst this article vests the rights concerning the disposal of natural resources in the people, the right to permanent sovereignty over natural resources is ultimately vested in the state. Equating states with peoples however, assumes that the interests of the people are adequately represented by the governing state. The intention of equating peoples with the state is not to take the ownership of natural resources away from the people, but rather to give control to the country, so as to enable it effectively to protect and administer those resources for and on behalf of those people. Obviously, to achieve this goal, it is imperative that the state be controlled by the people, in the democratic sense. Antonio Cassese, commenting on Article 1(2) of the Covenants, has insisted on the need for popular sovereignty in the economic as well as the political sphere:

"Article 1(2)...is not merely a reaffirmation of the right of every state over its own natural resources; it clearly provides that the right over natural wealth belongs to *peoples*. This has two distinct consequences. For dependent peoples, the right implies that the governing authority is under the duty to use the economic resources of the territory in the interest of the dependent people. In a sovereign state, the government must utilize the natural resources so as to benefit the whole people. The right of the people over natural resources, and the corresponding duty of the government, are but a consequence, in economic matters, of the people's right to (internal) self-determination in the political field. Just as the people of every sovereign state have a permanent right to choose their own form of government...so the people are entitled to insist that the natural resources of the nation be exploited in the interest of the people."[43]

However, caution has been expressed regarding the "state-centric" character of the Declaration on the Right to Development, 1986. If, and when the right does eventually find its way into an international and binding covenant, the question that needs to be asked, is whether it will serve the interests of the peoples within independent states, or whether it will serve the interests of the inter-state system. In other words, is this new right to development, which is to ostensibly create the conditions for the enjoyment of the peoples' right to social, cultural and economic self-determination, simply a form of neo-colonialism?

"Indeed, the extension of the principle [of self-determination] to concepts of economic and cultural self-determination (as opposed to political self-determination) portends an even further encroachment of the principle onto ground formerly considered the domain of other norms such as non-intervention and the proscription of force."[44]

The West's increasing encroachment upon the Third World's right to cultural self-determination gave rise to the fierce debate over the universality of human rights at the UN Human Rights Conference, 1993.

When the system of states expanded beyond the confines of Western Europe in the emergent global international system, the relations between the West European states in particular and the new member states of the international community were no longer based upon the erstwhile principles of mutual respect and fair play. Instead, verticality replaced horizontality with regard to relations between the West European states and the new member states of the international community. Verticality pointed to both the assumed superiority and the corresponding dominance of the

West European states in the conduct of international affairs. Despite the changed situation in international politics, especially in the aftermath of decolonisation, both the superiority complex and the persistent dominance of Western states remain more than apparent. This then captures the essence of the Western conception and conduct of international affairs and is amply demonstrated in the Declaration on the Right to Development.

The right to development generally belongs to states, as opposed to individuals and peoples. This is clearly expressed in the Preamble of the Declaration which "recognises [that] the creation of conditions favourable to the development of peoples and individuals is the primary responsibility of their States". It continues, "States have the right and duty to formulate appropriate national development policies", (article 2(3)); states have a duty to co-operate with each other in ensuring development (article 3(3)); and in formulating international development policies (article 4(1)); even popular participation is supposed to be encouraged by states (article 8(2)); and "States should fulfil their rights and duties in such a manner as to promote a new international economic order based on sovereign equality, interdependence, mutual interest and co-operation among all States, as well as to encourage the observance and realisation of human rights" (article 3(3)).

"The 'State' here, has been presented out from a fairytale as the embodiment of all virtues and interests of the people which, needless to say, flies in the face of historical evidence and is certainly nowhere close to the real-life authoritarian states...used ruthlessly by imperialism and compradorial ruling classes in the exploitation and oppression of the...people and nations".[45]

Underpinning the workings of the Declaration on the Right to Development, is a notion which sees development as a gift/charity from above. In the Declaration, the human person is regarded as a "participant and beneficiary" of development (article 2(1)), rather than being the creator of the struggling force for development. The people are both the potential victims of the state's excesses and the recipients of its handouts.

Faced with organised ethnic or regional groups who have been excluded from power and who have attempted to gain international support by exploiting great power rivalries and mobilising Western liberal opinion through human rights and other pressure groups, Third World governments have frequently argued that political instability is a result of the marginalisation of the Third World within the Western-dominated international economy. The way to resolve problems of third world instability, and by implication to reduce the destructive potential of communal and sub-national passions, they argue, is to restructure the world economy so that third world participation would contribute postively to economic development. "The identity of nationalism with anti-colonialism" has therefore been preserved, "or rather a way has been found to continue the anti-colonial struggle by other means."[46]

Such state practice is illustrative of an attempt to present the right to development under the banner of self-determination, as a pacifier and as a way of avoiding the fulfillment of both the external and the internal manifestation of the right to economic self-determination.

Development, which has achieved an unprecedented ideological hegemony in the Third World, is increasingly being presented as the moral equivalent of war, requiring the subordination of the individual and social groups to the state. In the hands of repressive elites, this often justifies a wide range of human rights violations. Even where the regime's commitment to development is genuine, rather than merely a cover for elite depredations, so that there is an attempt to provide the substance of some economic and social rights, enshrining development as an overriding social objective assures that individuals, groups and their rights will regularly be ignored. In general, in "development dictatorships",[47] individual and group rights, especially rights against the state, the essential agent of development, must wait until development has been achieved.

The reluctance on the part of many developing countries to have foreign development aid linked to issues of human rights is based on more than anti-imperialist sentiment. It is also and essentially based on capitalist aspirations. At the recent Human Rights Conference in Vienna, June, 1993, the Amnesty International secretary general, Mr Pierre Sane, reminded the countries attending that many governments in Asia considered international protection and monitoring of human rights not only as interference, but also as an attempt by the West to cut their competitiveness in the international economic order.

"What is at stake here is the rights of the workers in Asia...If they are respected, products coming from Asia will be more expensive. And therefore the economic competitiveness of countries like China, Indonesia, Malaysia - the new and emerging Tigers - will be threatened. It is a very linear concept of development whereby you fill the bellies first and then you provide people with freedom. Maybe 100 years ago, the universal consciousness could accept that to industrialise you crush a whole generation. But it is not acceptable in 1993."[48]

The debate over the new right to development, is a manifestation of a wider conflict between the universalist and the relativist, the adherents of a Western liberal interpretation of human rights on the one hand, and the proponents of alternative social goals based on a radically different conception of human dignity on the other.

The right to self-determination remains "still-born" even in the era of decolonisation. This is the case, not only because the peoples living within independent states, have often been denied their right to the political, social, economic and cultural aspects of the internal right to self-determination, and have hence become dependent upon the benevolence of their governors, but also because the governments of the Third World states themselves, often remain in a state of dependency upon the hand-outs of the West and are thus denied full expression of their external right to self-determination.

"The still-birth of self-determination in decolonisation means the institutionalisation of the condition of dependency to which the progeny of the conquered people continue to be subjected since the military defeat of their ancestors by the colonial conquerors. Thus, present-day international relations can be described, with particular reference to the so-called "Third World", as the ongoing experience of self-determination in decolonisation".[49]

In the Third World, the right to development is in reality, an insurance for "underdevelopment". In other words, the development that the dominant West continues to impose upon the Third World is in effect "development for servitude".

At present, it remains doubtful whether positive international law goes so far as to accept the new progressive understanding of the right to internal self-determination. However, "the continuing vitality and potential for expansion of the principle of self-determination, at least as a directive principle should not be underestimated".[50] Attacks have often been levelled at the international community for its "double standards" apparent in its differential treatment of colonial and non-colonial peoples. While it was reasonable to concentrate initially on the elimination of more blatant forms of colonial rule, today it is unreasonable and unjust to treat international law as static and incapable of further evolution.

The principle of self-determination shows no sign of disappearing from the language of international relations with the virtual demise of Western colonialism, nor is it likely that the principle of self-determination will disappear from the rhetoric used by minority and indigenous groups to legitimise their territorial claims and demands for greater regional autonomy and independence.

Each year, the UN General Assembly passes a resolution on "The importance of the universal realization of the right of peoples to self-determination and of the speedy granting of independence to colonial countries and peoples for the effective guarantee and observance of human rights",[51] in which it "declares its firm opposition to acts of foreign military intervention, aggression and occupation", since "they result in the suppression of the right of peoples to self-determination". The resolutions adopted in recent years have been concerned mostly with the right to self-determination of peoples which have been identified by name, (e.g., former Southern Rhodesia, South Africa and Palestine). Nowadays, resolutions concerning the right to self-determination are adopted by the General Assembly on rare occasions. The relevant resolutions of the General Assembly essentially confine themselves to addressing problems of external self-determination when elaborating on that right.

However, a cautious but apparent evolution is taking place in the attempt to identify the peoples to whom the right to self-determination applies outside of the decolonisation context. The principle of self-determination is no longer:

"...predominantly anti-colonial and anti-racist. If this were so, self-determination would inevitably lose its force (since colonial regimes have slowly disappeared and racist ones are, one hopes, dying out). In fact...this principle possesses at least one other virtue endowing it with a value and a potential which have nothing to do with historical colonialism (or its racist derivations): the condemnation of that form of oppression of another people involving occupation of its territory. This 'dimension' of the principle is destined to have effect even after the numerous contemporary historical situations have vanished. It will continue to lend a 'liberating' (or, if one prefers, 'libertarian') charge to the idea of self-determination."[52]

Whilst the international community's condemnation of Iraq's invasion of Kuwait, was evidence of the force behind this "dimension" of the principle of self-determination, it was evidence only of the "libertarian" charge of external self-determination, not internal self-determination. Such international condemnation of the oppression of another people involving internal territorial colonisation, is rarely to be found.

Clearly, the subjects of the right to self-determination are not only colonial peoples, but also peoples living under foreign domination, in racist systems and under the regime of apartheid. For example, Resolution 2649/XXV, which concerns South Africa and Palestine refers to peoples living "under alien domination" and Resolution 2787/XXVI refers to the right to self-determination of peoples within the context of "foreign domination and alien subjugation".

"The United Nations and the Member States must take effective measures to ensure the immediate and complete liberation of all peoples from any form of foreign subjugation, to eliminate all manifestations of exploitation and discrimination, racism, and *apartheid*, and to repress any action intended to revive such practices. With the same object, the United Nations must derive specific measures to end all support to the colonial and racist regimes that disregard the right of self-determination, and take practical action to support the movements for the liberation of peoples from colonialism, racism, *apartheid* and foreign occupation, and to ensure the adequate representation of such movements within the United Nations".[53]

A broader application of the right to self-determination suggests that peoples suffering from neo-colonialism are also subjects of the right. The threat of neo-colonialism, in the cloak of political and economic, social and cultural pressures, against newly independent or developing nations, is given expression in the following warning:

"While colonialism in the traditional sense, is nearing its end, imperialism and the policy of force and diktat continue to exist and may persist in the future, under the guise of neo-colonialism and power relationships. The exploitation by colonialist forces of the difficulties and problems confronting developing or recently liberated countries, interference in the internal affairs of those States and attempts to maintain, especially in the economic sector, a relationship based on inequality are serious threats to the new States. Economic pressure and domination, interference, racial discrimination, subversion, intervention and the threat of the use of force, are neo-colonialist devices against which the newly independent nations must guard".[54]

To sum up, the internal aspect of the right to self-determination, continues to be formulated in the international instruments in a very general manner, neither enriching the contents of the right, nor introducing new elements to it that would exceed its scope, resulting in "a lack of a commonly accepted concept of internal self-determination."[55]

The prospect of reaching a universal interpretation of the scope and content of the internal right to self-determination seems unlikely. In this light, it is suggested that the internal aspect of self-determination ought be analysed in close relation to the concept of human rights, since the international instruments have led to some uniformity in interpretation and in implementation of human rights on the universal scale.

"...when the rights and fundamental freedoms of members of a people are systematically denied this means that the people's right of self-determination is also infringed. From this point of view "internal" political self-determination is, therefore, the *synthesis and the summa of human rights*. Thus, "internal" political self-determination does not generically mean "self-government" but rather (a) the right to choose freely a government, exercising all the freedoms which make the choice possible (freedom of speech, of association, etc) and (b) the right that the government, once chosen, continues to enjoy the consensus of the people and is neither oppressive nor authoritarian."[56]

To date, "internal self-determination as a legal concept can only mean that full guarantees are provided for a democratic process in which every citizen can participate under conditions of full equality".[57] The centrepiece of internal self-determination, being the accountability of governments before the people, according to the maxim: government for and by the people, i.e., it does not accord to minorities or groups within sovereign states, the right to secede.

The odds are against a uniform interpretation of the whole body of political and economic, social and cultural rights, the interpretation and implementation of which, have basic implications for the definition of the contents and scope of the internal right to self-determination. In the meantime, whilst the "contents of the right to internal self-determination are not stated with precision in international norms because a settlement of this aspect is not feasible...the matter is therefore left to the domestic law and practice of particular States."[58]

Notes

1 Brownlie. I., "The rights of peoples in modern international law", in: Bull. Austl. Soc'y Legal Phil., Vol.9, (1985), pp.107-8, quoted in: Kiwanuka: R. N., "The meaning of "people" in the African Charter on Human and Peoples Rights", in: AJIL, Vol.82, pp.80-101, p.87.

2 Extract from UNESCO meeting of Experts on Further Study of the Rights of Peoples, Paris, February, (1990), quoted in: Jayawickrama. N., "Self-Determination", pp.3-4.

3 Aureliu Cristescu, "The right to self-determination, historical and current development on the basis of the United Nations instruments", para.279, UN Doc E/CN.4/Sub.2/404, Rev.1, (1981).

4 Capotorti, F., "Study on the rights of persons belonging to ethnic, religious and linguistic minorities", UN Doc.E/CN.4/Sub.2/384/Rev.1, (1979), quoted in: Kiwanuka. R. N., p.92.

5 Ermacora. F., "The protection of minorities before the United Nations", in: Recueil des Cours, 182, (1983), p.327, quoted in: Kiwanuka. R. N., p.92.

6 Ibid., p.483.

7 "The concept of equality", Dissenting opinion of Judge Tanaka, South West Africa cases (second phase), (1966), p.482.

8 Modeen. T., "The international protection of national minorities in Europe", (1969), p.144, cited in: Ryan. S., "Ethnic conflict and international relations", (1990), p.160.

9 The Saskatoon Statement and Recommendations on Self-Determination, adopted at the Martin Ennals Memorial Symposium on Self-Determination, Saskatoon, Canada, March 3-6, 1993, published by International Alert, College of Law, University of Saskatchewan.

10 For further analysis on the rights of self-determination to indigenous peoples, see Davies. M., "Indigenous rights: Minority rights, indigenous rights and self-determination", in: Macartney. W. J. Allan, (ed.), "Self-determination in the Commonwealth", pp.45-51.

11 Professor Erica-Irene Daes quoted in: Jayawickrama. N., in "Self-Determination", p.4.

12 Jayawickrama. N., "Self-Determination", p.6.

13 Zinn. C., "Aboriginal land claim recognised", in: The Guardian, October, 20th, (1993), p.9.

14 Brownlie. I., "Principles of international law", (1985), p.109, cited in: Crawford. J., "Outside the colonial context", in: Macartney. W. J. Allan., (ed.), "Self-determination in the Commonwealth", p.15, (emphasis

added).

15 Buchheit. L. C., "Secession. The legitimacy of self-determination", (1978), p.14.

16 Shivji. I. G., "The right of peoples to self-determination: An African perspective", in: Twining. W., (ed.), "Issues of self-determination", pp.33-48, p.37.

17 Ibid.

18 Ibid.

19 Ibid.

20 Ibid.

21 Lenin. V.I., "On the national question and proletarian international-ism", p.168, cited in: Shivji. I. G. p.37.

22 4 UN SCOR, Spec. Supp. 6, UN Doc. S/1417 (1949), cited in: Buchheit. L. C., p.14.

23 Ibid., pp.14-15.

24 Ibid., p.15.

25 Ibid., pp.15-16.

26 Michalska. A., "The right of peoples of self-determination in interna-tional law", in; Twining. W., (ed.), "Issues of self-determination", pp.71-90, p.86.

27 Sohn. L., "The new international law: Protection of the rights of indi-viduals rather than states", in: Am. U.L. Rev., 32, (1982), p.50, quoted in: Kiwakuka. R. N., p.93, (emphasis added).

28 Higgins. R., "The evolution of the right of self-determination: Commentary on Professor Franck's paper", p.3.

29 The Indian Government in ratifying the ICCPR, decided that in article 1 "...the words 'the right self-determination'...apply only to the peoples under foreign domination and...these words do not apply to sovereign independent States or to a section of a people or nation - which is the essence of national integrity", cited in: Crawford. J., p.2.

30 Principle VIII in the Decalogue in the First Basket, Final Act of the CSCE, (emphasis added).

31 Principle III does not, however, exclude the change of frontiers as a result of "negotiations conducted...between a State and a minority group".

32 Jan Helgesen, in: Rosas. A., & Helgesen. J., (ed.), "The strength of diversity: Human rights and pluralist democracy", (1992), p.166.

33 Figure taken from Jayawickrama. N., "Self-determination", p.2.

34 Ibid.

35 Cassese. A., "The self-determination of peoples", in: Henkin. L., (ed.), "The International Bill of Human Rights: The Covenant on Civil

and Political Rights", p.97.

36 Islam. M. R., "Bangladesh Liberation Movement", (1987), p.269.

37 Aureliu Cristescu, (Special Rapporteur of the Sub-Commission on Prevention of Discrimination and Protection of Minorities, of the Commission on Human Rights), "The right to self-determination: Historical and current development on the basis of United Nations instruments", (1978), p.2.

38 Issa. G. Shivji., "The right of peoples to self-determination: An African perspective in: Twining. W., (ed.), "Issues of self-determination", p.39.

39 Resolution 1803 (XVII).

40 Issa. G. Shivji., p.39.

41 Ibid.

42 Aureliu Cristescu, p.3.

43 Cassese. A., p.103.

44 Buchheit. L. C., p.16.

45 Issa. G. Shivji., p.45.

46 Mayall. J., "Nationalism and international society", (1990), p.125.

47 Donnelly. J., "Human dignity, human rights, and political regimes", in: <u>American Political and Science Review</u>, Vol.80, No.3, September, 1986, pp.801-817, p.813.

48 Amnesty International secretary general, Mr. Pierre Sane's statement made at the Human Rights Conference, Vienna, June, (1993), reported in *The Financial Times*, Friday 11 June, (1993).

49 M. B. Ramose., "Self-determination in decolonisation", in: Twining. W., (ed.), "Issues of self-determination", p.30.

50 Crawford. J., p.15.

51 See UN Docs. 45/130 (1990), 46/87 (1991).

52 Cassese. A., "The law in a divided world", p.136.

53 Aureliu Cristescu, p.2.

54 Ibid.

55 Michalska. A., p.88.

56 Cassese. A., p.154-55, quoted in Kiwanuka. R. N., p.100, (emphasis in original).

57 Tomushcat Christian, in: Rosas. A., & Helgesen. J., (ed.s), "The strength of diversity. Human rights and pluralist democracy", (1992), p.40.

58 Ibid., p.40.

CHAPTER 7

Self-determination and democracy

The preceding chapters have shown how self-determination, in the guise of a political postulate and *idee force*, has been advanced over the last century. Briefly, the right to self-determination has been advanced in three different ways. In an essentially anti-colonialist form, it was propounded above all by Lenin. His obvious aim was to disrupt colonial empires and redistribute power in the international community on the basis of the idea of equality among nations, thereby assisting in the emergence of new international subjects consisting of those very peoples which had previously borne the colonialist yoke. In a more moderate version, the principle was advanced as a criterion for "reshaping" existing states, with due emphasis on national and ethnic groups, by proposing such instruments as plebiscites and referendums. Seen from this point of view, the principle carried a less destructive charge with regard to the international community. It essentially addressed itself to sovereign states, and invited them to rearrange their territorial order so as to make allowance for the aspirations of various groups and communities. Lastly, especially in recent years, the principle has been interpreted, largely in the West, as impinging upon the internal self-determination of peoples living within independent states. In other words, as a criterion for the democratic legitimation of the governments of sovereign states.

"The only thing linking these three different versions is that all three 'intrude' upon the domestic affairs of sovereign States and concern themselves, more or less intrusively, with communities which are subject to those States."[1]

Faced with these various politico-ideological formulations, contemporary international law has sanctioned self-determination as an anti-colonial postulate, a criterion for condemning those forms of oppression of a people involving the occupation of territory, and as an anti-racist postulate. The principle of self-determination, however, has not been accepted as a principle protecting national or ethnic, linguistic or religious groups living within independent states, or as a postulate for defying autocratic regimes. Rather, the principle of state sovereignty has shielded states from the demands of minorities and the demand for democratic legitimation which could have had a radically unsettling effect on a significant number of states worldwide, although especially on the Second and Third World.

This chapter will examine the most recent version of the principle of self-determination, the interpretation of the principle as a standard for the democratic legitimation of the governments of sovereign states. Clearly, "any lingering doubt that use of the term 'self-determination' might have amounted to a mechanical, or at best a deferential hang-over from Wilsonian diplomacy, and not a radical decision that henceforth the internal authority of governments would be appraised internationally"[2] has been firmly dispelled. Furthermore, this chapter will determine to what extent this interpretation has served to emasculate the meaning and relevance of the right to self-determination, by presenting "democracy" under the banner of self-determination, as a pacifier and as means of avoiding the external form, thereby removing from the right any last vestiges of anti-imperialism. Moreover, it will reveal how the notion that the international community can impose standards on which the internal authority of sovereign states can be based, has been challenged by reference to the age-old principle of state sovereignty and non-intervention. The chapter will conclude by contrasting the fear expressed by many Third World states, that international electoral monitoring is being used to reimpose a form of neo-colonialism under the banner of democracy, with the ever-decreasing inhibition expressed by the West, about interference in the "internal jurisdiction" of states.

The two radical propositions manifested by the US Declaration of Independence, i.e., that governments instituted to secure the "unalienable rights" of their citizens derive "their just powers from the consent of the governed", and that a nation earns "separate and equal station" in the community of states by demonstrating "a decent respect to the opinions of mankind", are rapidly becoming normative rules of the contemporary international system, merging in the process, into what has collectively been labelled as the "democratic entitlement".[3]

Increasingly, modern governments are recognising that their legitimacy depends on meeting a normative expectation of the community of states. This recognition has led to the emergence of a community expectation, that those who seek the validation of their empowerment, patently govern with the consent of the governed. Democracy, is thus on the way to becoming a global entitlement, one that will increasingly be promoted and protected by collective international processes.

Whilst the transformation of the democratic entitlement from moral prescription to international legal obligation has evolved gradually, the tendency has accelerated in the last decade. As of late 1991, there are more than 110 governments, almost all represented in the UN, that are legally committed to permitting open, multi-party, secret-ballot elections with a universal franchise, many of which have joined during the last ten years. Whilst the growing demand for democratic entitlement by governments is testimony to the fact that it is "an immutable fact of life: government cannot govern by force alone",[4] many states continue to be democracies more in name than in character, thus suggesting that many of these new regimes only need to be seen to be complying with global standards of democracy.

Three related generations of rule-making and implementation have been responsible for the emergence of an international democratic order. The oldest and most highly developed subset of democratic norms are those that have emerged through the right of self-determination.

"Self-determination, postulates the right of a people organized in an established territory to determine its collective political destiny in a democratic fashion and is therefore at the core of the democratic entitlement".[5]

The right to self-determination is signified by the gradual growth of a tradition of maintaining observers on behalf of international and regional organisations, at elections in colonies and trust territories. The first observer missions developed operational procedures. They sent reports to their sponsoring international agency or committee, which helped the community's political organs and individual member governments to make decisions about the legitimacy of the decolonisation process. Over time, with many variations, the observer missions' methods became the standard operating procedure for validating an exercise of self-determination.

"Self-determination is the historic root from which the democratic entitlement grew. Its deep-rootedness continues to confer important elements of legitimacy on self-determination, as well as on the entitlement's two newer branches: freedom of expression and the electoral right".[6]

The second subset of democratic norms, is the freedom of expression which has developed as part of the growth of human rights since the mid-1950's and which focuses on maintaining an open market-place of ideas. The right of free political expression was first enunciated normatively in the Universal Declaration of Human Rights, 1948, which recognises a universal right to freedom of opinion and expression (article 19), as well as to peaceful assembly and association (article 20). These entitlements reappear in the ICCPR, 1966, which also upholds the right to freedom of thought (article 18) and freedom of association (article 22). Furthermore, article 19(2) states "Everyone shall have the right to freedom of expression; this right shall include freedom to seek, receive and impart information and ideas of all kinds, regardless of frontiers, either orally, in writing or in print, in the form of art, or through any other media of his choice". Article 19(2) is subject to restriction by law where "necessary...for the protection of national security or of public order...or of public health or morals" (article 19 3(b)). These restrictions, like the rule itself, are subject to case-by-case review and application by the Human Rights Committee.

The right to opinion, expression and association contained in the Universal Declaration of Human Rights, 1948, and in the ICCPR, 1966, were both a refinement of an aspect of the older right to self-determination, as well as constituting the essential preconditions for an open electoral process. This, the third and newest subset of democratic norms, seeks to establish, define and monitor a right to free and open elections.

Article 21(3) of the Universal Declaration of Human Rights, 1948, provided that "[t]he will of the people shall be the basis of the authority of government; this will shall be expressed in periodic and genuine elections which shall be by universal and equal suffrage and shall be held by secret vote or by equivalent free voting procedures". This statement signified that the "sovereign" had finally been dethroned. The concept of "popular sovereignty" had at last been enshrined in a fundamental international constitutive legal document.

The international human rights programme has been instrumental in shifting the fulcrum of the system, from the protection of sovereigns to the protection of people. It is becoming increasingly apparent that the notion of national sovereignty can no longer be invoked to immunise a state's human rights abuses from the writ of international law. International condemnation is increasingly being brought to bear on a state's discriminatory policies towards its subjects.

"International law is still concerned with the protection of sovereignty, but, in its modern sense, the object of protection is not the power base of the tyrant who rules directly by naked power or through the apparatus of a totalitarian political order, but the continuing capacity of a population freely to express and effect choices about the identities and policies of its governors."[7]

In the ICCPR, 1966, the participatory electoral process became a customary legal norm applicable to all. Article 25 extends to every citizen the right to take part in the conduct of public affairs, directly or through freely chosen representatives, and to vote and to be elected at genuine periodic elections which shall be by universal and equal suffrage and shall be held by secret ballot, guaranteeing the free expression of the will of the electors.

Article 25 of the ICCPR clearly supplements and compliments article 1 of the ICCPR (the right to self-determination).[8] Article 25 is concerned with the detail of how free choice (necessarily implied in article 1) is to be provided, by periodic elections, on the basis of universal suffrage. It is concerned with matters that are clearly beyond those touched on by article 1, namely, the entitlement to participate without discrimination in the public life of one's country.

The evolving notion of internationally validated political consultation has continued to permeate the General Assembly. At its forty-fifth session in 1991, it adopted a resolution entitled "Enhancing the Effectiveness of the Principle of Periodic and Genuine Elections".[9] This non-binding, yet important document, reaffirms and further specifies the electoral entitlement first outlined in the Universal Declaration of Human Rights, 1948, and later embodied in article 25 of the ICCPR, 1966. It "stresses" the member states':

"conviction that periodic and general elections are a necessary and indispensable element of sustained efforts to protect the rights and the interests of the governed and that, as a matter of practical experience, the right of everyone to take part in the government of his or her country is a crucial factor in the effective enjoyment by all of a wide range of other human rights and fundamental freedoms, embracing political, economic, social and cultural rights".[10]

The resolution also declared, "that determining the will of the people requires an electoral process that provides an equal opportunity for all citizens to become candidates and put forward their political views, individually and in co-operation with others, as provided in national constitutions and laws".[11]

The most dramatic, norm-creating activity in the process of making the democratic entitlement explicit and specific, was witnessed in the recent efforts made by the members of the Conference on Security and Co-operation in Europe (CSCE), constituted of the nations of Europe, Canada, the United States and the nations of Eastern Europe. At a meeting in

Copenhagen in June, 1990, the members of the CSCE affirmed that "democracy is an inherent element of the rule of law" and recognised "the importance of pluralism with regard to political organisations".[12] Among the "inalienable rights of all human beings," they declared, is the democratic entitlement, including, "free elections that will be held at reasonable intervals by secret ballot or by equivalent free voting procedure, under conditions which ensure in practice the free expression of the opinion of the electors in the choice of their representatives"; a government "representative in character, in which the executive is accountable to the elected legislature or the electorate"; and political parties that are clearly separate from the state.[13]

The thirty-five CSCE participants, also linked recognition of the democratic entitlement by governments to the validation of their right to govern. It stated "the will of the people, freely and fairly expressed through periodic and general elections, is the basis of the authority and legitimacy of all government".[14] The CSCE thereby implicitly deemed illegitimate, those regimes that deny their citizens their basic democratic rights. Whilst not explicitly endorsed, this must, by extension, also deem any government that denies a *section* of the population of the state their basic democratic rights, illegitimate.

Whilst the rules pertaining to the democratic entitlement do not yet address normatively the delicate issue of the right of a disaffected portion of an independent state to secede, "the idea of self-determination has evolved into a more general notion of internationally validated political consultation",[15] one that is beginning to be applied even to independent (post-colonial) states. At the same Copenhagen Meeting in June, 1990, a Conference on the Human Dimension of the CSCE was held, at which the democratic entitlement was implicitly extended to minorities, albeit without encouraging secession.

Part IV of the Copenhagen Document was entirely devoted to the issue of the protection of minorities. Taking place in a dramatically altered Europe, the CSCE negotiating table was heavily influenced by the proliferation of ethnic nationalist sentiment and violent ethnic conflict in Europe. Some of the CSCE delegates, only too aware of the political instability of the region, felt that the issue of minority protection should not be focused upon at all. Some felt that the very concept of the nation-state was at stake, whilst others argued that the issue of minority protection should have been left or reinterpreted decades ago. At the root of these disparate fears was the age-old and deep-seated fear of secession.[16]

Despite the reluctance of some delegates at the CSCE to tackle the issue of minority protection, the first operative paragraph in the Document revealed a decisive development in the approach of the CSCE states towards minorities. In addition to a "traditional" statement, declaring that minorities are entitled to effective enjoyment of human rights without any discrimination (prohibition of negative discrimination), it stated that "The participating States will adopt, where necessary, special measures for the purpose of ensuring to persons belonging to national minorities full equality with the other citizens in the exercise and enjoyment of human rights and fundamental freedoms".[17]

For the first time within an important norm-creating instrument, albeit only a regional and not an international instrument, a commitment to carry out positive discrimination was agreed upon. Few other international instruments contain such an obligation. However, it is important to note what the Copenhagen Document did *not* say. It did not require the participating states to adopt special measures to ensure full equality with other citizens to national minorities, *per se*. Instead, it required them to adopt special measures to ensure that "*persons* belonging to national minorities" might enjoy full equality (emphasis added). By reiterating the language of article 27 of the ICCPR, 1966, and attempting to substitute the protection of minorities in contemporary international law, with the principle of non-discrimination against individuals, the Copenhagen Document, failed to provide comprehensive protection to minorities.[18]

However, the Copenhagen Document recognised that respect for the human rights of persons belonging to national minorities "is an essential factor for peace, justice, stability and democracy in the participating States".[19] Having regard to the CSCE participant's open acknowledgement of the linkage of the democratic entitlement by governments to the validation of their right to govern, it must be inferred that a CSCE participant who does not respect the human rights of persons belonging to national minorities, should not call itself a democracy, and by implication, ought to lose its legitimacy to govern, at least its legitimacy to govern the minority group in question.

Moreover, the Copenhagen Document stated in the introductory part, that the effective protection of minority rights "can only be satisfactorily resolved in a democratic political framework based on the rule of law, with a functioning independent judiciary".[20] In other words, only in democratic governments, with pluralistic political organisations, can the issue of minority protection be truly resolved. It can be assumed that the Copenhagen Document intended to treat the democratic entitlement as inextricably linked, both conceptually and strategically to the protection of minorities. Whilst it does not explicitly treat the democratic entitlement as linked to the claim of minorities to secession, it does implicitly suggest that a government that does not respect the human rights of minorities, which is an "essential" factor for democracy, cannot presume to legitimately govern its people, and by implication cannot expect the approbation of the international community.

To those delegates involved in the drafting of the Copenhagen Document who wanted to make constructive progress in minority issues, the challenge was to find the proper balance between the right to internal self-determination for the minority populations and the necessary respect for the territorial integrity of existing states.

The principle that popular participation in societal life is the key-stone in a democracy, was clearly highlighted in the Copenhagen Document. Moreover, it openly accepted that this principle applies equally to both minority as well as majority populations. The participation of minority groups in the democratic governance of a state was courageously tackled in the Copenhagen Document. It was clearly recognised that separatist conflicts most often arise when groups become the victims of aggressive state centralisation, and are forced in turn, into marginal positions at the periphery of the political system. The Copenhagen Document acknowledged that such conflicts could be resolved, if not prevented, if such groups could be integrated firmly into the political decision-making process at the centre. It also recognised that an alternative option would be to leave the power to make decisions to the people most affected by the decisions, i.e., encouraging the delegation of powers, or the devolution of power, in other words, "grassroots democracy".

"In principle and in practice, this (local self-government) is but an element in the principle of self-determination, the 'internal' aspect of that right".[21]

Both the above forms of minority participation in the democratic governance of a state were addressed in the Copenhagen Document in the following paragraphs:

"The participating States will respect the right of persons belonging to national minorities to effective participation in public affairs, including participation in the affairs relating to the protection and promotion of the identity of such minorities.

The participating States note the efforts undertaken to protect and create conditions for the promotion of the ethnic, cultural, linguistic and religious identity of certain national minorities by establishing, as one of the possible means to achieve these aims, appropriate local or autonomous administrations corresponding to the specific historical and territorial circumstances of such minorities and in accordance with the policies of the State concerned".[22]

The latter part of the paragraph of the Copenhagen Document created more complications for the CSCE states than the first part of the paragraph. In many of the CSCE states, minority populations are already represented in the national legislative, executive and judicial systems. Indeed, in some states, minorities have some kind of quota-system, for instance, minorities are allocated particular seats in parliament. Indeed, few states fear that their national unity is threatened by such participation from the marginal groups. Despite different methods of accommodation, such groups will of course always constitute a "minority", not only within the state, but also within the various legislative, executive and judicial bodies.

The other form of popular participation by minorities, proved much more threatening to the CSCE states. The issue of local self-government is often one of the key issues on a minorities' agenda. Some of the CSCE states have already accepted some form of local self-government for minority populations. Mostly, this has been organized on a territorial basis. In cases where the members of the minority group have been living in specific areas, they have been granted some kind of autonomy. Legally though, this has quite often been seen as granting autonomy to a geographical region, not to a group of individuals constituting a minority in a demographic sense. The text from the Copenhagen Document reflects this position rather well, but also represents a possible opening for a progressive evolution. The provision refers both to "local" administrations according to "territorial" circumstances, as well as to "autonomous" administrations according to "historical" circumstances.[23]

Those more general and theoretical problems, the concept of "peoples", and the theoretical implications of self-determination, were not discussed in the CSCE framework. The negotiations were conducted on a more pragmatic level, and questions of local democracy were handled in a very concrete manner. This is due to the fact that most governments represented were reluctant to discuss problems which touched upon or questioned the principle of territorial integrity. The significance of the principle of territorial integrity becomes evident when the Document declares that these committments, entered into by the states cannot be interpreted so as to imply any right for individuals to engage in activities in contravention of other norms, "including the principle of territorial integrity of

States".[24]

In the same year that the Copenhagen Declaration was passed, the leaders of the thirty-four CSCE states joined in Paris to declare "a new era of democracy, peace and unity".[25] Unanimously, they endorsed an extraordinary Charter, which committed them "to build, consolidate and strengthen democracy as the only system of government of our nations".[26] The Charter of Paris, as it came to be known, restates the older entitlement to free expression, but adds the right of every individual, without discrimination, "to participate in free and fair elections,"[27] backed by the leaders' pledge to "co-operate and support each other with the aim of making democratic gains irreversible".[28]

Although the Charter of Paris is not a treaty, its language is weighted with the terminology of *opinio juris*, and is therefore deliberately norm-creating. It is significant that the Charter of Paris builds on the assumption that electoral democracy is owed not only by each government to its own people, but also by each CSCE state to all other independent states in the international community. According to Judge Thomas Buergental, an US participant in the Copenhagen meeting, today:

"...no domestic institution or norm, in theory, is beyond the jurisdictional reach of the CSCE Here the traditional domestic jurisdiction doctrine, which has tended to shield the oppressive state practices and institutions from international scrutiny, has for all practical purposes lost its meaning. And this notwithstanding the fact that non-intervention in the domestic affairs of a state is a basic CSCE principle. Once the rule of law, human rights and democratic pluralism are made the subject of international commitments, there is little left in terms of governmental institutions that is domestic".[29]

More recently, during September - October, 1991, the CSCE representatives unanimously endorsed the Document of the Moscow Meeting of the Conference on the Human Dimension of the CSCE. It reaffirmed "that issues relating to human rights, fundamental freedoms, democracy and the rule of law are of international concern, as respect for these rights and freedoms constitutes one of the foundations of the international order". The participating states "categorically and irrevocably declare[d] that the commitments undertaken in the field of the human dimension of the CSCE are matters of direct and legitimate concern to all participating States and do not belong exclusively to the internal affairs of the State concerned".[30]

To safeguard the rights concerned, the Paris Charter established an institutionalised process for monitoring compliance with the electoral duties of states. It gives the CSCE several organs, including a secretariat at Prague and an Office for Free Elections at Warsaw. The latter is to "facilitate contacts and the exchange of information on elections within participating States".[31] The Paris Charter also envisages the eventual creation, after further consultations, of a "CSCE parliamentary assembly, involving members of parliaments from all participating States", to achieve "greater parliamentary involvement in the CSCE."[32]

The evolution of textual determinacy with respect to the electoral entitlement is a relatively recent development. In practice, however, the monitoring component of the entitlement has a long history. Since the close of the Cold War, the UN has increasingly supervised elections in independent member states. Moreover, in the final report on ONUVEH (the mission established on October, 10, 1990, to oversee Haitian elections), the Secretary-General warned that if electoral democracy is to be more than a one-time event in the history of a state with little experience in such matters, a far more sustained effort will have to made under the auspices of the community of nations. He suggested the need for a long-term preemptive assistance programme and implied the need for a longer-term international effort to create the grass-roots elements of democratic political institutions and processes in nations without that tradition. He suggested that international election monitoring cannot be limited to guaranteeing the citizen's right to vote, but rather, must also ensure a far broader panoply of democratic rights of the sort enunciated in the Covenant on Civil and Political Rights and the Charter of Paris.

The capacity of the international system to validate governments, is rapidly being accepted as an appropriate role of the UN, the regional systems and supplementarily, international NGOs The democratic entitlement has its roots in the still radical principle, that the community of states has the power to create and implement codes governing the behaviour of governments toward their own citizens. Indeed, such an assumption once justified "enlightened" colonialism, the residue of which can still be found in article 38(1)(c) of the International Court's Statute, which authorises the judges to consult "general principles of law recognised by *civilised* nations" (emphasis added). Clearly, the notion that governments can be graded for deportment is not new. The UN Charter limits UN membership to states that are "peace-loving" (article 4(1)) and enjoins governments to respect the "equal rights and self-determination of peoples" (article 1(2)). The Genocide,[33] and the Racism Conventions,[34] also qualify as rules of deportment imposed on all states by the community of nations. Having become customary as well as treaty law, if not also rules of *jus cogens*, these Conventions may be said to exemplify the principle that states collectively have the authority to determine minimum standards of conduct from which none may long deviate without eventually endangering their membership in the club.

But the notion that the community can impose such standards on which the democratic entitlement is based, is challenged by reference to another equally venerable principle of international law, embodied in article 2(7) of the Charter, which upholds the age-old principle of state sovereignty. It provides that the UN shall not interfere in matters "essentially within the domestic jurisdiction of states". While as noted above, this conflict may have been resolved within the regional context of the CSCE, with the recognition by the Copenhagen Document and the Paris Charter of the paramountcy of the democratic entitlement, the clear-cut supremacy of that entitlement is not yet apparent in the global context.

A head-on conflict between proponents and opponents of election monitoring as a general normative democratic entitlement is likely, however, as long as the conflict of deep-seated principles, such as the emerging right to free and fair elections and non-intervention in domestic affairs remain unreconciled, such conflict will generate a clash of political wills in the global and regional communities. The very idea of general international monitoring of elections in sovereign states arouses anger, not only of the few remaining totalitarian regimes, but also of nations with long memories of humiliating interventions by states bent on "civilising" missions. Opponents are mostly motivated by the fear that monitoring is being used to reimpose a form of neo-colonialism under the banner of establishing democracy. While many states will accept occasional monitoring of elections to end a civil war or regional conflict, these same states consider it a necessary exception, not a normal manifestation of an universal democratic entitlement.

The most unyielding opposition to the right of secessionist self-determination, has come not from erstwhile Imperial Western Powers, but from those nations that have themselves only recently emerged from the process of colonial self-determination. The articulated justifications for the desire of the Third World to limit the doctrine of self-determination to classic instances of Western colonialism (or, at least to remove from it any secessionist implications), entails more than an appeal to the probable disruptive consequences of any endorsement of secession, in view of the unstable, heterogeneous character of many of these states. Instead, an alternative justification has been advanced, which seeks to categorize any movement toward 'balkanisation', as a species of neo-colonialism. In other words, the practice of balkanisation is not limited to the process of the disintegration of an independent state into smaller, autonomous enti- ties, it includes any constitutional or political scheme, such as federalism or local self-government, which in any way dilutes the political authority of the central government.

"Now that Africa has asserted itself and has been achieving its inde- pendence, the irreconcilable and scheming former colonists are viewed as seeking through constitutional and political devices, such as federalism,... multiparty political systems, local self-government, and entrenched bills of rights, to prevent the development of strong, unified and economically as well as politically independent African States. Thus federalism is seen as a refined neo-colonialist extension of the colonial balkanisation prac- tice, designed to enfeeble or split up independent African States".[35]

In this context, any suggestion that political decentralisation might pre- serve the national unity of states in the face of strong parochial sentiment, is not viewed as advice for the strengthening of the developing states, but rather as a sinister attempt to perpetuate the evils of colonialism, by encouraging debilitating divisions in the newly independent states. Fears of neo-colonialism on behalf of many of the newly independent states, are often reflected in both their internal state structures and in their poli- cies advocated before the international forum. Whilst states continue to reject a political structure based on a devolution of political power to the component regions of a state, they will clearly deny their people the right to internal self-determination, and thus increase the risk that these peo- ples will demand greater regional autonomy, escalating into a demand for separation and in the final instance, secession and independence.

Although the CSCE seems poised to pioneer a generalised duty to be monitored, even this regional body has not made the duty mandatory for all. In the international community, while there may be a duty under arti- cle 25 of the Covenant on Civil and Political Rights, 1966 to permit free and open elections and a review of national compliance by the Human Rights Committee, there is as yet no obligation to permit actual election monitoring by international or regional organisations. Indeed, one should expect resistance to any effort to transform an election-monitoring option, exercisable at the discretion of each government, into an obligation owed by each government to its own people and to the other states of the global community.

This deficiency was demonstrated by the General Assembly's recent ambiguous attitude towards the democratic entitlement. The members passed two seemingly incongruent resolutions on monitoring, which largely reflected the concerns of many states in the Third World, as they contemplate the apparently relentless evolution of an entitlement to democracy, including free elections and resultant international supervision. In General Assembly Resolution 45/150 February 21, 1991, the democratic entitlement was restated by the General Assembly and election monitoring commended as one way to ensure its implementation. Almost in the same breath however, the second resolution affirmed "that it is the concern solely of peoples [of each State] to determine methods and to establish implementation according to their constitutional and national legislation";[36] and it urged all states "to respect the principle of non-interference in the internal affairs of States".[37]

Not long ago, international efforts to implement the right of self-determination were vigorously opposed as imposing upon the right of governments, under article 2(7) of the UN Charter, to administer their colonies without outside interference. That opposition gradually abated as the principle of self-determination gained in determinacy. Efforts to monitor compliance with the right to freedom of expression have encountered similar expressions of outraged *amour-propre* by states called to task for arbitrarily silencing their own citizens. It is not surprising therefore, that passionate resentments should also arise in some quarters at the prospect of seeing the international community insinuate itself into the intimate political process by which governments are empowered by the people.

Inhibitions about interference in the "domestic jurisdiction" of states, are less compelling than they used to be. "We are arriving at the conclusion", the erstwhile Soviet Foreign Minister Boris D. Pankin observed, "that national guarantees [of human rights] are not sufficient. So we have to review the principle of non-interference in affairs of other governments".[38]

"It thus appears that support is increasing even - perhaps *particularly* - among former totalitarian states for the proposition that the democratic entitlement enhanced by linkage with other basic human rights and the accompanying international monitoring of compliance, has trumped the principle of non-interference..."[39]

This support, however, demonstrates not the debunking of the principle of non-intervention, nor the universal belief that undemocratic electoral processes imposed upon a people by their government are counter-normative and not beyond the purview of the international community, but rather the reaction by many states to the consequences that can reasonably be expected to ensue for those who "fail the test". If the democratic entitlement evolves into a systemwide obligation, unwelcome consequences will ensue for governments unwilling to be monitored or to hold free elections.

The international community has long asserted for example, in the case of South Africa, a right of all states to take hortatory, economic and, in extreme cases, even military action to enforce aspects of the democratic entitlement,[40] but only when duly authorized by the UN in accordance with its Charter. Article 2(7), in barring UN intervention "in matters which are essentially within the domestic jurisdiction of any State", stipulates that "this principle shall not prejudice the application of enforcement measures under Chapter VII".

"It is no longer arguable that the United Nations cannot exert pressure against governments that oppress their own peoples by egregious racism, denials of self-determination and suppression of freedom of expression. That litany is being augmented by new sins: refusals to permit demonstrably free elections or to implement their results. However, if the sin is committed, the international community may only invoke collective enforcement measures such as sanctions, blockade or military intervention in limited circumstances - as when the Security Council finds that a threat or breach of the peace has occurred - or if it collectively determines that it is not engaging in enforcement against a member but is acting at the request of a legitimate government against a usurper. These prerequisite determinations, however, must be made by the appropriate collective machinery of the community and not by individual members."[41]

As Judge Buergenthal observed, regarding the effect of the Copenhagen Document and the Paris Charter, there is bound to evolve a "linkage of human rights to other questions (trade, security, environment, etc.)...Linkage permits the participating States...to condition their bilateral and multilateral relations in general upon progress in the human dimension sphere".[42]

The Special Rapporteur of the Sub-Commission on Prevention of Discrimination and Protection of Minorities, of the Commission on Human Rights has endorsed this development:

"The progress achieved in social development must therefore be analysed in conjunction with the progress achieved in the sphere of human rights. This requires more effective co-ordination between the work of the United Nations bodies which deal with social questions and those which deal with fundamental human rights".[43]

Since the end of the ideological crusading of the Cold War, the West has become ever more discriminating about who it backs in the Third World, its ostensible goal being to "break the paternalistic cycle of aid dependence."[44] Human rights, trade concessions and development aid have become the pivot of today's North-South conflict. The row, evidenced in all its colours at the United Nations World Conference on Human Rights, held in June 1993 in Vienna, the first in twenty-five years, symbolised the enduring and at times bitter debate between advocates of the "universality" of human rights, represented primarily by the developed countries of the North on the one hand, and many developing countries on the other hand, who prefered to stress economic development and cultural relativism, seeing the strictures of the North, i.e., the practice of "conditionality", tying development aid to concessions on political and civil rights, as badly disguised interference and imperialism.

Addressing the Conference, the UN secretary general, Boutros-Boutros Ghali said that countries attending should aim to improve the human condition by backing democratic development, accepting that human rights were universal and indivisible and ensuring that their observance was guaranteed. He said that the cloak of national sovereignty should not be used as a cover to perpetrate human rights abuses unchecked, and affirmed that regional and international organisations had the right to intervene to protect individuals and communities from governments violating their rights. In response, the representative from Beijing, insisted that individual rights were inferior to those of the state and rejected all notions of outsiders "interfering" in a country's sovereignty in human rights. The hardliners' stance on human rights was laid out in a statement issued in Bangkok in April, 1993, after a meeting of thirty-four Asian and Arab countries. It stressed regional, cultural and religious factors, suggesting that rights were relative rather than universal, and insisted that human rights should not be used "as an instrument of political pressure", and rejected the linkage of trade and aid with human rights issues.[45] Furthermore, in his address to the Conference, Yasser Arafat, the Palestine Liberation Organisation leader echoed their views, accusing the West of using human rights as a pretext for intervention "to achieve their objectives".[46]

Any expression of autonomy and independence in the Third World in the post-Cold War era, continues to be interpreted as antithetical to the interests of the West. This antithesis, which "is most adequately represented through the cultural framework of a traditional clash of civilisations",[47] was clearly illustrated in the coverage of the United Nations World Conference on Human Rights, 1993. Underlying much of the coverage of the debates at the Conference was the idea of a "societal cold war", "a hi-tech crusade to defend the Western way of life".[48]

Discernable in the coverage of the discussions, was a more fundamental thesis based on the idea that this "clash of civilisations" will one day dominate global politics. Implicit in this fear, is the demand for greater Western military vigilance against Eastern civilisations. The idea that all non-Western interests will eventually coagulate to change the balance of global power, was prevalent in the coverage of the debates at the Conference.

Behind the discourse on the democratic entitlement and in the coverage of the debates at the UN World Conference on Human Rights, 1993, lay the assumption that there is a fundamental North-South divide over the concept of national sovereignty, and that it is Third World nationalism rather than Western nationalism, which is the obstacle to the gradual transcendence of the national idea, and the creation of a global supra-national sentiment. In reality, however, nationalism in both the Third World and the West is equally subversive of any wider international order. The internal and external policies of Western and Third World states are governed equally by national interest, regardless of how desirous Western states appear to be to rise above nationalism. The attainment of a post-national order:

"...is impossible so long as politicians attempt to manipulate (or appropriate to their own favoured policies), the mass public opinion on which they ultimately rely. Such efforts inevitably limit how far they can pursue international policies (or committ themselves to schemes for international cooperation) when these run counter to perceived national interests. In other words, in all industrial societies, nationalism is a powerful constraining or mobilising force; but it is generally invisible, embedded in the social fabric and institutional practices of the state."[49]

Clearly, nationalism has become structurally embodied as the basis of the modern state. Whilst the nation-state (or the would-be nation-state) remains the basic political unit:

"...there is no immediate prospect of transcending the national idea, either as the principle of legitimisation or as the basis of political organisation for the modern state. Hence, for the time being, international society cannot develop in ways which are inconsistent with the continued existence of separate national states. Islands of supra-national authority may arise here and there, but the principle of popular sovereignty will not easily translate into supra-nationalism in general."[50]

As such, the right to self-determintion continues to be the principle of state legitimisation. Since communities do not exist within natural boundaries, there seems little alternative but to define the principle of popular sovereignty by reference to historical communities, or those whose collective identity is being created within frontiers that were demarcated in the decolonisation period. Whilst the "domestication" of the concept of self-determination has allowed it to support the sovereignty of existing states rather than subvert it, the principle continues to have enormous subversive appeal to all those actual and potential secessionists, in both the Third World and the West, who remain convinced that their fundamental rights have been denied. The principle of self-determination continues to provide one of the few instruments left, through which people can successfully mobilise themselves politically and socially in opposition to the increasingly internalised totalitarianism of the New World Order.

Notes

1 Cassese. A., "International law in a divided world", p.135.

2 W. M. Reisman., "Sovereignty and human rights in contemporary international law", in: AJIL, Vol.84, (1990), pp.866-876, p.876.

3 Professor Franck. T. M., "The emerging right to democratic government", in: AJIL, Vol.86, (1992), pp.46-91, p.46.

4 Ibid., p.48.

5 Ibid., p.52.

6 Ibid.

7 Reisman. W. M., p.872.

8 Higgins. R., "Self-determination", (1991), Hague lecture, (unpublished paper), pp.1-25, p.13.

9 General Assembly Resolution 45/150, February 21, (1991).

10 Ibid., Paragraph 2.

11 Ibid., Paragraph 3.

12 Conference on Security and Co-operation in Europe (CSCE), Document of the Copenhagen Meeting of the Conference on the Human Dimension, June 29, (1990), para.3.

13 Ibid., Paragraph 5.

14 Ibid., Paragraph 6.

15 Franck. T. M., p.55.

16 Jan Helgesen., in: Rosas. A., & Helgesen, J., (ed.s), "The strength of diversity. Human rights and pluralist democracy", (1992), p.172.

17 Ibid., p.173.

18 Thornberry. P., "Minorities and human rights law", in: Minority Rights Group Report, No. 73, (1987).

19 Jan Helgesen., p.173.

20 Ibid.

21 Ibid., p.178.

22 Ibid.

23 Ibid., p.179.

24 Ibid.

25 CSCE, Charter of Paris for a New Europe and Supplementary Document to Give Effect to Certain Provisions of the Charter, November 21, (1990), Preamble, reprinted in 30 ILM 190, p.193, (1991), cited: in Franck. T. M., p.67.

26 Paris Charter, p.193.

27 Paris Charter, p.194.

28 Paris Charter, p.195.

29 Buergenthal, CSCE Human Dimensions: The birth of a system, 1 Collected courses of the academy of European law, No. 2, pp.42-43 (forthcoming), cited in: Franck. T. M., p.68.

30 CSCE, Document of the Moscow Meeting of the Conference on the Human Dimension of the CSCE, October 3, (1991), Preamble, at 2, (unofficial text of the US delegation), reprinted in 30 ILM 1670, (1991), cited in: Franck. T. M., p.68.

31 Charter of Paris, p.206.

32 Ibid.

33 Convention on the Prevention and Punishment of the Crime of Genocide, December 9, 1948, UNTS 277, entered into force January 12, (1951).

34 International Convention of the Elimination of All Forms of Racial Discrimination, opened for signature March 7, (1966), 660 UNTS 195, entered into force January 4, (1969).

35 Rivkin. A., "Nation building in Africa: Problems and prospects", p.87, (1969), cited in: Buchheit. L. C., "Secession: The legitimacy of self-determination", (1978), p.104.

36 General Assembly Resolution 45/151, paragraph 2 December 18, (1990).

37 Ibid., Paragraph 4.

38 *New York Times*, September 10, (1991), cited in Franck. T. M., p.83.

39 Franck. T.M., p.83

40 International Convention on the Suppression and Punishment of the Crime of *Apartheid*, General Assembly Resolution 3068, 28 UN GAOR Supp. (No. 30) at 75, UN Doc. A/9030 (1973), entered into force July 18, (1976).

41 Franck. T. M., p.85.

42 Buergenthal, CSCE Human Dimension: The birth of a system, in: Franck. T. M., p.84.

43 Aureliu Cristescu, (Special Rapporteur of the Sub-Commission on Prevention of Discrimination and Protection of Minorities, of the Commission on Human Rights), "The right to self-determination: Historical and current development on the basis of United Nations instruments", (1978), p.4.

44 Palmer, J., "Brussels links Third World aid to human rights and democracy", in: *The Guardian*, 10th September, (1993).

45 Traynor, I., "Lofty aims felled by squabbling", in: *The Guardian*, 22nd June, (1993).

46 Ibid.

47 Furedi, F., "The new ideology of imperialism: Renewing the moral imperative", (1994), p.3.
48 Ibid.
49 Mayall, J., "Nationalism and international society", p.112.
50 Ibid.

Part 2

Sri Lanka: A case study

The Right to self-determination: The Sri Lankan Tamil national question

On 4 February, 1948, Sri Lanka attained her independence from the United Kingdom, and by implication, the people of Sri Lanka instrumentalised their right to self-determination. In less than a decade however, the Island of Sri Lanka,[1] once the erstwhile jewel of the Indian Ocean and the epitome of beauty and tranquillity, and regarded not long ago as a model of liberal democracy in the "Third World", had been engulfed by devastating violent inter-ethnic conflict. Communal disharmony led to a series of riots and to the particularly disgraceful and bloody clashes that occurred between the majority Sinhalese community and the minority Tamil community in 1956 and 1958. By the year 1977, the leaders of the main Tamil political party, the Tamil United Liberation Front (TULF) had obtained a clear mandate from the Tamil-speaking community for the creation of an independent sovereign state of Tamil *Eelam*. This state was to be constituted of "all the geographically contiguous areas that have been the traditional homeland of the Tamil-speaking people in the country".

The legal legitimacy of the Sri Lankan Tamils' demand for an independent state, is based upon the assumption that in positive international law, "all peoples" have the right to self-determination. It was made apparent in Part One of this study, however, that the right to self-determination in positive international law does not apply to "all peoples", especially minorities and ethnic or communal groups living within independent states, but rather, it is a principle whose usage is confined to instances of traditional colonialism and occasionally neo-colonialism, in the case of racism, *apartheid* and alien occupation. However, it was established in Part One that the principle of self-determination has been bifurcated and has two component parts; an internal and an external aspect. The right to internal self-determination, in contrast to the established right to external self-determination (which implies the right to sovereignty, and territorial integrity, with its implicit right to non-intervention), rests ultimately upon the doctrine of liberal democracy, and is anti-imperialist in intent. The right to self-determination that the peoples of an independent state are entitled to, is the right to determine their own political, economic, social and cultural destiny. To date, internal self-determination as a legal concept, means that full guarantees must be provided for a democratic process in which every citizen can participate under conditions of full equality. In other words, the centre-piece of the internal right to self-determination is the accountability of governments before the people, according to the maxim; government for and by the people.

Moreover, it was also recognised in Part One that the principle of popular participation in societal life, which is the key-stone in a democracy, applies to minority populations as well as to majority populations. It was clearly recognised that separatist conflicts most often arise when groups become the victims of aggressive state centralisation and are forced in turn, to occupy marginal positions at the periphery of the political system. It was acknowledged that such conflicts could be prevented/resolved, if such groups could be integrated firmly into the country's political decision-making process. In principle and in practice, local self-government is a fundamental element of the principle of self-determination, i.e., the internal aspect of this right.

The problems associated with minority participation in the democratic governance of a state, i.e., the fulfilment of a group's claim to the internal right to self-determination, are outlined in the following empirical case study. Part Two of this study, clearly reveals how successive denials of the Sri Lankan Tamils' claim to the right to internal self-determination, i.e., the right to local self-government, by each of the Sinhalese-dominated governments, has ultimately led to the demand for secession and independence, i.e., the right to external self-determination, and has resulted in the ethnic civil war that is now consuming the Island.

Whilst there have been several violent inter-ethnic and intra-ethnic cleavages apparent in the Island, viz: between the Sinhalese and the "Tamils"[2]; the Low-Country Sinhalese and the Kandyan Sinhalese; the Jaffna-based Tamils and the Eastern-based Tamils; the Tamils and the Muslims, and the ruling Sinhalese elite and the youthful Sinhalese Marxist contingent, the Janata Vimukti Peramuna (JVP), the focus of this study is predominantly on the violent inter-ethnic conflict between the two main ethnic groups in the Island, the majority Sinhalese-Buddhist community and the native minority Tamil Hindu community, constituting respectively, approximately 74% and 12.6% of the total population of the country. (See Table 1)

However, three other ethnic groups also inhabit the Island; the

Muslims (Malays and Moors), the "Up Country" or "Plantation" Tamils and the Burghers. It is useful to provide at the outset a brief account of the status of the Muslim and the "Up Country" Tamil communities, for they have both played and continue to play an important role in the ethnic conflict between the Sinhalese and the Tamil communities.

The Muslim community is the third largest ethnic community in Sri Lanka. They are predominantly Tamil-speaking, and have historically inhabited the Eastern Province of the Island, constituting the largest population in what is popularly deemed to be part of the traditional "homeland" of the Sri Lankan Tamil-speaking people. Thus, the Muslim community also share a cultural affinity with the Sri Lankan Tamils. Over the last few decades, however, the Muslim community has increasingly found itself in the unsavoury role of piggy-in-the-middle, being exploited by both parties to the conflict and trusting neither. They have therefore begun to take an increasingly independent role in the civil war, to safeguard their rights as Muslims *qua* Muslims.[3]

The Plantation or "Up Country" Tamils, the fourth largest ethnic community in Sri Lanka, were brought to the Island from India during the nineteenth century to work on the coffee and tea plantations. Whilst the Up Country Tamils and the indigenous Tamils can profess to having shared few common ties over the last few centuries, and even today harbor distinctly variant grievances, the Tamil separatists have nevertheless sought to embrace the interests of the Up Country Tamils. In a similar fashion, S. Thondaman, President of the Ceylon Worker's Congress (CWC), the main political and trade union party of the "Up Country" Tamils, and long-standing party member of the ruling United National Party (UNP), has openly supported the Tamil separatists on numerous occasions and has often played the mediator between the ruling Sinhalese-dominated government and the Tamil separatists.[4]

In the early 1950's and 1960's, at the height of the decolonisation process, the majority of newly independent states were multi-ethnic states. In other words, they did not conform to the nationalist principle that had been so prevalent in the early years of the century, which purported that states and nations should be congruent. During the era of decolonisation, the nationalist principle was replaced by a new panacea, the principle of integration, by which the newly independent multi-ethnic states, such as Sri Lanka, were regarded as being capable of attaining political and perhaps even national integration. Furthermore, it was regarded as axiomatic, that nations could be "built" from above.

"Thus 'nation-building' made its entry into the jargon, an incongruent concept which in fact implied "empire-building" and at best, "state-building" by way of "nation-destroying".[5]

Whilst beneath the veneer of symbols of unity and nationalist fervour that greeted the first years of the anti-colonial struggles, there lurked rival loyalties and disintegrative tendencies, the nation-building edifice held its ground. The "primordialism" that was considered characteristic of the "developing" states, was regarded as pathological and a denial of the secular essence of modern politics. Developing states were therefore urged to domesticate these disruptive ascriptive ties. However, the real world was not so compliant. In the Third World, "detribalisation" proved evanescent, giving way instead on many occasions to "retribalisation", even among the elites who were considered to be the natural nation-builders.

The new governors of independent Sri Lanka, attracted by the concept of nation-building and integration, popularly expounded by political scientists in the early 1950's and 1960's, duly attempted to incorporate this new edifice into the governance of independent Sri Lanka. Like many other newly independent states however, Sri Lanka's ethnic make-up did not sit easily with the principle of nation-building. Indeed Sri Lanka has at no time in her history of Independence actually been a nation-state. Sri Lanka has always been and remains a multi-national state.

In 1948, Sri Lanka adopted upon independence from the United Kingdom the boundaries that had been the administrative divisions of her former ruler. It was always understood by states emerging from colonialism, that there would be problems associated with the fact that their boundaries had been demarcated by the colonial powers, inspired by political interests that rarely coincided with their own. But the inherited boundaries were accepted by the newly independent states, in full knowledge of what they were doing. The importance of the stability and finality of frontiers was viewed as the paramount consideration. The acceptance that these colonial boundaries were not to be challenged after independence came to be known as the principle of *uti possidetis*. This principle has found general reflection in many newly independent states.

"General Assembly Resolutions 1514 (XV) and 1541 (XV), with their balancing of self-determination with the importance of national unity and territorial integrity, necessarily entail the consequence that they intended that the colonial boundaries function as the boundaries of the emergent state."[6]

By the end of the 1960's, the optimistic assumptions of the assimilation theorists were increasingly coming under attack. As the experiences of multi-ethnic states, in both the developed and the developing world, revealed the flaws inherent in the nation-building theory, a new interest developed in the theory of the plural society, which posited that multi-ethnic societies could not remain both stable and democratic. Even a cursory examination of the recent experiences of multi-ethnic states, such as the Baltic states and the former Yugoslavia, to name but a few, will tend to support the plural-society hypothesis. It is indeed the case, that many multi-ethnic states have experienced either severe ethnic violence or have created regimes which are responsible for gross violations of human rights and fundamental freedoms.

It is generally recognised that the various strategies that can be pursued by governments in multi-ethnic states can be placed under two headings, policies of "denial" of an ethnic group or minority, and policies of "acceptance". Under the heading "denial", can be included strategies such as; removal or elimination (genocide), coercion (subjugation, state terrorism), domination within a framework of institutionalised cultural divisions and assimilation, as well as individualisation of the problem by way of non-discrimination and human rights. Under the heading "acceptance", can be included the following strategies; integration in the sense of equal and joint contribution by both groups involved into a new superordinate nation and culture, minority protection and safeguards, consociational democracy in a unitary system, federalism or extended autonomy, very loose federalism akin to confederation, and in the final instance, secession and independence.

Clearly, policies of denial will generally lead to instability and inter-communal violence, whilst policies of acceptance will more often than not provide for a stable and democratic multi-ethnic state. The plural-society theorists, highlight the deep problems that exist when trying to create stable and democratic multi-ethnic states. They demonstrate that all too often claims for the fulfilment of the right to self-determination by minority or ethnic groups living within multi-ethnic states are denied, leading to violence, human rights abuses and civil war. The consociationalist on the other hand, offers an analysis of how ethnic groups can manage their conflict within stable democracies. The consociationalist suggests that minority and ethnic groups can be offered a stake in the political system, through a policy of acceptance. They demonstrate that only through the fulfilment of a minority or ethnic groups' claim to the right to internal self-determination can a multi-ethnic state remain both stable and democratic.

Due to Sri Lanka's historical and colonial heritage, the country that Sri

Lanka's new governors received upon independence was a multi-ethnic state. The immediate task before the new governors therefore, was to integrate these parochial tendencies, whilst recognising the disparate needs and aspirations of the different ethnic groups. However, the first Sri Lankan government, intent on nation-building, adopted policies which in the long run accentuated the ethnic differences in the Island, and which were ultimately responsible for the disintegration of the Island into what today constitutes, "psychologically and at the grass-roots, two separate States".[7]

Some of the direct theories of disintegration and its kindred concepts of separatism and secession are mentioned here, in an attempt to construct a theoretical paradigm within which to determine, when and why the Sri Lankan Tamils demanded greater regional autonomy, and when and why they opted for the more extreme option of independence (secession). Three approaches of the last decade can be regarded as direct theories of disintegration, or of the breakdown in state-building: internal colonialism, ethnicity or primordialism, and communalism. Whilst each theory in itself, cannot predict or explain the reason for all, or even the majority of secessionist movements, in conjunction, they do act as helpful indicators when assessing the relative causes of violent ethnic conflicts, and can be of use in constructing policies of conflict resolution.

The proponents of internal colonialism, claim that the cause of separatism is fundamentally economic, and that it essentially amounts to a question of injustice. The fundamental tenet of the ethnicity or primordialist approach on the other hand, is that ethnicity, ethnic identity or ethnic consciousness, is the essential independent variable that leads to political assertiveness and militant separatism, regardless of the existence of inequality or dominance. In other words social and economic discrepancies *per se* create discontent, but only discontent founded on ethnic symbols such as language, religion, culture, origin or race can lead to separatism. Communalism is a more general approach, which acts as a useful bridge between the above two opposed theories of disintegration. The main focus of the various communalist approaches is modernisation, the rise of aspirations, scarcity, the distribution of rewards, elite interests and the compartmentalisation of institutions on communal grounds. The roots of separatism are located in elite disputes over the direction of change and grievances linked with the scarcity of resources. Separatism develops when previously acquired privileges are threatened or alternatively when underprivileged groups realise that the moment has arrived to address inequality.

Whilst the aforementioned theories of disintegration, internal colonialism, ethnicity or primordialism and communalism do account, in part, for the breakdown in state-building in Sri Lanka, three different but related elements are recognised as the fundamental and independent variables which made the Sri Lankan Tamils' claim to the right to self-determination legitimate, possible and indeed inevitable.

The first variable is territory, (territorial contiguity), and a territorial base for a collectivity; the second is the existence of a sizeable human grouping, a collectivity that is cognizant of its distinctiveness, and the third is the type of relationship existing between the centre and this collectivity. (Some form of disadvantage, inequality, or discrimination, will undoubtedly cause the collectivity to resist integration and tilt towards separatism). All three variables interact with each other and all three in conjunction, make separatism at one historical point, meaningful to the ingroup and a credible threat to the centre. Each of these variables or facilitating conditions, are present in the ethnic conflict in Sri Lanka.

Firstly, let us consider the element of territory to the separatist. What distinguishes separatist claims from other minority claims, is the fact that the separatist wishes to establish a new state on a particular piece of land, and can justifiably assert a claim to the territory. A potential separatist territory should appear to those concerned as having historical roots, (separatists typically seek to right historical territorial wrongs or injustices), and be seen to be viable as an independent state. Secessionist claims invariably involve disputed claims to territory.

"Groups which are able to create a fully-fledged separatist movement, seriously challenging the Centre, are those with a strong territorial base, that is, groups which constitute a clear majority by living fairly compactly in a distinct and integral territory within a state."[8]

Whilst the typical secessionist claim links an argument about ethnic distinctiveness with a claim to a particular piece of land, "[T]he mere fact that the secessionist group constitutes a distinct people does not by itself establish a right to secede. To be persuasive a separatist argument must also present a territorial claim."[9] Similarly, "[M]altreatment alone does not give rise to a territorial claim; such claims must be independently established."[10]

Secondly, let us consider the element of a collectivity who is cognisant of its distinctiveness.

"For a group to become a separate community or distinct society able to mobilise and politicise those concerned, it must be in the position to erect a psychological boundary, a "communal" boundary between itself and outsiders."[11]

Certainly, any student of what has come to be known as the doctrine of self-determination, must begin with the "fact of entrenched parochial sentiment."[12] The psychological momentum of the principle of self-determination lies in the fundamental human desire to associate primarily with one's immediate fellows (family, clan, tribe or village). The moral appeal of the principle, seems to arise from a recognition of the severe treatment and exploitation that have historically been the fate of groups governed by an "alien" people. In other words, the unfamiliar is often equated with the hostile, and until a degree of trust can be established, the fear of the unknown can rarely be breached.

It is generally acknowledged, however, that this "urge to parochialism", suggesting a political structure which satisfies an emotional need for self-government, will frequently come into conflict with the equally natural desire for the economic, social, and military benefits provided for by wider participation in a larger grouping such as a city, province or state.

"If left entirely alone, therefore, the centripetal effect of the desire for economic or military strength will presumably be occasionally offset by the centrifugal demands of parochialism whenever the loss of group identity or the fear of alien domination becomes unbearable for the people concerned."[13]

In reality however, these forces have rarely been left alone to operate in this fashion.

"If history were a chronicle of the voluntary association and disassociation of human groups, there would be no need for a doctrine of self-determination. Without the effects of conquest, forced annexation, subjugation, dynastic union, and colonial expansion, the world's peoples would presumably now be arranged into freely chosen political units. It is the distinct absence of such a peaceful evolution of mankind's social organisation which ultimately gave rise to the principle of self-determination as the twentieth century's primary expression of disapproval of involuntary political association."[14]

Lastly, let us consider the relationship between the centre and the collectivity who is cognisant of its distinctiveness and which can present a territorial claim.

"[T]he type of policy chosen by the Centre in order to resolve the conflict is of cardinal importance for the road to secession and violent separatism".[15]

It is both the perceived and the concrete situation existing within a state, that gives rise to the communal boundary in the first instance.

"For separatism to be born there should exist some kind of disadvantage (inequality or differential), past or present, actual or conjectured. Without such a relationship, which is perceived by the potential separatists as existing, no group will conceive of territorial separatism."[16]

To conclude, a distinct community or society in a disadvantageous relationship with the centre and living apart in an integral territory, together with a combination of some of the aforementioned disintegrative tendencies, such as internal colonialism, primordialism and communalism, can be defined as being in a situation of "latent separatism". However, politicisation and separatism can only occur with the intensification of interaction with the centre. Interaction can give rise to the need to establish a communally or territorially-based political organisation. The various events prior to, and in particular, after territorial-communal politicisation, function as precipitants of separatism and secession. The precipitants consist of the actions (and non-actions) and reactions of the centre (or actions attributable to the central government) to the rising demands of the community.

The decision on the part of the separatist group to resort to an armed struggle for independence, or unilaterally to declare independence, can be based on considerations of feasibility and the prospects of future viability as an independent state. But, in reality, it is more often the case that regional groups seeking autonomy through largely peaceful means are left with very little choice but to resort to armed violence. Once a secessionist war ensues and the issue is no more a peaceful process to autonomy or a federal framework, then an international dimension is inevitably injected into the conflict. An intra-state ethnic conflict takes on an international dimension as soon as third-party states intervene, whether directly or indirectly. For instance, India's tangible but indirect military involvement outside the secessionist terrain, through the provision of sanctuary, training camps, base of operations, arms and other military equipment to the Liberation Tigers of Tamil Eelam (LTTE) during the 1980's, at once transformed the ethnic conflict in Sri Lanka from an internal affair into an international affair.

Other forms of international involvement also have a significant impact on the outcome of intra-state ethnic conflicts. The unconditional provision of unilateral development aid to a country suffering from inter-ethnic violence, i.e., aid which is not linked to considerations of a human rights nature or to the social, economic, and cultural conditions of the country concerned, will more often than not be used to further inflame the communal tensions. In a similar fashion, military arms sold to a country embroiled in a civil war, without due regard for the use to which they will be put, will in the majority of cases be used by the government against the separatist group.

Total third-party intervention and recognition by foreign states of a group's claim to secession or a unilateral declaration of independence are a rarity. In most instances, the internationalisation of an intra-state ethnic conflict favours the centre, for the international system is typically disinclined to encourage an attack on the principle of territorial integrity. Two basic weapons exist for the secessionist, military prowess, i.e., military striking capability (the ability to inflict serious damage upon the centre in the field, thus raising the costs), and the ability to present an exceptionally good case for extended autonomy or independence.

The time of the secessionist has not yet come, but autonomy, federalism and a degree of power-sharing as the only way of accommodation within a multi-ethnic state has come of age. With regard to the etiology of separatism, it can be concluded that once a separatist process has begun, it can only be arrested if the centre redefines its position and accords extended autonomy and power-sharing to the regional separatist group. That is only if the centre is prepared to meet the real needs of the separatists. On the one hand, there is no acceptance of independence as such for the secessionist movement, and territorial integrity is upheld. At the same time, there is no assimilation of the secessionist group, or attempts on the part of a central government to dominate the separatist community. The maximalist aims of both parties are rejected, whilst the real needs of the parties concerned are met.

Part Two of this study, illustrates that the violent and protracted ethnic conflict between the majority Sinhalese community and the minority Tamil community in Sri Lanka, arose primarily as a result of the Sinhalese-dominated government's continued denial of the Tamil speaking people's claim to the right to internal self-determination. It is hoped that by providing a comprehensive account of the Sri Lankan government's consistent failure to accord to the Tamil-speaking people their legitimate right to internal self-determination, it will amply demonstrate that the determination of such claims should not be left in the hands of the concerned government or self-interested third-party states. In other words, it is submitted that a group's claim to the right to internal self-determination should be recognised as a supra-national and supra-regional affair.

Part Two provides a historical and contextual framework within which to analyse the Sri Lankan Tamils' claim to the right to self-determination. It focuses on the events which have occurred since Sri Lanka attained her independence in 1948, which have led to the genesis and development of the Sri Lankan Tamils' claim to the right to self-determination, and which have subsequently led to the violent armed conflict that presently exists between the Sinhalese-dominated government and the Liberation Tigers of Tamil Eelam (LTTE).

Part Two begins by analysing the growth of what is considered to be one of the main proponents of the ethnic conflict in Sri Lanka, i.e., communalism. It examines the transfer of power from the British to the Sri Lankan people, during which intercommunal strife first manifested itself in a bloody and violent fashion. It is revealed that the Sri Lankan electoral system that was finally established after independence, was inimical to ethnic accommodation between the Sinhalese and Tamil communities.

Part Two examines the evolution of the Tamil separatist movement after Sri Lanka became independent. It focuses on the transformation of the Sri Lankan Tamils' ideology, from that expressed by the Tamil Federal Party (FP), in 1949, of *sectional nationalism*, to that which manifested itself in 1974, of *separatist nationalism*, which ultimately led to the invocation by the Tamil United Liberation Front (TULF), in 1976, of the principle of self-determination, after which Sri Lanka witnessed the gradual descent of the ethnic conflict into civil war.

Inherent in the Sri Lankan Tamils' claim to self-determination, is the demand for Tamil autonomy in the Northern and Eastern Provinces, which are popularly deemed to be the traditional "homelands" of the Tamil-speaking people. It is maintained that an historical and territorial interpretation of the Sri Lankan Tamils' claim to the right to self-determination is necessary in order to fully understand the sentiments underpinning the demand for Tamil "Eelam". Part Two therefore provides a survey of the demographic history of the Island and analyses what is probably the most contentious issue facing the Tamil-speaking minority, after language and education rights, the government-sponsored "colonisation" of the Tamils' traditional homeland.

Part Two analyses the Sri Lankan government's various political strategies to solve the Tamil national question. Even upon a cursory review of the Sri Lankan government's attempts to solve the Tamil national question through political measures, it is apparent that the successive Sinhalese-dominated government is unwilling to concede to the Tamil-speaking people even their most minimalist aims, viz. a substantial devolution of legislative, executive and judicial power, ensuring meaningful autonomy to an unified politico-administrative entity, i.e., the permanently merged Northern and Eastern Provinces.

Part Two examines in detail what is considered to be one of the Sri Lankan government's most genuine political strategies to solve the Tamil national question, viz. the Provincial Councils Bill, and the Thirteenth Amendment to the Constitution, 1987, passed under the aegis of the Indo-Sri Lanka Accord, 1987. A careful examination of the provisions devolving administrative, judicial and legislative powers to the Provincial Councils, reveals that the Sri Lankan government has considerably fallen short of according to the Tamil-speaking people their right to internal self-determination. An analysis of the constitional provisions on which the Thirteenth Amendment rests, reveals the difficulties that are entailed, due to the unitary nature of Sri Lanka's Constitution, when a federalist solution to the Tamils' demands for greater regional autonomy is pursued.

Part Two concludes with an analysis of the Sri Lankan government's two most recent attempts to solve the Tamil national problem through political measures, the All Party Conference, 1989 and the Parliamentary Select Committee, 1991-1993. A close examination of these attempts at a political solution to the ethnic conflict, reveals that the Sri Lankan government remains instransigent in its unwillingness to make concessions to the Tamil-speaking people. It is clear that whilst the Sri Lankan government continues to refuse to negotiate participatory democracy for the Tamil-speaking people and devolution of power for the Northern and Eastern Provinces, in other words, to recognise the Tamil-speaking people's legitimate right to internal self-determination, the representatives of the Tamil community are left with no credible alternative but to seek a solution to the ethnic crisis outside of the Parliamentary process.

Part Two concludes with an analysis of the events that have taken place in Sri Lanka since the election of President Wijetunge in May, 1993, in an attempt to determine what the Tamil-speaking people will face in the near future and the hopes that can be realistically entertained for a peaceful solution to the Tamil national question.

Notes

1 The Island was known as Ceylon until the first Republican Constitution enacted in 1972 changed its name to Sri Lanka.

2 For the purposes of this study, "Tamil" is used to denote the "indigenous" Sri Lankan Tamil population, as opposed to the "Up Country" Tamils. However, the expression "Tamil-speaking peoples" is used to denote both communities.

3 For a more detailed account of the Muslim community's present political stance, see "Muslims should vote only for SLMC", an interview with Mohamed Hussain Mahamed Ashraff, leader of the Sri Lankan Muslim Congress (SLMC), in the run-up to the May, 1993 Provincial Council elections, in: *The Island*, 14th April, (1993), p.9.

4 For a more detailed account of the "Up Country" Tamils' present political stance, see: "UNP accepts CWC despite our stand on N-E-merger", an interview with Saumiamoorthy Thondaman, leader of the Ceylon Worker's Congress (CWC), in the run-up to the Provincial Council elections held in May, 1993, in: *The Island*, 7th April, (1993), p.9.

5 Heraclides. A., "The self-determination of minorities in international law", (1991), p.3.

6 Higgins. R., "Self-determination", (unpublished Hague lecture), p.16.

7 Wilson. A. J., "The break-up of Sri Lanka: The Sinhalese-Tamil conflict", (1988), p. 214.

8 Heraclides. A., p.13.

9 Brillmayer. L., "Secession and self-determination: A territorial interpretation", in: <u>Yale Journal of International Law</u>, Vol.16, (1991), pp.177-202, p.179.

10 Ibid., p.188.

11 Heraclides. A., p.16

12 Buchheit. L. C., "Secession. The legitimacy of self-determination", (1978), p.1.

13 Ibid., p.3.

14 Ibid.

15 Heraclides. A., p.11.

16 Ibid., p.17.

CHAPTER 8

The transfer of power: Communal versus territorial representation

"Ceylon was for some years after it became independent on 4 February 1948 held up as a model for all the world of the way in which a colony might peacefully and by easy stages attain full independence without suffering those communal tensions that severed Pakistan from the Republic of India. Then unheralded by premonitary rumbles felt in the outside world there came in 1956 a period in which politics suddenly took on an air of instability: in which Cabinet dissension, the assassination of the Prime Minister (Mr. S. W. R. D. Bandaranaike) and states of emergency followed each other in quick succession; and in which communal disharmony led to a series of riots and to the particularly disgraceful clashes of 1958."[1]

What happened to the seemingly peaceful, well-governed and harmonious inter-community life of 1948? Was the show of national unity on the eve of independence purely cosmetic? Have the ethnic tensions that presently consume the Island a long history, or are they the result of more recent forces and events? In an attempt to answer such questions, this chapter shall examine the genesis and growth of what is considered to be one of the main proponents of the ethnic conflict in Sri Lanka, i.e., communalism.

It will examine to what extent the communal conflict in Sri Lanka was due largely to the attempt on the part of the British to develop a unified territorial system of government in the Island and to produce a Sri Lankan nation along the lines of the nation-building paradigm. It will focus upon the transfer of power from the British to the Sri Lankan people and the attendant debates over the future framework of independent Sri Lanka. An analysis of the dissentions apparent in the pre-independence period, highlights issues which continue to be prevalent in Sri Lankan politics today, i.e., the battle waged over the concepts of unitarianism versus federalism, the conflict between theories of accommodation and assimilation, and inherent in each of the above, the conflicting principles of tolerance and intolerance.

Whilst British rule remained autocratic in Sri Lanka, communal rivalries remained well below the surface. However, once the mechanisms for the transfer of power from foreign rule to domestic rule had been set in motion, the 1920's, 1930's and 1940's witnessed a protracted debate over how to evolve representative institutions for Sri Lanka, and a battle began to be waged over communal versus territorial representation. The dilemma between the two concepts was inescapable. On the one hand, territorial electorates, drawn with no eye to the distribution of communities, would mean rule by the majority community with no safeguards for the minorities, whilst on the other hand, safeguards for the minorities would inevitably deepen the divisions of the nation along communal lines.

The dilemma between the two concepts, however, was not resolved with the interests of the Sinhalese and Tamils in mind. Rather, it was managed by the British, in the interests of British Rule. On the grounds that the Sri Lankans, including the middle class, were divided racially and were therefore not a homogeneous people, deserving of the title "nation", the British were unwilling to concede to the Sri Lankan English educated middle class, comprised of both Sinhalese and Tamils, even the beginnings of parliamentary government. Instead, the British pursued reforms that they hoped would ultimately forge a Sri Lankan "nation", whilst staunchly preserving British Rule and making it impossible for the Sinhalese and Tamils, who were clamouring for greater autonomy, to outvote the officials and other minorities in the Legislative Council. Indeed, behind the Governor of Sri Lanka's avowed object, to make it impossible for one community to dominate over the rest, there lay a well-worn policy of "divide and rule".

The single most important historical event that enabled the Sri Lankan English-educated middle class to develop some sense of national identity and attain full independence peacefully, were the Donoughmore Reforms. These reforms equipped the middle classes with a semi-responsible form of government. They encouraged a move towards nationhood in the broadest sense and ultimately brought about the end of British Rule. These very reforms, however, which took away the control of Sri Lanka from the English-educated middle class and placed it in the hands of the mass of the people, who in the main, continued to cling to their traditional and primordial ascriptive ties, were partly responsible for the emergence of communalism in the Island. To understand better the present conflicts, it is necessary at this stage to briefly mention the Colebrook Reforms, which first contributed to this development in a substantial way.

The main pattern of political, constitutional, economic and social practice during the British period was laid down by the Colebrooke Reforms, leading to the development of a territorial form of government in Sri Lanka and the growth of a corporate Sri Lankan spirit, sufficiently strong to unite the English-educated middle classes against British Rule.

"The Colebrook Reforms were not based so much on conditions in Ceylon, though they were not ignored, or on changes that were feasible in Ceylon on comparison with a similar stage of development in Britain. They were more an attempt to transform the system in Ceylon as far as possible according to the latest ideas proclaimed in Britain and accepted by those in power in Britain at the time."[2]

The British at that time were being influenced in the realms of government, economics, law and religion by writers such as James Mill, Adam Smith and Jeremy Bentham, and were beginning to alter their political, economic and social organisations accordingly. The rising middle-class in Britain began to object to privileges based on birth or tradition and demanded that utility be made the main basis of assessment, and that the law should reflect this line of reasoning. They demanded further equality for all persons and a democratic form of government for the greatest good of the greatest number. They considered religious toleration and freedom of thought, speech and action essential ingredients in society and that the individual should be freed from the customary restraints of the family or of the community based on kinship, so that he/she may form new associations in accordance with the changed economic and social developments of the time.

Arriving in Sri Lanka therefore, the Colebrooke Commission, constituting of British citizens accustomed to one of the best models of a nation-state and a national system of government on a territorial basis, found many of the institutions in the Island archaic. They found not one, but three quite separate and distinct systems of administration. In the south-west there was a low-country Sinhalese system, influenced by the Portuguese and even more by the Dutch. In the north there was a similarly influenced Tamil system. In the central Kandyan area there was a Sinhalese Buddhist system based on the ancient Sinhalese form of government. The Commission recommended the establishment of a single unified form of government on a territorial basis in their place. The Colebrooke Reforms led to the development of a bureaucratic form of government on a territorial basis in place of a medieval form of government by chiefs for races and castes.

The Colebrooke Commission proposed the re-division of the existing districts, ignoring race and caste, and the reduction from sixteen to five.

They recommended that the country should be governed from Colombo and that the recruitment of officials should be made as far as possible from all parts of the Island. They recommended the grant of equal rights to all and the opening up of the government services to all irrespective of race and caste. These reforms they hoped would encourage the assimilation of the three former districts of Low-country Sinhalese, Kandyan and Tamil. Thus, Sri Lanka having come under a single government in 1815, had by 1832 come under a unified system of territorial administration where all citizens were treated as equals before the law.

In 1908, the English-educated middle class in Sri Lanka demanded that the electoral system be established on a territorial basis in harmony with the administrative and economic unification which had already taken place. The British government, however, deviating from the liberal objectives underpinning the Colebrooke Reforms on the grounds that the Sri Lankans were not ready to assume a territorial form of government, established communal electorates.

However, the Donoughmore Commission, appointed to visit Sri Lanka to report on the working of the Colebrooke Reforms and on any difficulties of administration which may have arisen in connection with them, found that the provision of these communal electorates had not led to unity among the various communities or to a diminution of the growing demand for such territorial electorates. Hence they saw no justification for their continuance, and had no alternative but to suggest the abolition of communal electorates and the extension of the territorial system, in order to assimilate and unite the different communities and to stimulate the development of a national as against a sectional outlook. The Donoughmore Commissioners declared:

"We have unhesitatingly come to the conclusion that communal representation is, as it were, a canker of the body politic eating deeper and deeper into the vital energies of the people, breeding self-interest, suspicion and animosity, poisoning the new growth of political consciousness and effectively preventing the development of a national or corporate spirit. There can be no hope of binding together the diverse elements of the population, in a realisation of the common kinship and an acknowledgement of common obligations to the country of which they are citizens, as long as the system of communal representation, with all its disintegrating influences, remains a distinctive feature of the constitution."[3]

Despite the grant of equal rights to all and the opening of government services to all, irrespective of race and caste by the Colebrooke Reforms, at the beginning of the twentieth century, all key posts in the administration of the Island were still held by the British. In response, the English-educated middle class, influenced by the British ideas that had filtered down as a result of the spread of English education, began, in an attempt to secure power, to agitate for a reform of the Legislative Council. Influenced by British liberalism, they demanded that members of the Legislative Council should be elected instead of being nominated, and should be made responsible to the people. Furthermore, they asked that Sri Lankans themselves be associated with the administration which had hitherto been British and that one or two Sri Lankans be included in the Executive Council.

Whilst the British government was reluctant to concede to the English-educated middle class even the trappings of parliamentary government, they did nevertheless concede a nominated seat to the English-educated middle class and an extra nominated seat each to the Sinhalese and the Tamils, thereby assuring that they retainined the majority of seats as before. The Liberal Secretary of State went a step further and granted the right of election to the English-educated middle class and a nominated seat to the Europeans and the Burghers also, thus creating in the process, communal electorates which disregarded all principles of territorial administration. Hence, the first legislative assemblies in the Island were entirely communal in composition. From 1833 to 1889, three Europeans, a Sinhalese, a Tamil, a Muslim and a Burgher were nominated to the Council to represent their respective communities. However, the principle of territorial representation was gradually introduced, finally triumphing in the 1931 Constitution based on the report to the Earl of Donoughmore.

Only five years after the British government's concession to the English-educated middle class, they began to press for further reforms in the Legislative Council. The Ceylon National Congress (CNC) asked for a Council of fifty members, forty of which were to be territorially elected, whilst ten were to be officials and nominated unofficials, the control of the budget, an elected speaker, a wide male franchise and restricted female franchise.

The British government, unwilling to hand over the government to the Sri Lankans quite so soon, granted instead in 1920, a Council of 37, with 23 unofficials and 14 officials, but in which the British executive was still able to maintain itself in power. Of the 23 unofficials, only 16 were to be elected and of these 16, only 11 were to be territorially elected. In any crisis, the 14 British officials could expect the support of the 3 British members and the 7 nominated members who owed their seats to the

Governor. Hence the government was able to influence 24 votes of out of a Council of 37.

The CNC objected to the reforms and accordingly boycotted them. In response, the Governor agreed to give a further instalment of reforms based on the recommendations of the new Council. The CNC cooperated on this assurance and the new constitution came into operation in 1921.

By 1921, however, a new consideration had come to the forefront. Would any member of any community be elected to a territorial electorate on pure merit? If a territorial system was adopted, would not the Tamils be reduced to a small minority as in 1920, whilst the other minorities would perhaps secure no seats at all? The representatives of the Sri Lankan Tamil middle-class refused to accede to such a system and joined by members of the "Up Country" Tamils and the Muslims, petitioned the Secretary of State on the dangers of Sinhalese domination in the legislature, openly expressing fears based upon their minority status in the country.

The prospect of the transfer of power, forced the Sri Lankan Tamil representatives to reconsider the most effective mechanisms for their protection as an all-Sri Lankan minority. In the process of reconsideration which necessarily accompanied the prospect of the transfer of power, it is apparent that the Sri Lankan Tamils began to develop a sense of identity as a separate people, rather than as a minority in need of special safeguards and protection.

After the reforms were fully discussed in the Legislative Council, the British government proposed a Council of 47 members. Of these, 12 were to be officials, 3 Europeans, 2 Burghers and 8 nominated representatives or 25 in total. Under this system, the British government was still able to secure a majority in the Council. The Governor gave the Tamils 8 seats as against 3 in 1920, including a Western Province elected Tamil seat to which the Sinhalese strongly objected, whilst giving the Sinhalese only 14 seats, as against 11 Low-country Sinhalese and 2 Kandyan seats in 1920.

The Secretary of State, however, agreed to increase by 2 the number of members for the Sinhalese areas, by giving the Sinhalese who were nearly six times the population of the Sri Lankan Tamils, 16 members as against the 8 seats occupied by the Tamils. These additions only increased the territorially elected members to 23 in a Council of 49, and only increased the Sinhalese and Tamil representatives to 24, thus leaving the Sinhalese and Tamils in the minority. However, the Secretary of State allowed the Muslims and the "Up Country" Tamils to elect their own members and thus increased the elected non-British members of the Council to 31.

Thus, the reforms of 1924 gave to Sri Lanka a representative government, in form but not in content. Whilst the reforms made it impossible for the Executive to command a majority in the Legislative Council, thus removing its power to act as it wished, the Legislature did not have the power to enforce its decisions through the Executive or to take the place of the government when it defeated it.

The genesis of communalism in Sri Lanka and the subsequent rise of the Sri Lankan Tamil separatist movement, can be found in the early 1920's, when the fledgling CNC was split asunder as the majority of Tamil political leaders and the Kandyan Sinhalese leadership broke away and set up their own respective associations. All subsequent efforts to patch together some sort of unity proved abortive. The failure to bring together the principal Tamil and Sinhalese associations during the period dating from the split to the formation of the United National Party (UNP), highlighted a divergence in material interests and the weight of primordial loyalties, as well as the influence of the West European model of the nation-state, which considerably hindered any concessions to communalism.

The conflict between the pluralist and accommodationist approach on the one hand, and the dogmatic, unitary nation-state outlook on the other, emerged in striking fashion during an attempt at reconciliation during the mid-1920's. In June 1925, negotiations took place, in what came to be known as the Mahendra Agreement, regarding the distribution of seats in the Legislative Council. Well esconsed in one corner of the debating ring, sat Francis de Zoysa, whose underlying rationale was the West European model of a single nationality nation, presented within the idiom of the Gandhian Sublime:

"There is too much communalism with us yet. A mere pretence of unity will not do. A unity brought about by pacts and agreements based on communal prejudice, communal distrust and communal selfishness is nothing but a pretence and a fraud, and pacts between the two largest communities in the Island guaranteeing to each a certain proportion of the loaves and the fishes are revolting in the extreme and deserve unqualified condemnation. The only real and lasting unity is based on mutual trust, mutual good-will and a recognition of the community of interest,..."[4]

Behind this anti-communalism, there no doubt lay fears that even the smallest concessions would only go to further whet the appetites of what had increasingly appeared to be sectional interests in the Island. Across the debating table from the nation-statists, sat in stark contrast those whose aim at reconciliation was through appeasement and accommodation. C. E. Corea, President of the CNC, attacked "Western institutions", maintaining that they were essentially inappropriate for a country like Sri Lanka. With a pluralistic view of Sri Lankan society, he stated that:

"Racial difference in human society was in the order of Nature, and Ceylon's social fabric was built on the wholesome and holy principle of nationality".[5] He further demanded that his Sinhalese brothers "reject the silly notion that political union required the absorption of the small by its big neighbour".[6]

C. E. Corea, was seconded on this occasion by S. W. R. Dias Bandaranaike, who argued that "communities could retain their identity and yet act together as one nation for the benefit of the whole country".[7] Indeed, Bandaranaike took this approach to its logical conclusion by advocating the establishment of a federal state as a means of bringing about a better understanding among the different communities in Sri Lanka. Whilst the Sri Lankan Tamil leaders did not advocate federalism at this time, the pluralist vision certainly attracted them. Their demand for minority rights in the decades before 1948, were couched within a framework of thought, in which they regarded themselves first and foremost as Sri Lankan, and in which the future polity was to be a multi-ethnic state.

"The conception of corporate unity...in the minds of the Sinhalese is in the nature of a merger, an absorption of the minorities in the major community. A just and more correct idea of an united Ceylon is that of a rich and gorgeous many-coloured mosaic, set and studded with the diversities of communal consciousness within a glorious one-minded solidarity,..."[8]

At the same time as the Simon Commission was deciding on schemes for electoral and constitutional safeguards for minorities in India, only twenty-five miles away across the Palk Straits, the Donoughmore Commission in Sri Lanka, appointed to revise the existing constitution, rejected such measures and instead pinned its faith on the progress of national integration through increased participation in the political process by all people.

The Donoughmore Commission was influenced not only by the conditions prevailing in Sri Lanka, but also by those in Britain. Britain was no longer governed by a mere parliamentary form of government based on liberal lines, but by a form of government on socialist or more correctly, on welfare lines. One of the members of the Donoughmore Commission was Drummond Shiels, a member of the Labour Party, and led by him the

Commission felt impelled to establish a welfare state in Sri Lanka also. They believed that if Sri Lanka was to be granted self-government, the government should represent not merely the middle classes, but the entire nation. In 1931 therefore, the franchise was granted to all adults, both men and women.

Thus, the Donoughmore Commission for Constitutional Reform, 1928, granted a semi-responsible form of government through a legislature territorially elected by the entire community of adults, irrespective of wealth or education. In other words, the Commission accepted that the ward had come of age and that power had to be transferred from the Secretary of State and the British Parliament to the Legislative Council and the people of Sri Lanka. It therefore recognised the end of British Rule in Sri Lanka and the Sri Lankan peoples' right to self-determination.

The Legislative Council however, whose representation remained largely based on communal lines, naturally objected to the abolition of communal representation. Whilst the Sinhalese supported the Commission, for the obvious reason of numerical strength, and the Muslims and the Burghers supported it, for they believed it was their only safeguard against extinction as a community politically, the Sri Lankan Tamils objected to the establishment of electorates based on numbers, for they believed it would diminish their political influence.

In the event, the final recommendations made by the government were accepted by only 19 votes to 17. Under the reforms of 1924, the Sinhalese had 17 members, the Sri Lankan Tamils 8, the Europeans 3, the Burghers 2, the Muslims 3, and the "Up Country" Tamils 2. By 1945, when the Soulbury Commission arrived to prepare Sri Lanka's independence constitution, of the 50 territorially elected members, 39 were Sinhalese, 8 were Sri Lankan Tamils, 2 were "Up Country" Tamils, and 1 was a Muslim. Thus in 1945, the Sinhalese had more than double the number of seats that they had occupied in 1924, while the number of Sri Lankan Tamil members for the Northern and Eastern Provinces remained static.

By the time the Soulbury Commission arrived in Sri Lanka in 1944, to draw up the country's independence constitution, communal battle lines had already been well drawn between the two main ethnic communities in the Island, the Sinhalese and the Sri Lankan Tamils. With the passing of the Soulbury Constitution in 1946 and the attainment of independence in 1948, Sri Lanka's communal politics had entered a new and bloody phase.

When the Soulbury Commission came to Sri Lanka, the Sri Lankan Tamil leaders naturally asked for a revision of the system of representation introduced by the Donoughmore Commission, in an attempt to recover the position that they had lost, and to obtain some nominal concessions and assurances that their minority status would be protected.

It is worth noting at this junctrue, what provision the Donoughmore Commission made for the protection of the minority communities in the Island. It proposed that all matters affecting the salaries and emoluments, pensions and gratuities, of all government services should be left to the decision of the Secretary of State and the appointments to the decision of the Governor, thus removing appointments to the public services away from the political sphere. They further recommended the appointment of a Public Service Commission to advise the Governor regarding appointments, promotions and other matters connected with the services. It ensured that minority representatives in the Executive Committee system in the State Council had a knowledge of the matters that arose for discussion and an opportunity of stating any objections they might have to any proposals. It recommended that the Governor be granted the power to refuse assent to any bill "where persons of any particular community or religion are made liable to any disabilities or restrictions to which persons of other communities or religions are not also subject to or made liable or are granted advantages not extended to persons of other communities or religions."[9]It recommended the establishment of Provincial Councils, in the opinion that the special views and needs of the different communities predominant in the different parts of the Island would have effect in the administration of those parts. Lastly, it reserved twelve seats for nominated members so that unrepresented minorities may be represented in the State Council.

The main Tamil political party, the Ceylon Tamil Congress (CTC), established in 1944, based their demand on the principle, already abandoned by the British, that one community should not dominate over the rest. They asked that the Legislative Council be based on a fifty-fifty system, limiting the Sinhalese to half of the seats in the legislature, whilst reserving the other half for the minorities. The Tamils also proposed that not more than half of the members of the Cabinet should belong to one community. Whilst the Soulbury Commission admitted that the problem of the Sri Lankan Constitution was essentially the problem of reconciling the demand of the minorities for adequate representation in the conduct of affairs, so as to ensure that their interests received a due measure of consideration, it rejected the view that one community should not dominate over the rest, admitting the fact that the Constitution must preserve for the majority, the proportionate share in all spheres of government activity to which their numbers entitled them. In other words, the Soulbury Commission refused to restore communal representation in any form, believing that such a system would hinder the development of "nationhood" in Sri Lanka. They accordingly rejected the fifty-fifty idea. They did not, however, object to any adjustment of the form of representation, provided it was done on territorial lines. They agreed to give the minorities an opportunity to secure more seats, by agreeing to electorates which were smaller in size, basing them on area as well as population. (75,000 people per constituency, plus one constituency for every 1000 square miles). Weightage in favour of the Tamil minority was further enhanced by the creation of some multi-member constituencies in the North.

The problems entailed in a system which demarcates electoral constituencies along territorial lines, were clearly revealed soon after independence, when this form of legislative representation was exploited in favour of the majority community. Between the years 1948 to 1949, independent Sri Lanka's new government, the United National Party (UNP), passed the Citizenship Act, No. 18, (1948) and The Ceylon (Parliamentary Elections) Amendment Act, No.48, (1949), which disenfranchised approximately one million "Up Country" Tamils. While enjoying no vote, the "Up Country" Tamils were counted for the purpose of delimitation, thus creating thirteen seats in the legislature for Sinhalese members and ensuring in the process that the government could increase their percentage of seats in the legislature from 67% in the 1947 election to 73% in the 1952 election.

Thus, the first general election held in independent Sri Lanka in 1947, was based upon territorial representation. Whilst the total Sinhalese population constituted barely 70% of the legislature, the Sinhalese community were able to enjoy more than 80% representation in the 1947 general election. Of the 151 elected members in parliament, 124 were Sinhalese. In other words, Sri Lanka became one of the only countries in the world, which has given weightage in representation to the majority community in the legislature, at the expense of the minority.

However the Soulbury Constitution of 1946, did attempt to go some way towards allaying minority apprehensions, at least partially, by continuing to preserve the safeguards for the minorities already granted in the Donoughmore Commission. In other words, providing in explicit terms, that parliament could not confer on any community benefits which were not equally available to other communities, nor impose on any community disabilities which did not likewise attach to other communities,[10] except by having recourse to a special procedure which required a two-thirds majority in parliament.[11] The Commission wrote:

"We are however strongly of opinion that until parties develop in Ceylon on lines more akin to Western models, the leader of the majority group would be well advised in forming a government, to offer a proportion of the portfolios to representatives of the minorities and, in selecting those representatives, to consult the elected members of the group or groups to which they belong."[12]

In an appeal to the Tamils as Sri Lankan citizens, Mr D. S. Senanayake, President of the CNC, and who was to become Sri Lanka's first Prime Minister asked "Do you want to be governed from London or do you want, as Ceylonese, to help govern Ceylon?"[13] Urging the minority communities to accept the new Constitution, he promised:

"On behalf of the Congress and on my own behalf, I give the minority communities the sincere assurance that no harm need they fear at our hands in a free Lanka".[14]

The Sinhalese leaders who stood to inherit a potential monopoly of communal power through the arithmetic of the ballot box, gave assurance that this position would never be abused. The British, the Tamils and the other minorities whose interests were vitally affected, all accepted the assurance, and the transfer of power accordingly took place. However, it was not long before disappointment set in and the respective communities began to look to their own, for solidarity, strength and security.

Just one year later in Jaffna, the capital of the Northern Province and home to the majority of Sri Lankan Tamils, the Tamil people overwhelmingly elected the Tamil Congress leader, Mr G. G. Ponnambalam, defeating a member of the Board of Ministers, thereby giving clear notice of their continued preference for communal leadership.

Whilst since 1925, S. W. R. Dias Bandaranaike had been developing the views that he had presented at the Mahendra negotiations, i.e., rejecting the foreign model of a single nationality "nation" and adopting instead a solution based on pluralism, on becoming head of state in 1956, he was unable to take this approach very far. It made its appearance only once, in the Bandaranaike-Chalvanayakam Pact, of 1957. Had this Pact materialised, it would have perhaps safeguarded the position of the Sinhalese, while at the same time have reasonably met the fears of the Tamils. Unfortunately, Bandaranaike was unable to impose his views on the forces that had picked him up as their leader and symbol. Both the pluralist approach and its advocate, were submerged by an emergence of Sinhalese-Buddhist revivalism in the 1950's, which eagerly recognised the symbolic and material rewards that control of the country's state apparatus would accord them.

The fate of Bandaranaike's pluralist approach and with it, the 1957 Pact and the rise of communal politics in the Island, signalled the end of a move towards the establishment of a federalist independent Sri Lanka, and witnessed the growth and escalation of Tamil separatism, in the face of an intransigent government bent on the establishment of a communal, majoritarian political process.

Lord Soulbury, the main architect of Sri Lanka's independence Constitution, later attributed his disappointment in Sri Lanka's fate, to the death of the first Prime Minister, Mr. D.S. Senanayake, who according to Soulbury, "would have scorned the spurious electoral advantages that a less far-sighted Sinhalese politician might expect to reap from exploiting the religious, linguistic and cultural differences between the two communities".[15] He further claimed, that he had thought that his Constitution had "entrenched in it all the protective provisions for minorities that the wit of man could devise".[16] Subsequently, however, he stated: "Nevertheless - in the light of later happenings - I now think it is a pity that the Commission did not also recommend the entrenchment in the constitution of guarantees of fundamental rights, on the lines enacted in the constitutions of India, Pakistan, Malaya, Nigeria and elsewhere".[17] In retrospect, the Tamil community have also come to feel that it was "a pity" to have left so much on trust, and on a "sincere assurance", and many have now come to share the regret, held by Mr. S. J. V. Chelvanayakam's Federal Party, from as early as 1975, that the system had not been federal from the outset, and now share his opinion, that it is not too late for Sri Lanka to adopt a federalist system.

The attainment of independence signalled the beginning of a shift away from liberal democracy in Sri Lanka.[18] Since then, not only have the Tamil minority community been largely excluded from the benefits of state patronage, but they have also been unable to resist a whole series of "Sinhalisation of the state" policies. The Sri Lankan electoral system that was finally established in 1946, revealed itself to be inimical to ethnic accommodation between the Sinhalese and the Sri Lankan Tamils. Given the first-past-the-post system of elections to parliament, governments are regularly elected and then overthrown as a result of relatively small shifts in electoral preference in mainly Sinhalese electorates. Governments can almost always be constructed on the basis of clear parliamentary majorities for one or other of the two main Sinhalese-dominated party blocs. Whilst the Sri Lankan Tamil community, the Plantation Tamil community, and the Muslim community constitute important voting blocs, the two main Sinhalese-dominated parties, the UNP and the Sri Lankan Freedom Party (SLFP), have nevertheless often preferred to outbid one another in Sinhalese chauvinism to gain votes, rather than make their policies agreeable to the minority communities.

Notes

1 Professor B. H. Farmer., "Ceylon: A divided nation", (1963), cited in: Mendis. C.G., "The evolution of a Ceylonese nation" in: <u>Journal of Royal Asiatic Society</u> (Ceylon), Vol.XI, (New Series), (1967), pp. 1-22.

2 Ibid., p.4.

3 Ibid., p.15.

4 Francis de Zoysa in: Handbook CNC (1928), pp.661-4, cited in: Roberts. M., "Ethnic conflict in Sri Lanka and Sinhalese perspectives: Barriers to accommodation", in: <u>Modern Asian Studies</u>, 12,3 (1978), pp.353-376, p.358.

5 Ibid., pp.692-701.

6 Ibid.

7 Ibid., pp.701-2.

8 Memorandum from the President of the All Ceylon Tamil Conference to the Secretary of State for the Colonies, 14 July, (1937), cited in: Roberts. M., "Ethnic conflict in Sri Lanka and Sinhalese perspectives: Barriers to accommodation", in: Modern Asian Studies, Vol.12, No.3, (1978), p.259.

9 A similar worded safeguard for minorities was included in the final draft of The Ceylon (Constitution) Order-in-Council, (1946), in Section 29(2).

10 The Ceylon (Constitution) Order in Council, 1946, Section 29(2).

11 Section 29(4). However, the Sinhalese government, enjoying majority status in the legislature has been able to introduce two new constitutions through a two-thirds majority.

12 Cited in: Mendis. G.C., p.19.

13 Schwartz. W., "The Tamils of Sri Lanka", in: <u>Minority Rights Group Report</u>, No.25, p.6.

14 Ibid.

15 Lord Soulbury in his foreword to B.N. Farmer, "Ceylon, a divided nation", p.viii, cited in: Schwartz. M., p.5.

16 Sir Charles Jeffries, "Ceylon: The path to independence", cited in: Schwartz. M., p.5.

17 Lord Soulbury, p.ix, cited in: Schwartz. M., p.5.

18 See Mick Moore, "Retreat from democracy in Sri Lanka?" in: <u>Journal of Commonwealth and Comparative Politics</u>, Vol.30, No.1, March, (1992), pp.64-84.

CHAPTER 9

Post-Independence: The evolution of Tamil separatism

Up until Sri Lanka attained her independence in 1948, the demands of the Sri Lankan Tamils had been invoked in the language of human rights and minority rights, i.e., their claims as a nationality were not advanced. In this sense, their ideology was one of Sri Lankan Tamil sectional patriotism,[1] i.e., they were a sectionalist group willing to work within and for Sri Lankan nationalism. The Tamils were in the vanguard of Sri Lanka's struggle for the right to self-determination, in the full confidence that they also, as a people, would regain their independence from foreign rule.

It was not until independence in 1948 and thereafter, that the Tamil peoples' ideology became founded on "sectional nationalism".[2] In 1949, the Federal Party (FP), representing almost the entire Tamil-speaking population of the Island was established, seeking in its mandate regional autonomy on the grounds that the "Tamil-speaking people in Ceylon constitute a nation distinct from that of the Sinhalese by every fundamental test of nationhood".[3]

This chapter shall focus predominantly on the transformation of the Sri Lankan Tamils' ideology, from that expressed by the FP in 1949 of "sectional nationalism", to that which manifested itself in 1973/4, of "separatist nationalism", which ultimately led to the invocation by the Tamil United Liberation Front (TULF), the then main Tamil-speaking political party, of the principle of self-determination in 1976, and the gradual descent of the ethnic conflict into civil war, thereafter.

It is generally acknowledged, that there have been four distinct phases in the evolution of the Sri Lankan Tamil separatist movement form 1948/9 to the present, each phase reflecting the escalating demands of the minority in the face of an intransigent government. The four major periods in the deterioration of Tamil-Sinhalese relations can be grouped as follows: (i) a period of "responsive cooperation" between the English-educated middle-class of both communities, from independence in 1948 until the election of the Sri Lanka Freedom Party (SLFP), on a platform of

Sinhala-Buddhist nationalism in 1956: (ii) the emergence of a reciprocal Tamil demand for a federalist state marked by the *Satyagraha* movement or Gandhian non-violent resistance, and civil disobedience from 1956 until the adoption of the new Republican Constitution of Sri Lanka in 1972; (iii) the emergence of political violence and a growing ideology of separatism from 1972 until 1983, culminating in the July riots in Colombo; and (vi) the armed struggle of the Tamil separatists and the gradual descent into civil war from 1983 until the present day.

In an attempt to account for the transformation of the Sri Lankan Tamils' ideology from sectional nationalism to separatist nationalism and the gradual descent of the ethnic conflict into civil war, this chapter shall analyse the events in accordance with the paradigm provided above. The first part of this chapter, will focus briefly on the period of "responsive cooperation" between the English-educated middle class from independence until 1956 and the emergence of a reciprocal Tamil demand for a federalist state from 1956 until 1972. The latter half of this chapter, shall focus upon the events that led up to the bloody riots in July, 1983.

(i) Sri Lankan Tamil sectional nationalism: 1948-1972

What were the events that led to the disintegration of the unity, based on shared interests, that appeared to exist between the Tamils and Sinhalese before independence? Why, once the imperial yoke had been dismantled, and the object of nationalist fervour had been achieved, did the Sri Lankan polity split into geographical parochial units? The answers to these questions, lie partly in an understanding of the language issue, which was to dominate Sri Lankan politics in the first decade of independence and which ultimately contributed to the development of Tamil separatism in the early 1970's.

The growth of Sri Lankan nationalism in the early twentieth century, was intimately linked to a religious revival among the Sinhala Buddhists and to a lesser degree among the Tamil-speaking Hindus. On the one hand, the Buddhist revivalist movement was in part a reaction against Christian missionary teaching in the Island, and was therefore part of a wider feeling of anti-imperialism. After the Donoughmore Reforms, as a result of the adult franchise which made equality of opportunity possible, the Buddhists became conscious that owing to their numbers they could secure for Buddhism a status which they had been deprived in the past, and at the same time secure equal rights alongside the Christians. However, it was also a revolt by people literate in Sinhala, but not in

English, against the privileges of the English-speaking elite, and was thus an expression of a growing class consciousness, and part of a wider class struggle. In its early days, this religious revivalism was not only alien from, but also hostile to, the Westernised leaders of the CNC The Sinhalese-educated Buddhists also realised that their language, in which Buddhism was intimately expressed, could be made the language of government in place of English, the language of British Christianity. The government had come to be increasingly conducted in English, despite the fact that over ninety per cent of children were receiving their education in Sinhalese and Tamil. However, it was not long before the revivalist ideas were adopted as an essential component of the political game and the language issue had taken centre stage in the growing reliance of Sri Lankan party politics on communalism.

In the last decades of British Rule, the emphasis was gradually switched to vernacular education, and the *swabasha* or "own language" movement, became a central feature of the nationalist movement. How the "Sinhala Only" movement came to be adopted to the point in 1972, when it was enshrined in Sri Lanka's Constitution, is the story of how the arithmetic of politics gradually overcame more tolerant and enlightened attitudes.

The *swabasha* movement was not originally a communal issue, but the Tamils, with greater literacy in English had less incentive than the Sinhalese to support it. The British government's reliance on English as the language of administration had fostered the dominance of a small class of English-speaking civil servants and professionals. In this field, the Tamils occupied a preponderance of positions disproportionate to their numbers. In 1911, 4.9% of Sri Lankan Tamil males were literate in English, compared with only 3.5% of the (Kandyan) Sinhalese males. As a result of the lack of employment opportunities in the Tamil-speaking Northern Province, many of these young English-educated Tamil men found it expedient to migrate to the southern areas of Sri Lanka, especially to the capital of Colombo, to seek employment in the public sector or the professions. Thus, the English-educated Tamils were reluctant to forfeit the privileged status that they enjoyed under the British system. However, it was clear to the Sinhalese that the adoption of Sinhala in place of English, would automatically eradicate the competition that marked the relations between the English-educated Sinhalese and Tamils, and in the process address the imbalances of the past.

At first, as pressure rose among the Sinhalese electorate to make *swabasha* into a Sinhala Only movement, the ruling UNP resisted it and remained loyal to its commitment to pluralism. However, Mr S. W. R. Dias Bandaranaike succumbed to the pressure and the temptation of electoral success, and formed his Peoples United Front (MEP) on a Sinhala-Only platform, which accordingly won the 1956 general election. The first act of the new government was the Official Language Act, No.33 of 1956, declaring that "the Sinhala Language shall be the one official language of Ceylon". The new government was also the first not to include a Tamil in its Cabinet.

The Official Language Act of 1956, directed that unless a Tamil public servant passed a proficiency test in Sinhala, his annual increment would be suspended and he would eventually be dismissed. Mr Kodiswaran, a Tamil in the executive clerical service, declined to sit for the exam and in 1962 his increment was stayed. He sued the government on the ground that the regulation was illegal as the Official Language Act transgressed the prohibition against discrimination provided for in Section 29(2) of the Soulbury Constitution, 1946. The trial judge upheld the plea, but it was set aside on appeal in the Supreme Court, on the grounds that a public servant could not sue for his salary. Mr Kodiswaran, accordingly appealed to the Privy Council in London, which set aside the Supreme Court's decision on suing for a public servant's salary and directed that the Supreme Court should rule on the constitutional question. The government ensured that legislation was accordingly passed through parliament which abolished all appeals to the Privy Council, thereby disposing of the case. Sri Lanka's new Republican Constitution, 1972, did not include Section 29(2).

Inherent in the Sinhalese Buddhist revivalist movement, making Tamil revivalism a necessity, was the assertion of an exclusive right in the Island and an implied tolerance of minorities. It was asserted by the Sinhalese, that Buddha had chosen Sri Lanka to be the home of Buddhism, and that by implication, Buddhism and the language of its home, Sinhala, had to be protected. One sees in the Official Language Act, although not expressly stated, the first assertion of a desire on behalf of the Sinhalese to assimilate and reduce to oneness the other cultural and linguistic traditions of the Island.

For a brief period in 1960, the Tamil Federal Party held the balance in parliament, having consolidated its influence in the North of the Island. In the 1960 General Elections the FP won 10 of the 13 seats in the Northern Province and all 5 Tamil seats in the Eastern Province. The more accommodating All Ceylon Tamil Congress (ACTC), established in 1944, had now become virtually defunct. The FP, according to its 1956 convention, stood for the adoption of a federal constitution and the creation of one or more linguistic states, enjoying "the widest autonomy and residuary powers consistent with the unity and external security of Ceylon".[4] It also sought absolute parity of status for the Tamil langauge, citizenship on the basis of residence and an immediate end to state-sponsored land "colonisation".

In the early 1960's, in the absence of any progress on the language front, the FP launched a *satyragraha* in the North, setting up their own postal service, and issuing their own stamps. A state of Emergency was declared and FP leaders were kept in detention for the next six months. The frustration that followed produced the first appearance of a schism in the party, although it did not yet figure in official pronouncements. In 1964, however, the FP Secretary warned in parliament that:

"If the leaders of the Sinhalese people persist in this attitude, I will say that when you will be advocating federalism, we will rather choose to have a division of this country even at the cost of several lives".

As the language bill was being passed in parliament in 1956, Sri Lanka witnessed the first outbreak of deliberately provoked communal violence between Tamils and Sinhalese. In response, Mr. Bandaranaike and Mr. Chelvanayakam, leader of the FP, met in an effort to resolve the differences of opinion that had been growing and creating tension in the Island. The resulting Bandaranaike-Chelvanayakam Pact, of 1957, embodied one of the few statesmanlike compromises ever to be attempted in Sri Lanka between the Sinhalese-dominated government and the leaders of the Tamil community. Had it been promulgated, it is possible that it would have safeguarded the position of the Sinhalese, while at the same time have reasonably met the fears of the Tamils. In the event:

"[T]he Pact envisaged a sort of federal set-up for Ceylon, and though never implemented, furnished the agenda of Tamil demands for the next thirty years."[5]

At an early stage of the discussions between Bandaranaike and Chelvanayakam, the question that arose was whether it was possible to explore the possibility of an adjustment without the FP abandoning or surrendering any of its fundamental principles or objectives. As a result, the FP dropped their demand for parity of status between the languages, and they came to an agreement by way of compromise. It was agreed that the proposed legislation should contain recognition of Tamil as the language of a "national minority" of Sri Lanka, and that the language of administration of the Northern and Eastern Provinces would be Tamil and that any necessary provisions would be made for the non Tamil-speaking minorities in the Northern and Eastern Provinces.

Furthermore, it was agreed that provision was to be made for the direct election of regional councillors. It was agreed that regional councils should have powers over specified subjects, including; agriculture, co-operatives, lands and land development, colonisation, education, health, industries, fisheries, housing, social services, electricity, water schemes and roads. It was agreed that in the matter of the government's land "colonisation" schemes, the powers of the regional councils would include the power to select allottees to whom lands within the area of authority shall be alienated and also the power to select personnel to be employed for work on such schemes. The regional councils were also provided with powers of taxation and borrowing.

The publication of the Pact however, was the immediate invitation for violent agitation by extremist militant Buddhists. The UNP, the main opposition party, made an expedient *volte-face* and supported them, thereby giving a foretaste of the demagogic cynicism which continues to characterise party politics in Sri Lanka today. In response to the Buddhist agitation, the Tamils retaliated, thereby giving a foretaste of the indiscriminate policy of attack and counter-attack, which also continues to characterise the warfare between the Sinhalese and Tamils today. In 1958, Sri Lanka experienced a major bloody communal riots and the Pact in turn, became no more than a dead letter.

In the same year, in a desperate attempt at reconciliation Mr. Bandaranaike enacted the Tamil Language (Special Provisions) Act, 1958, providing for the "reasonable use" of Tamil in education, Public Service entrance examinations and for certain administrative purposes in the Northern and Eastern Provinces. However, the Act remained on paper, since its implementation required the promulgation of certain regulations which the government failed to adhere to. However, these were framed in 1966, by the ruling coalition party which included the FP The FP had decided to temporarily drop its demand for Tamil-Sinhala parity and to accept Sinhala as the official language, provided that district councils allowing greater autonomy for the various Provinces were set up and appropriate regulations framed to implement the Tamil Language (Special Provisions) Act, 1958. These provisions found temporary expression in the Dudley Senanayake-Chelvanayakam Pact, of 1965. However, the government failed to appease the extremist Buddhists, with the result that the 1965 Pact suffered a fate similar to that suffered by the 1958 Pact. The FP accordingly resigned from the coalition in 1968.

(ii) Sri Lankan Tamil separatist nationalism: 1972-1986

Until 1970, it is clear that the Tamil people had conceived of their political future within the framework of a united Sri Lanka. Their aspirations were for Sri Lanka to implement a constitution modelled on the Indian Constitution, recognising and protecting religious, linguistic and cultural diversity. By 1972, however, the ideology of the Tamil community had been transformed from its earlier Sri Lankan Tamil sectional nationalism into Sri Lankan Tamil separatist nationalism,[6] when it became clear that the Tamils could not secure their political and human rights on the basis of equality with the Sinhalese in a united Sri Lanka. It was in this climate, of discrimination and oppression, that the Tamil community first sought legal justification for their demands in the international doctrine of the right to self-determination.

The latter half of this chapter, shall focus predominantly on the events that transformed the Sri Lankan Tamils' demand for "domestic political fairness" through "domestic political reform", into an aim to redraw Sri Lanka's political boundaries, by invocation of the right to self-determination, thereby internationalising the conflict. The events analysed, can be grouped into two phases. Firstly, the emergence of political violence and a growing ideology of Tamil separatism from 1972 onwards, and secondly, the subsequent adoption of armed struggle by extra-parliamentary forces, culminating in the riots of July, 1983, and the country's gradual descent into civil war from 1983 until the present day.

With the enactment of Sri Lanka's first Republican Constitution in 1972, the Tamil FP, who had participated in the deliberations of the Constituent Assembly, withdrew in despair after its attempts to insert certain amendments in some basic resolutions were dismissed by the government. While Sinhala was declared to be the official language, guarantees for the "reasonable" use of Tamil were not forthcoming. Basic Resolution 12(b), stipulated only that "the use of the Tamil language shall be in accordance with the Tamil Language Act of 1958". At this pronouncement, the FP complained that their demand for more regional autonomy had been ignored and that the United Front, consisting of the Sri Lankan Freedom Party (SLFP), the Communist Party (CP) and the Lanka Sama Samaja Party (LSSP), had stuck to the principle of a "unitary republic". Thus further alienated, the FP felt obliged to push further their earlier demand, the parity of Sinhala and Tamil as official languages.

During the final stages of the drafting of the constitution, at a press conference held in Madras, the leader of the Tamil FP, S. J. V.

Chelvanayakam, disclosed that he had come to India to mobilise "outside sympathy, if not assistance"[7] for the idea of an autonomous Tamil province in Sri Lanka, to be achieved through non-violent struggle. He declared that the Bandaranaike government had spurned all the efforts of his party to assure Tamil citizens of a "position equal to the Sinhalese"[8] in the new republican constitution. Chelvanayakam even wondered aloud, whether the time had not yet come for Sri Lanka to start thinking in terms of an "independent sovereign state"[9] for the Tamil population in the Northern and Eastern Provinces of the Island. Chelvanayakam's comments gave voice to a situation, which because of Emergency regulations imposed by the Sri Lankan government as a result of the JVP insurrection in April, 1971, had been almost unknown to the outside world. Indeed, the protest resolution adopted by the Tamil party's special convention at Jaffna in January, 1971, was censored by government authorities. This resolution demanded recognition of the right to self-rule for the "Tamil nation in their traditional homeland".[10] Chelvanayakam proclaimed: "At this moment in the country's history, when a republican constitution is to be inaugurated, all reasonable demands of the Tamil people have been completely rejected, and the actions of the government are inexorably driving the Tamil nation into separation". The Tamils, a FP leader warned, had to be ready for any sacrifice for the cause, and declared that "[W]e will win our freedom whatever the price".[11]

These and other statements by FP leaders, assumed special significance at the time, when seen in a demographic context, the Tamils being heavily concentrated in the Northern and Eastern Provinces. In the early 1970's, the Tamils accounted for almost three-quarters of the population in the Northern Province, while in the East they represented almost half. The FP's dominant position among the Tamils in these areas had long been evident, in each of the Provincial elections during 1956 to 1971, it had won 13 to 15 of the 23 seats in the Northern and Eastern Provinces.

Despite their feelings of disillusionment, however, the Tamil leaders formulated a programme that incorporated the lowest denominator of Tamil needs and aspirations. The programme, later called the Six Point Plan, contained six elements:

(1) equal constitutional status between the Tamil and Sinhala languages;

(2) extension of citizenship to all who had settled in Sri Lanka and who had been rendered stateless by the citizenship laws;

(3) commitment to a secular state, ensuring equality of religions;

(4) constitutional guarantees of fundamental rights and freedoms,

based on equality of citizens on ethnic and cultural grounds;

(5) abolition of caste and untouchability;

(6) the establishment of a decentralised structure of government that would enable participatory government to flourish, and where "power would be people's power rather than state power".[12]

The six elements clearly presupposed a commitment to constitutionalism. They represented a desire among the Tamil leaders to work towards equality within a pluralistic society. At the 1971 Constituent Assembly however, the committee rejected the Tamil FP's proposals for a federal state, and the FP responded by boycotting the formal inauguration of the Republic of Sri Lanka in 1972. Furthermore, S.J.V. Chelvanayakam, resigned his seat in the National State Assembly with a view to seeking a mandate for the Six-Point Plan.

During this period, other forces were contributing to the dramatic escalation of Tamil demands. In addition to the demand for language concessions, the Tamil Language (Special Provisions) Act, 1958, still not having been implemented, the Tamils complained of a conscious policy of discrimination in access to employment and education, and the marked absence of developmental programmes in the Northern and Eastern Provinces. In land use and land settlement, the government was accused of pursuing a policy directed towards transforming the demographic composition of traditional Tamil-speaking areas in the Northern and Eastern Provinces. Political resistance to and agitation against such discrimination was further repressed through preventive detention and harassment of Tamil youths in the Northern Province. The politics of hostility, supported by repression and the arbitrary exercise of Emergency powers, hardened Tamil resistance to the government.

These events had an important bearing on the emergence of a new Tamil awareness and the Kankesanthurai by-election of 1974, became the focal point of agitation for the emerging aspirations of the Tamil people. The Tamil United Front, the new party representing the Tamil-speaking people, fighting the election on the issue of the Six-Point Plan, won an overwhelming majority of the votes. After the results, S. J. V. Chelvanayakam said:

"Throughout the ages the Sinhalese and Tamils in the country lived as distinct sovereign people till they were brought under foreign domination. It should be remembered that the Tamils were in the vanguard of the struggle for independence in the full confidence that they also will regain their freedom. We have for the last 25 years made every effort to secure our political rights on the basis of equality with the Sinhalese in a united

Ceylon. It is a regrettable fact that successive Sinhalese governments have used the power that flows from independence to deny us our fundamental rights and reduce us to the position of a subject people. These governments have been able to do so only by using against the Tamils the sovereignty common to the Sinhalese and the Tamils. I wish to announce to my people and the country the verdict at this election as a mandate that the Tamil Eelam nation should exercise the sovereignty already vested in the Tamil people and become free. On behalf of the Tamil United Front, I give you my solemn assurance that we will carry out this mandate".[13]

By this historic statement, the conceptual transformation and the demands of the Tamil people were crystallised. Chelvanayakam's statement represented a shift away from the struggle for equality to an assertion of freedom, from the demand for fundamental rights and minority safeguards, to the assertion of the right to self-determination, from the acceptance of the pluralistic experiment, to the surfacing of a new corporate identity. In the event, the first Republican Constitution of Sri Lanka, enacted in 1972, removed the existing safeguards of the minority communities, by failing to incorporate a provision corresponding to Section 29(2) of the 1946 Soulbury Constitution.

The 1970's were duly characterised by punctuated political and cultural persecution. In 1972, at the annual international Tamil Conference held in Jaffna, the police attacked Tamil participants and visas were refused to visiting Tamil scholars. In the same decade, the Jaffna Public Library, home to invaluable sources of Tamil cultural heritage, was burnt down.

In 1971, the world witnessed the first successful secessionist movement outside of the decolonisation era. It is worth noting at this juncture, what features of the Bangladesh case qualified it as an exception to the international ban against secessionist self-determination, for these formed the basic criteria on which a decision was made to place the demands of self-determination above those of "territorial integrity" and above a "non-interventionist" stand on the part of the United Nations. These features were, firstly, the physical separation of the mother state and the territory to which the claim to self-determination was tied, secondly, the political dominance of Western Pakistan over Eastern Pakistan, i.e., neo-colonialism, marked by the regional disparity in economic growth between the two regions, thirdly, the electoral results of the separatist political party as a mandate for regional autonomy, fourthly, the brutal suppression of the Bengali community by the government of West Pakistan, akin to genocide, and lastly, the economic and political viability of the future independent state of Bangladesh.[14]

The events in East Pakistan in 1971, did not go unnoticed by the FP in Sri Lanka, and it is probable that Tamil ambitions for the establishment of a separate Tamil state in the Northern and Eastern Provinces were further fuelled as a result. However, whilst leaders of the FP might have compared their own situation with that of the pre-December Awami League in Bangladesh, the FP could not claim to be the Awami League of Sri Lanka for one major reason. The FP leaders could not hope for India to intervene on their behalf on the scale of its intervention on behalf of Bangladesh. Indeed in 1958, in the wake of communal rioting in Sri Lanka, the then Indian Prime Minister, Jawaharlal Nehru, warded off any future discussions in the Indian parliament on the plight of Sri Lankan Tamils, by declaring the matter to be an "internal" affair. Similarly, Chelvanayakam's appeal in Madras failed to gain an encouraging response from the Tamil Nadu state leadership, since many of them expressed their inability to intervene in what they too considered to be essentially a domestic affair. Instead, after India's intervention in the secession of Bangladesh, for which she received little approbation from the international community, Prime Minister Indira Gandhi, was keen to smooth relations with India's neighbours.

Moreover, the successful secession of Bangladesh is often used to reinforce rather than to cast doubt on the existing principle of self-determination, for it happens to fit well with what is assumed to be the very essence of the principle, that it applies only and exclusively to majorities.[15] Indeed, only a few years before the Bangladesh incident, it was reiterated that "self-determination refers to the right of a majority within a generally accepted political unit to the exercise of power", and that minority interests on the other hand, are to be safeguarded by state "obligations on human rights and the protection of minorities".[16]

It is interesting to note here, the response of the Sri Lankan representative of the United Nations to the Bangladesh crisis:

"This is surely not a liberation movement in the classical and universally understood sense of the term, we would be creating a deadly precedent if we regarded it as such. It could be claimed that not only majorities that have a right to be liberated but, even more logically minorities. Most countries in the assembly have substantial minorities - my country has - and must bear in mind the implications of treating the East Pakistan Awami League Movement as a Liberation Movement. The East Pakistan leaders must renounce all secessionist demands. We do not however, question their right to negotiate secession with the Government of Pakistan, but we cannot condone or encourage the use of force in the pursuit of their objectives."[17]

Clearly, the Sri Lankan government adopted a state-centric approach to the issue of secession, claiming that when the territorial disintegration of a sovereign independent state is at stake, the issue does not fall within positive international law, but is instead considered to be a domestic affair, in which the international community should not interfere.

"Self-determination as it is generally understood in international law and relations refers to freedoms from colonisation. It has never been taken or understood under international practice as applicable to self-determination for a part of a state. That is a matter left to the domestic jurisdiction of the state itself and to the section of its people who want their status altered".[18]

Clearly, the response of the Sri Lankan representative of the United Nations to the Bangladesh crisis reiterated the common belief held among the international community that "if secession is to be allowed it must again be on conditions determined within the larger group, and compatible with its character. The question of unity or secession is a question of national determination not of self-determination".[19] To conclude, it is generally accepted by most members of the international community, including Sri Lanka, that "[H]ow such an issue of the group seeking independence from the mother state is to be settled, amicably or by force, is a problem of the mother state".[20]

In 1976, the Tamil United Front (TUF), which was established in 1972, and which was a coalition of the Federal Party (FP), All Ceylon Tamil Congress (ACTC) and the Ceylon Workers Congress (CWC) reconstituted itself into the Tamil United Liberation Front, (TULF). This coalition marked the emergence of a forceful Tamil separatist political party. The central tenet of the TULF was the creation of a separate Tamil state. The Ceylon Workers Congress (CWC) however, representing the Up Country or Plantation Tamils, refused to continue to be part of the coalition, issuing a statement proclaiming that the creation of a separate state may be a course of action to solve the problems of the North-East Tamils, but would not solve the grievances of the Plantation Tamils.

The principle of self-determination was first invoked by the TULF in their 1976 Resolution. (See Appendix I) The resolution, which marked the first clear committment of a Tamil party to a separate state of Tamil Eelam, read as follows:

"The first National Convention of the Tamil United Liberation Front meeting at Pannakam (Vaddukoddai Constituency) on the 14th day of May 1976, hereby declares that the Tamils of Ceylon, by virtue of their great language, their religions, their separate culture and heritage, their history of independent existence as a separate state over a distinct territory for several centuries till they were conquered by the armed might of the European invaders, and above all by their will to exist as a separate entity ruling themselves in their own territory, are a nation distinct and apart from the Sinhalese and their constitution announces to the world that the Republican Constitution of 1972 has made the Tamils a slave nation ruled by the new colonial masters, the Sinhalese, who are using the power they have wrongly usurped to deprive the Tamil nation of its territory, language, citizenship, economic life, opportunities of employment and education, thereby destroying all attributes of nationhood of the Tamil people...This convention resolves that the restoration and reconstitution of the Free, Sovereign, Secular, Socialist State of TAMIL EELAM based on the right of self-determination inherent to every nation has become inevitable in order to safeguard the very existence of the Tamil nation in this country".[21]

The theoretical basis upon which the Tamil-speaking people claim the right to self-determination, is that the sovereignty of the Tamil kingdom or nation, which existed in 1621 at the time of the Portuguese conquest, necessarily reverted to the Tamil community when legal ties with the United Kingdom were severed in 1972. The Tamils maintain that they have never given up their sovereignty, and that the Sinhalese nation has never obtained sovereignty over them by conquest or consent.

"In international law, the principle of self-determination is applied to people who have been deprived of it - deprived of the right to determine their own political, social and economic structure. What it provides for, therefore, is in reality a *restoration* of the status of which they were deprived by the colonial power. What is involved here is not secession from the colonial power, nor is it a case of granting some new right, for it is simply a restoration to the colonised people of a right of which they were forcibly deprived".[22]

In their resolution, the TULF clearly draw on the idea of the "restoration and reconstitution" of the status of which they were forcibly deprived when the Tamil kingdom was first occupied by colonial forces in the early seventeenth century. Thus, the theoretical basis upon which the Tamils assert their right to self-determination, is that when the legal ties with the United Kingdom were severed, both the Tamil nation and the Sinhalese nation, should have had their sovereign rights restored.

In the general election of July, 1977, the TULF was elevated to principal opposition after capturing all 14 seats in the Northern Province and a further three out of the ten seats in the Eastern Province. In the North, the TULF, fully pledged to separate Tamil statehood, won 68.5% of the 400,000 votes cast. In the Eastern Province, which had a mixed population of some 300,000 Tamils, 245,000 Tamil-speaking Muslims and 167,000 Sinhalese, the TULF scored 31.4% of the vote.[23]

In its election manifesto of 1977, the UNP, took due account of the continuing escalation of the grievances and discontent of the Tamil-speaking people. Their manifesto accordingly declared:

"The United National Party accepts the position that there are numerous problems confronting the Tamil-speaking people. The lack of a solution to their problems has made the Tamil-speaking people support even a movement for the creation of a separate State. In the interest of national integration and unity so necessary for the economic development of the whole country the Party feels such problems should be solved without loss of time. The Party when it comes to power will take all possible steps to remedy their grievances in such fields as:

(1) Education
(2) Colonisation
(3) Use of the Tamil language
(4) Employment in the public and semi-public corporations".[24]

One of the new government's first steps, was to constitute a Constitutional Select Committee to draft a new constitution for Sri Lanka. However, the TULF declined invitations to join the committee. Its leader, Appapillai Amirthalingam, summarised its refusal to participate in the formation of the new constitution thus:

"The United National Party had a clear, unequivocal mandate to assert the sovereignty of the Sinhala nation and enact a new constitution. The mandate of the majority of the Tamil nation pointed to a different duty".

This statement symbolised the major conceptual transformation that took place during 1972 to 1977, resulting in a debate over the relevance of "constitutionalism" to the problems of a multi-ethnic society. The conceptual transformation was connected to the assertion of a corporate identity by the Tamil people which was shaped by their perception of a distinct history, language, and culture. This identity was seen by others however, as incompatible with, and antagonistic to, the corporate, collective identity of the Sinhala people, causing a deep ideological and political crisis in Sinhala-Tamil relations.

The Constitutional Select Committee reached a remarkable degree of consensus on several matters relating to the rights of the Tamil people, including: the recognition of Tamil as a national language and a language of the courts and administration in the Northern and Eastern Provinces, the removal of the insidious distinction between citizens by descent and those by registration, and the recognition of justiciable fundamental rights. Despite these constitutional advances, however, Tamil discontent continued to be unleashed, especially in the town of Jaffna, the capital of the Northern Province, where Tamil youths began to sporadically attack police stations manned by Sinhalese. In response to rising communal antagonism in the South, where the Janata Vimukti Peramuna (JVP) were launching violent attacks on members of the government, the government introduced a state of Emergency, and passed the harsh Prevention of Terrorism Act (PTA) in 1979. At the same time, the government began to consider structural arrangements that could provide a measure of self-government to Tamil-speaking areas. The need for such an approach was reiterated by other party leaders. N. M. Perera, leader of the Trotskyist Lanka Sama Samaja Party (LSSP), argued that the language provisions of the constitution were no longer satisfactory:

"What might have satisfied the Tamil community twenty years ago cannot be adequate twenty years later. Other concessions along the lines of regional autonomy will have to be in the offing if healthy and harmonious relations are to be regained".[25]

As a result, informal discussions were initiated with political leaders of the UNP on regional arrangements that would go some way towards satisfying the Tamil peoples' aspirations.

Due to the extreme sensitivity of the issue, discussions on alternative structural arrangements proceeded with caution. Government leaders had not forgotten that previous accords with Tamil leaders on schemes for decentralisation of authority, such as the Bandaranaike-Chelvanayakam Pact of 1958, and the Senanayake - Chelvanayakam Pact of 1965, had been thwarted by Sinhala extremism. Similarly, they were aware that political solutions mooted in the 1950's and 1960's were no longer durable or viable, given rising Tamil aspirations. In the event, two alternative proposals were considered. The first, based on the models of devolution in Scotland and Wales, was designed to respond to the special economic and political needs of the Northern and Eastern Provinces. The second proposal was designed to strengthen and democratise the existing district ministry scheme, formally instituted in March, 1978, but containing no specific assignment of functions. This proposal illustrated the government's political commitment to a system of district ministers who were representatives of the executive president.

In the event, on 4 June, 1978, the government presented to parliament a White Paper, which envisioned the greater integration of the district ministry scheme with a more comprehensive programme of decentralisation. The White Paper stated that its purpose was to strengthen the representative character of the democratic system by grafting on to it a scheme of self-management by the people of a district. The objectives of the district ministry scheme were to:

(a) enable the people to participate in the administration at the district level through their elected representatives and through institutions established in the district;

(b) enhance the accountability of the district minister to the president, the cabinet ministers, and parliament; and

(c) facilitate control and co-ordination and secure the expeditious functioning of administrative functions at the district level.[26]

It was the White Paper that set forth the concept of the District Development Council (DDC), its representative character, its powers, functions, and the devolved subjects over which it would enjoy jurisdiction. The Development Councils Law became one of the most controversial pieces of legislation of post-independent Sri Lanka. Whilst some welcomed the legislation as a response to the need for regional autonomy in the Tamil populated Northern and Eastern Provinces, and considered it to be a compromise between the demand for a separate state of Eelam and an undiluted and highly centralised unitary form of government, others considered the measure as an attempt to deflect the drive for a separate state by legitimising further inroads into the "traditional areas" of the Tamils. On the other hand, some Sinhalese condemned the scheme as an attempt to undermine the unitary character of the constitution. Siri Perera, Q.C., summarised the fears of some Sinhalese in the following words:

"Since time immemorial this country has had a unitary system of government and the people [have] all along regarded this [as] one country, and that a Buddhist country. If these development councils are set up, the Buddhists have great fears not only as to the loss of their rights and privileges as citizens of the land, [but] also for their survival."[27]

For the purposes of this study however, the plan for development councils is viewed as a structural arrangement that was designed to ease the ethnic tensions that had begun to erode the multi-ethnic polity of Sri Lanka. It is necessary to examine therefore, to what extent the devolution of powers anticipated by the DDC's actually succeeded in alleviating some of the grievances at the root of the ethnic conflict.

Despite the internal debate that ensued after the issue of the White Paper, no meaningful steps were taken to strengthen the position of the district ministers, or to create a participatory organisation at the district level to complement the de-centralisation of executive power. At this stage, appreciating the advantage of democratic decentralisation for accelerating development and promoting participatory democracy, the government decided to constitute a Presidential Commission to make recommendations regarding a scheme of devolution and decentralised administration.

Whilst the SLFP declined to participate in the process, believing it to be no more than a ruse to translate into action by means of a commission the very regional council system that was rejected by the people of Sri Lanka in 1957 and 1968, the TULF decided to nominate a member. In its final composition, the Commission reflected the ethnic balance of the country. The Commission was headed by a former Chief Justice who was a Kandyan Sinhalese, and included three other Sinhalese, three Tamil members and three Muslims.

However, while it was originally thought that the broad concepts of the scheme had been determined in the terms of reference, and that the Commission would concentrate on the details of the mechanism, there was little agreement on fundamentals. Disagreements arose over such issues as the powers and functions of development councils, the subjects to be devolved, and the borrowing and taxing powers of the councils. These differences were reflected in the final majority report, which was a compromise between those who viewed the development councils as an advisory body and those who wanted it clothed in the powers of a decision-making body.

Clearly, there were competing and conflicting conceptions of the decentralisation scheme, of which the district development councils formed a part. Whilst some urged that the unitary character of the state would be strengthened by reinforcing the district ministry scheme, feeling that such a scheme would enable the centre to project itself more effectively at the periphery, others called for more authentic devolution through democratically constituted institutions at the district level. A brief review of two of the main elements of the legislation, illustrates the accommodations reached between these competing conceptions.

First, it is necessary to examine the representative character of the development councils. Although the development council was supposed to be a democratically constituted decision-making body, there was no provision for nomination of members or appointment of officials. Most members of the council were to be members of parliament elected from the districts, whilst the remainder were to be elected directly on the basis of proportional representation. The chairman of the council was to be the candidate whose name appeared first in the list of the political party which received a majority in the DDC elections. It was pointed out by the opposition parties, that weightage in favour of members of parliament would, in effect, ensure that in twenty of the twenty-four districts the UNP, which had a five-sixths majority in the legislature, would exercise control of the councils. For this reason, the SLFP, the CP, and the LSSP did not participate in the elections to the councils held in May, 1981. The TULF, however, did participate in the elections, though in the seven districts in which it presented candidates, it enjoyed a weighted majority only in the Jaffna district.

A second aspect central to the scheme was the district development plan. The plan represented a compromise between those seeking to devolve certain limited and specific subjects to the exclusive control of the council and those advocating a more flexible approach. The legislation expressly defined the devolved subjects as including; agriculture and food, land use and settlement, animal husbandry, co-operatives, small and medium-scale industries, fisheries, rural development, housing, education, health services, cultural services, irrigation of an intra-district nature, and agricultural marketing, social services, and employment. The council was required to formulate a plan for a programme of development in the district relating to each devolved area. This plan had to be submitted to the centre for appraisal and approval. Only after the plan had been approved, could the executive authority assume the responsibility for the administration of the plan.

The system of executive presidency instituted in Sri Lanka in 1978, reinforced the tendency toward centripetal authority that prevails in the political culture of the country. The tendency for power to inevitably gravitate towards the centre, which aborted previous efforts to achieve devolution of power and authority in the 1950's and 1960's, similarly thwarted all hopes that the DDC scheme might prove to be a bold experiment in participatory democracy, or that it would redress some of the grievances felt by the Tamils in the Northern and Eastern Provinces.

Whilst the TULF must have expected the DDC to have solved at least some of the basic problems faced by the Tamil community, in reality the DDC plan turned out to be only an administrative arrangement, designed by the government to transfer some of the functions of the central ministries to the districts. The other severe constraint that affected the functioning of the DDC's, was the lack of financial resources. The treasury under the control of the central government failed to allocate sufficient funds to these councils. By restricting the flow of funds, the government strangled development activities in the Tamil areas. The overall manner in which these councils functioned, demonstrated that these were not even a partial cure for the maladies affecting the Tamil-speaking people. Indeed, the DDC's were clearly partially intended to satisfy foreign donors, who had recently stressed the need to decentralise specific decision-making functions to provincial governments in order to develop rural areas.[28]

Whilst discussions were in progress over the formulation of the DDCs, communal antagonism had escalated in the Island and increasing pressure had been placed on the government by the more chauvinistic elements of the Sinhalese community to combat "terrorism by terrorism". These developments were the logical outcome of two parallel, but complimentary developments, the betrayal of promises to solve the "Tamil Problem" at successive stages, proceeding hand in hand with the uninterrupted induction of chauvinistic anti-Tamil hysteria in the country, followed by the emergency and military intervention.

By 1978, the separatist struggle had to a large extent been taken over by armed Tamil youths, who had resolved to guerrilla tactics to win their demands. They dubbed the TULF as a moderate party, unable to secure the promise of a separate state of Eelam. In April, 1978, one of these dissatisfied groups called the Tamil New Tigers announced that its name had changed to the Liberation Tigers of Tamil Eelam (LTTE). By the mid-1980's, the LTTE were at the helm of the Tamil separatist movement. Only one month later, on the 23rd May, 1978, the LTTE were proscribed by the Sri Lankan government.

The Tamil leaders' demand for separate statehood could still be interpreted at this juncture as an extreme form of what the majority of Tamils really wanted, i.e., reasonable autonomy in running their own administration, security from the fear of being "over-run" and placed in a minority in their "own" areas, through state-sponsored land colonisation projects, and equal opportunities in the economic and educational spheres of life. The intensity of Tamil resentment directed against the Sinhala-dominated state was attributable to the actual and perceived, deliberate and sustained discrimination practised against them in the various spheres of public life. Tamil leaders continued to complain about discrimination in state employment, especially in the armed forces and in the police force, and the non-enforcement of the language safeguards in the constitution. The issue of university admissions continued to be a source of racial antagonism and ethnic friction. The government's formula of district quotas and preferential treatment of backward areas caused bitter resentment among

Tamil university aspirants in Jaffna and Colombo.

However, in the absence of government concessions towards self-government through decentralisation, the original demand of the Tamils for "fair shares", developed gradually into a demand for independence, as moderate leaders came under pressure from extremists. Concessions towards greater autonomy were regarded by the more chauvinistic elements of the Sinhalese-dominated government, as the thin end of the wedge, and accommodationist policies were subsequently dropped in favour of militant policies, in an attempt to appease the electorate. The slide towards extremism and "direct action", that was precipitated following the TULF Resolution in 1976, gradually culminated into a steady growth of guerilla action by the mid-1980's. The armed struggle continues today, albeit, in a slightly more conventional and institutionalised manner.

In July, 1983, communal violence erupted on an unprecedented scale in Sri Lanka, and exacerbated gravely if not irreversibly, harmonious inter-communal relationships in the Island. By 1983, the Sri Lankan armed forces had become deeply embroiled in a bloody civil war with the armed Tamil separatist guerrillas. Since then, political violence has become a fundamental and de-stabilising element in the Sri Lankan political system, and its continued growth remains a threat to the very foundations of society and state.

Notes

1 Roberts. M., "Ethnic conflict in Sri Lanka and Sinhalese perspectives: Barriers to accommodation", in: Modern Asian Studies, Vol.12, No.3, (1978).

2 Ibid.

3 Federal Party manifesto, 1949.

4 Federal Party Convention manifesto, 1956.

5 Hellmann. D., "The concept of a 'Tamil Homeland' in Sri Lanka - its meaning and development", in: South Asia, Vol.XIII, No.2, (1990), pp.79-110, p.102.

6 Roberts. M., p.370.

7 Cited in: Urmila Phadnis., "Keeping Tamils internal" in: Far Eastern Economic Review, March 25, (1972), p.21-22.

8 Ibid.

9 Ibid.

10 Ibid.

11 Ibid.

12 Tiruchelvam. N., "The politics of decentralisation and devolution: Competing conceptions of District Development Councils in Sri Lanka", in: Wilson. A., (ed.), "From independence to statehood: Managing ethnic conflict in..." (1984), pp.196-209, p.197.

13 Statement of S. J. V. Chelvanayakam, at the Kankesanthurai by-election, 1974.

14 Nanda. V. P., "Self-determination in international law: The tragic tale of two cities -Islamabad (West Pakistan) and Dacca (East Pakistan)", in: AJIL, (1972), Vol.66, pp.321-336.

15 Heraclides. A., "The Self-determination of minorities in international law", (1991), p.24.

16 Higgins. R., "The development of international law through the political organs of the United Nations", (1963), pp. 104-105.

17 Saxena. J. N., "Self-determination: From Biafra to Bangladesh", (1978), p.19.

18 R. S. Bhalla., "The right of Self-determination in international law", in: Twining. W., (ed.), "Issues of Self-determination", pp.91-101, p.91.

19 Ibid., p.93.

20 Ibid., p.94.

21 The Tamil United Liberation Front National Convention, Pannakam (Vaddukoddai Constituency), 14 May, 1976.

22 R. S. Bhalla., p.91, (emphasis added). Whilst Bhalla maintains that

the right to self-determination belongs solely "to the people who were deprived of it" (p.98), he is nevertheless "in favour of the more restricted interpretation of the principle, as applying to decolonisation only" (p.94).

23 Figures cited in: Schwarz. M., p.11.
24 Tiruchelvam. N., p.199.
25 Ibid., p.201
26 Ibid., p.202
27 Siri. Perera., Q.C., cited in: Tiruchelvam. N., p.196.
28 Manogaran. C., p.161.

CHAPTER 10

The Sri Lankan government's response to the Tamil national question: 1983-1986

The question that clearly prevails in an analysis of the Sri Lankan government's policy towards the Tamil national question, is whether the ethnic struggle can be solved through "domestic political reforms". In other words, is the Sri Lankan Tamils' claim to the right to self-determination an internal affair or is it an international affair? This chapter aims to reveal that all attempts on the part of the Sri Lankan government to solve the Tamil national question, have more often than not, been marked by political expediency in the light of short-term gains. Because the ethnic conflict in Sri Lanka has been categorised as an internal affair, not only by the Sri Lankan government itself, but also by the international community, Sri Lanka has witnessed the irrevocable deterioration of the ethnic conflict into civil war.

This chapter will examine the various attempts that were made to ostensibly solve the Tamil national issue by the Sri Lankan government during 1983 and 1986. These include, the establishment of the Sixth Amendment to the Constitution in 1983, the All Party Conference (APC) in 1984, the Thimpu negotiations in Bhutan in 1985, and the Political Parties Conference in 1986. Moreover, it briefly examines the gradual "internationalisation" of the ethnic conflict, as the Sri Lankan government attempted to solve the Tamil issue by military force.

From 1983 onwards, the leadership of the Tamil secessionist movement passed with increasing momentum into the hands of extra-parliamentary forces and was assumed in due course by a variety of militant groups who advocated guerrilla warfare as the vehicle for the redressal of their grievances. The militant groups have continued to gain strength and support among sections of the Tamil community in their campaign for the establishment of the separate state of Tamil *Eelam*.

Whilst the electoral results of the TULF in the 1977 general election were a clear mandate for separatism, the TULF forfeited its representation in parliament in 1983, by refusing to subscribe to an oath of allegiance to the unitary Sri Lankan state which was compulsorily required by the Sixth Amendment to the Constitution, certified on 8th August, 1983, in the wake of the widespread ethnic disturbances in 1983. (See Appendix II) Articles 157A and 161(d), required all Members of Parliament, public officers and professionals to solemnly declare and affirm to uphold and defend the Constitution and not to "directly or indirectly, in or outside Sri Lanka, support, espouse, promote, finance, encourage or advocate the establishment of a separate State within the territory of Sri Lanka".

As a result of the communal violence in 1983, the ethnic conflict in Sri Lanka was "internationalised". Due to a massive refugee exodus of up to 25,000 Sri Lankan Tamils into Tamil Nadu, South India, India was unable to ignore what was happening on her southern flanks and could no longer ascribe to her initial summarisation of the ethnic conflict in Sri Lanka as an "internal" affair. The early 1980's witnessed not only the tangible involvement of India with the Sri Lankan Tamil separatists, through the supply of arms and the provision of military training and refuge camps in Tamil Nadu, but also the active involvement of India in the negotiating process with the Sri Lankan government. In response to the 1983 massacre, and the enactment of the Sixth Amendment, India's Prime Minister, Indira Gandhi sent her special envoy to mediate between the Tamils and the Sri Lankan government.

As a result, an All Party Conference (APC) was summoned by the Sri Lankan government in January, 1984. The TULF indicated that the agenda of the APC should be based on proposals which had emerged in earlier discussions in Colombo and New Delhi, as contained in "Annexure C", which provided for substantial devolution of power to regional councils rather than district councils. However, the government rejected "Annexure C" and any form of regional autonomy, and while the Conference was still in session, made the first of many subsequent attempts to impose a military solution to the Tamil national question by repressive action in the Northern and Eastern Provinces. Thus, the government began its protracted attempt to solve the Tamil national question by military rather than political measures. The Sri Lankan government has continued to step-up its policy of military repression over the last decade.

The Sri Lankan army, however, was not formed for combat, but for parade ground ceremonies. Even during the second world war, the Allies did not call upon it for any major operations. Its one taste of action before the Tamil war started, was against the large but ill-equipped JVP in 1971. That rebellion was put down swiftly and brutally, but with foreign help.

An assortment of strange bed-fellows was called upon to help Sri Lanka fight its battle against the armed Tamil separatists in the mid-1980's. Israel, China and Britain supplied patrol boats to guard the coastline. Italy sold a squadron of six Siai-Marchetti light aircraft. South Africa shipped about thirty of its armoured personnel carriers, especially designed to deflect explosions from landmines, the most effective weapon of the Tamil-guerillas. More than twenty American Bell helicopters were brought through the international arms market in Singapore. Israeli anti-insurgency experts were used as advisors. Up to 2,000 Sri Lankan troops were being trained in Pakistan. A shadowy firm known as Keeny Meeny Services, based in the Channel Islands, trained an elite unit of police commandos, the Special Task Force. The firm used Western mercenaries, many of them former members of the Special Air Services (SAS), who were paid between £2,000 and £3,000 a month for their work.[1]

In 1985, the Tamil party leaders and the Sri Lankan government met in Thimpu, the capital of Bhutan under Indian auspices and during a three month cease-fire, to discuss the possibilities of pursuing a meaningful solution to the ethnic conflict. The TULF and five other Tamil militant parties; the LTTE, the *Eelam* Revolutionary Organisation of Students (EROS), the Peoples Liberation Organisation of Tamil *Eelam* (PLOTE), the *Eelam* People's Revolutionary Liberation Front (EPRLF), and the Tamil *Eelam* Liberation Organisation (TELO) declared in a joint statement at the Thimpu negotiations:

"It is our considered view, that any meaningful solution to the Tamil national question must be based on the following four cardinal principles:

1. Recognition of the Tamils of Ceylon as a nation;
2. Recognition of the existence of an identified homeland for the Tamils in Ceylon;
3. Recognition of the right of self-determination of the Tamil nation;
4. Recognition of the right to citizenship and the fundamental rights of all Tamils in Ceylon.

In the face of continued lack of acceptance by both the Indian and Sri Lankan government for all of the principles tabled at Thimpu, the Tamil groups, determined not to compromise on the four clauses, decided that there was little point in the discussions. Their decision to withdraw from the discussions was finally made when the Sri Lankan security forces massacred a number of Tamils in Vavuniya. The Sri Lankan government, having rejected the demands of the joint statement at the outset, asked that the Tamil party leaders would not re-open the principles put forward at Thimpu in any future negotiations in any form whatsoever, thereafter confining its discussions to the Indian government. In September 1985, the "Terms of Accord and Understanding" between the Sri Lankan and Indian government were made public. The "Terms of Accord and Understanding", whilst providing for regional councils, concentrated all state power on the president, including the power to dissolve the elected councils.

In January 1986, the TULF presented to the Indian Prime Minister its proposals for a solution to the Tamil national question. These proposals were then forwarded to the Sri Lankan President, Mr. J. R. Jayewardene. The TULF concept of a political and constitutional structure was based on federal principles. Part one of the proposals read:

1. Sri Lanka, that is *Ilankai*, shall be a union of states,

2. the North and East Provinces shall constitute one Tamil linguistic state, and

3. the Territory of a state, once established shall not be altered without its consent.

With regards to parliament, part one of the proposals stated that the legislative power of the union shall vest in the parliament, and that the membership of parliament shall reflect the ethnic proportion of the union. The parliament was accorded exclusive power to make laws in respect of any matter enumerated in List 1, which included; 1. Defence, 2. Foreign Affairs, 3. Currency, 4. Post and Telegraph, Telecommunications, 5. Immigration and Emigration, 6. Foreign Trade and Commerce, 7. Railways, 8. Airports and Aviation, 9. Broadcasting and Television, 10. Custom, 11. Election, and 12. Census.

Part two of the proposals concerned special constitutional provisions, including; the grant of citizenship to all those who were resident in Sri Lanka on November 1, 1981, and their descendants, the recognition of Tamil as an official language, and provisions to ensure that the ethnic proportion of the Island is reflected in all union services, including the public sector and the armed forces.

With regard to the states, part three provided that there shall be a governor for each state, appointed by the president of the union in consultation with the chief minister of the state. There shall be an elected assembly for each state, and provision shall be made to ensure adequate representation of Muslims in the Tamil linguistic state. The legislative power of the state shall vest in the assembly and will have exclusive power to make law for such state in respect of any of the matters enumerated in

List Two which included included; 1. Police and Internal Law and Order, 2. Land and its uses, 3. Education including universities and technical education, 4. Archaeology, 5. Culture, 6. Industries, 7. Fisheries, 8. Local Government, 9. Excise, 10. Agriculture, 11. Irrigation, 12. Agrarian State Transport and Roads, and 16. Co-operative Development.

The executive power of the state shall vest in the chief minister and the council of ministers. The governor shall appoint the leader of the largest party in the assembly as chief minister and the chief minister will select members of the council of ministers. The state assembly shall have power to levy taxes and mobilise resources through loan and grant. All revenue received by the state and all loans raised by the state shall form one "Consolidated fund of the state". Some duties and taxes shall be levied and collected by the union government. The president shall appoint a finance commission to be presided over by the governor of the central bank, which shall include three members, one of whom will be Sinhala, one Tamil and one Muslim. There shall be a high court in each state, while the Supreme Court shall deal with constitutional matters.

Part four concurred special provisions for the "Up Country" Tamils, in order to meet their specific needs and to ensure that they enjoy a sense of security and to provide for their participation in the government of the country.

In June, 1986, a Political Parties Conference (PPC) was convened to discuss the establishment of provincial councils. In the Sri Lanka government's Peace Proposal, President Jayewardene declared that Sri Lanka was a multi-racial and multi-religious country and said: "Let the past suspicion of these different groups be forgotten to secure a better future for all".

In the contentious sphere of law and order, the Sri Lanka government peace proposal provided that the provincial police force was to be headed by a Deputy Inspector General of Police (DIG) who was to be recruited by the central government. Under the package, the president, upon the declaration of a state of Emergency, could assume the powers and responsibilities of the chief executives of the provincial councils and the provincial administration in respect of public order within the provinces. If public order was threatened by grave internal disturbance, the president, without declaration of emergency but in consultation with the chief minister can deploy any unit of the national police or army to restore public order in the province concerned.

In the similarly contentious area of land settlement, the package envisaged the setting up of a national land commission for the specific purpose of evolving a national land policy and provincial committees would have representation on this commission. Under the package, inter-provincial irrigation schemes and major irrigation schemes would be implemented by the central government. Settlement of people in such a scheme would be on the basis of national ethnic proportion.

With regards to the allocation of funds, the package provided that the provincial council would have the power to levy taxes, and to mobilise resources through loans, which would be credited to the provincial fund. Financial resources would be appointed to the provincial council on the recommendation of a representative finance commission appointed from time to time by the president. The provincial council would have to get the sanction of the central government for foreign loan and grant, while the nature of taxes to be levied by the provincial council would be defined by parliament by law.

Under the package the president would appoint a governor, who in turn would appoint a chief minister. The chief minister would be entitled to choose a board of ministers from the members of the provincial council.

Mr. Jayewardene, in presenting the package said that the proposals would not require representation but an amending of the constitution. The bill to amend the constitution to enable the creation of provincial councils would be enacted by the parliament by a 2/3 majority. Once the Provincial Councils Act had been passed, he said that it shall not be revoked or altered in any manner except by an act of parliament passed by a 2/3 majority after consultation with the councils concerned.

Thus, it is clear that the government's proposals for the establishment of provincial councils were far removed from that envisaged by the TULF The proposals once again gave all power to the central government and the president. As a result, the TULF refused to participate further in the deliberations. However, the PC was to set the agenda for what was to become one of the most far-reaching, but fundamentally flawed agreements, namely, the Indo-Sri Lanka Accord of 1987.

Notes

1Humphrey Hawksley, "Toy soldiers who became military monsters", in: *The Guardian*, 11th August, (1986).

CHAPTER 11

A historical and territorial interpretation of the Sri Lankan Tamils' claim to self-determination: The government-sponsored colonisation of the Tamils' traditional "homeland"

"Only in Sri Lanka has the right of an ethnicity to a precisely circumscribed territory and the rejection of state-sponsored colonisation of that territory been made the basis of successive election programmes and manifestoes and even the basis of the secession demand."[1]

It is generally recognised that "what distinguishes separatist from other minority claims is the fact that the group wishes to establish a new State on a particular piece of land".[2] Even upon a cursory review, one finds that most contemporary separatist movements include claims to a particular territory. However, the discourse surrounding the debate over the status of the right to self-determination all too often neglects to highlight the territorial claim inherent in a separatist group's claim to the right to self-determination, focusing instead on whether the concerned group constitutes a distinct "people", or whether the group is subjected to marked oppression. In other words, the discourse focuses upon the quality of the relationship between the "people" and the state. What is at issue however, "is not a relationship between peoples and states, but a relationship between people, states, and territory".[3] Indeed, a separatist group's claim to the right to self-determination makes little sense unless it is interpreted in a territorial light.

This chapter shall adopt a historical and territorial analysis of the claims of secessionist groups to the right to self-determination, which necessarily contrasts sharply with the traditional analysis based on ethnic differentiation and discrimination. In the first instance, a distinction must be drawn between ethnic minority claims to the right to self-determination and secessionist claims. "Although some ethnic struggles concern issues of domestic political fairness, many involve secessionist claims.

Secessionist demands, unlike claims about domestic political fairness, cannot be satisfied through domestic political reforms. Instead they aim to redraw the political boundaries."[4] Traditionally the self-determination norm on which separatist groups base their claims, is assumed to turn on democratic principles of consent and popular sovereignty. Accordingly, self-determination represents a liberal democratic value (with secession as the liberal democratic alternative), while the principle of territorial integrity remains "feudal, undemocratic and oppressive". The traditional linkage of the theory of democratic participation and popular consent with a right of secession, is contested by the fact that "separatists typically would not find satisfaction in rights of democratic participation. What makes them separatists is their desire to leave and form a new state. The fact that some states deny certain groups the right to participate does not explain why secession, rather than full participation, is the appropriate remedy."[5]

The standard account pits the principle of self-determination against the principle of territorial integrity. The first assumes that government is defined as a collection of individuals, the latter, as an area of land. Defining government in terms of land, however, better explains what secessionists are trying to accomplish. When an ethnic group wishes to secede, they are making a claim to territory. They wish a piece of land for their future, a piece of land on which they will be able to make their own claims to territorial integrity. A separatist group's claim to the right to self-determination is typically centred on a piece of land which they claim to have possessed in the past, and upon which they once claimed territorial integrity.

"Territorial integrity properly understood accommodates the principle of self-determination. Whatever conflict exists is not between principles, but over land."[6]

However, it is apparent that the secessionist group must not only wish to establish a new state on a particular piece of land, it must also somehow establish a claim to the territory on which it wishes to found its new state. Such claims to territory do not flow automatically from ethnic distinctiveness or from marked discrimination. It is evident that groups which are ethnically distinct and which are the victims of discrimination, but who possess no independent territorial claims, have very poor chances of convincing anyone of their right to secede. Most secessionist groups will claim that a territorial justification exists. A secessionist group will typically argue that they have a right to the particular piece of land on which they seek to establish their nation-state. This territorial right represents an integral part of any secessionists' claim to the right to self-determination.

A theory of secession necessarily depends upon a theory of legitimate sovereignty over territory. Separatists are typically motivated by a perceived historical injustice, in which land that was rightfully theirs was taken by another group. "Secessionist claims involve, first and foremost, disputed claims to territory".[7] Often, the secessionist group will argue that the land upon which they wish to establish their state properly belongs to them and only came under the dominion of the existing mother state by way of some unjustifiable historic event. The secessionist group will often harbor a "historical grievance over territory" and will typically seek to right "historical wrongs". Two types of argument are often used by secessionist groups to demonstrate that the current state boundaries are illegitimate and that secessionists have a superior claim to the land that they seek. The first proposes that the contested land was acquired through conquest by the state from which the ethnic group wishes to secede. For example, the separatists in the Baltic Republics based their claim to territory upon a charge of improper annexation. In this type of "historical grievance over territory", it is alleged that the currently dominant state is responsible for improperly including the group's land base into its own. The second argument purports that the wrong-doer was a third-party state, who at some point in history joined the territory inhabited by the separatist group with the territory of the currently dominant state. This type of "historical wrong" occurred when the European colonial powers demarcated colonial borders to satisfy their own interests and then left the borders intact when their empires receded.

Such an analysis highlights a major defect in the standard account of self-determination, namely its insufficient focus on the history of the dispute. An account which concentrates solely on the issue of whether an identifiable group constitutes a people, and whether the group is subject to alien subjugation, discrimination or oppression, cannot fully capture a significant normative feature of the separatist group's claim to the right to self-determination, namely that the asserted historical grievance confers on it the right to a particular territory.

A historical and territorial analysis of a separatist group's claim to the right to self-determination will go further than the standard account in determining the most important question, namely, whether the group in question actually constitutes a separate people and is thereby entitled to the right to self-determination, or whether it is merely a minority group within the state. Only in the former case is the separatist movement justified. A historical and territorial analysis which focuses on historical and territorial equities can go some way towards determining on what exactly the question of nationality turns.

An enquiry into the historical legitimacy of a group's claim to territory will necessarily involve the extent to which the status quo should be altered to rectify past wrongs. This has been labelled as the problem of "adverse possession". One controversial factor in determining whether the status quo is currently settled enough to give rise to a defense of "adverse possession", is the extent to which the disputed territory is currently settled by members of the dominant group.

"From the point of view of the separatists, such new settlement ought to have no significance whatsoever. They did not ask for these new inhabitants. Had the secessionists' territory not been improperly annexed the newcomers could have been excluded entirely. Taking the newcomers' presence into account compounds the original injury."[8]

However, it is often the case that the new settlers tend to legitimise the territorial status quo. Thus, the reason that members of the separatist group often resist such migration, is precisely because they realise that it undercuts the legitimacy of their territorial claim and hence their claim to the right to self-determination.

A secessionist group's claim to the right to self-determination depends largely upon the existence of a contiguous, and the possession of a sustained territory. Indeed one of the legal criteria of "statehood", is a defined territory, "statehood" requires that there must be a reasonably stable political community, which is also in control of a definable area. Article 1 of the Montevideo Convention on Rights and Duties of States, signed 26 December, 1933, provides, "The State as a person of international law should possess the following qualifications: (a) a permanent population; (b) a defined territory; (c) government; and (d) capacity to enter into relations with other States."[9] However, it is clear from past state practice that the existence of fully defined frontiers is not of paramount importance, and that what matters is the effective establishment of a political community.[10] Furthermore, the principle of self-determination may compensate for a partial lack of certain desiderata in the fields of statehood and recognition.[11]

To conclude, a secessionist group's claim to the right to self-determination makes little sense unless it is interpreted in a historical and territorial light. When a group seeks to secede it is typically claiming a right to a particular piece of land, and one must necessarily inquire into why it is entitled to that particular piece of land, as opposed to some other piece of land, or to no land at all.

This chapter shall interpret the Sri Lankan Tamils' claim to the right to self-determination in a territorial light. The Sri Lankan Tamils' claim to the right to self-determination is based not only upon the grounds that they are a distinct people, sharing a common heritage, culture and language and who suffer from marked discrimination, but also on the grounds that they inhabit an homogenous and contiguous territory, constituted of the temporarily merged Northern and Eastern Provinces. This chapter shall attempt to analyse the historical and territorial legitimacy of the Sri Lankan Tamils' claim to the Tamil-speaking people's hereditary motherland, or what is now called Tamil *Eelam*, the country of gold.

In 1956, at its fourth annual convention, the Federal Party passed the Resolution of Trincomalee, which demanded "a Tamil linguistic state or states incorporating all geographically contiguous areas in which the Tamil-speaking people are numerically in a majority...and the immediate cessation of colonising the traditionally Tamil-speaking areas with Sinhalese people."

In 1976, in what came to be known as the "*Vaddukoddai*" Resolution, the TULF declared:

"that the Tamils of Ceylon, by virtue of their great language, their religion, their separate culture and heritage, their history of independent existence as a separate state over a distinct territory for several centuries till they were conquered by the armed might of the European invaders, and above all by their will to exist as a separate entity ruling themselves in their own territory, are a nation distinct and separate from the Sinhalese."

By this historic resolution, the conceptual transformation and the demands of the Tamil people were crystallised. The *Vaddukoddai* Resolution signified a shift away from the demands of a minority group for the devolution of state power and greater participation in the democratic system of government, to the claim of a secessionist group for a particular territory, which they claimed to have possessed in the past and upon which they wished to make their own claims to sovereignty and territorial integrity.

Integral to the transformation of the Sri Lankan Tamils from a minority group to a secessionist group, has been the Sinhalese-dominated government-sponsored "colonisation" schemes in the sparsely populated Dry Zone of Sri Lanka, which covers regions in what is now known as the North Central, Northern, and Eastern Provinces, i.e., the so-called traditional Tamil-speaking "homelands".(See Map 2)

This chapter shall provide a historical and sequential account of how the Sinhalese-dominated government-sponsored colonisation scheme has fed and fuelled the Tamils' demand for a separate state of *Eelam*. The political, economic, and ideological consequences and implications of the state-sponsored colonisation scheme are accordingly analysed. This chapter shall examine how the colonisation of the Tamil's traditional homeland has become one of the principle grievances of the Tamil-speaking people, and it analyses the attempts of successive Sinhalese-dominated governments to address these grievances. In this context, it examines to what extent the Tamils' demands for the devolution of power over the subject of land settlement and colonisation were addressed in the Bandaranaike-Chelvanayakam Pact, 1957, the Senanayake-Chelvanayakam Pact, 1965, and the District Development Council's Act, No.35, 1980. A cursory examination of the above provisions, which ostensibly granted greater autonomy over the issue of land settlement and colonisation to the local level, reveals a consistent attempt on the part of the Sri Lankan government to further centralise the state's power and resources. It is made apparent in this chapter that the settlement of this principle area of concern, remains a pre-requisite to finding a lasting and satisfactory solution to the Tamil national question.

The demographic history of the Dry Zone, has been infused with mythicised historical arguments used by both Sinhalese and Tamil elites for political purposes. However, an unbiased historical review of the demographic history of the Dry Zone is attempted here. Such a review serves two purposes, it places recent changes in population and ethnic composition into historical perspective, and it provides a context for the conflicting interpretations of the past invoked on both sides of the ethnic crisis.

The island of Sri Lanka, separated from India by the Palk Strait, just twenty-five miles at the narrowist crossing, has been intimately connected with the history of the Indian sub-continent. However, whilst the Indian influence has been strong, the geographical isolation of the Island has ensured that the civilisation which evolved in Sri Lanka developed characteristics which made it more than just a variant of an Indian prototype, or hybrid. It is to the characteristics of Sri Lanka's unique civilisation that we shall now turn.

The earliest settlements in Sri Lanka have been recorded with surprising accuracy (albeit riddled with a strong Sinhala-Buddhist bias) in the *Mahavamsa* (believed to have been compiled in the sixth century AD), and its sequel, the *Culavamsa* (composed by *bhikkus*, priests or monks of the Buddhist order). The founding of the Sinhala race is treated in elaborate detail in the *Mahavamsa* with great emphasis on the arrival of Vijaya (the legendary founding father of the Sinhalese) and his band on the Island. Their advent is made to coincide with the parinibbana (the passing away of the Buddha), in a deliberate attempt to emphasise the historical role of the Island as a bulwark of Buddhist civilisation. These sources indicate that the Sinhalese were a people of Aryan origin who came to the island from Northern India about 500 BC.

It was in the Dry Zone of Sri Lanka that the earliest settlements arose. These were riverine in character and rice was the staple crop. The earliest colonists were wholly reliant on the NorthEast Monsoon to cultivate a single annual crop of rice. The climate was harsh and the rains were seasonal, but not reliable. With the expansion of the settlements, the great problem was to provide insurance against the not infrequent droughts. By the beginning of the first century AD, highly sophisticated irrigation systems had been constructed using water from the *Mahavali Ganga* and other rivers whose sources lay in the Wet Zone. Increasing sophistication over the next five centuries witnessed an extension of these activities to cover the water resources of the Dry Zone, and to the development of major complexes of irrigation works based on the Mahavali and its tributaries and drawing on the waters of the *Malvatu* and *Kala Oyas*.

Two important cores of Sinhalese civilisation developed, and control of these gave the Sinhalese rulers the resources to extend their power over the whole Island. The two cities of Anuradhapura and Polonnaruva became in time, and in succession, the capitals of the Sinhalese kingdom.

The introduction of Buddhism to the Island influenced and moulded every aspect of the life of the people. According to the *Mahavamsa*, the introduction to Buddhism in Sri Lanka occurred during the reign of Devanampiya Tissa (307-267 BC). From around this time, Buddhism became the bedrock of the culture and civilisation of the Island, and Anuradhapura became the centre of Buddhist civilisation. Furthermore, Buddhism, as the state religion, became the indispensable bond between the ruler and the ruled. This connection between religion, culture, language and national identity has continued to exert a strong influence on the Sinhalese.

Whilst there is little firm evidence concerning the dates of the first Tamil settlements on the Island, an isolated but very strong body of archaeological material relating to a probable Tamil settlement has been found at Pomparippu on the north-western littoral of Sri Lanka. This group of megalithic burials "which are datable to a time between the second century BC and the second century AD, are the earliest and perhaps the most definate evidence regarding any Tamil settlement in the Island."[12]

As early as 237 BC, two Tamil adventurers usurped the Sinhalese throne and ruled for twenty-two years. Ten years later, came a Cola general Elara, who ruled at Anuradhapura for a further forty-four years. The long fifteen year campaign waged by Dutthagamini, a Sinhalese prince, which culminated in the defeat of Elara, is dramatised as the central theme of the *Mahavamsa* and is developed there into a major confrontation between the Sinhalese and the Tamils.

Both the Sinhalese and the Tamils have used the argument of seniority to legitimise their respective territorial claims. Whoever can claim or prove to "have been there first", before the "other" "invaded", claims to have the moral-historical high ground to demand possession of the Island, regardless of whether the invaders have been living in the area for centuries or whether the original inhabitants left it long ago. However, what is of concern here, is not who were the first settlers on the Island, let it suffice that it is generally acknowledged that Aryan settlement and colonisation preceded the arrival of Dravidian settlers by several centuries, but the nature of the first settlements.

Until the complexion of Sri Lankan society changed with the arrival of the first of the colonial powers, social pluralism in Sri Lanka meant essentially the existence of the two social groups, the Sinhalese and the Tamils. The Sinhalese and the Tamils claimed descent from distinct racial stocks, from the Aryans and the Dravidians respectively, and as the claims were deeply embedded in their consciousness, the ethnic difference was always important in the structuring of plurality in pre-colonial times and indeed thereafter. But the ethnic difference alone was not responsible for the emergence of the Sinhalese and Tamils as distinctive social groups, above all because neither of them ever succeeded in retaining anything resembling a "racial purity". Furthermore, there is little reason to suppose that tension was the normal state of affairs between the Sinhalese and Tamils.

"It is more appropriate to describe Sri Lanka in the first few centuries after the Aryan settlement as a multi-racial society (a conception which emphasises harmony and a spirit of live and let live) than a plural society (in which tension between ethnic or other distinctive groups is a main feature)."[13]

There were a number of other factors which helped to amplify the original ethnic differences. Among these was religion. Since the Sinhalese embraced Buddhism and the Tamils retained their Hindu faith, religion became a divisive factor in society. Religion was to become even more crucial, since it germinated an ideology among the Sinhalese which was politically emotive and potent. This ideology was built up around the special destiny claimed for the Sinhalese and the land they inhabited as the chosen guardians of Buddhism, and it brought together, with what proved to be of profound consequence, two distinct elements, nation and religion. The unity of Sinhaladipa (Island of the Sinhalese) and Dhammadipa (Island of Buddhism) was the fruit. The appearance of this ideology, as early as the sixth century AD, was reflection enough of a group identity among the Sinhalese vis-a-vis the Tamils. However, contrary to popular thinking the development of a group identity did not result in constant tension and conflict in society, and there is no reason to suppose that the ideology constantly clouded relations between the Sinhalese and the Tamils. The ideology seemed to have surfaced only in times of crisis. Let us examine those episodes in which the ideology of the unity of Sinhaladipa and Dhammadipa were threatened.

In the fifth and sixth centures AD, a new factor of instability was introduced into the politics of Sri Lanka with the rise of the Pallava Hindu state in South India, in addition to the Pandyas, the Cheras and the Colas. The flourishing but very vulnerable irrigation civilisation of Sri Lanka's Dry Zone proved a tempting target for invasion from South India. There was a special quality of hostility in the threat from this quarter. This emerged from the fact that these Dravidian states of South India were militantly Hindu and that Buddhism, which had maintained its hold in that region up to this time, disappeared in the face of this aggressive Hinduism. This development was not without its effect on the Tamils in Sri Lanka who became "more conscious of their ethnicity - which they sought to identify in terms of culture, language and religion - Dravidian, Tamil and Hindu."[14] Moreover, the Tamil settlements in the Island became sources of support for the South Indian invaders. From this period: "Sri Lanka, from being a multi-racial polity, became a plural society in which two distinct ethnic groups lived in a state of sporadic tension."[15]

By the middle of the ninth century, the Sinhalese kingdom was drawn into the vortex of South Indian politics in the wake of the Pandyans. The ascendancy of the Pandyans in South Indian politics had immediate consequences for Sri Lanka in the shape of a Pandyan invasion and the inevitable sack of Anuradhapura. In the tenth century, after the withdrawal of the Pandyans, the Sinhalese sent an invading army to the mainland in support of Pandya against the rising Cola power. The Pandyans were defeated and the Sinhalese had to face the wrath of the victors. Under

Rajaraja the Great (985-1018), the Colas having conquered all of South India extended their control to Sri Lanka, attaching the Rajarata, the king's country, the heartland of the Sinhalese kingdom to the Cola empire. With the destruction of Anuradhapura, the Colas established their capital at Polonnaruva in the north-east of the Dry Zone. For the next seventy-five years Sri Lanka was ruled as a province of South India.

Tamil settlements reached a fairly impressive scale in the eleventh century AD, after the Colas annexed Sri Lanka to their empire in 1017. During this period, although there was undoubtedly some migration of peaceful settlers in the wake of the Cola conquest, the mercenary and mercantile bodies remained the predominant elements among the Tamils present in the Island. It is worth noting, however, that the main areas of Tamil settlement in the eleventh and twelfth centuries lay not in the Jaffna Peninsula, which today has the highest concentration of Tamils, but in the north-eastern littoral and in the western region or what is now known as the North-Western Province. Of the areas presently designated as the traditional homelands of the Tamil-speaking people, i.e., the Northern and Eastern Provinces, only the upper half of the Eastern Province was settled by Tamils during this period.

The Tamils in the Eastern Province trace their origin back to the Mukkuvars, a tribe or lineage of fisher people who are said to have come from Kerala and follow matrilinear traditions. The outlook and the perceptions of the Tamil-speaking peoples in the North and East, enhanced by the differing immigration myths, were different. It was not without some effort that the interests of the Tamil-speaking people of the North and East were finally brought together under the influence of the Federal Party in the early 1950's.

In 1070, the Colas were driven out by Vijaya Bahu I. While Vijaya Bahu regained control of Anuradhapura, he retained Polonnaruva as the capital and so began the era of the Polonnaruva kingdom. During his reign of forty years, the country recovered significantly from the ravages of Cola disrule. Buddhism had suffered a severe setback during the reign of the Colas when Hinduism flourished, and Vijaya Bahu devoted his attention to organising its recovery and restoration to its once vigorous condition.

From 1153-1186, Parakramabahu I ruled at Polonnaruva. His reign marks the last major phase in the development of irrigation in ancient and medieval Sri Lanka. After the death of Parakramabahu there was a brief decade of order and stability under Nissanka Malla (1187-96), during which Polonnaruva reached the peak of its development as a capital city.

With Nissanka Malla's death there was dissension among the Sinhalese and dynastic disputes contributed to the collapse of the Polonnaruva kingdom. The ensuing political instability attracted South Indian invasions.

It was during the thirteenth century, that the second and most important stage in the process of Tamil settlement, which eventually led to the transformation of the present Northern Province into an exclusively Tamil-speaking area occured. During the thirteenth century, the Jaffna Peninsula was occupied by new Tamil settlers. The Jaffna Tamils refer to a mixed immigration tradition with connections to Tamil Nadu and Kerala where the matrilinear law is overlaid with patrilineal accretions. They were joined by Tamil members of the invading armies, often mercenaries, who chose to settle in Sri Lanka rather than return to India with the rest of their compatriots. The permanent dislodgement of Sinhalese power from northern Sri Lanka and the subsequent migration of many of the Sinhalese to the south-west regions, led to the transformation of northern Sri Lanka into a predominantly Tamil-speaking region and led directly to the foundation of a Tamil kingdom there.

Polonnaravu, the heartland of the old Sinhalese kingdom was abandoned in the mid-thirteenth century. Before the Dry Zone was abandoned, it is believed that the elite strata of the Sinhalese kingdom were heterogenous and that the Tamil and Sinhalese cultures were in close contact.[16] Certainly, by the time of the Cola conquests, a distinct Tamil-speaking population existed within the kingdom. The polarisation of Sinhalese and Tamil linguistic regions is seen primarily as a product of the period after the capitals were moved out of the Dry Zone. The Sinhalese, in the face of repeated invasions from South India retreated further and further into the hills of the Wet Zone of the island in search primarily of security, but also for some kind of new economic base to support the truncated state that they now controlled.

The population decline in the Dry Zone continued well into the seventeenth century. The abandonment of the ancient Sinhalese kingdom which remains "one of great unsolved puzzles of Sri Lanka's history" is generally attributed to a combination of three interrelated factors. The natural internal decay of the irrigation works, compounded by the destructiveness of the South Indian invasions and the spread of malaria. The advent of malaria defied all attempts at large scale re-settlement, till the discovery in 1946 and the subsequent administration of the insecticide DDT.

"Malaria - coming on the heels of invasion and thriving on disused irrigations works - played a critically important part in multiplying obstacles to re-settlement."[17]

The Dry Zone soon reverted to forests thinly occupied by a mixture of Sinhala and Tamil-speaking cultivators and by forest-dwellers (*Veddas*), the original inhabitants of the country who spoke some archaic form of Sinhala, while the population grew along the coasts. For the past millenium, both communities in the Dry Zone have been subject to famine, disease and drought, and individuals have assimilated to one of the locally dominant cultures.

Thus the ideology established upon the special destiny claimed for the Sinhalese and the land they inhabited as the chosen guardians of Buddhism, seems to have surfaced only in times of crisis. It was invoked in the eleventh century against the South Indian Colas who had conquered much of the Island and in the post-Cola period against divisive tendencies on the local political plane.

"The evocation of the ideology had its measure of success, but the impact was never to be lasting; a political entity which could be described as Sinhalese-Buddhist was rarely to be meaningful in an all-island framework."[18]

The political reality became more than apparent with the emergence in the early thirteenth century of a separate Tamil kingdom in the north, and after the thirteenth century there was even to be a geographical separation of the social groups with the migration of the Sinhalese from their original settlement areas in the *Rajarata* to the south-west coastal belt. However, neither of these factors brought about the total isolation of the two social groups from each other:

"...latterly the original propinquity was lost, but there was no break in the social and economic relations between the two peoples, and underlying all these was a strong cultural affinity."[19]

Aberrations obviously existed, but it is generally acknowledged that the early history of Sri Lanka largely reveals a picture of harmonious social relations between the Sinhalese and the Tamils. However, the collective memory of the Sinhalese especially, has tended to concentrate not upon the more general conditions which prevailed but on the tensions and hostility which were generated at times of unrest. Thus much has been made of the South Indian invasions, their destruction of the ancient polity and the subsequent migration of the Sinhalese from their heartland. The resistence which emerged to these invasions from among the Sinhalese has been glorified and sanctified, while the heroes which the struggle elevated have found permanence in the popular imagination.

"Much of the responsibility for this tendancy has been placed upon the *Mahavamsa*, the sixth century "Great Chronicle" which is the primary historical source for early Sri Lanka; its perspective, strongly Sinhalese-Buddhist, has coloured not only popular thinking over the years, but also the historiography of the land until recent times. Later chauvinists were to take up from where the *Mahavamsa* left off."20

The years 1200 to 1500, witnessed four major political developements. The drift of Sinhalese power to the south-west and centre, the establishment and consolidation of a Tamil kingdom in the north, the eventual emergence in the centre of the Island of a separate political entity with aspirations to the status of a separate kingdom, the early beginnings of the Kandyan kingdom and the arrival of the first European colonists, the Portuguese.

During this period, the centre of power in the Sinhalese kingdom gradually shifted further south to Kotte, near what is now the capital of Colombo. Despite the political instability which characterised the history of the Sinhalese kingdom during these years, economic activity thrived. Cinnamon emerged as one of the main export commodities with the increased demand for spices in Europe after the Crusades. The emphasis on trade led to an important development, the settlement of Muslims in the Island, especially along the east coast and in the ports. However, the Sinhalese rulers remained unwilling to accept the position and status of a satellite state of South India, or to abandon the aspiration, harbored by so many Sinhalese kings in the past, to rule over the whole country. However, despite repeated attempts, the Sinhalese rulers failed to establish control over the Tamil kingdom in the north of the Island.

From the thirteenth century to the beginning of the seventeenth century, the Tamil kingdom in the north with the Jaffna Peninsula at its centre, maintained its independent position. Indeed, as the Sinhalese power in the Island waned, the Tamils' power seemed to wax. By the middle of the fourteenth century, the Tamil kingdom is believed to have extended as far southwest as Puttalam. The Sinhalese kingdom in the southwest, however, had become embroiled in turmoil, instability and dissension. By the close of the fifteenth century, the Sinhalese rulers were being confronted by the emergence of a claim by the central region to an independent political role of its own. Indeed, the turmoil in the Kotte kingdom in the late fifteenth and early sixteenth centuries, afforded the Kandyans the opportunity to assert their independence from the control of Kotte. Moreover, the Kotte rulers were in no position to re-establish their control over the Kandyans. Thus the decline of Kotte proved to be a necessary condition for the rise of the Kandyan kingdom. The result was that when the Portuguese arrived in the Island in the first decade of the sixteenth century, they found three separate and distinct kingdoms in Sri Lanka, the Tamil kingdom in the north, the Kotte kingom in the south-west, and the Kandyan kingdom in the central region.

The impact of the rule of the Portuguese, and the Dutch and the British thereafter, on the configuration of Sri Lanka's social polity was profound. Upon entering the Island, the Portuguese found the kingdom of Kotte on the brink of disintegration. After the partition of Kotte into three distinct entities, the ruler of the old capital of Kotte found himself confronted with the increasing power and influence of the ruler of Sitavaka, who was soon pressing for domination not only of the kingdom of Kotte, but also the whole Island. The Sitavaka, whilst unable to exert its authority over the kingdom of Jaffna, did manage to bring the kingdom of Kandy under its sway during 1581-1591. In 1591, however, the kingdom of Kandy regained its independence. In 1593, Rajasinha I, the ruler of Sitavaka died, leaving the Portuguese to extend its control over the south-west littoral. The establishment of Portuguese control over the Tamil kingdom came about at much the same time as the collapse of Sitavaka. In 1591, the king of Jaffna was killed and a Portuguese protege was placed on the throne.

One of the two objectives of the Dutch colonists arriving on the Island at the close of the sixteenth century, was to complete the process of control over the Jaffna kingdom and to subjugate the Kandyan kingdom. By 1619, the Dutch had successfully annexed the Jaffna kingdom and in so doing they brought to an end the independent existence of a Tamil kingdom in Sri Lanka. Never again did it recover its independence. Indeed the subjugation of the Jaffna kingdom was one of the more lasting effects of Portuguese rule. The Dutch and the British after them, continued the policy of treating Jaffna as a mere unit of a larger political identity.

For two decades after it regained its independence, the Kandyan kingdom was confronted by a concerted Portuguese attempt to bring it under their rule and thus complete their domination over the whole Island. The annexation of the Tamil kingdom in 1619, impeded the Kandyans by depriving them of a potential ally and a bridgehead for communication with South India. By 1628, however, the Portuguese had seized and fortified the two major ports of Batticaloa and Trincomalee, which were acknowledged as being part of the Kandyan kingdom.

The district of Batticaloa, whilst overwhelmingly Tamil-speaking, was never under direct Tamil rule or part of the kingdom of Jaffna, it was actually a fief of Kandy. Trincomalee, on the other hand, seems to have enjoyed more independence. While Jaffna sometimes claimed suzerainty, this was mostly rejected on the plea that the Vanniyar chieftans of Trincomalee held their areas as a fief from a Chola king, Kulakkottan. Traditionally, Kulakkottan is said to have built the temple in Trincomalee and to have given the area as a fief to Taniamma Pupalan, the ancestor of the Vanniyar. Attempts by the Jaffna kings to encroach on this independence were fiercely resisted by the Vanniyar chieftans. The Vanniyars are regarded as a treacherous and fickle lot who have always created trouble and rebellions for the Jaffna king by joining the side of the Sinhalese. Most traditions attribute their existence to a caste or a group of families called the Vanniyar from Tamil Nadu who came over under either under the Colas (under Kulakkottan, i.e., during the Cola invasion of the ninth and tenth centuries) or under Magha in the thirteenth century and got their lands as fiefs in return for services rendered to the temple in Trincomalee.

In 1639, however, both Trincomalee and Batticaloa were captured from the Portuguese by the Dutch and handed back to the Kandyans. Up until 1762, relations between the Dutch and the Kandyans bordered on cordial. In 1766, however, the Dutch reduced the Kandyan kingdom to the position of a landlocked power. The demise of the Kandyan kingdom followed shortly after, with the arrival of the British. In 1815, after successive acts of resistence to invasion, the Kandyan kingdom was ceded to the British. Thereafter, the British effectively became the rulers of the whole of Sri Lanka. In 1833, in acceptance of Colebrooke's proposals, the separate existence of the Kandyan provinces were abolished and they were duly amalgamated with the "Maritime" provinces in a single unified administrative structure for the whole Island. The provincial boundaries within the two administrative divisions, the Kandyan and the Maritime provinces, were replaced by a new set of provincial units, five in all, in which only one, the Central Province was purely Kandyan. In so doing, an administrative, legislative and judicial unification was imposed on the Island and all sense of nationality among the Kandyans was accordingly obliterated.[21]

From the mid-1930's, the British consolidated the process of unification set in motion by the administrative, legislative and judicial reforms of the 1832, through the introduction of plantation crops, thereby providing the economic basis for the further unification of the Island. While the focus of the colonial administration was on plantation agriculture, the traditional agricultural system was neglected as was the welfare of the peasant population. Under the Governorship of Sir Henry Ward however (1855-60), a concerted effort was made to rehabilitate the Dry Zone through the revival of the ancient irrigation works there. For the first time since the days of the Polonnaruva kings, a positive attempt was made to rejuvinate the irrigation facilities of the heartland of the ancient civilisation of the Sinhalese kingdom.

However, the principal achievement and object of this programme of irrigation activity was to convert irregular cultivation into regular cultivation rather than to open up new areas for peasant agriculture. The irrigation programme did not represent a comprehensive policy of peasant agriculture. Only during the Donoughmore era, especially in the period of the second state Council (1936-47), when the impulse towards social welfare began to manifest itself, was the welfare of the agricultural peasant catered for. This welfare package included the establishment of peasant colonisation schemes in the Dry Zone, with conditions of land tenure designed to prevent fragmentation of holdings. D. S. Senanayake's schemes for the restoration of the irrigation works of ancient Sri Lanka were among the major achievements of the Donoughmore era.

Thus by the end of the nineteenth century, a steady stream of people had migrated back into the Dry Zone. However, resettlement of the Dry Zone did not begin in earnest until the twentieth century, by which point the revitalisation of the area had been taken out of the hands of the British and had become a matter of particular urgency for Sinhalese nationalist politicians.

"Only when, in the 1930s and after the discovery of quinine, the future prime minister Senanayake suddenly discovered his sympathy for colonisation to 'restore the ancient glory of the Rajarata', did colonisation take off with massive government help."[22]

By this time, land had become scarce not so much in the Wet Zone, but in the Kandyan highlands due to the development of the tea estates. D. S. Senanayake infused Sinhalese nationalism with the vision that the colonisation of the Dry Zone was a return to the heartland of the ancient irrigation civilisation of the Sinhalese. Though his scheme envisaged land to be opened up for "Ceylonese" of all descriptions, it transpired to mean mainly Sinhalese colonisation. Overall, the government's policies increased the control of land by members of the majority community, thereby providing broader bases of political support to its elite.

"...it was no longer a question merely of opening up arable land for rice cultivation and easing the congestion in the highlands and the Southwest. Instead it became the task of taking the Sinhalese land back for the Sinhalese, i.e., it became an ideological issue - the reconquest of the Rajarata. It was never said from whom it should be reconquered, though this became clear soon enough".[23]

A land commission in 1927, declared that the government must hold crown land in trust for all the people and allocate it for their benefit. With this mandate the State Council, under D. S. Senanayake's leadership, planned colonisation schemes in the Dry Zone, in which landless Sinhalese peasants were to become independent peasant proprietors. The colonisation scheme was particularly important for the Low-Country Sinhalese elite, for whom it was a means of appealing to the Kandyan Sinhalese, the people identified as suffering most from landlessness. The Land Development Ordinance of 1935, created the mechanisms for the colonisation scheme, and the first pioneers settled under the Ordinance in 1939. The state objectives of colonisation were to relieve unemployment in the Wet Zone, to increase food production, and to establish prosperous settlements in the Dry Zone.

Whilst the colonisation of the Dry Zone began before independence, it was during the 1950's and 1960's that it was continuously implemented on a large scale as the major form of agricultural development in the Island. By the late 1960's, the government had alienated more than 300,000 acres of land to 67,000 allottees in major colonisation schemes.[24] Large capital-intensive multipurpose enterprises such as the *Gal Oya* Scheme in the Eastern Province, which created an area of irrigation for more than 120,000 acres between 1948 and 1952,[25] and the *Mahaweli* Programme were part of this development initiative.

The Tamils, though for a long time not very interested in settling the Dry Zone, still considered not only Batticaloa and Trincomalee but also the "Vanni" down south to Anuradhapura, the few scattered people living there being Sinhalese and Tamil cultivators and *Veddas*, as Tamil country. The current dispute between the Tamils and the Sinhalese rages over the "Vanni", the North-Eastern, North-Central and North-Western districts of the Island, whilst focusing predominantly on the North-Eastern districts of Trincomalee and Batticaloa and on fixing the borders of what were the majority Tamil settlements there to the west.

For a long time after the decline of the Rajarata kingdom, and the Sinhalese shift to the Southwest, the Vanni was a border area and one of confrontation and conflict. Not only were Sinhalese said to be instigating trouble and rebellion against the king of Jaffna among the Vanniyars, but the latter were themselves considered of dubious loyalty swinging back and forth between Jaffna, Trincomalee, Kandy, and in later centuries the Portuguese and the Dutch. Even under the Dutch and the British, it was from the Vanni that the opposition to foreign rule came, and it was not until the late nineteenth century that the British could finally eradicate such resistance by capturing and killing the last of the Vanniyars.

Thus from the time of the decline of the civilisation in the Rajarata, the Vanni had always been a wild country, a no-man's land between the Sinhalese and Tamil settlements. For Jaffna, the Vanni was an uncertain region of dubious value, for the Vanniyars of Trincomalee and Batticaloa, their legitimate, albeit hardly populated hinterland. Indeed the unwillingness of the Jaffna Tamils to allow the Sinhalese to settle the Vanni, suggests that this region functioned as a buffer zone to protect the Tamils from what they considered as Sinhalese encroachments.

Whilst the question has always been how far the Tamil homeland stretches to the West, into the interior, into the Vanni, and in turn, how far the Sinhalese can enter without encountering hostility, what concerns the Tamils now is the attempt by the government to use colonisation schemes as a strategy to separate the Tamils' traditional homelands, i.e., the Northern and Eastern Provinces, by driving a wedge of Sinhalese colonised land between them, principally in the strategic Trincomalee area. Consequently, the colonisation of the Vanni, has led to friction precisely in the disputed areas bordering on Batticaloa, Trincomalee and the Northern Province, where the population was to an extent already mixed, and most of the fierce fighting between the Sri Lankan armed forces and the Liberation Tigers of Tamil *Eelam* has taken place in the Trincomalee district, in an attempt to secure control of vital areas where the North and Eastern Provinces merge.

Tamil leaders insist that the merger of the North and Eastern Provinces is a pre-requisite for commencing any serious negotiations with the government. The Tamils consider the colonisation issue to be the most serious of the problems facing them, since maintaining their traditional homeland is axiomatic for the preservation of the Tamil language, for providing employment opportunities to Tamils, and for Tamils to live without fear in their own land. The merger of the Northern and Eastern Provinces is regarded as essential to the future viability of Tamil *Eelam*, for the North would provide it with its human resources and the East with its natural resources.[26]

Whether or not it was D. S. Senanayake's conscious objective to change the demographic profile in these areas in favour of the Sinhalese is unclear. If he thought about the reconstitution of the *Rajarata*, he would most probably have seen it as largely unpopulated. But change the demographic profile it did. The Tamils were not driven out of the areas where they lived, but they were made a minority in what they considered to be their own territory. What the Sinhalese-dominated government regarded as the peopling of an empty area, meant for the Tamils an invasion of what was rightfully theirs and the deterioration of their quality of life, their political and social influence and their right to live within secure borders. They began to feel threatened in their very own living space.

The Island's political evolution changed fundamentally after the Constitutional reforms in the early and late 1920's. Instead of two majority communities, the Sinhalese and the Tamils, there was now just one majority community, the Sinhalese. The Tamils henceforth regarded themselves and were regarded as a minority community. Colonisation threatened to make them into a minority community in their very home. The debates in the 1920's and 1930's over communal versus territorial representation and the fifty-fifty proposal have to be seen in this light. The Tamil leaders who argued for communal representation, did so for the reason that the Tamils in spite of their numerical minority, are a significant part of the population, "with a history going back more than 2000 years and with certain ancient and established homelands and settlement areas in the North and East."[27]

In the event, the Donoughmore Constitution which stipulated territorial representation, confirmed the worst fears of the Tamils about their rights and status in the country and made it all the more important for the Tamils to hold on at least to the territorial bases where the power of the Tamil vote could be guaranteed.

"Whether intended or not, a factual change of the demographic profile was brought about by colonisation, but even this was not the real problem; the real problem was a legacy of British rule, territorial representation. The question of the majority in the area only became virulent when constitutional reforms came on the agenda. Because the principle of territorial representation was accepted, colonisation meant not that Sinhalese would live there, but that they would vote there, and the Tamil vote would be lost".[28]

Although "traditional areas of contiguity" was a catchphrase during the debates over communal versus territorial representation in the 1920's and 1930's, it was not yet a debate over homelands, since the Tamil majority in these areas was as yet undisputed. Nor did the Tamils try to deny the Sinhalese generally the right to live there. On the contrary, it is assumed that the different ethnic communities to a large extent continued to live in relative harmony. After independence however, with colonisation ever gaining pace, the Eastern Tamils began to define this region as exclusively Tamil and Tamil-speaking.

By 1949, however, the FP, had made colonisation a political issue for Tamil-speaking peoples. Between 1921 and 1946, the Sinhalese population in the Eastern Province had almost doubled. Census figures of the government reveal that the population of the Eastern region was 279,112 in 1946, and comprised of 146,059 Tamils, 109,024 Muslims and 23,456 Sinhalese. Others numbering less than 2,000, included the Portuguese Burghers, "Up Country" Tamils and the *Veddas*. The population in 1981, was 976,475, comprising of 411,451 Tamils, 315,201 Muslims and 243,358 Sinhalese, others accounted for the balance. (See Table 2)

Table 2, which shows the population figures for 1946, 1951, 1963, 1971 and 1981 on an ethnic basis, provides a clear picture of the overall growth rate during the last four decades and the changing trend in the ethnic composition of the total population of the Eastern region. The growth in population due to natural increases in the past four decades is insignificant though birth rate ranged around the national average of three percent, when compared to the increase induced through movement of people into the region from other Provinces. The figures indicate the large numbers of Tamil-speaking people who have moved out of the region with the escalation of the ethnic conflict.

Within seven years of splitting from the Jaffna based Tamil Congress in 1949, the FP had become the main Tamil party, not only in Jaffna but also and especially in the East. Long before the language question became virulent in 1955, Chelvanayakam had said in 1949 in the FP's founding manifesto, that the Tamil-speaking peoples of Ceylon in the North and East belonged together as one nation:

"From many indications it becomes clear, that the opinion of the Tamil speaking people in Batticaloa, and the opinion of our brothers in Trincomalee and the North support us in this matter...In short, they are conscious of being a nation of their own."[29]

This went far beyond anything the Tamil Congress had ever claimed. In its early conventions, the first topic to be raised and given priority by the FP was always that of the Tamil homelands in the North and East and the threat that the government-sponsored colonisation constituted. At its fourth annual convention on August 19, 1956, it passed a resolution which stated that "the colonisation policy pursued by successive Governments since 1947 of planting Sinhalese population in the traditional homelands of the Tamil-speaking peoples is calculated to overwhelm and crush the Tamil-speaking people in their own national areas." The Resolution of Trincomalee resembled closely the four points that were put forward during the Thimpu conference in Bhutan by the main Tamil parties in 1985. The four resolutions were:

(1) demand for a Tamil linguistic state or states "incorporating all geographically contiguous areas in which the Tamil-speaking people are numerically in a majority..."

(2) giving the Tamil language its rightful place,

(3) repeal of the Citizenship laws which discriminated against the Indian Tamils', and

(4) "the immediate cessation of colonising the traditionally Tamil-speaking areas with Sinhalese people".[30]

From the outset, the FP spoke of the Tamil-speaking peoples, and in doing so, included the Muslims in its sweep. To allay the fears of Tamil domination, the FP always took pains to assure the Muslims their fair representation in a federal, Tamil-dominated set-up and very early demanded that Amparai, a Muslim majority district, be made into an autonomous unit in this set-up. For the same reason, colonisation was denounced for allegedly making the Muslims a minority in the only area where they were the majority. In political debates, the government has consistently attempted to delink the Muslims of the Eastern Province from the Tamil autonomist demand and co-opt them by concrete material enticements to pro-centrist positions.

Although there were no new initiatives in colonisation under the United Front government (UF) which came into power in 1970, Sinhalese-Tamil relations actually worsened during the 1970's and colonisation remained one of the issues that eventually led to separatist demands. The TULF created to contest elections on an explicitly secessionist platform, listed the colonisation of traditional Tamil homelands by Sinhalese in the *Vaddukoddai* Resolution of May 14, 1976, as one of the nine justifications for the separate state of *Eelam*.

It is generally recognised that the Tamil separatist demand did not emerge merely because of cumulative grievances of discrimination. Rather, the forging of a positive separatist vision was underpinned by the realisation that the Northern and Eastern Provinces could constitute a viable autonomous politico-economic entity.[31] The geopolitical rationale for separatism emerged from the dynamics of various political and economic processes, but the chief of these was the peasant resettlement in and the colonisation of the Dry Zone, which favoured the Sinhalese, dramatically changed the population ratio among the Sinhalese, Tamils, and Muslims, creating competition for a limited set of opportunities, thereby deepening the ethnic divide. Certainly the potential for agricultural prosperity in the Dry Zone must have made the Tamils conscious of the agricultural possibilities and economic viability of their alleged homelands, to be further supplemented by an industrial hinterland around Trincomalee as a harbour. In other words, for the Tamil secessionists, the case for Eelam was made as a positively viable project, and not merely as a negative refuge.

After independence, the economic potential of the Dry Zone was realised in the shape of the reconstruction of the ancient irrigation works. However, this was not done for the economic benefit alone, but for reasons of national ideology. The Rajarata was the country of the Sinhalese, not the Tamils. The economic benefits of these areas was now recognised by the Tamils. The economic argument was of supreme importance for the FP throughout the 1950's, since the economic potential of the Vanni district was exploited by the successive Sinhalese-dominated governments to benefit the Sinhalese community and not the Tamil population. This was resented by the Tamils, and hence the demand (which took a back seat in the late 1960's and early 1970's) that colonisation be put under the responsibility of the district authorities, as opposed to the central authority, came to the fore. "If the Tamil areas were under Tamil government" they asked, "would there be room for talk about Sinhalese colonisation?"[32]

The economic argument, together with the accusation of changing the demographic profile, brought the Tamils from Jaffna and those from the East together on common ground. From now on, it was no longer merely a political question over rights to settle and administrate, but a politico-economic conflict over the right to control and exploit the economic resources of the area. The new- found co-operation was strong enough to give the proposal for a merged province wide support.

"...the concept of Eelam was intimately rooted in both the development and the discrimination experienced by the region and its population. The development of the region demonstrated to the Tamils its potential for economic growth and opportunity. The manner in which that development was being effected, through the instrumentalities of the unitary state and majority rule consolidated in ethnic terms, made them acutely aware that they would not be shareholders in this development but would be its casualties. Although their declining stake in the system explains their alienation from it and their acceptance of the separatist option, the region's perceived potential for development provided a strong, intense motivation to struggle for the goal of a separate state."[33]

Sinhalese-dominated governments from both ruling parties have sporadically acknowledged Tamil concern over settlement policy. S.W.R.D. Bandaranaike recognized the concept of the traditional Tamil homeland when he was willing to devolve administrative powers to regional councils in the Northern and Eastern Provinces, under the provisions of the Bandaranaike-Chalvanayakam Pact, 1957. One major point of the Banda-Chelva Pact, was the stipulation that colonisation by Sinhalese in the North-East and North-Central areas, should be stopped and newly opened up land in this area be given to Tamils or "people living in contiguous areas" on a priority basis so as not to disturb the demographic profile of the region, since these were the "traditional homelands" of the Tamils. No new colonisation schemes were to be started until the details had been negotiated with the FP The control of colonisation should be under the provincial governor in the federal set-up envisaged by the FP, and not under the central government. The *Gal Oya* project in the East should be discussed and adapted in accordance with Tamil demands. The proposed regional councils were to be granted powers for selecting allottees to colonization schemes that would be established in Tamil districts. The Pact also included provisions that recognized Tamils as a distinct nationality and Tamil-speaking areas as traditional Tamil homelands, by permitting the use of Tamil for administrative purposes in the areas to be administered by separate regional councils.

In 1963, however, the massive *Gal Oya* project, launched for the re-settlement of families in the southern corner of the Eastern Province, prompted the government to adjust the boundaries of the province to create a new district of Amparai. At the time of independence, Sri Lanka comprised of nine provinces. The administrative units of each province were districts. The Eastern Province was demarcated into two districts, namely, the Batticaloa and Trincomalee districts. Batticaloa was the capital. The creation of the new district of Amparai, was done by dissecting the existing district of Batticaloa, thus increasing the number of districts in the Province to three. District administration is co-ordinated through sub-divided units of administrations called divisions. With the creation of the new district of Amparai it was inevitable that the number of divisional units had also to be increased. The change in ethnic composition added a new dimension to parliamentary representation of the region. The colonisation strategy which diluted the majority Tamil-speaking representation of the Eastern region in parliament, and the gerry-mandering of district boundaries, made it possible to carve out two Sinhalese majority seats in the Amparai and Trincomalee districts composing mainly of the *Gal-Oya* project area and the *Allai, Kantalai* project areas. The election of two

Sinhalese members of parliament from these two constituencies thereafter accelerated the pace of lop-sided development as these members of parliament were able to lobby successive governments to divert adequate financial resources for over-all development of these two electorates.

The abolition of provincial boundaries as recongnised administrative units and the shift to districts in 1963 as the desirable subnational units for administration and decentralisation, facilitated the increasingly dense nature of state activity at the local level. It fragmented the units of Tamil claims and demands, the provinces (units the Banda-Chelva Pact had recognised) into smaller units that could be made more limited in their functions and responsibilties. This strategy is apparent in the centre's attempts thereafter to retain all policy-making responsibility and delegate only administrative functions to district-level bodies. With the Tamils losing majority status in Amparai and Trincomalee districts, central spokespersons could also argue that the Tamils' claim to the Eastern Province as their homeland was an exaggerated one.

The concept of a traditional Tamil homeland was later recognised by Dudley Senanayake, head of the coalition government formed by the UNP and the FP as a coalition partner, when he agreed under the provisions of the Senanayake-Chalvanayakam Pact in 1965, to specify the priorities that would be observed by district councils of the Northern and Eastern Provinces when granting lands to allottees under colonisation schemes. Land in the Northern and Eastern Provinces should be granted:

(a) to landless peasants in the District;

(b) to Tamil-speaking persons resident in the Northern and Eastern Provinces; and

(c) to other citizens of Sri Lanka, preference being given to Tamil residents in the rest of the island.

Under the Senanayake-Chelvanayakam Pact, there would have been little opportunity for colonisation of Tamil homelands by Sinhalese. However, in the event, Dudley Senanayake did not enact the Pact into law, but his government was compelled to formulate the Tamil language (Special Provisions) Regulations in 1966, in order to administer the predominantly Tamil-speaking areas. These language provisions acknowledged that the Northern and Eastern Provinces were distinctly Tamil areas and that they could not be administered unless special provisions were formulated to transact all government and public businesses and maintain all records in Tamil. Had the provisions of either the Bandaranaike-Chelvanayakam Pact or the Senanayake-Chelvanayakam Pact been enacted into law, the policy of settling large numbers of

Sinhalese people in Tamil districts would have been automatically discontinued. Instead, the policy of colonising Tamil districts with Sinhalese peasants continued unabated, and the ethnic composition of these districts, especially in the Eastern Province, continued to change drastically from the mid-1950's.

"Overall, the effort by the center to undertake an expansionary role and to respond to, protect, and project majority interests into minority areas was clearly part of the process of centralisation of power that was taking place at the national level and the logical obverse of its failure to carry out promises of decentralisation to the Tamils."[34]

It will be made apparent in the analysis of the land settlement and colonisation provisions made in the Thirteenth Amendment to the Constitution, 1987 in Chapter 12, that the Sri Lankan government accorded less autonomy and devolution of power in this legislation, than had previously been provided by both the Bandaranaike-Chelvanayakam Pact and the Senanayake-Chelvanayakam Pact.

The UNP acknowledged the importance of colonisation for Tamils by including it in its election manifesto of 1977, as one of the Tamil grievances that needed to be resolved. According to A. J. Wilson who mediated between the Jayawerdene government and the TULF during this period, whilst "the President had pledged not to disturb the demographic composition of the traditional Tamil homelands",[35] he nevertheless "turned a blind eye" toward Sinhalese colonisation under the Accelerated Mahaweli Programme.

In December, 1985, the TULF proposed that colonisation be devolved to the provinces. It objected to the government's use of the phrase "national settlement schemes" to exclude the Accelerated Mahaweli Programme and other large projects from devolution and "national ethnic ratio" to justify Sinhalese colonisation in the Northern and Eastern Provinces. It demanded that the remainder of land under the Accelerated Mahaweli Programme be reserved for Tamils and Muslims. The government rejected the TULF proposals outright and proposed a Natural Resources Development Commission to determine colonisation policy.

Government proposals in 1986, specifically discussed the distribution of land grants in the colonisation projects. These appear to have been unchanged in subsequent developments leading to the India-Sri Lanka Accord of July, 1987, and the devolution of power to Provincial Councils. A detailed account of the provisions relating to land settlement and colonisation in the Indo-Sri Lanka Accord, 1987, are provided in Chapter 12. The proposals included an addendum on the devolution of power in respect to land and colonisation. They stated, "Rights in or over land, land tenure, transfer and alienation of land and land improvement will devolve on Provincial Councils,"[36] except land required for the purposes of the central government and interprovincial projects such as the Accelerated Mahaweli Programme. Land use must agree with national land policy set by a National Land Commission, the government allocated the estimated 101,483 remaining allotments of the Accelerated Mahawali Programme to population distribution; 75,504 Sinhalese, 12,787 Sri Lankan Tamils, 7,509 Muslims, and 5,683 "Up Country" Tamils. Allotments previously made to Tamils and Muslims in Trincomalee and Batticaloa districts (882 and 1,481 respectively) were to deducted from their totals.[37] Within the provinces, "the ethnic proportions within the Province would be the best applicable principle" for the distribution of land grants.[38] Government policy therefore, adopted a quota system with a limited amount of devolution to the provinces. In the Mahaweli Programme it made no concessions to the existing population structure but adjusted the figures in favour of the Sinhalese.

To sum up, the government-sponsored colonisation scheme transformed the Dry Zone from "a sparsely populated and unhealthy but ethnically diverse region to a rapidly growing and almost exclusively Sinhalese and Buddhist one."[39] Tamil protests against this transformation, and demands for the Tamil-speaking peoples' control of the traditional homelands have often been followed by intensification rather than moderation, culminating in the escalation of violence between the security forces and the LTTE in the contested areas of the Dry Zone, especially in the Northeastern districts of Trincomalee and Batticaloa. At the heart of the dispute remains the problem of who has the right to control the East, in other words, who will have access to its natural resources. In an attempt to gain further control of the East, the Sri Lankan government continues to push forward with forcible resettlement programmes, arming the resettled Sinhalese with arms, and creating civilian buffer zones between itself and the Tamil Tiger separatists in the disputed regions of the North-East. In the meantime, it continues its policy of driving a wedge of colonised land between the temporarily merged North and Eastern Provinces in an effort to further discredit the Tamil-speaking people's claim to their traditional homeland, the regions where Tamil-speaking people have traditionally lived and governed themselves.

Notes

1 Hellmann. D., "The concept of a 'Tamil Homeland' in Sri Lanka - its meaning and development", in: South Asia, Vol.XIII, No.2, (1990), pp.79-110, p.103.
2 Brillmayer. L., "Secession and Self-determination: A territorial interpretation", in: Yale Journal of International Law, Vol.16, (1991) pp.177-202, p.193.
3 Ibid., p.179.
4 Brillmayer. L., p.179.
5 Ibid., p.185.
6 Ibid., pp. 201-202.
7 Ibid., p.178.
8 Ibid., p.200.
9 Brownlie. I., "Principles of International Law", (1979), p.72.
10 Ibid., p.72.
11 Ibid., p.598.
12 K. Indrapala., "Early Tamil settlements in Ceylon", in: Journal of the Royal Asiatic Society (Ceylon), Vol.XIII, (1969), pp. 43-63, p.511.
13 K. M. de Silva., "Historical survey", in: K.M. de Silva., (ed.), "Sri Lanka: A Survey", (1977), pp.31-85, p.38.
14 Ibid., p.38.
15 Ibid., p.38.
16 Peebles. P., "Colonisation and ethnic conflict in the Dry Zone of Sri Lanka", in: Journal of Asian Studies, Vol.49, No.1, February, (1990), pp.30-55, p.33.
17 Ibid., p.43.
18 Samaraweera. V., "The evolution of a plural society", in: K.M. de Silva., (ed.), "Sri Lanka: A survey", (1977), p.87.
19 Ibid., p.87.
20 Ibid., p.88.
21 Between 1873 and 1889, three Kandyan Provinces - the North Central, Uva and Sabragamuwa - were carved out, giving expression to the fact that the Kandyan problem, in the sense of a "traditional" nationalism, had ceased to be a serious threat to the continued stability of British rule.
22 Hellmann. D., p.95.
23 Ibid.
24 Peebles. P., p.37.
25 Ibid.

26 See Manorgaran, M., "Ethnic conflict and reconciliation in Sri Lanka", (1987), for a more comprehensive account of the economic benefits of the inclusion of the Eastern Province in Tamil "*Eelam*".
27 Hellmann. D., p.97.
28 Hellmann. D., p.110.
29 S.J.V. Chelvanayakam, "Tirkktaricanamiku Talaimaipperuari", 18 December, (1949), Part 1, p.7, cited in: Hellmann. D., p.100.
30 I.T.A.K. Resolution passed at the 4th annual convention held at Trincomalee on 19 August, (1956), in Velli Vila Malar, Part 1, Annex. A, p.14, cited in: Hellmann. D., p.100.
31 See Shastri. A., "The material basis for separatism: The Tamil *Eelam* movement in Sri Lanka", in: The Journal of Asian Studies, Vol.49, No.1, February (1990), pp.56-77.
32 K. Vanniyacinkam, Party Congress, 17 April, (1955), Trincomalee, in Velli Vila Malar, Part 1, Annex A, p.15, cited: Hellmann. D., p.105.
33 Shastri. A,. p.75.
34 Shastri. A., p.69.
35 A. J. Wilson., "The break-up of Sri Lanka", (1988), p.161, cited in: Peebles. P., p.46.
36 Peebles, P., 47.
37 Ibid.
38 Ibid.
39 Ibid., p.51.

CHAPTER 12

The Indo-Sri Lanka Accord, 1987: Provincial Councils Bill and the Thirteenth Amendment

During 1987, the Indian government came under increasing domestic pressure especially from the state government of Tamil Nadu, to intervene on behalf of the Sri Lankan Tamils. In May and June 1987, over 3,000 Tamil refugees joined more than 130,000 Sri Lankan Tamil refugees already living in India in state-run camps in Tamil Nadu. The Indian Prime Minister, Mr. Rajiv Gandhi, appealed to the Sri Lankan government to exercise restraint in its dealings with the Tamil separatists, and to work towards a negotiated settlement which would go some way towards satisfying the Tamils' aspirations.

The events of June 1987, proved to be characteristic of India's subsequent stance on Sri Lanka's ethnic civil war. Unwilling to witness the outright success of either the Sri Lankan security forces or the LTTE, India has attempted to maintain the momentum on both sides. Therefore, at the height of a military campaign which gave the Sri Lankan armed forces access to regions in the immediate vicinity of Jaffna, the nerve centre of the Tamil militant movement, India proposed to send a flotilla of unarmed vessels under the auspices of the Indian Red Cross, to deliver relief supplies to the Tamil civilians living in the Jaffna peninsula. Regardless of the Sri Lankan government's objection to such "unilateral action", regarding it as a violation of Sri Lanka's "independence, sovereignty and territorial integrity", however, the Indian Air Force invaded Sri Lankan air space and dropped food parcels in the area, ostensibly as an "humanitarian" measure. The Sri Lankan government immediately complained of "naked violation" of it's territorial integrity. Strong nationalist reaction in Colombo, with talk of acquiring ground-to-air missiles from Pakistan, led Indian and Sri Lankan leaders to agree that events were getting out of control. There is little doubt that had the Sri Lankan air force resisted, the Indian aircraft would have used force.[1] They accordingly moved from the brink of war into a comprehensive alliance.

Clearly, this confrontation with India acted as a keen reminder to Sri

Lanka that her neighbour not only considered herself to be the regional "super-power", but also that Sri Lanka could not hope for India to remain a silent spectator, ignoring the ethnically based human rights violations that were occurring on her southern flanks. The confrontation opened the way for the signing of the Indo-Sri Lanka Accord. The negotiations that had been held between the representatives of the Indian and Sri Lankan governments in Colombo, New Delhi and Bhutan, India's mediation with the Tamil militant groups, as well as with the TULF in 1986, and the work of the PPC, contributed to the drafts that were made of the Thirteenth Amendment to the Constitution and the Provincial Councils Act, which later came to be part of the Indo-Sri Lanka Accord of 1987, that was signed by Mr. J. R. Jayewardene, the President of Sri Lanka and Mr. Rajiv Gandhi, the Prime Minister of India.

The signing of the Indo-Sri Lanka Accord was a logical extension of India's past involvement in the Sri Lankan conflict. Indian concern in Sri Lanka's ethnic conflict was officially registered as far back as 1981, when following upon the anti-Tamil riots in the South of the Island, an all-party delegation from Tamil Nadu visited New Delhi and persuaded Indian Prime Minister, Indira Gandhi, to officially announce India's active concern in the welfare and security of all Tamils in Sri Lanka. J. R. Jayewardene, however, gave in to the intolerant forces of Sinhala chauvinism and made no effort to win the sympathy and co-operation of the Indian government. Although it was evident that without India's active co-operation in denying to the Tamil separatist groups the facilities in India which were necessary for the guerrilla struggle, there was absolutely no possibility that the Sri Lankan government could cope with the political and military problems posed by the Tamil separatist groups.

In the absence of the necessary political understanding between the two countries, it was inevitable that India resorted to other measures to secure her interests. During the 1980's, the Indira Gandhi government supplied retired and inservice military officers to train Tamil militants. Political reality thereafter, forced the Jayewardene government to recognise India's interest in Sri Lanka's ethnic crisis, and the necessity of involving India in the effort to find a political solution acceptable to the contending parties.

The Thirteenth Amendment to the Constitution of Sri Lanka, and the Provincial Councils Act, were duly enacted in pursuance of the Indo-Sri Lankan Accord, and were presented to parliament on 9 October, 1987. The provisions contained in the Thirteenth Amendment to the Constitution and the Provincial Councils Act had the effect of accepting the division of the Republic of Sri Lanka into nine provinces and of establishing, in respect of each province, a provincial council vested with legislative, executive and judicial powers in regard to specified topics within the boundaries of the province.

The Accord provided for a conditional merger of the Northern and Eastern Provincial Councils, whilst imposing upon the Indian government the duty of exercising surveillance in the Northern and Eastern Provinces of the Island and of ensuring that the Tamil militants surrendered their arms within a stipulated period of time. Reciprocally, the Sri Lankan government undertook to confine its own armed forces to barracks in the Northern and Eastern Provinces.

The immediate presence of a huge and powerful neighbour has always played a major role in Sri Lanka's domestic and foreign affairs. It was therefore natural that Sri Lanka looked to India, often regarded as a model of federalism and secularism, in drafting the model for the devolution of powers to the provincial councils. The Indian Constitution, being federal in structure, provides for central and state legislatures. It has three lists, each identifying the powers of the state and central legislatures. A Union List reserves subjects for control by the centre, a State List sets out the subjects for which states alone have competence and a Concurrent List contains the subjects over which both the centre and the states can exercise competence. The Thirteenth Amendment to the Sri Lankan Constitution, purported to adopt the same strategy in dividing powers between the parliament in Colombo and the provincial councils.

The Ninth Schedule to the Thirteenth Amendment consists of three lists designated respectively, the Provincial Council List, the Reserved List, and the Concurrent List. The first list sets out the topics in respect of which legislative authority is assigned to the provinces, the second list envisages matters regarding which legislative power is retained by the central parliament, whilst the third list pertains to a variety of matters which involve the sharing of power between the central legislature and the provincial law-making bodies.

It is worth noting at this juncture, however, that whilst the Indian Constitution is couched in terms of federalism, containing a framework within which the interests of minorities and other indigenous groups are safeguarded, it does not provide for the secession of minorities or territorially-based ethnic groups. In discussing the question of secession within the framework of the Indian Constitution, and in particular, the significance of the Constitution's description of India as a "Union of States", it has been remarked:

"The distinction may lie not in the use of the word "Union" but in the antecedent, historical background which establishes that the constituent states were at no time independent or autonomous states which entered into a voluntary compact to surrender some of their powers to the general government. The States constituting the Indian Union were thus at no time "indestructible states". Having no existence as states anterior to the Constitution they could never claim a right to secede."[2]

Similarly, the Drafting Committee of the Indian Constitution, wanted to make it clear at the outset that "...[a]lthough India was to be a federation the Federation was not the result of an agreement by the States to join in a Federation and that the Federation not being the result of an agreement no State has the right to secede from it".[3]

The government of India claimed that the provincial councils system would fulfil the political aspirations of the Tamil people and provide political autonomy comparable to that provided by the Indian Constitution to regional states. The Indian understanding, was that if regional autonomy, based on the Indian model was provided to the Tamil-speaking provinces, it would go some way towards solving the ethnic crisis. Rajiv Gandhi, articulated this conception in parliament in the following words:

"The Agreement meets the basic aspirations which animated the Tamil struggle, namely, the desire to be recognised as a distinct ethnic entity, political autonomy for managing their political future, and appropriate devolution of governmental power to meet this objective, the recognition of the Northern and Eastern provinces of Sri Lanka as areas of historical habitation of the Tamils and the acknowledgement and designation of Tamil as an official language".[4]

In an address made at a public meeting in Madras, Rajiv Gandhi made further statements observing that the Accord "provides autonomy, approximately like that of an Indian state, to the Tamils of Sri Lanka". At a later stage of his speech he observed:

"The Agreement secures everything that the Sri Lankan Tamils had demanded, short of breaking Sri Lanka's unity. In fact it goes well beyond the initial demands of the Sri Lankan Tamils. Under the Agreement, approximately one-third of Sri Lankan territory will be made into a single Province where the Tamils will have a clear majority. They will have regional autonomy comparable to State Governments in India".[5]

Clearly, a minority group's claim to the right to self-determination can only be met when meaningful concessions are made by the majority community. It is important therefore, to look carefully at the Thirteenth Amendment to the Sri Lankan Constitution, for within its framework the government ostensibly laid down concessionary provisions to the Tamil people in an attempt to find a balance between local-self government, i.e., the satisfaction of the Tamils' demand for the right to internal self-determination and territorial integrity, i.e., the refusal to accede to the Tamils' demand for the right to external self-determination.

From the outset, however, it was clear that, in spite of Rajiv Gandhi's eloquent conciliatory rhetoric, the grafting of India's consitutional model onto Sri Lanka would not appease the Tamils' claim to internal self-determination, since the same model has failed to respond to similar aspirations on the part of the Sikhs in the Punjab, the Muslims in Kashmir and the Christians in Nagaland. India's reluctance to recognise regional claims to internal self-determination on its own soil, has pushed once manageable political and ethno-cultural problems into full-scale insurgencies.

Moreover, a detailed study of the Thirteenth Amendment, reveals that it did not even accord with the Indian division of powers, thus defeating the objectives of the Indo-Sri Lanka Agreement.[6] If it had provided for a similar devolution of power, it is feasible that it could have presented an adequate framework within which to find a lasting solution to the ethnic problems in Sri Lanka. In order to understand why a similar devolution of powers was not implemented, it is important to look initially at the legal basis of the Thirteenth Amendment.

A brief perusal of the Supreme Court of Sri Lanka's verdict on the Thirteenth Amendment, will show not only that the constitutional foundations on which it is built are very shaky, but also that Sri Lanka's constitutional provisions continue to fail to provide for an effective solution to the present conflict in the Island. An analysis of the constitutional provisions on which the Thirteenth Amendment rests, highlights the difficulties entailed, due to the unitary nature of Sri Lanka's constitution, in pursuing a federalist solution to the Tamils' demand for greater regional autonomy.

An attempt shall be made in the latter part of this chapter to examine to what extent the provisions of the Thirteenth Amendment have satisfied what are considered to be two of the major grievances of the Tamil speaking-people, i.e., the issue of land settlement and colonisation and higher education. Only after such an analysis has been made can the true worth of the amending legislation be satisfactorily jugded.

The structural framework of the provision made by the amending legislation for the devolution of legislative and executive power to the provinces, engendered serious doubts as to its constitutionality in the light of the fundamental unitary characteristics pervading the constitution of Sri Lanka. The jurisdiction vested in the Supreme Court, to determine whether any amending legislation or any provision thereof, is inconsistent with the constitution was accordingly invoked.

Article 120, of the Sri Lankan Constitution, 1978, provides for such a challenge. In the case of such a challenge being made, the function of the Supreme Court in Sri Lanka is limited. It merely has to decide on the manner in which the legislation has to be passed. Unlike in India, where the Supreme Court has the power to hold that the legislation is void for being inconsistent with the provisions of the constitution, the Supreme Court of Sri Lanka, having a much reduced role of being a constitutionally subserviant body, can merely state whether the legislation is one which can be passed by a two-thirds majority in parliament or is one which must be submitted to a referendum as well. Article 83 of the Constitution, contains a list of constitutional provisions which cannot be changed except through a referendum, and the Supreme Court's function is merely to state whether the legislation that is being contested, impinges on those provisions to an extent which requires its submission to a referendum.

The issue concerning the Thirteenth Amendment, was heard by a full bench of the Supreme Court, which consisted of nine judges in total. In the event, the Supreme Court was split four to five. Four judges held that the Amendment need not be subject to a referendum, whilst the other five judges held that it would be unconstitutional if it was not subjected to a referendum. Judge Ranasinghe agreed with the latter view, but suggested that the Thirteenth Amendment would be valid if the clause entrenching it was altered, so as to remove the need for a referendum for any future change to the Amendment. Chapter XVIIA, 154G(2) of the Thirteenth Amendment to the Constitution, stated:

"No Bill for the amendment or repeal of the provisions of this Chapter or the Ninth Schedule shall become law unless such Bill has been referred by the President, after its publication in the Gazette and before it is placed on the Order paper of Parliament, to every Provincial Council for the expression of its view thereon, within such period as may be specified in the reference, and -

(a) where every such Council agrees to the passing of such Bill and such Bill is passed by a majority of the Members of Parliament present and voting; or

(b) where one or more Councils do not agree to the amendment or repeal such Bill is -

(i) passed by the special majority required by Article 82; and

(ii) approved by the people at a Referendum."

In the event, Ranasinghe J provided the swing vote and the government took up his suggestion and enacted the Thirteenth Amendment without the entrenching provision requiring a referendum for the alteration of the Amendment. This judgement was significant, for it weakened any protection given to the Thirteenth Amendment. It could henceforth be altered by a simple two-thirds majority in parliament. It is worth noting that an identical provision was conferred by Section 29(4) of the Soulbury Constitution, 1946. Section 29(2) of the Soulbury Constitution which prohibited communal discrimination and was intended to safeguard the rights of minorities, was protected by Section 29(4), requiring a two-thirds majority for change. Clearly, since the government is Sinhalese-dominated, it does not find it difficult to secure a majority in parliament.

It is important to briefly examine the judgements heard in the Supreme Court, since: "[T]he themes which underscore the judgements in the case are of perennial importance, involving as they do the balance to be achieved between centralising and devolutionary impulses, subserving respectively the objectives of qualified self-determination and residual control, within the framework of federal or quasi-federal structures".[7]

The major argument addressed to the Supreme Court, was that the Thirteenth Amendment which sought to create a federal structure, must necessarily be inconsistent with Article 2 of the Constitution, which states categorically that "The Republic of Sri Lanka is a Unitary State".[8] The Sri Lankan Constitution identifies the core provisions which are incapable of amendment except by resorting to the special procedure of a two-thirds majority and the people's approval obtained at a referendum. There are in total, ten articles entrenched by Article 83 in this manner.[9] Included, among these is Article 2. Needless to say, since the Sinhalese community constitute the majority in Sri Lanka, it is obvious that any efforts made to alter Article 2 are at once doomed to failure. Indeed, President Jayewardene, in drafting the 1978 Constitution, had devised a provision which precluded the possibility of any meaningful devolution of powers ever being accorded to the Tamil community.

The provincial councils established by the Thirteenth Amendment, were invested with extensive legislative, executive and judicial powers. Let us examine firstly, the legislative powers accorded by the Thirteenth Amendment.

Among the legislative powers included in the Provincial Council List are; police and public order (including recruitment to, and aspects of disciplinary control of the provincial police force), land settlement, education, local government, housing and construction, social services, and rehabilitation and agrarian services.[10] Where the central legislature purports to legislate in respect of a matter falling within the ambit of the Provincial Council List and where one or more of the provincial councils declines to accept the proposed legislation, a special procedure is obligatory to render legislation passed by the central parliament effective.[11] The special procedure requires a two-thirds majority in the central parliament, combined with the postulate of endorsement by the people at a referendum.[12]

Whether or not these legislative provisions entailed conflict with the Constitution of the Republic of Sri Lanka 1978, was a question that gave rise to a vigorous difference of opinion between the majority and the minority judgements of the Supreme Court. Article 76(1) of the Constitution precludes parliament from abdicating, or in any manner alienating, its legislative power, nor is it permissable for parliament, in terms of the paramount law, to set up any external authority invested with legislative power.

The majority judgement held that the degree of............legislative power invested in the provincial councils by Articles 154G(2) and (3) of the Amendment, did not amount to........................a limitation of the sovereign power of parliament, but..........implied only an...............imposition of procedural constraints. The majority judgment accordingly declared:

"No abridgement of legislative sovereignty is involved when rules prescribe as to how legislative authority can be exercised. Articles 154 (2) and (3) merely set out the manner and form for the exercise of its legislative power by Parliament to repeal or amend the Ninth Schedule or to legislate in respect of any matter included in the Provincial Council List."[13]

The judgement of the majority was based on the premise that requirements....declaring the content and scope of legislation in certain instances,.... constitute no erosion of the doctrine of legislative sovereignty and are thus not *ultra vires* Article 76(1) of the Constitution.

The minority on the other hand, perceived the purport of the Thirteenth Amendment in this area as transcending considerations linked with procedural restraints and as involving a substantial curtailment of the sovereign powers conferred on the legislative by the Constitution. The minority sought to reinforce this view, by appealing to the political realities permeating it. Wanasundera J, referring to the introduction of proportional representation as an integral feature of the election laws of the Island, indicated that once "the first past the post" principle is replaced it would be improbable in the extreme that any government would enjoy a two-thirds majority in parliament. He further contended, that it would be exceedingly difficult, if not impossible, to make use in practice of the procedure spelt out in the Thirteenth Amendment for the exercise of legislative power by the central legislature in respect of matters allocated to provincial councils. The essence of this reasoning, was that since the amending legislation entails an almost complete abdication of legislative power by the central parliament in decisive respects, the consent of the people expressed at a referendum represents an irreducible prerequisite for such a significant restructuring of constitutional provisions controlling the exercise of legislative power.

Let us turn next to the executive powers accorded by the Thirteenth Amendment to the provinces and the responses invoked in the Supreme Court by the minority and majority respectively.

The provincial councils established by the Thirteenth Amendment are invested with executive power, which is exercised by the Governor of the province directly or through the Board of Ministers or via officers subordinate to him.[14] The attack in the Supreme Court mounted on the above provisions, was based on the argument that the executive power, professedly assigned to the Governor of a province, could scarcely be reconciled with the unambiguous constitutional provision upholding that the executive power of the people shall be exercised by the president of the Republic elected by the people.[15]

The majority further held, that the Governor of a province, as an official appointed by the President of the Republic and holding office during the "President's pleasure",[16] could appropriately be labelled a delegate of the President. It also stressed, with reference to provisions of the amending law, that the President is entitled to give directions to the Governor and to supervise the Governor's exercise of the executive power vested in him.[17] Where the Governor of the province is required to determine a matter in his own discretion, the amending legislation mandates that the Governor's discretion is to be exercised only in accordance with Presidential directions.[18]

In this respect, the majority were content to accept the view, that so long as the President retained the power to give the Governor directions with regard to the exercise of his executive functions and the Governor was bound by such directions, which had the effect of overriding the advice of the Board of Ministers, there could be no encroachment upon the domain of the executive power as demarcated by the Constitution.

The minority by contrast, held that the effect of the provision in the Amendment, was to bring about an unwarranted dilution of the executive power of the President, by channelling it into repositories incapable of being accommodated readily within the entrenched constitutional framework.

Lastly, let us consider the judicial powers accorded by the Thirteenth Amendment to the provinces.

With respect to the enhanced jurisdiction of the High Courts, established within the provincial council system, the responses by the majority and the minority were wholly disparate. The principal provision made by the Constitution, is that the judicial power of the people shall be exercised by parliament through courts, tribunals and institutions created and established or recognised by the Constitution, or created and established by law.[19] The impact of the amending legislation on the structure and powers of the courts, is that it confers on High Courts of the provinces; jurisdiction in respect of writs of *habeas corpus* vis-a-vis persons illegally detained within each province,[20] the power to issue writs of *certiorari*, *mandamus* and the power to prohibit any person from exercising within the province, any power under any law or statute made by the provincial council in respect of any matter included in the Provincial Council List.[21]

In response to this provision, the majority held that the vesting of this additional jurisdiction in the High Court of each province, would be beneficial, in so far as it would serve to bring justice closer to the citizen and to reduce the delay and cost of litigation. Since the power of appointment of judges of the High Court remained with the President and the power of nominating them continued to be exercised by the Chief Justice, while the transfer and dismissal of judges of the High Courts in the different provinces was the responsibility of the Judicial Service Commission sitting in Colombo, the majority had no doubt that the centre continued supreme in the judicial sphere.

The fears of the minority, however, were not allayed by the above considerations. The minority viewed with considerable apprehension the assignment to the High Courts functioning at the provincial level, of responsibility for the disposal of writs of *habeas corpus*, involving as they do the core of individual liberty.

To conclude, the majority opinion purported to demonstrate that the sum total of legislative, executive and judicial powers devolving upon the periphery, under the terms of the amending legislation, leave intact the unitary complexion of the Republic of Sri Lanka.

With regard to the devolution of legislative power, the majority judgement adopted as the governing criterion, the question whether the provincial legislatures were subordinate to the central parliament or whether the two categories of law-making bodies were co-ordinate and independent within the spheres allotted to them. The basic assumption, was that under the aegis of a federal system, the central legislature is sovereign in some matters, while responsibility for other matters is allocated in terms of a power-sharing mechanism to provincial legislatures. The result, is that the central legislature and the provincial legislatures, each exercises its assigned powers within its own sphere without having to accept a position of subordination to, or exposure to control by, the other.

The majority, in holding that this characteristic of a federal constitutional structure was not discernible in the content of the Thirteenth Amendment, was influenced by the consideration that the central parliament continued to enjoy competence, by invocation of the special procedures prescribed in the Thirteenth Amendment, not only to override provincial councils and to legislate directly in respect of matters entrusted to their care, but even to completely dismantle the constitutional arrangements representing the differences between central and provincial legislative vires.[22] In keeping with this conception of the basis of transfer of legislative power in limited contexts to the periphery, the majority asserted that there was no competition, in the sense relevant to identifying the indispensable attributes of federalism, in the scheme embodied in the Thirteenth Amendment.

In other words, the majority judgement found it expedient to whittle the powers of the provincial councils, in order to circumvent the argument that the Thirteenth Amendment was inconsistent with the entrenched constitutional provisions and had to be submitted to a referendum if it were to be validly enacted. In the process, the majority judgement effectively emasculated the motion of regional autonomy, as contained in the Indo-Sri Lanka Accord, initially forming the back-bone of the solution to the ethnic conflict in Sri Lanka. Moreover, the juridical basis on which the majority judgement rested the validity of the Thirteenth Amendment, did not provide an acceptable basis for the solution of the Tamil national problem. In seeking to overcome the need for a referendum, the majority produced an effect, which made the Thirteenth Amendment useless as a political device on which any meaningful solution of the ethnic conflict could be based. They also exposed the fact that there is at present, no constitutional mechanism in Sri Lanka through which any meaningful devolution of power could be given to the Tamils.

In order to overcome the argument that the Thirteenth Amendment was inconsistent with Article 2 of the Constitution, the majority sought to reduce the provincial council to little more than a glorified municipal council. The majority judgement had to play down the powers of the provincial council in order to overcome the argument that the Thirteenth Amendment sought to change the unitary structure of Sri Lanka and introduce a federal structure. If there had been a transfer of power in an irrevocable manner to the provincial councils, the argument that it was inconsistent with Article 2 would have had validity. On the other hand, if the view was taken that parliament had merely sought to delegate powers to the provincial assemblies, parliament would have remained a supreme institution and the unitary structure of the Constitution would have been unaffected by the Thirteenth Amendment. The majority judgement, which was intent on ensuring that the Thirteenth Amendment did not necessitate a referendum, held that there was no irrevocable transfer of power from parliament. What the Thirteenth Amendment accomplished therefore, according to the majority judgement, was merely to delegate revocable powers to the provincial councils.

Neither the majority nor the minority judgement were able to free themselves from actively participating in political controversy in the Supreme Court. Subjective impressions of the strengths and weaknesses of Sri Lanka's national policy permeated the predilections of majority and minority alike. The majority laid great store by the advertence to decentralisation of administrative power in the Directive Principles of State Policy, which are recognised by the Constitution as a set of aspirations intended to guide parliament, the President and the Cabinet of Ministers, in the enactment of laws and the governance of Sri Lanka.[23] Paramount among these normative principles, is the injunction that:

"The State shall strengthen and broaden the democratic structure of government and the democratic rights of the People by decentralizing the administration and by affording all possible opportunities to the People to participate at every level in national life and government."[24]

The majority, in determining the constitutionality of the Amendment, allowed their priorities to be conditioned by a positive appraisal of devolution, as a policy bringing in its wake abundant benefit to the people. This rationale, underlying the process of devolution, pervaded the majority's assessment of the provisions of the amending legislation, and enabled them to declare its constitutionality.

The minority on the other hand, upon deciding that it was incongruous for the legislature to attempt to infuse into the terms of the Thirteenth Amendment concomitants of a federal structure which sat uneasily with the basic unitary features of the Constitutional framework, insisted upon the conduct of a referendum as a prerequisite for the legality of the Amendment. In sharp contrast with the point of departure above, the minority substantiated their conclusion by calling in aid a detailed narration of the sequence of events culminating in the attempt to enact the legislation under consideration.

The minority expressed a keen interest in the role of India and her intervention in Sri Lanka, and to what they perceived as a grudging and hesitant response on the part of the government of Sri Lanka to escalating demands by militant Tamil groups, especially the LTTE, for a substantial measure of autonomy. In particular, the minority was perturbed by the cumulative effect of the amending Constitutional provisions in giving a considerable degree of legitimacy, as a matter of practice to the consistent Tamil demand for recognition of the Northern and Eastern Provinces of Sri Lanka as the traditional homelands of the Tamil-speaking people.

The Accord entered into between the governments of India and Sri Lanka in July 1987, was interpreted by the minority as the source of insidious pressures inducing Sri Lankan statesmen to abandon positions, diametrically opposed to the homelands concept, which they had espoused over a sustained period with unrelenting vigour. The proposed merger of the Northern and Eastern Provinces, with a view to establishing a single provincial council responsible for the governance of the entire territory comprising those provinces, considerably strengthened the apprehension felt and articulated by the minority, that the practical effect of the proposed constitutional arrangements would make the whole of the North and East, accounting for approximately 30% of the land area of the Republic and almost 60% of its coastline, inaccessible to the Sinhala community. These fears supplied the impetus of the reasoning which impelled the minority towards its conclusion, in respect of the extent to which the amending legislation dissolved the cement binding together the different organs of government under the aegis of a unitary state.

The provisions of the Provincial Councils Act were three in number, a Provincial Governor, a Provincial Board of Ministers with a Chief Minister, and a Provincial Council. At the head of this constitutional trinity stood the Provincial Governor. Article 154B(2) of the Provincial Councils Act reads: "The Governor shall be appointed by the President by warrant under his hand, and shall hold office, in accordance with Article 4(b) during the pleasure of the President". In compliance with the

Sri Lankan Constitution, 1978, in which all executive power was vested in the President, the Thirteenth Amendment provides that in relation to provincial matters, all executive power will reside in the Provincial Governor, who is appointed by the President.

Below the Governor, lies the Provincial Board of Ministers with a Chief Minister at its head. Article 154F(1) of the amending legislation reads: "There shall be a Board of Ministers with the Chief Minister at the head and not more than four other Ministers to aid and advise the Governor of a Province in the exercise of his functions. The Governor shall, in the exercise of his functions, act in accordance with such advice, except in so far as he is by or under the Constitution required to exercise his functions or any of them in his discretion". The Governor shall be responsible for appointing the Chief Minister,[25] and shall, on the advice of the Chief Minister, appoint the other Ministers.[26] Thus, the executive power remains firmly in the hands of the Governor, who holds office at the President's "pleasure".

It is important at this juncture, to examine the extent to which the Thirteenth Amendment addressed itself to two of the most significant grievances of the Tamil-speaking people, i.e., the issues of land settlement and colonisation and higher education. Firstly, let us examine the provisions relating to land settlement and colonisation.

Whilst the President of Sri Lanka and the Prime Minister of India recognised in the Indo-Sri Lanka Accord signed on July 29 1987, "that the Northern and the Eastern Provinces have been areas of historical habitation of Sri Lankan Tamil-speaking peoples", the Thirteenth Amendment ensured that the question of colonisation and decisions made as to the selection of settlers would remain firmly in the hands of the Sinhalese-dominated government.

The Thirteenth Amendment deals with the issue of colonisation in the following provisions; Provincial Council List, No.s 9.1, 18, and 19, Appendix II to Provincial Council List, and No.17 of the Concurrent List. Whilst the Thirteenth Amendment initially speaks of colonisation as a subject which falls within the Provincial Council List, Appendix II, dealing with: "Land and Land Settlement", proceeds to strip away the last vestiges of the provincial council's power and vest it in the government of Sri Lanka instead. List 1 of the Ninth Schedule, the Provincial Council List, contains the subjects over which the provincial councils have control. Land settlement is mentioned on three occasions in List 1. Firstly, power is given over agriculture, but land settlement schemes, state lands and plantation agriculture are excluded (item 9.1 in List 1). Secondly, when power over land is mentioned (item 18 in List 1), an impression is created that complete powers are given, but in fact these powers are significantly curtailed by not appropriately devolving state land (Appendix II to List 1). Thirdly, powers over irrigation are provided, but irrigation schemes relating to inter-provincial land development schemes are excluded (vide XIth subject in List II viz. Rivers and Waterways; items 9.1 and 19 of List I). All the services relating to inter-provincial land and irrigation are placed in the Concurrent List (vide item 17.2 in List III), thus enabling the government to exercise control over land development schemes associated with inter-provincial rivers. Appendix II contains limitations on the provincial council's power over land, by use of an arbitrary concept of state land quite contrary to the basic concepts of devolution and the exemption of control over inter-provincial irrigation and land development projects. State land within the province can be freely utilised by the government as required in respect of a reserved or concurrent subject. Since irrigation, forestry and tourism are on the Concurrent List, the potential for the government to take over the use of land in the provinces is vast.

Likewise, the treatment of inter-provincial irrigation and land development projects, ensures that the central government takes over responsibility for land settlement. Appendix II (2.2) boldly states that land development projects will be the responsibility of the government. The power to select allottees is given to the provincial councils, although the selection criteria are to be determined by the government of Sri Lanka. Distribution of the land "will be on the basis of national ethnic ratio"(2.5). Accordingly, the mandatory tone of the provision ensures that the majority of the allotments will be accorded to the majority Sinhalese community. Appendix II goes on to add, "The distribution of allottments in such projects on the basis of the aforesaid principles would be done as far as possible so as not to disturb very significantly the demographic pattern of the province and in accordance with the principle of ensuring community cohesiveness in human settlements"(2.7). Such provisions are so open-ended as to provide for the continuation of the land settlement schemes to which the Tamils have consistently been opposed.

The treatment of the subject of land settlement and colonisation under the Indian Constitution is relevant, for the government of India's proposals, under the July, 1987 Accord, required that the Provincial Council List should be similar to the State List in the Indian Constitution. In the Seventh Schedule of the Indian Constitution, matters relating to land, including colonisation and irrigation are included only in the State List (item No.18). Thus the provisions relating to land settlement and coloni-sation in the Thirteenth Amendment, fell short of the provisions of the Indian Constitution, which the Indo-Sri Lanka Accord was ostensibly modelled upon.

At the core of the Sinhalese-Tamil ethnic conflict, which invokes and generates passions of Sinhala Buddhist nationalism and the separatist claims of the Tamil-speaking people, is a cluster of interest-based issues. These concern the official language(s) of administration, the linguistic medium of education, and their linkage with the issues of educational opportunities, including admissions to universities and places of higher learning, and of recruitment to administrative services and professions. The systematic squeezing out of the Tamil-speaking people from higher education and from the administrative services and professions, consti-tutes one of the major grievances of the Tamil-speaking people, consis-tently fiding prime of place in articulated demands made by Tamil party leaders over the years. The settlement of this principle area of concern remains a pre-requisite to finding a lasting and satisfactory solution to the Tamil national question. In this respect, it is essential to examine to what extent the Tamils' demands in the sphere of higher education were addressed in the Thirteenth Amendment to the Constitution. Only after such an analysis has been made, can the effectiveness of the amending legislation as a basis on which to address the Tamil national question, be satisfactorily judged.

There has been a consistent pattern of discrimination practiced in high-er education against the Tamil community by successive Sinhalese gov-ernments.[27] Tamil party leaders have complained particularly about the system of "standardisation" inaugurated after 1972, by which marks obtained by candidates for university admissions were weighted by giv-ing advantage to certain linguistic groups and/or certain districts. The problem was complicated for the Tamil-speaking people because of their relatively high level of education in English, which has traditionally given them a disproportionally high share of places in university education.

At the time of Independence, the Sri Lankan Tamils who constituted 10% of the population occupied 31% of the places in universities. At that time, all secondary and higher education was conducted in English, a lan-guage in which less than 7% of the population was literate.[28] The nation-alist movement therefore, considered the *Swabasha* movement, the switch over to the vernacular system, as one of its most urgent tasks. Accordingly, in 1961, all state-aided schools were nationalised. By 1970, the proportion of Tamils at university had fallen to under 16%.

However, one of the first acts of Mr. Jayewardene's UNP government in 1977, was the abolition of standardisation. In 1974, the Ministry of Education supplemented this system with district quotas. The aim was to favour the rural, hitherto underprivileged child. There is little doubt that ethnically, the Tamil-speaking people faired worse than their Sinhalese counterparts under this system. As a result of the standardisation scheme, the percentage of Tamil medium students entering courses in engineering fell from 40.8% in 1970/1 to 24.4% in 1973, and as a result of the quota system, fell from 24.4% in 1973 to 16.3% in 1974.[29]

It is necessary to examine to what extent the Thirteenth Amendment granted power to the Tamil-speaking people to manage their own educational institutions, in order to assess whether or not it satisfactorily meets the Tamil-speaking peoples' demands, and hence goes some way to solving the Tamil national question.

Appendix III to List I of the Ninth Schedule, accords to the provincial council in Section 2(a) and (b), the supervision of the management of all pre-schools and all state schools. In order to ensure standards, the Minister of Education retains the right to inspect and supervise the management of these schools. The appointment of the Principles of these schools,[30] is made by the Secretary to the Minister in charge of the subject of Education or the Public Service Commission, the criteria for which,[31] will be laid down by the Minister of Education.[32] The training of teachers and other educational personnel will come within the purview of the National Institute of Education. Provincial authorities will indicate their needs to the National Institute of Education.[33] The appointment of Provincial Boards of Education which will have advisory functions will be the responsibility of the Minister of Education. However, this will be done with the concurrence of the Chief Minister of the Provincial Authority.[34] Production and distribution of school textbooks can only be made after approval by the Ministry of Education.[35] The organisation and development of school libraries can only occur in accordance with guidelines by the National Library Services Board. It is clear that while an appearance is created that some control over secondary and primary education is transferred to the provincial council, effective control over all levels of education remained firmly with the central government.

The Reserved List, List II of the Thirteenth Amendment, includes Professional Occupations and Training. This includes: (a) institutions such as universities, declared by parliament to be institutions of national importance; (b) institutions for scientific or technical education, declared by parliament to be institutions of national importance; (c) provincial agencies and institutions for, (i) professional, vocational or technical training, including the training of police officers or (ii) the promotion of special studies or research; and (d) co-ordination and determination of standards in institutions for higher education or research and scientific and technology.

The Concurrent List, List III of the Thirteenth Amendment includes higher education. This includes: 4:1 the establishment and maintenance of new universities; 4:2 the establishment of degree awarding institutions under the Universities (Amendment) Act, No. 7 of 1985, and other institutions for tertiary, technical and post-school education and training.

Thus, the central government continues to have control over admission to institutions of higher education, including universities, and retains the power to determine the standards in these establishments. The Reserved List concerns Professional Occupations and Training, i.e., the medical, legal, and engineering sectors. Hence the central government remains in control of those sectors of higher education over which there has been so much contention. Those areas of higher education left for joint control, mentioned in the Concurrent List, are the Arts and Social Sciences.

The provincial council's authority over the subjects on the Provincial Council List itself, such as the maintenance of public order and the collection and disposition of state funds were similarly curtailed. The subject of "Police and Public Order" within the province lay outside the competence of the provincial council, ensuring that this subject was effectively retained in the hands of the President and the Inspector General of Police. The amount of moneys available for the provinces was determined by the President, in so far as central government grants were concerned, and by the Governor in so far as provincial taxes and levies were concerned. The custody of the Provincial Fund, the payment of money into the Fund and all other connected matters were regulated by the Provincial Governor. No moneys could be expended from the Provincial Fund except on the recommendation of the Governor.

To conclude, the provisions for land settlement and colonisation and higher education found in the Thirteenth Amendment, offer in reality only a nominal transference of power to the provincial councils. The preceding analysis of the provisions of the amending legislation with regards to land settlement and colonisation and higher education, which are of perennial importance to the Tamil-speaking people, is sufficient to show that what has been offered to the Tamil-speaking people consists of nothing more than a series of subterfuges. The Thirteenth Amendment failed to devolve power on the Tamil-speaking people, offering form without content. The Thirteenth Amendment, far from making concessions to the Tamil people's right to internal self-determination, establishes a framework within which the central government, the dominant Sinhalese majority, may more effectively govern the periphery, i.e., the Tamil minority.

The provincial council, as anticipated by the Indo-Sri Lanka Accord, is in reality no more than a glorified local government authority, with power to enact statutes in respect of a few innocuous matters, and these too, subject at all times to the overriding control of the central government. Moreover, the powers of the provincial councils may themselves be altered from time to time, by a simple majority of members present and voting in parliament. The above perusal of the provisions of the Thirteenth Amendment, which ostensibly devolve power to the provinces, highlights how the Sri Lankan government, in response to escalating international pressure, made what appears to be another ineffectual effort to evade a settlement of the real question.

Since 1987, no real transfer of powers to the provincial councils, as provided in the Thirteenth Amendment to the Constitution, has taken place. Administratively, President Premadasa used his powers to undercut the provincial councils in areas of activity in which the centre has concurrent powers with the provincial councils. The appointment of Divisional Secretaries under his direct and exclusive authority and the subjection of the *Pradeshiya Sabha*'s activity to them, was for instance, a direct violation of the provision that all local government should come exclusively under the purview of the provincial councils. Backed by the forces of Sinhala communalism, whilst simultaneously providing the LTTE with facilities to destroy the EPRLF-governed Northern and Eastern Provincial Council, President Premadasa successfuly disrupted the merged Northern and Eastern Provincial Council. The wholly subservient nature of the provincial administrations elsewhere in the country, proved to be beneficial to Premadasa in this exercise.

The referendum to enable the people of the Eastern Province to decide whether the Eastern Province should remain linked with the Northern Province as one administrative unit, and to be governed with the Northern Province, which was supposed to be held on or before the 31st December 1988, as provided in the Accord, has still not been held, and subsequent governments have consistently back-slided on the condition of merger of the two provinces, and have failed to offer a viable alternative solution. Six years after the signing of the Indo-Sri Lanka Peace Accord, the issue of the "temporarily" merged Northern and Eastern Provinces has become the sticking point. The majority Sinhalese community will not hear of a permanent merger of the two provinces, whilst the main plank of the Tamils' manifesto continues to be the demand for the merger of the North and East. To sum up, it is clear that the aspirations of the Tamil-speaking people can only be met if their demand for a substantial devolution of power ensuring meaningful autonomy to an unified politico-administrative entity, comprising of the permanently merged Northern and Eastern Provinces is recognised.

Notes

1 Greenwood. C., "Is there a right of humanitarian intervention?" in: The World Today, Vol.49, No.2, February, (1993), p.35.

2 Setalvad. M., in: "Union and state relations under the Indian Constitution", p.29, 1974, cited in: Buccheit. L.C., "Secession: The legitimacy of self-determination", (1978), p.98.

3 Ibid.

4 Prime Minister's statement on the Indo-Sri Lanka Agreement in Parliament on July 31, (1987).

5 Cited in: "An autopsy on autonomy: A provisional assessment of the Thirteenth Amendment to the Constitution of Sri Lanka", (1988), The Liberation Tigers of Tamil *Eelam*, p.6.

6 The extent to which the Amendment fell short of the Indian model is detailed in: Satyendra. N., "Sri Lanka's ethnic conflict and the Indo-Sri Lanka Agreement - Thirteenth Amendment to the Sri Lankan Constitution", (1988), London, Tamil Forum, p.6.

7 Peiris. G.L., "Provisional autonomy within a unitary constitutional framework: The Sri Lankan crisis", in: CILSA, 22, (1989), pp.165-189, p.170.

8 Article 2 of the Constitution of the Democratic Socialist Republic of Sri Lanka, (1978).

9 Among these are Article 3, which vests the source of sovereignty in the people. The sovereignty is inalienable, it includes the powers of government, fundamental rights and the franchise.

10 List 1 in Ninth Schedule.

11 Article 154 G(3).

12 Article 83 of the Constitution of Sri Lanka, (1978).

13 Ninth Schedule, cited in: Peiris. G.L., p.171.

14 Article 154C.

15 Article 4(b) of the Constitution of Sri Lanka, (1978).

16 Article 154B(2).

17 Article 154F(2).

18 Ibid.

19 Article 3(c).

20 Article 154P(4)(a).

21 Article 154P(4)(b).

22 Article 154G(2) and Article 154G(3).

23 Article 27(1).

24 Article 27(4).

25 Article 154F(4).

26 Article 154F(5).

27 For a detailed account of the discrimination practised in higher education against the Tamil-speaking people, see: C.R. de Silva, "Weightage in University admissions : Standardisation and district quotas in Sri Lanka", in: <u>Modern Ceylon Studies</u>, Vol.5, No.2, July, (1974), and C.R. de Silva, "The impact of nationalism on education: The school take-over and university admission crisis, 1970-1975", in: Roberts. M., (ed.) "Collective identities, nationalism and protests in modern Sri Lanka", (1989).

28 Walter Schwartz, "The Tamils of Sri Lanka", in: <u>The Minority Rights Group Report</u>, No.25, p.9.

29 Ibid.

30 Section 7, Appendix III to List I of the Ninth Schedule to the Thirteenth Amendment to the Constitution.

31 Section 6.

32 Section 8.

33 Section 9.

34 Section 23.

35 Section 24.

CHAPTER 13

Post-Accord: 1987-1993

It was made apparent in Chapter 12, that the Indo-Sri Lanka Accord failed to provide any meaningful devolution of power to the Tamil-speaking people in the Northern and Eastern Provinces. The LTTE, who by 1987 had come to be generally regard as "the sole legitimate representative of the Tamil people", rejected the basic provisions of the Thirteenth Amendment to the Constitution on the grounds that the Indo-Sri Lanka Accord rejected the fundamental political demands of the Tamil national struggle, demands which were proclaimed at the Thimpu talks in 1985, and which gave expression to the unanimous will of the Tamil people, viz: the demand for the recognition of the Tamil homeland, the demand for the recognition of the Tamil-speaking people as a nationality, and the demand for the recognition of the Tamil-speaking peoples' right to self-determination. The LTTE maintained that the Thirteenth Amendment and the Provincial Councils Act, which the Sri Lankan Parliament had passed to give effect to the Indo-Sri Lanka Accord, rather than addressing the specific grievances of the Tamil people, had instead proposed the creation of an Island-wide administrative structure rigidly controlled by the centre.[1]

This chapter will focus on some of the most recent attempts made by the Sri Lankan government to ostensibly solve the Tamil national question. The first section will analyse the convening of the All Party Conference (APC) on the 13th September 1989, established with a view to devising a formula based on a national consensus, to bring about political and economic stability, and primarily to restore law and order in the Island, and the attempt on the part of India and Sri Lanka to restore their somewhat strained post-Accord relations, in the proposed "Twenty Years Friendship Treaty", 1990, and the subsequent intensification of hostilities between the two countries after the LTTE emerged as the chief suspects of the assassination of the Indian Prime Minister, Rajiv Gandhi in May 1990. The second section will analyse the appointment of a Parliamentary Select Committee (PSC) in 1991, established to actively engage in discussing proposals made by its members with a view to evolving a national consensus solution to the Tamil national question, involving a devolution package to the Northern and Eastern Provinces.

However, before addressing the government's above attempts at a political solution to the Tamil national issue, this chapter shall begin by briefly analysing the events that occured immediately after the signing of the Accord, which finally culminated in the appointment of the All Party Conference (APC) in 1989. In other words, the arrival of, and the abrupt departure of the Indian Peace Keeping Force (IPKF), the collapse of peace talks and the resumption of civil war between the Sri Lankan forces and the LTTE.

Immediately after the signing of the Indo-Sri Lanka Accord, on 30th July 1987, the IPKF, comprising of more than 30,000 troops was deployed to the Northern and Eastern Provinces, to "guarantee and enforce the cessation of hostilities".[2] Only days later, in response to the LTTE's rejection of the basic provisions of the Thirteenth Amendment, the so-called IPKF launched a widespread and indiscriminate attack on the Tamil people with the object of bending them to the will of the Indian government who sought to persuade the Tamil militants to surrender their arms and enter the electoral process by participating in the elections for the temporarily merged Northern and Eastern Provincial Council. With the arrival of the IPKF, other Tamil rebel groups, such as the *Eelam* People's Revolutionary Liberation Front (EPRLF), and the Tamil *Eelam* Liberation Organisation (TELO) laid down their arms and proceeded to assist the IPKF in identifying Tamil Tigers for IPKF operations. Thus began a protracted and bloody war of infratricide between the rival Tamil groups.

In 1988, the temporarily merged Northern and Eastern Provincial Council elections took place. In early October, in the Northern Provincial Council elections, representatives of two Indian-backed Tamil rebel groups, the EPRLF and the *Eelam* National Democratic Liberation Front (ENDLF) were returned unopposed, securing seats in the Jaffna, Mullaitivu, Mannar and Vavuniya districts. On 19 November, in the Eastern Provincial Council elections, the ENDLF and the Sri Lanka Muslim Congress (SLMC) each secured seventeen seats, whilst the ruling United National Party (UNP) took only one seat in the Amparai electoral district. The LTTE and the Sinhalese People's Liberation Front, *Janata Vimukti Peramuna* (JVP) boycotted the elections.

The merged North-East Provincial Council set up with limited autonomy under the Accord did not have an easy existence. The Council had serious problems in getting the government to define and transfer devolved and concurrent functions. The central ministries were reluctant even to transfer devolved functions on which there was consensus, and there was a stranglehold on the allocation of resources to the Council for capital investment. The Council was eventually dissolved by a Presidential Decree in 1991.

By late December 1989, Sri Lanka's beleaguered Northern and Eastern Provinces were spectacularly poised between war and peace, as military units of the LTTE and the Indian-backed Tamil National Army (TNA) vied to fill the political vacuum left by the retreating IPKF. After a bloody war with the LTTE and enormous civilian suffering in the North and East of the Island, the IPKF was finally withdrawn in March 1990. In thirty-two months of bitter fighting with the LTTE, the Indians lost 1,200 men in an operation costing over $1 billion. Over 10,000 civilians died. Lured into Sri Lanka to sap Tamil separatism by the erstwhile President J. R. Jayewardene, the IPKF had quickly become bogged down in a politico-military quagmire that has since elicited comparisons with America's humiliation in Vietnam. All illusions that India had previously entertained of being the South Asian "super-power" were quashed:

"Post mortems on the Indian military misadventure in northern Sri Lanka have veered towards the polite, pointing to the futility of regional superpowers trying to impose a settlement from the outside. The truth is much simpler. The Indians were out-fought and out-thought while trapped in the grand illusion of their post-colonial status".[3]

At its height, 100,000 Indian troops with sophisticated air and artillery support were ranged against a small but dedicated guerilla army, hostile terrain and an increasingly hostile population. President Premadasa's UNP government, elected into office in December, 1989, and vehemently opposed to India's intervention, supplied arms and ammunition to the LTTE and also allowed the import of highly sophisticated electronic and communication equipment when the IPKF was engaged in disarming the LTTE.[4]

A brief but bloody chapter in Sri Lanka's history was finally closed on 25 March 1990, when the last 2,000 soldiers of the IPKF set sail from Trincomalee, following President Premadasa's unilateral deadline for withdrawal. By late January 1990, the LTTE were able to take control of the town of Jaffna. In early March 1990, the leaders of the Indian-backed EPRLF, who were running the North-East Provincial Council, were air-lifted to India, and from mid-March the Tiger takeover of the administration of the Northern and Eastern Provinces was virtually complete. The

LTTE established a temporary skeleton civil administration. Hours after the Indian exodus, President Premadasa declared President's Rule in the Northern and Eastern Provinces.

Subsequent negotiations over the following year between the Sri Lankan government and the LTTE, failed to produce any lasting results. The LTTE sought speedy dissolution of the Northern and Eastern Provincial Council, repeal of the Sixth Amendment to the Constitution outlawing separatism, and fresh provincial council elections to be held under international observation. The government in return, required that the Tigers disarm as a prerequisite to admitting them to participate in the democratic process, and permitting them to contest in fresh elections to the Northern and Eastern Provincial Council. The result was a stalemate.

The fragile peace that had existed between the Sri Lankan government and the Tamil Tigers, based largely on their mutual distrust for, and distaste in the presence of the IPKF in Sri Lanka, disintegrated in early June 1990, when growing tension between the Sri Lankan security forces and the LTTE flared into full-scale warfare. As the Sri Lankan air force began to indiscriminately bomb the Northern and Eastern Provinces, peace talks became firmly part of the distant past. The armed conflict between the government forces and the LTTE, which resumed in June 1990, has continued unabated ever since. The LTTE continues to hold effective territorial control of the Northern peninsula, whilst government forces have regained control of small coastal areas, including some of the offshore islands. Whilst fighting continues in the contested areas bordering the so-called Tamil homelands, the government forces have sporadically regained control of some of the main towns in the Eastern Province, leaving the LTTE in control of the surrounding areas of the countryside.

(i) The All Party Conference (APC), 1989

After the signing of the Accord and the arrival of the IPKF in Sri Lanka, the Sinhalese rebel movement, led by the JVP, unleashed a wave of political violence that threatened the very basis of democracy and the institutions of government. In the midst of the "political instability, social anarchy, mass murders and the reign of terror, the virtual collapse of the law and order machinery and the deteriorating economic situation",[5] the various political parties who were ostensibly committed to peace and stability, convened the All Party Conference (APC), with a view to devising a formula based on national consensus, to bring about political and economic stability, and to restore law and order in the Island.

Although the APC gave an opportunity to most of the political parties of the country to examine the major issues of the Island's political crisis, it failed to establish a political consensus in respect of the fundamental issues facing the country.

"Above all, it also demonstrated the competitive character of the party system, in the context of the multiplicity of political parties based on ideologies and ethnic loyalties. This aspect of the Sri Lankan system, as demonstrated in the mechanism of the All Party Conference, militates against the development of consensus politics in the country."6

In the event, the APC was dubbed by Mrs Sirimavo Bandaranaike, leader of the opposition SLFP, as an "expensive gimmick", which "staged the grand political fiasco of the decade."7

However, it is useful to briefly analyse the events and the final demise of the APC, for it was initiated by the Sri Lankan government, in part, to accommodate the LTTE during their "honeymoon" period in 1989-1990. President Premadasa had by this time, made considerable progress in respect of his dialogue with the LTTE to bring about peace and order in the Northern and Eastern Provinces. It is also useful to analyse the proposals made by the various political parties at the "political party consultation process" initiated by the President, in order to understand the different positions adopted by the political parties, in particular, regarding the continuance of the executive presidential system of government, and by implication, the Tamil national question. The failure of the APC to overcome ideological and ethnic loyalties and to achieve national reconciliation, provided a precedent and a foretaste for the Parliamentary Select Committee (PSC) debacle that was to take place only two years later.

The All Party Conference which was convened on the 13th September 1989, included 69 delegates from twenty-one political parties. Amongst the political parties which participated in the APC, were several Tamil political parties, including amongst others, the TELO, the TULF, and the EPRLF, the Democratic People's Liberation Front (DPLF), the Eelavar Democratic Front (EDF), and the CWC, and two Muslim political parties, the SLMC and the Sri Lankan Muslim Party. President Premadasa, making his opening address at the Conference, stated that the political parties that were represented at the Conference, had placed as their first priority, the cessation of violence and the restoration of peace and normalcy in the country. He stated that when he assumed office in January 1989, he made a declaration to the effect that "consultation, compromise and consensus" would be the articles of faith in the conduct of state affairs under his lead-

ership. The APC, he stated, epitomised these principles, which constituted the basis of co-operation to achieve national consensus and national
reconciliation.

On the 4th October 1989, the polit-bureau of the JVP, participating in
the process of consultations with President Premadasa and the government delegation, issued a dramatic statement implying that the APC only
helped "Indian imperialism",[8] further stating that they were fighting and
laying down their lives for the realisation of the following:

1. Abrogation of the Indo-Lanka Peace Accord;
2. abolition of the provincial council system;
3. freeing the country from the autocracy of the Northern and
   Eastern Provinces;
4. driving away the invading Indian armies;
5. solving the national problem democratically without foreign
   interference; and
6. disbanding of the illegal fascist forces.[9]

The JVP's intransigence on the issues facing the current political situation in the country and its refusal to enter into the democratic process,
enabled the government to defeat the call made by the political parties in
the joint opposition, comprising the SLFP, the Mahajana Eksath
Peramuna (MEP), the Lanka Sama Samaja Party (LSSP), the Nava Sama
Samaja Party (NSSP), SLMC and EPRLF, for the establishment of a provisional government and the dismantling of the executive presidency system. The opposition formulated a number of specific proposals pertaining
to the political crisis and addressed themselves to the specific issue of the
failure of the presidential system of government in Sri Lanka, demanding
its abolition and its replacement with a provisional government consisting
of political parties represented in parliament. The opposition maintained
that the prime ministerial form of parliamentary government, with
accountability to an elected parliament, needed to be brought into existence through constitutional reforms, and that steps needed to be taken to
hold free and fair parliamentary elections so that the political forces now
on the extra-parliamentary road could be given an opportunity to enter
parliament. In other words, the opposition made a call for the restoration
of democracy in Sri Lanka. Instead, however, the UNP, at the meeting of
its Working Committee held on 2nd October, 1989, agreed to a dissolution of parliament and the formation of a caretaker government to initiate
a process of national reconciliation. The major parties in the joint opposition viewed this move with suspicion, regarding it as an attempt to form a
national government while retaining the executive presidential system.

The proposals of the joint opposition, including the demand for the formation of a provisional government, as opposed to a national government, became the major issues before the APC, and were examined by all the main political parties represented at the Conference.

The first major attack on the proposals of the joint opposition came from parties close to the Premadasa government. Ranil Wickremasinghe, a front rank Minister in the government, argued that fundamental constitutional changes would be necessary for the implementation of the proposals of the joint opposition. He argued that the abolition of the executive presidency, would require a referendum, because it affected Article 3 of the 1978 Constitution, which includes the franchise in the sovereignty of Sri Lanka. However, President Premadasa agreed to consider holding a referendum on the continuance of the presidential system of government. The various positions of the political parties in respect of this matter were polarised, one group of parties supported the abolition of the presidency whilst the other demanded its retention. It would be relevant at this stage, to examine some of the different positions adopted by the political parties at the APC.

The CWC, led by Minister S. Thondaman, who has been actively associated with the UNP government since 1977, adopted a hostile attitude to the main proposals advocated by the joint opposition and it rejected the charge that the executive presidential system was responsible for the current political crisis in the country. The CWC pointed out that the powers enjoyed by the executive president were not very different from what prime ministers had enjoyed in the past, and that under the 1972 Constitution which was based on the Westminster model, there was a similar concentration of power in the hands of the prime minister. The CWC suggested that the proportional system of representation introduced under the 1978 Constitution, afforded opportunities to the opposition to play an important role in the affairs of the country. According to the CWC, the failure to recognise the multi-ethnic, multi-linguistic, multi-religious and multi-cultural aspects of the Sri Lankan society, was the root cause of the cult of violence which had become a part of the political culture of Sri Lankan society. It argued therefore, that the multi-ethnic nature of the country should be accepted as a fundamental reality and that all policies and programmes should be framed on the basis of this reality. The CWC argued for the retention of the executive presidency, on the grounds that it gave an opportunity to all ethnic, religious, linguistic and other groups to have a say in the election of the president. It also advocated the continuation of the proportional system of representation as the method of representation, with an elimination of some of its shortcomings.

The TULF maintained that the authoritarian and anti-democratic trends in the country could be reversed by transforming the present presidential system to a parliamentary system. The TULF insisted that "a truly autochthonous constitution be evolved consistent with the pluralistic character of the country consisting of distinct minorities."10

The All Ceylon Tamil Congress, led by G. G. Ponnambalam jr., made no reference to constitutional changes, though it did argue for the participation of the JVP in the deliberations of the Conference.

Three other main Tamil militant groups, the DPLF, the TELO, and the Eelavar Democratic Front (EDF), made representations before the APC, refering to a wide variety of issues affecting the Tamil community. The EDF advocated a political solution to the national question on the basis of the principles adopted in Thimpu, between the government of Sri Lanka and the Tamil groups in 1985, including the following:

1. The Tamil-speaking people of Sri Lanka constitute a distinct nationality;
2. recognition of the traditional homeland of the Tamil-speaking people;
3. recognition of the right of self-determination; and
4. the right to establish appropriate organs of state.11

The Democratic Peoples Liberation Organisation (DPLF), advocated fundamental changes to the 1978 Constitution, with a view to bringing about a transformation of the constitutional order imposed by the Constitution. The DPLF advocated a constitution that could truly command a bi-partisan consensus, using the Constitution of the U.S.A. as a model.

The Sri Lanka Progressive Front (SLPF), which was hastily formed by S. D. Bandaranaike during the presidential election of 1989, presented a set of proposals, some of which fell in line with the agitational campaign of the JVP and its clandestine military wing, the Deshapremi Janata Viyaparaya (DJV). The SLPF submitted a seven point formula to the APC which included:

1. Disbanding of all unofficial armed groups and the declaration of cease-fire;
2. abrogation of the Indo-Sri Lanka Accord together with the provincial councils system;
3. removal of the Emergency and all other forms of repressive legislation;

4. release of all political prisoners;

5. opening of all universities and schools in the country;

6. allowing the younger generation to mobilise the masses, i.e., the militant Sinhalese youths who formed the base of the JVP; and the

7. holding of a fair and free general election and presidential election under a caretaker regime.[12]

A Monitoring Committee appointed to monitor the "cease-fire", was to undertake the implementation of items no.1 to 6, and it was on the basis of this formula, that the JVP, the DJV and the LTTE were to participate at general and presidential elections. The caretaker regime was to comprise of seven representatives from the JVP, the DJV and the LTTE.

The process of consultation at the APC, conducted through a series of consultative meetings, from 18th September to 6th October 1989, was given wide publicity on an unprecedented scale, primarily on national television, in order to "enable the entire country to participate in this national search for consensus".[13] During Premadasa's address at the Conference, he identified the issues on which there was total unanimity, these included: (a) restoration of peace and normalcy, (b) prevention of violence, and (c) bringing into the mainstream of politics those forces which are today outside the democratic process.[14] He also noted that there was a consensus achieved in regard to the means to be adopted to restore peace and normalcy, including: (a) surrender of arms, (b) the disbanding of illegal para-military forces, (c) lifting the state of Emergency, (d) suspension of the Prevention of Terrorism Act (P.T.A.), (e) releasing of detainees and the declaration of a general amnesty, and (f) redressing of legitimate grievances perceived by various groups. In addition to these fundamental issues affecting the stability of the political system, there was an overall concern on general matters such as: (a) ensuring of equal rights for all peoples, (b) reducing of socio-economic disparities, and (c) restructuring of the political, economic and administrative systems.

Clearly, the most sensitive issue facing the Conference was the demand for the abolition of the executive presidency. The government, however, managed to show that there was no real consensus on this issue, and therefore avoided a discussion of the presidential system, which could have led to a popular demand for its abolition. Although there was consensus on the need for an interim government to restore peace and normalcy, there was a divergence of opinion on the type of interim government.

The soft-pedalling attitude of the government to the major issues that were placed before the Conference, showed that it was attempting to buy time. One view was that the government, through its military offensive against the militants of the JVP-DJV, could put a stop to violence and thereby stabilise itself in power. Another argument was that peace moves through the forum of the APC were necessary before the government negotiated with the aid-giving agencies, whose support was necessary to tide over the numerous economic difficulties of the government. This criticism was not entirely unfounded. For instance, the International Committee of the Red Cross (ICRC), which was invited at the instigation of the political parties who continued to raise the issue of the violations of human rights, especially those committed under Emergency Regulations, to provide "their traditional humanitarian services in Sri Lanka", was invited primarily to placate international opinion on the issue of Sri Lanka's violations of human rights.

Apart from the arrival of a team from the ICRC to visit Sri Lanka, President Premadasa recognised what he considered to be two other "very substantial achievements of the All Party Conference". The first was the declaration of the cease-fire, under the auspices of a Ceasefire Monitoring Committee. On the whole however, the cease-fire was a failure, because even the call to surrender received no response from many of the militant groups. The second achievement was the appointment of a commission to probe the youth unrest in the country. The commission was set up on 19th October, 1989 under the Commission of Inquiry Act, with powers to investigate into disquiet, unrest, and social discontentment among the youth and to investigate into factors that had contributed to the growth of youth violence in the Island. In the event however, the main issues were not pressed at the APC, due primarily to the partisan attitude adopted by the government, and several political parties, including the SLFP which withdrew from the consultations. The withdrawal of several of the political parties, dissatisfied with the outcome of the APC, signalled the speedy demise of the APC, leaving national and international political observers with the impression that the APC had been nothing more than a "grand fiasco".

It was made apparent during the APC, that the JVP, the Sinhalese rebel movement, was keen not only to abrogate the Indo-Sri Lanka Accord, and to abolish the provincial councils system, but also to free Sri Lanka of the "invading Indian armies". Certainly, relations between India and Sri Lanka had been severely strained during the intervention of the IPKF in the Island, albeit with the approbation of the erstwhile President Jayewardene. However, with the assumption of the presidential office by Premadasa in December, 1989, relations actually worsened, when

President Premadasa issued a "unilateral deadline" and ordered the IPKF to withdraw. This was obviously done in part, to appease the JVP and other Sinhalese contingents who shared the JVP's desires, and to give Premadasa the electoral support he required. However, the IPKF were withdrawn amongst strong feelings on the part of the Indian government of humiliation and regret, for what had become one of its greatest foreign policy blunders. Similarly, the former reliance that the Tamil-speaking population and the LTTE had had on India, seemed to have been curtailed forever. In the post-Accord climate therefore, it seemed that India wanted nothing more to do with the ethnic struggle in Sri Lanka.

However, thirty-two months after the Indo-Sri Lanka Accord was signed, in the context of the changed political scenario in both countries, relations between India and Sri Lanka were reviewed. The result was the proposed "Twenty Years Friendship Treaty", 1990. The proposed Treaty was expected to assist the process of political reconciliation in the violence prone Island and assign a new role for India to play in Sri Lanka's ethnic conflict. However, it was clear that the Indian government's primary concern was to secure India's security and regional interests, and the proposed Treaty appeared to be nothing more than an appendage to the Indo-Sri Lanka Accord, intended to regain the trust and confidence from Sri Lanka, which had been damaged during the IPKF intervention.

The Indo-Sri Lanka Accord, expressly stated India's concern with regard to the Jayewardene government's concessions to the USA. In an exchange of letters annexed to the Accord, Sri Lanka accepted the obligation not to enter into particular types of transactions or relationships with other states without the concurrence of the Indian government. In the following excerpt from the text of Prime Minister Rajiv Gandhi's letter of July 22 1987, to President Jayewardene, it is evident that the Accord gave India a firm hand in Sri Lanka's affairs:

"Conscious of the friendship between our two countries stretching over two millennia and more and recognising the importance of nurturing this traditional friendship, it is imperative that both Sri Lanka and India reaffirm the decision not to allow our respective territories to be used for activities prejudicial to each other's unity, territorial integrity and security.

2. In this spirit, you had, during the course of our discussions, agreed to meet some of India's concerns as follows:

(i) Your Excellency and myself will reach an early understanding about the relevance and employment of foreign military and intelligence personnel with a view to ensuring that such presences will not prejudice

Indo-Sri Lankan relations.

(ii) Trincomalee or any other ports in Sri Lanka will not be made available for military use by any country in a manner prejudicial to India's interests.

(iii) The work of restoring and operating the Trincomalee oil tank farm will be undertaken as a joint venture between India and Sri Lanka.

(iv) Sri Lanka's agreements with foreign broadcasting organisations will be reviewed to ensure that any facilities set up by them in Sri Lanka are used solely as public broadcasting facilities and not for any military or intelligence purposes.

4. India and Sri Lanka have agreed to set up a joint consultative mechanism to continuously review matters of common concern in the light of the objectives stated in para. 1 and specifically to monitor the implementation of other matters contained in this letter".

The basic difference between the Accord and the proposed Friendship Treaty, was that while through the Accord, India tried to impose its "big brother" attitude on its small neighbour, the Friendship Treaty encouraged Sri Lanka to become India's semi-client.

"The core expectation from the Indian diplomatic circles will be that the Sri Lankan territory will not be made available for military use by any third country in a manner prejudicial to the security interest of India".[15]

Whilst the Friendship Treaty appears to be a permanent and durable solution to re-establish the traditional relations between India and Sri Lanka, India continues to refuse to recognise the political reality of Tamil nationalism, and remains unwilling to lend its powerful support to secure a constitutional structure in Sri Lanka which recognises the political forces of Tamil nationalism and Tamil interests. Moreover, it remains unwilling to let go of the status of "regional superpower", which it gained at the time of Bangladesh's liberation in 1971, and which it continues to covet. The question that remains to be asked, is whether India's current non-interventionist attitude justifies the state terrorism and human rights violations that are continually being perpetrated by the racially biased Sri Lankan government? Clearly, the Indian government's reaction towards such political developments should be reaffirmed and openly stated, for it is possible that a silent or non-committed approach, will in due course of time undermine the strength of Indian diplomacy and its style of functioning.

By 1991, the relations between India and Sri Lanka had once again been tested. In this year, the LTTE emerged as the chief suspects of the assassination of the Indian Prime Minister, Rajiv Gandhi.[16] Almost a year after the assassination, the Indian government proscribed the LTTE in May, 1992. Announcing the ban in parliament on 14 May, Indian Home Minister, S. Chavan accused the LTTE of conspiring with collaborators for the separation of Tamil Nadu, and posing a threat to the sovereignty and territorial integrity of India. Following the assassination of Rajiv Gandhi, all support that had previously been felt in the Indian state of Tamil Nadu, for fellow Sri Lankan Tamils, was virtually eroded. Sympathy was further removed with the electoral defeat of the Dravida Munnetra Kazhagham (DMK) party in Tamil Nadu, and the defeat of its Chief Minister, D. Karunanidhi, who had been an active supporter of the separatist Eelam movement in Sri Lanka.

The ban on the LTTE was imposed under the Unlawful Activities (Prevention) Act, becoming effective once it is approved by a tribunal and then remaining in force for just two years. The fact that the ban was not issued under the harsh Terrorism and Disruptive Activities (Prevention) Act, seemed indicative of India's continued "soft approach" towards the LTTE. President Premadasa's refusal to ban the LTTE despite pressure from India, was proof that he also opted for a mild stance, planning to keep his options open for future talks with the LTTE. Similarly, President Premadasa side-stepped all questions relating to the extradition of the LTTE supremo, V. Prabhakaran, to India, for complicity in the assassination.

However, India's ban on the LTTE did inaugurate an intensified campaign on a global scale against the LTTE The erosion of the international standing of the LTTE as a legitimate national liberation struggle, was clearly evidenced when in 1993, the Sri Lankan government was able to deny that there was an "ethnic problem" in Sri Lanka, maintaining instead that there was only a "terrorist" problem. Certainly, the role of India in future peace negotiations seems doubtful at present. It seems that India clearly wishes to avoid future protracted confrontations with the LTTE. Likewise, the LTTE described the ban as a political trick designed to prevent the Sri Lankan government from negotiating with them, thus sending clear signals to India to keep out of Sri Lanka's affairs.

(ii) The Parliamentary Select Committee (PSC), 1991

As a bloody climax to the June 1990 War appeared increasingly inevitable, and following the collapse of the APC, the government took the decision to initiate yet another process in the hope of attaining national reconciliation. Accordingly, a motion was moved in parliament by a

Mr. Mangala Moonesinghe of the opposition SLFP, clearly in consultation with the government, to set up a forty three-member Parliamentary Select Committee (PSC), which was to actively engage in discussing proposals made by its members with a view to evolving a national consensus solution to the conflict in the Island, involving the devolution of power to the North and East. This motion was unanimously adopted by parliament on 9th August, 1991 and the PSC commenced its sittings on 20th November, 1991.

It was rumoured that President Premadasa's choice of Mr. Mangala Moonesinghe, as the Chairman of the PSC, was primarily to "shut the mouth of the opposition", which had ostensibly been clamouring for meaningful action to solve the ethnic crisis.[17] It is apparent that one outcome of the APC deliberations, was the opposition's demand for the establishment of a joint select committee to look into the Tamil national question. The appointment of Mr. Mangala Moonesinghe was inevitable, given the support that he enjoyed from the members of the ruling UNP at the instance of President Premadasa himself. At the annual South Asian Association for Regional Cooperation (SAARC) discussions in New Delhi, on 1st October 1992, President Premadasa stated that in the light of the opposition that was invoked in response to the Indo-Sri Lanka Accord and because many felt that they had not been adequately consulted, he clearly did not want to do anything that would enable the opposition or any other political elements, to sabotage new measures being worked out to restore ethnic peace in the Island.[18]

The Select Committee was appointed to realise the following objectives:

(a) to arrive at a political solution to the question involving the devolution of power to the Northern and Eastern Provinces;

(b) to prevent -

(1) the disintegration of the nation;

(2) the killings of innocent civilians, members of the armed forces and youths fighting for a cause;

(3) the increased militarisation of the culture of violence in our country; and

(4) to achieve peace and political stability and utilise the reduced defence expenditure for rapid economic growth and national development.[19]

The Tamil political parties maintained that it was clear from its inception, that the terms of reference of the PSC, as well as its composition, was biased against Tamil interests. For instance, the earlier formation of the terms of reference which referred to the need for a political solution to the "National Question" was amended by Mr. Mangala Moonesinghe to read, "to arrive at a political solution to the question involving the devolution of power to the Northern and Eastern Provinces." The Tamil political parties interpreted this amendment as a clear bias in favour of de-linking the presently merged Northern and Eastern Province.

Similarly, the composition of the PSC, which had a total membership of forty-five, was weighted decisively in favour of the Sinhala parties, with the ruling UNP having an absolute majority. As a result, the PSC, dominated by Sinhala parties, lacked sensitivity towards the legitimate grievances and aspirations of the Tamil-speaking people. This was clearly demonstrated by the low turn-out of members at the sittings of the PSC, often resulting in the chairman having to send out the personnel in his secretariat to round-up sufficient members to ensure the quorum of fourteen.

In the event, the PSC negotiations included amongst others; the ruling UNP, and the opposition SLFP, the SLMC, the CWC, five Tamil Parliamentary parties, including TULF, EPRLF, EROS, TELO, ENDLF, and two Tamil parties not represented in parliament, the All Ceylon Tamil Congress (ACTC), and the Peoples Liberation Organisation of Tamil Eelam (PLOTE).

Thus despite the above limitations, seven Tamil parties who had prior to the Indo-Sri Lanka Accord, been engaged in the armed struggle for a separate nation-state, laid down their arms, entered the democratic mainstream and decided to extend their full co-operation to the PSC, on the basis that a political system could be evolved within a united Sri Lanka that would ensure the identity, security and autonomy for the Tamil-speaking people. Indeed, it was seen by many as the last chance for a political solution to the ethnic question:

"We feel that the Select Committee under your Chairmanship is the most important Forum instituted to date to evolve a consensus on the Tamil Question...We are also mindful of the fact that your Committee is the last chance that has been afforded to this country to save it from what may be utter chaos."[20]

Accordingly, the Tamil parties proceeded to place their proposals individually before the PSC and also sent their respective delegates to the PSC in response to the invitation by the chairman to make their oral submissions.

In a Joint Memorandum of 22nd April 1992, seven Tamil political parties, in addition to reiterating their expectations of the PSC, stressed the need for a unified politico-administrative entity for the permanently merged Northern-Eastern Province as a basic prerequisite for a broadly acceptable solution. It stated:

"We are of the considered view that, as far as the Tamil people are concerned, any meaningful attempt at solving the Tamil Question can only be on the basis of an unified politico-administrative entity for the permanently merged Northern and Eastern Province. Our opposition to a de-merger stems from politico-administrative, socio-economic and security criteria.

What the Tamil people and the polity that represents them seek, is a political system that guarantee their linguistic and cultural identities and security, in addition to providing the base for socio-economic progress. This could be achieved either through secession or by evolving a political system within a united Sri Lanka that addresses the Tamil Question. We now seek the latter. The precondition, however, is a permanent merger of the Northern and Eastern Provinces and substantial devolution of power to that unified politico-administrative unit. In order to ensure a permanently merged unit of the two provinces, we are mindful of the fact that the position of the Muslims and the Sinhalese must be considered.

In conclusion, we earnestly urge that your Committee adopt our proposal for a permanent merger and proceed immediately to the opening of negotiations on a substantial devolution package that shall ensure regional autonomy for the unified politico-administrative unit of the North-East region.

In the meantime, we urge on the Select Committee to impress on the Sri Lankan Government to freeze forthwith all ongoing colonisation in the North-East region."[21]

President Premadasa had said on several occasions, that the government would accept the decision of the Select Committee. However, it became abundantly clear that his intention was never to allow the Committee to arrive at a proper and acceptable solution. Whilst the Tamil parties were engaged in placing their proposals before the PSC, neither President Premadasa's ruling UNP, nor the main opposition party, the SLFP, led by former Prime Minister Sirimavo Bandaranaike, submitted a proposal to the PSC. In true "cat and mouse" style, each party waited to see what the other party would propose, before shooting its proposals down and presenting its own proposal. Indeed, attempts to out-do one another with Sinhalese chauvinism, has been the standard practice of the two main Sinhala parties in Sri Lanka since 1956. Despite this, the other political parties at the negotiating table continued to place their individual proposals before the Select Committee. Each one in turn was accordingly rejected.

A year after the inauguration of the PSC, and after a year of protracted deliberations, the credibility of this government peace ploy had all but dissolved. On 14 December 1992, six Tamil parties, (excluding the TELO), said in a public statement that the Parliamentary Select Committee had denied the Tamil people their legitimate aspirations and proclaimed that the decisions of the Select Committee on the 11 December, were held by a majority vote and not by a Tamil-Sinhala consensus, and were a "gross betrayal of faith", making the deliberations an "utter farce".[22] At the December meeting, a discussion of the Tamil parties' "Four-Point formula" was refused, and the PSC instead endorsed the "Srinivasan proposals", promoting a watered-down federalism on the Indian model and the demerger of the temporarily merged Northern and Eastern Provinces.

It is important to make an assessment of the PSC, in order to determine its scope and limitations. An attempt is made here to shed some light on what transpired in the PSC. It is apparent that the primary obstacle to the resolution of the Tamil national question in the past has been the lack of political will of the major Sinhala parties, the UNP and the SLFP. This study reveals that the Select Committee proceeding was yet another example of this lack of political will.

After elaborating on their proposals and formulating what is now commonly known as the "Four Point formula", the seven Tamil political parties, following a meeting with the President and leading members of the ruling UNP, met the main opposition parties, the SLFP, the Democratic United National Front (DUNF), the Communist Party (CP), the LSSP, and the NSSP, in an attempt to forge a Tamil-Sinhala consensus on the basis of the Four Point Formula. Except for the NSSP, all the other political parties were either non-committal or non-supportive of the proposal. The Four Point Formula was endorsed by the CWC, headed by Mr. Thondaman, and formally placed before the Parliamentary Select Committee on 17 June 1992. It proposed:

(1) Permanently merged North-Eastern Province shall be the unit of devolution.

(2) Substantial devolution of power ensuring meaningful autonomy to the unified unit.

(3) Institutional arrangement within the larger framework of the unbifurcated North-Eastern Province for the Muslim community ensuring its cultural identity and security.

(4) Sinhalese will enjoy all the rights that other minorities have in the

rest of the country.[23]

On the same day, the Chairman of the PSC, Mr. Mangala Moonesinghe circulated what was termed a "Concept Paper", which provided for two district councils for the Northern and Eastern Provinces, respectively. Further, it suggested an "Apex Assembly", whose powers and structure were left ambiguous and vague. The seven Tamil parties and the CWC responded separately to the Concept Paper expressing dissatisfaction at the proposals contained.

The joint response of the seven Tamil political parties to the Concept Paper, stated that its proposal, "completely disregards the proposals of the various Tamil Political Parties that were placed individually and collectively before the Select Committee".[24] Moreover, it stated:

"The Concept Paper's proposals have totally disregarded the Tamil consensus providing for a Unified Politico-Administrative entity for a permanently merged North-Eastern Province as the basis for a political solution to the national question."[25]

In the response of the CWC to the Concept Paper presented to the PSC, S. Thondaman, President of the CWC, stated: "The Concept Paper does not so much as seek even to understand the problems much less to evolve strategies for resolving them." Thondaman reminded the Committee that when the Tamils speak of an unbifurcated North-East Province, they were not proposing anything new. Indeed, the Bandaranaike-Chelvanayakam Pact of 1957 conceded the North-East Province as a single unit. Similarly, under the Senanayake-Chelvanayakam Pact, 1965, land in these two Provinces was earmarked for distribution permanently among the Tamil-speaking people of the Northern and Eastern Provinces. Moreover, the Reasonable Use of Tamil Act, of 1958, evolved a special arrangement for the North-East Province in respect of language. Furthermore, the Indo-Sri Lanka Accord of 1987, recognised the North-East Province as the traditional homeland of the Tamil-speaking people and the unit of devolution. Thondaman maintained that to advance a two council formula to the Tamils thirty years after a one council solution was offered "betrays a heartrending capacity to resolve a political tragedy of vast magnitude." He concluded: "It is needless to say that to bifurcate the North-East Province is to bifurcate the country."[26]

Following this, the Chairman of the PSC and his advisory panel, held informal discussions with the TULF on 7th October 1992 on ways and means of narrowing the differences in relation to the unit of devolution. It appeared at these discussions, that the chairman was agreeable to substantial devolution to the merged North-Eastern region, while providing some institutional arrangements to safeguard the interests of the minority Sinhalese and Muslim communities in this region. Similar assurances were given by the Chairman in separate discussions to the EPRLF and PLOTE.

However, these assurances proved to be no more than lip service, when at the PSC meeting on October 14th 1992, the Chairman of the Select Committee, circulated what was called an "Option Paper". The Option Paper was an elaboration of the earlier Concept Paper and failed to reflect the inputs that the EPRLF, TULF and some other Tamil parties had suggested in the earlier informal discussions with the Chairman and his advisory panel. The Concept Paper called for:

(1) Two separate provincial councils for the Northern and Eastern Provinces;

(2) a regional council to cover both provinces and to exercise solely the concurrent powers now being shared by the centre and the Provinces, and;

(3) a second chamber which would enable the minority ethnic groups to share power at the centre.

The Tamil parties and the CWC were unanimously of the view that these proposals did not meet the Four Point Formula placed by the seven parties and the CWC before the PSC, and were accordingly forced to reject the paper on the grounds that it did not constitute a basis for negotiations, asserting that whilst they were willing to negotiate on all proposals made by the Select Committee, the Northern and Eastern Provinces must remain permanently merged.

On November 14, 1992, a Tamil member of parliament for the Jaffna district, Krishnapillai Srinivasan, who had earlier been expelled from the ENDLF, caused a furore in the Parliamentary Select Committee by submitting a ten-point proposal. It was suggested that in the circumstances, the government needed someone within the Tamil community, to make proposals for the demerger of the North-Eastern Province, hence the sudden emergence of K. Srinivasan. As a former member of PLOTE and ENDLF, there was suspicion amongst the Tamil parties, that Srinivasan had become involved in a plot by the Sri Lankan government to break the unity of the Tamil parties.[27]

The proposal sought to "compensate" the de-linking of the presently merged North-Eastern Province by replacing the present unitary constitution with a federal one, based on the Indian model. The proposals read as follows:

(1) The unitary nature of the Sri Lankan Constitution be converted into a federal one.

Provided however that subject to the undertaking by the parties to the Select Committee that they shall not canvas and/or participate, the question whether Sri Lanka should have a federal constitution or not may be put to the determination of the people of Sri Lanka through the democratic mechanism of a referendum.

(2) The Northern and the Eastern Provinces shall each be treated as a distinct unit of devolution.

(3) That the maximum powers as agreed upon be devolved to each such unit.

(4) That a Boundary Commission be appointed to demarcate ethnic orientated grass root institutions of power with maximum authority.

(5) Within the area of jurisdiction of each grass root institution, as far as possible people of the same ethnic community together with their respective residential, agricultural and pastoral land holdings be brought.

(6) Special institutional arrangements be made for the security of the Muslims of each unit.

(7) A Land Commission to distribute unalienated state lands within each unit among the different communities living in each district of the said unit; in keeping with its demographic proportion.

(8) The ethnic balance of each unit should be maintained as at the year 1971 without anyway displacing any Sinhalese settlement that has already taken place.

(9) In working out the land distribution, it must be ensured that wherever communities had already been displaced in the past, they be restored to possession of their original land holdings.

(10) Subject to the aforegoing principles of land distribution in all districts in each of the said unit of devolution, and with particular reference to Amparai district, the remaining land area of the former Amparai electorate be embraced within the boundaries of the Moneragala district.[28]

Even before these proposals could be discussed at the PSC, Mr. Hameed convened a meeting of all Muslim members of parliament on the 21st November 1992, to obtain an endorsement of the "Srinivasan Proposals". This meeting assumed significance, not only because it was clearly orchestrated to give legitimacy to the Srinivasan Proposals, but it simultaneously undermined the negotiations that the TULF were then holding with the SLMC, regarding the third point of the Four Point Formula, namely, the "Institutional arrangement within the larger framework of the unbifurcated North-Eastern Province for the Muslim community ensuring its cultural identity and security".

At the meeting on the 14th November 1992, Mr. Mangala Moonesinghe, announced that SLFP leader Mrs Bandaranaike, had verbally extended her support for the Srinivasan Proposals. At which point, Justice Minister, Mr. Hameed, intervened and assured that the ruling UNP would also back the proposal. In the face of opposition by former UNP ministers, Lalith Athulathmudali and Gamini Dissanayake, who had formed their own DUNF party, President Premadasa, by rejecting the merger, assured that he would retain substantial support from his Sinhala strongholds, for his UNP.

At this turn of events, the representatives of the TULF and the EPRLF in the PSC, inquired if this was the official view of the UNP and the SLFP The chairman then requested all parties to place their official position on the Srinivasan Proposals at the PSC's next meeting. That very evening, Mrs. Bandaranaike told reporters from India that she did not accept the federal system of government. The UNP and the SLFP subsequently stated that they would abide by any consensus at the PSC These official releases, however, made no reference to the federal form of government as proposed in the Srinivasan Proposals.

In the welter of confusion emanating from the contradictory statements from the UNP and the SLFP, as well as the euphoric interpretations in sections of the local and international media that federalism had finally been accepted by the Sinhala polity, the PSC met on 3rd November 1992. It was at this meeting, that all members were expected to place their official positions regarding the federal form of government.

No official positions were forthcoming from any other parties at this meeting, except the Tamil parties who placed their official response to the Srinivasan Proposals. At this meeting, the representatives of the TULF and the EPRLF inquired of Mr. Hameed, the precise nature of the UNP's commitment to federalism. He replied that federalism was only a "deal" if the Tamils were prepared to abandon their demand for the permanent merger of the Northern and Eastern Provinces. In response the Tamil parties insisted that the Four Point Formula be taken up for meaningful discussion. Accordingly, on two successive dates, land and law and order were discussed. However, the Tamil parties' demand that all state land be vested with the provincial councils, was summarily rejected. Leading Sinhalese Buddhists, writing to President Premadasa in December 1992, publically opposed even the partial devolution of land and law and order powers to the Northern and Eastern Provincial Councils, as established under the Provincial Councils Act. In suitable retaliatory style, LTTE leader Prabhakaran, told senior cadre in Jaffna, that the only alternative to Tamil *Eelam* was Tamil *Eelam*.[29]

At the next meeting on December 11 1992, instead of discussing the first point of the Four Point Formula, the second point of the Srinivasan Proposals was taken up for discussion. On the basis of a hand-vote called by the chairman, the majority voted for the second point of the Srinivasan Proposals, which referred to the demerger of the Northern and Eastern Province, while rejecting the proposal to convert the existing unitary Constitution of 1978 into a federal one.

In response to the Srinivasan Proposals, the EPRLF and the CWC jointly agreed that a federal constitution was the most viable constitutional arrangement to assure the minorities of their rights. However, Article 2 of the 1978 Constitution states that the Republic of Sri Lanka is a unitary state. To transform the unitary constitution into a federal one, would necessitate a two-thirds majority in parliament and approval by the people at a referendum, in terms of Article 83 of the Constitution. The EPRLF and the CWC did not consider it practicable to steer this amendment through parliament or have it endorsed at a referendum. They stressed that it was purposeless proffering a federal arrangement unless there be a commitment by both the government and the opposition that they would frame and adopt a federal constitution. On the assumption that such a commitment would be forthcoming, the EPRLF agreed to support the proposal, stressing however, that one of the federal units must be the presently merged North-Eastern Province:

"This principle that the unit of devolution for the Tamil-speaking people, whether be it under a unitary constitution or a federal constitution, should comprise of a unified politico-administrative entity is, both, basic and inalienable for the resolution of the National Question in Sri Lanka."[30]

However, upon enquiring from the parties present at the meeting, whether they all accepted the conversion of the unitary constitution of Sri Lanka for a federal one, as stipulated in the first point of the Srinivasan Proposals, Mr. Hameed replied "there is no need for federalism. It is not possible in the present context. It is not a reality. We will give the powers enjoyed by States in India."[31]

On 14th December 1992, the Tamil political parties issued a press release giving an elaborate account of the manner in which the PSC had deviated from the tasks that were originally intended and how it had consistently failed to recognise the legitimate grievances and aspirations of the Tamil-speaking people. The statement declared that the decisions at the PSC of the 11th December 1992, by majority vote, and not by way of Tamil-Sinhala consensus, represented "a gross betrayal of faith" and made the deliberations of the PSC an "utter farce". It stated that it was: "...now abundantly clear that the entire process of the PSC had been designed to give effect to the promise, contained in the UNP manifesto for the Presidential Elections of 1988, to demerge the presently merged North-East Province. This design suited the SLFP as well. Federalism, hence, was only a bogey floated by these two parties to achieve these ends."[32] It concluded:

"[D]uring the entire process of the PSC, there was no serious consultation, no sign of any compromise by the UNP or the SLFP and certainly no consensus with the Tamil parties on any matter. History will, instead, record that consultations were purely diversionary and compromises blatantly farcical and dishonest. And, the resulting "consensus" was nothing but the unilateral imposition of the narrow, chauvinist outlook of the major Sinhala Political Parties on the long-suffering Tamil people".[33]

In a note to the Speaker of Parliament on 16th December 1992, the chairman indicated that a "majority decision" had been reached to de-link the presently merged North-Eastern Province and to devolve powers to these two units along the lines of the Indian Constitution. It was also announced that an Interim Report would be submitted in due course.

In view of these developments, the CWC, at the instigation of Mr S. Thondaman, a powerful intermediary, with the confidence of both the Tamil political parties and the Sri Lankan government, decided to dissociate itself from partaking in any future proceedings of the PSC. On 22 December 1992, it withdrew on the grounds that the Committee had deviated from the purpose for which it was appointed and that none of the proposals of the CWC had been considered. Moreover, it pledged its renewed allegiance to the Four Point Formula. The EPRLF and the TULF opted to wait for the publication of the Interim Report of the Committee before deciding on their appropriate course of action.

On the 11th January 1993, at the meeting of the PSC, the chairman circulated what was called a "Draft" Interim Report. Under the heading "Matters agreed upon by a majority of the members", the report stated that the members of the Committee, constituting the UNP, the SLFP, the SLMC, the CP, the LSSP, as well as the independent members, Mr. K. Srinivasan, and Mr. Basheer Segudawood, member for Batticaloa district, had reached agreement:

(a) on the establishment of two separate units of administration for the Northern and the Eastern Provinces.

(b) to adopt a scheme of devolution on lines similar to those obtaining in the Indian Constitution; and

(c) to devolve more subjects that are in List 3 (Concurrent List) or to dispense with the List.[34]

Accordingly, the EPRLF took the decision to dissociate itself from a process that relied on a "consensus of the majority" rather than on a "consensus of all", and convened a meeting of all Tamil political parties on the same day. At this meeting, unanimity was reached that the seven Tamil political parties should reject the so-called "majority agreement" and that a written response to the Draft Interim Report be forwarded. In addition, the Tamil political parties represented in the PSC, took the decision to dissociate themselves from any future deliberations of the PSC, and appealed instead "to the secular democratic forces working against the Sinhala people as well as to the International community to expedite a solution to the National question that is just, rational and equitable."[35]

In the joint response by the seven Tamil political parties to the Draft Interim Report submitted to the PSC on 11th March 1993, as far as the devolution package was concerned, it was noted with some relief that the Draft Interim Report conceded on the basis of evidence that it had received from public servants, that "the devolution contemplated in the legislation relating to provincial councils (set up under the Indo-Sri Lanka Accord, 1987), had not been fully implemented". "However", the joint response continued, "what is inconsistent and misleading is the majority agreement to adopt a scheme of devolution on lines similar to those obtaining in the Indian Constitution".[36] It stressed the fact that Sections 2, 3, 4, 75 and 76 of the 1978 Sri Lankan Constitution, which militate against meaningful devolution, are not found in the Indian Constitution. Furthermore, it maintained that the scheme of devolution recommended under the "majority agreement", especially with regards to crucial subjects such as land and law and order, could not be said to be in any way synonymous with the scheme of devolution contemplated by the Indian Constitution.

After the issue of the Draft Interim Report, a group of intellectuals, convened at the instigation of a Colombo Tamil lawyer, Neelan Tiruchelvam, were briefed by Dayan Jayatilleke, one of President Premadasa's inner circle, on the realities of the government's room for manoeuvre over the peace issue. Whilst the widely discredited PSC process had yet to reach any final conclusions, Jayatilleke said that the federal option would engender pathological opposition from the majority Sinhalese community, and suggested that the only pragmatic route for the government, was firstly to marginalise the Tigers militarily and secondly, to impress upon the Tamil parties the desirability of making the best of the provincial councils system, introduced by the Thirteenth Amendment to the Constitution, in 1987.

To sum up, it seems that the establishment of the PSC was not intended to find a meaningful solution to the Tamil national question, but to provide legitimacy for the division of the temporarily merged Northern and Eastern Provinces, i.e., the Tamil homeland and to keep the concern of the international community at bay. Whilst the PSC discussions were taking place during 1992, government-sponsored colonisation was actually intensified in the Northern and Eastern Provinces, particularly in the Trincomalee and Mullaitivu districts, in effect bringing about the physical separation of the Northern and Eastern Provinces, to coincide with the decision of the PSC. Moreover, in late December 1992, the Sri Lankan government rejected an offer made by the LTTE to hold a New Year's ceasefire and the establishment of peace talks. Instead, it launched Operation *Jeyaganga* in the Eastern Province, killing a number of Tamil civilians and destroying Tamil property. Moreover, the economic blockade and air bombing in the Northern Province continued into the new year. The fate of the PSC, the denial of peace negotiations and the escalation of military operations, were clear indications that the government had not relented from its intention of imposing a military solution to the ethnic conflict consuming the Island and the destruction of the traditional Tamil-speaking homeland.

The PSC debacle, reveals how little has changed over the last few decades and how far away the Sri Lankan government and the main opposition party, the SLFP, remain from making true concessions to the Tamil community. Leader of the LTTE, Prabhakaran, and the various Tamil paramilitary groups came to power, precisely because Sinhalese politicians consistently refused to negotiate participatory democracy for minorities and devolution of power for the Northern and Eastern Provinces. The continuing intransigence of the Sri Lankan government that was demonstrated during the PSC, which was considered to be "the most important Forum instituted to date to evolve a consensus on the Tamil Question", presents the Tamils with no credible alternative but to seek a solution to the Tamil national question and the redressal of their grievances, outside of the parliamentary process. Indeed, it seems that President Premadasa never intended to offer more devolution than the puppet-like provisions of the provincial council system and that the PSC and the associated sideshows were merely an elaborate circular tour of the issues designed to bring the Tamils back to the starting point.

Notes

1 See the statement made by the Political Committee of the Liberation Tigers of Tamil *Eelam* (LTTE), at the International Tamil Conference, London on, May, (1988), cited in: "The Indo-Sri Lanka Accord and the Thirteenth Amendment to the Sri Lankan Constitution", The LTTE Branch, London.

2 In the Annexure to the Agreement, paragraph 6 stated: "The Prime Minister of India and the President of Sri Lanka also agreed that in terms of paragraph 2.14 and paragraph 2.16(c) of the Agreement, an Indian peace-keeping contingent may be invited by the President of Sri Lanka to guarantee and enforce the cessation of hostilities, if so required".

3 Cited in: "The end of an illusion", in: *The Sri Lanka Monitor*, No. 26, March, (1990), p.1.

4 See: "Sri Lanka: Death of a general", in: *Link*, September 20, (1992), p.15.

5 Warnapala. W. A., "The All Party Conference in Sri Lanka", in: India Quarterly, No.47, (1991), pp.39-62, p.40.

6 Ibid., p.61.

7 Ibid.

8 Statement of JVP in: *The Island*, 4th October, (1989), p.2, cited in: Warnapala. W. A., p.45.

9 Ibid., p.46.

10 TULF Proposals, All Party Conference Document, 3. 14, cited in: Warnapala. W. A., p.52.

11 Ibid., p.53.

12 Ibid.

13 President Premadasa's address at the All Party Conference, 12 October, (1989).

14 Ibid., p.2.

15 Viswanathan. V. N., "Indo-Sri Lankan relations -Towards confidence building", in: India Quarterly, 46, (1990), pp.90-95, p.92.

16 See: "Tigers tipped as Gandhi assassins", in: *The Sri Lanka Monitor*, No.40, May, (1991), p.1.

17 "Select Committee Decides to Dismember the Tamil Homeland", in: *Tamil Information*, No.17, December, (1992), p.2.

18 Manoj Joshi, "With savvy, from Sri Lanka: Premadasa in India", in: *Frontline*, November 6, 1992, p.41.

19 "An assessment of the Parliamentary Select Committee (PSC): Its scope and limitations", Department of Information, *Eelam* Peoples

Revoluntary Liberation Front (EPRLF), 20 March, (1993), Appendix 1, p.4.

20 Joint Memorandum of seven Tamil political parties to the Chairman of the Select Committee of Parliament to recommend ways and means of achieving peace and political stability, 22 April, (1992), Appendix 2.

21 Ibid., p.7.

22 "Select Committee decides to dismember the Tamil homeland", in: *Tamil Information,* No.17, December (1992), p.1.

23 "An assessment of the PSC: Its scope and limitations", Appendix 3, p.9.

24 Ibid., Appendix 5, p.12.

25 Ibid.

26 Ibid., Appendix 6, p.14.

27 "Select Committee decides to dismember the Tamil homeland", in: *Tamil Information,* No. 17, December (1992), p.2.

28 "An assessment of the PSC: Its scope and limitations", Appendix 10, p.21.

29 "Kittu dies in mystery ship blast", in: *The Sri Lanka Monitor,* No.60, January, (1993), p.1.

30 "An assessment of the PSC: Its scope and limitations", Appendix 11, p.22.

31 Ibid., Appendix 13, "Statement of Tamil political parties regarding the deliberations at the Parliamentary Select Committee on the Tamil Question", p.26.

32 Ibid.

33 Ibid.

34 Ibid., Appendix 1, "Interim Report -Draft", p.6.

35 Ibid., Appendix 14, "Joint response by seven Tamil political parties to the Draft Interim Report submitted to the Parliamentary Select Committee by its Chairman on 11.3.93", p.28.

36 Ibid.

CHAPTER 14

Prospects for peace in Sri Lanka 1993 -1994

Between the 23rd April, 1993, and the 1st May, 1993, Sri Lanka was plunged into one of the most serious political crisis in recent decades, when both Democratic United National Front (DUNF) leader, Lalith Athulathmudali, and President Ranasinghe Premadasa, leader of the ruling United National Party (UNP) were assassinated. Whilst few considered that Sri Lanka had the resilience and potential to withstand the shock, let alone evolve an alternative arrangement to keep the Island's political system intact, a smooth transition took place, with Premadasa's Prime Minister, D. B. Wijetunge, becoming acting President and being unanimously elected by parliament as the President who will complete the remaining part of Premadasa's elected term, and with Cabinet spokesman and Minister of Industries, Science and Technology, Ranil Wickremasinghe, becoming Prime Minister. Whilst in the wake of these assassinations, many recognised in the election of a new President and a new government, the beginning of a new chapter in Sri Lanka's history, it is clear that if Sri Lanka wishes to lay claim to a genuine democracy in the future, it is critical that the country recognises the urgent and immediate need to address the grievances of the Tamil-speaking people in the North-East.

President Premadasa was widely regarded as the political leader most likely to succeed in evolving a political resolution of the Tamil national question, and yet his approach was deeply flawed. Firstly, he endeavoured to isolate the North-East economically and psychologically from the South and to insulate the South from the consequences of the civil war. It was a strategy which enabled him to project the South as a haven for investment, trade and infrastructural development. This strategy, however, further accentuated the economic disparities between the North-East and the South and made the populace in the South indifferent to the severe deprivations which more than 600,000 internally displaced peopke continue to be exposed to in the North and East. The Premadasa Government down-played the financial and human costs of the civil war and thereby did little to develop a peace constituency.

Secondly, President Premadasa distanced himself from the efforts of the Parliamentary Select Committee (PSC), ostensibly engaged in the search for a political solution. While he undertook to implement a consensus, he did very little to forge such a consensus and allowed the Committee to drift for months without political direction. Furthermore, the Premadasa government eroded the existing devolutionary arrangements set up under the Provincial Council system, under the aegis of the Indo-Sri Lanka Accord, 1987, by creating divisional secretariats which have in effect further strengthened the centralised and authoritarian character of the state.

With the assassination of Ranasinghe Premadasa, the critical problem of addressing the ethnic conflict has been placed in the hands of the new Sri Lankan President, D. B. Wijetunge. However, by the end of the year, the honeymoon seemed to already be over for the new President, and the general view within and outside Sri Lanka, that he will not be able to deliver the goods, seemed to be gaining ground.

In the newly-elected head of state's interview with local and foreign journalists at the President's office, after parliament concluded its session on May 7th, 1993, Wijetunge clarified his assessment of the situation in the North-East. When asked what his first priority would be, he replied "To unify the nation".[1] He pledged to do his utmost to resolve all outstanding issues, including the North-East crisis. When asked whether the government was planning to intensify the military campaign in the North, he replied that there was no military campaign in the North, and that what the government was trying to do, was to disarm the armed militants in the North. When asked whether there was a "Tamil problem" in the country, he replied "There is no 'Tamil problem'; only a terrorist problem".[2] In reply to a question concerning the government's design to hold talks with the LTTE, now widely held responsible for the assassination of President Premadasa, the new President said:

"They were our friends at one time, but now they are our enemies. If they wish to talk with us the doors are open. They are welcome. We never closed the door; they can talk to us if they so desire".[3]

Furthermore, he stressed the need for the leaders of all parties, including Prabhakaran, leader of the LTTE, to meet and make a joint effort to find solutions to the problem. In a final reply to a question concerning the future possibility of foreign intervention in Sri Lanka's ethnic conflict, Mr. Wijetunge ruled out all foreign mediation in resolving the North-East issue, claiming "We can solve our problems ourselves".[4]

Speaking to reporters at Puttalam on May 23rd, 1993, the new Prime Minister, Ranil Wickremasinghe, indicated that while seeking a political solution to the ten year separatist war, the government would continue the campaign to military weaken the LTTE Moreover, he expressed the hope that by the end of 1994, when the next Presidential election is due, a political solution to the ethnic conflict in the Island would be finalised.

In the light of the above remarks and the events that have taken place since the election of President Wijetunge and his new government, it is clear that the new government is pursuing a "war and peace" strategy towards the Tamil separatist struggle. The new government's emerging military strategy seems to have several trajectories. Firstly, to write off the North, whilst sporadically engaging in protracted, bloody, and indecisive confrontations with the LTTE in the contested areas of the Vanni, in a continuing effort to lay siege to the Jaffna peninsula, thereby tightening the noose around the Tigers' neck. Secondly, to enforce normalcy in the East by "clearing" it of the LTTE, and instituting a referendum, planned to be held on February 18th, 1994, by which the people of the Eastern Province can choose to permanently merge, or de-merge with the Northern Province[5]. Thirdly, to establish a security ring around the South, by pushing Colombo-based Tamils back to the war-torn East.

The new government's emerging political strategy on the other hand, seems to be to maintain that there is no "ethnic" conflict in the Island, whilst implying that what is happening in the North and East of Sri Lanka, is simply the shedding of blood by a power-hungry group of "terrorists", i.e., the LTTE, who are simply ambitious of capturing political power. Furthermore, the government has stressed that the conflict is an "internal terrorist" problem, thereby refusing all international mediation, and maintaining that peace efforts are continuing through the Parliamentary Select Committee, despite the widespread evidence that it is now defunct.

It is hoped that a brief analysis of those occasions on which the new government has clearly demonstrated its emerging military and political strategy towards the separatist movement in the North-East, will go some way towards furnishing a more comprehensive picture of what the Tamil-speaking community will face in the near future, and the hopes that can be realistically entertained for a peaceful solution to the Tamil national question.

Only two weeks after President Premadasa's assassination, the new President and his government were faced with their first major challenge when the Provincial Council elections were held on May 17, 1993. In the event, Sri Lanka's ruling UNP secured a narrow vote of confidence, holding four out of seven provinces, and appointing UNP Chief Ministers in two others despite combined opposition majorities. Provincial council elections were not conducted in the North-East Province for security reasons.

The ruling UNP gained overall majorities in Uva, North Central, Central and Sabragamuwa Provinces. Although the UNP was the party with the largest number of seats in the Southern and North West Provinces, it failed to gain an overall majority. However, the Governors of these Provinces invited the UNP to form provincial governments, despite a combined opposition from the majority for the People's Alliance (PA) and Democratic United National Front (DUNF) candidates. Chandrika Kumaranatunge, daughter of Sri Lanka Freedom Party (SLFP) leader Mrs Sirimavo Bandaranaike, won the key Western Province containing the capital of Colombo, for the opposition People's Alliance (PA).

The results constituted a mixed mandate. DUNF, the breakaway party set up by former UNP minister Lalith Athulathmudali, assassinated only days before President Premadasa, the new third force in Sri Lankan politics, stole votes from both sides. DUNF and PA combined, polled 3.2 million votes to the UNP's 2.9 million registering a technical knockout if viewed as a presidential plebiscite on the Premadasa years. But the UNP performed disproportionately well in many rural areas, the legacy of Mr Premadasa's populist poverty alleviation programmes. The long-term question, however, is whether former UNP Gamini Dissanayake will shepherd DUNF's one million voters back to the ruling party or attempt to supplant the fractious Bandaranaike dynasty as opposition candidate before the Presidential elections in December, 1994?

In February, 1994, President Wijetunge revealed plans to short-circuit the next election by rewriting the Constitution to effectively marginalise the Tamil community. President Wijetunge said that he wanted to abolish the direct national presidential poll and replace it by a vote in parliament to choose the president. In parliament, the UNP has almost always been the largest single party. At a public rally President Wijetunge said: "What we have proposed is to shorten the journey to the presidency...I think an executive president elected by parliament is as good as a president elected by a country as one electorate."[6] This decision has come at a time when the Sinhalese are sharply divided between the main opposition Sri Lankan Freedom Party (SLFP) and the UNP, giving a decisive vote to the minority Tamil population. The UNP are confident, however, that in the event, the opposition dissidents in parliament will support them in getting the two-thirds majority, necessary for amending the current constitution.

The Provincial Council elections, seen largely as a trial of strength for the UNP Government, since previous PC elections in 1989 were uncontested after an opposition boycott, also symbolised the first "fair trial" of the Provincial Council system itself. With over 73.98% of the 9,301,304 registered voters in Sri Lanka participating in the elections, it would seem that this was tantamount to an acceptance and endorsement of the recently created institution. However, the Provincial Council system is still often criticised as being an "imposition" on the country and that it does not have the concurrence of the Sinhala majority community. Indeed, the newly elected President is reported to have suggested that the Provincial Council system be substituted by some other institutional device, which has yet to be formulated.[7]

Despite its many shortcomings, on the face of the legislative provisions, the Provincial Council system offers for the first time in Sri Lanka, a genuine, albeit small measure of regional autonomy. How that autonomy will operate in practice has not yet been tested, since all the functioning provincial councils have up until now been controlled by the same political party that forms the government at the national level. It is clear that the new President needs to remain conscious of the calamitous consequences that have overtaken Sri Lanka over the last decade, as a result of the over concentration of power at the centre.

As part of the new government's strategy to end the military stalemate and to smash the alleged security threat to Colombo from the LTTE, 100,000 Tamil refugees in the capital are expected to be pushed back to the war-torn North-East. Over 8,000 Tamils have been arrested in Colombo in the wake of the President's assassination, despite long-standing residence or employment in the city and despite *bona fides* identity documents. Revised Emergency regulations now require householders in Colombo to provide local police with a full list of occupants. However, registration does not offer protection from arbitrary arrest. Tamils in the Eastern Province are being forced to remain where they are, and only Tamils with special clearance will be allowed to travel to Colombo. This new security *apartheid* is expected to be gradual, but it seems inevitable as long as the government in Colombo feels threatened by the LTTE.

This regional carve-up is part of an emerging military strategy to write off the North and enforce normalcy in the East. After major operations in northern Batticaloa in early June, 1993, army officials said the district was now "safe" for all internally displaced refugees, including those in Colombo, to return home. The announcement followed the 10th June,

1993, "unanimous" decision by the widely-discredited Parliamentary Select Committee, proposing a referendum in the Eastern Province. The Indo-Sri Lanka Accord, 1987, including a provision which refers to the holding of a referendum in the Eastern Province *only*, to decide whether the "temporarily" merged North and Eastern Provinces are to remain merged or to be separated, requires a two-thirds majority is required to push the decision through parliament.

The General Officer commanding the Eastern Province, Major General Lucky Algama, assured the PSC Chairman, Mr. Mangala Moonesinghe, that they had the strength and capacity to "clear" out the Tamil Tigers from the entire Eastern Province, to pave the way for the holding of the referendum, by October, 1993. The referendum has since been postponed. However, whilst the decision to hold a referendum has been hailed by political observers as a "major-breakthrough" in the on-going joint exercise to evolve a peaceful solution to the North-East conflict, others recognised in the PSC decision, a prelude to the Sri Lankan Aid Group meeting which was held in Paris on 19th June, 1993.[8] Indeed, foreign investors are keenly observing the government's current attempts to stop the war in the North-East, which in the event of success, could boost Sri Lanka's economic growth by more than ten per cent in one year. Certainly, there would be no dearth of international monitors keen to supervise such a referendum, which would be seen to ostensibly afford an opportunity to the people in the Eastern Province, to express their opinion on such a crucial matter, in a suitably democratic fashion.

Tamil politicians, however, who were boycotting the PSC sessions were stunned, and then enraged by the prospect of a referendum. The objection to the referendum has been unanimous among the Tamil groups and parties, and both militants and moderates, proclaiming that "the Tamil homeland" concept is indivisible.

"Today, the issue of the merger is the sticking point. The majority community will not hear of it, whilst the main plank of the Tamils is the demand for the merger of the North and East. It would seem to be that merger has now crystallised to being the alternative to the demand for a separate state as far as the Tamils are concerned".[9]

Clearly, the reports in the national press about the referendum and Moonesinghe's ambiguous conduct gave rise to a feeling among some Tamil leaders that the ethnic issue had gradually been pushed back to square one by the new leadership of the UNP.

"This prospect is particularly bothersome to the Colombo-based Tamil parties, (which, despite their Tamil nationalist sentiments, have to ultimately depend on the goodwill of the government and its law enforcement and intelligence agencies), because they would simply be rendered impotent back at square one of Sri Lanka's ethnic conflict; whereas it would be business as usual for the LTTE in the north and east. It is this apparent unease, felt, as it were, at one of the most inconvenient junctures of the political career of the anti-LTTE groups, that seems to have prompted them to reiterate, with a nostalgic nationalist fervour, their commitment to the cause of the Tamil Homeland".[10]

There have been two recognisable reactions to the prospect of a referendum among the Tamil political parties and groups. The one rejects the referendum as such, while the other accepts it, but draws attention to the fact that a referendum in the East is not viable or even legal, until all Tamils who have been displaced by the war and colonisation are re-settled.

The first reaction is based upon the belief that the very idea of a referendum negates the concept of a Tamil homeland in the North and East. The demand for a merger was initially based on the theory of the traditional homeland of the Tamil-speaking people and that the North and East are predominantly Tamil-speaking regions. Indeed, when the Tamil parties were apprised by the government of India concerning the nature of the Indo-Sri Lanka Accord, all the Tamil parties opposed the clause on the referendum on these grounds. In the event, it seems that they accepted it on the assurance purportedly given by Rajiv Gandhi, that he would ensure that the referendum would be indefinitely postponed, until such a time that it would become a *fait accompli*.[11] Moreover, it seems that the Indian authorities believed that the referendum clause was the only way J.R. Jayewardene could sell the devolution package to the Sinhalese, and that Jayewardene would co-operate with Delhi once the Accord was signed in making the North-East merger permanent.[12] Furthermore, it seems that when the Tamil militants were consulted in New Delhi about the referendum, just prior to the signing of the Accord, they unanimously indicated to India that they were against a referendum being held *only* in the Eastern Province.[13]

The above reaction to the proposed referendum, presupposes the second principle enunciated at the Thimpu Conference in 1985, that any solution to the ethnic question in Sri Lanka, should be based on the recognition of the North and East as the traditional homeland of the Tamil-speaking people.

The second reaction to the proposed referendum, whilst accepting the possibility of a referendum, maintains that certain matters have to be taken into consideration if the referendum is to be fair and acceptable. The recommendations are as follows:

a) Voters in the Eastern Province should be determined on the basis of the 1971 voter's register, to rectify the systematic demographic engineering in the East since 1953, which has deliberately altered the ethnic voter composition in the Eastern Province in favour of the Sinhalese.

b) Tamils of the Eastern Province who have been made refugees since 1983 and who are currently living in India and in the Northern Province, should be properly resettled and registered as voters.

3) Persons from outside the Eastern Province who have illegally settled on private and temple property should be precluded from the referendum.

Those who advocate the above approach, stress that the attention of the international community needs to be drawn to the fact that any failure to address the question of the politically motivated alteration of the demographic complexion of the Eastern Province, would result in the government purposefully moving large numbers of outsiders into militarily-secured settler schemes and having them registered as voters before it is possible for the international team, that the PSC is reportedly inviting, to monitor the referendum.

It is likely that in the event of the matter of the referendum being pushed further by the government, the latter approach to the referendum would receive greater support. However, the fact remains that the future of the East lies in the hands of the Muslims who constitute the second largest minority community in the Eastern Province.

The Muslim community who are caught up in the middle of the battle raging over the referendum question, seem to be in a no-win position. If the Muslims vote for the de-merger, it is possible that the LTTE would not shirk from massacring both the Muslim and the Sinhalese communities in the East. On the other hand, if the Muslims vote against the de-merger, it is possible that the Sinhalese-led government would misunderstand the Muslim's intention and consider them to be joining ranks with the "terrorists" and treat them likewise. In either case, the Muslims are liable to be the losers, and it is expected that the "Referendum in the East will lead to untold bloodshed."[14]

Mohamed Hussain Mahamed Ashraff, leader of the Sri Lanka Muslim Congress (SLMC), who has laid claim to the leadership of all Muslims in Sri Lanka, claiming that the SLMC today packs enough punch to represent a "special Muslim political identity" in Sri Lanka, is candid about his objective concerning the ethnic conflict, including the referendum issue. In the run up to the Provincial Council elections in May, 1993, Mohamed

Ashraff urged the Muslim community not to vote for the UNP or the SLFP, which he identified as Sinhala-led "chauvinist" parties. In an interview for *The Island*, Mohamed Ashraff listed the "irritations" which he believes symbolise the continued existence of "majority community chauvinism" in Sri Lanka. Among the irritations that he mentioned, were, the issue of language rights, the issue of state-sponsored colonisation of traditional Muslim areas, the issue of security and minority rights, the question of an equitable share in the administration of the country and an equitable share of the nation's resources. He maintained that the above issues could not be solved by a Sinhalese-led government, and that unless there was a package solution to the North-East problem, these issues could not be solved. When asked why the SLMC did not collaborate with the Tamil parties over minority issues, he replied:

"I consider the LTTE a fascist group. Simply because they have guns we will not be cowed by them. We do not believe in either collaborating with the Tamil parties against the Sinhalese, or in collaborating with the Sinhalese to undermine the Tamils. There is a chauvinistic strategy to make use of the Muslims to deny something to the Tamils. There are also some Tamil groups trying to use the Muslims against the Sinhalese. We are against all this. But I have always advocated a better understanding between the Tamils and the SLMC for the purpose of putting forward to the nation a joint set of proposals that will be acceptable to both the Tamils as well as the Muslims so that the majority community will find it difficult to say "no"".[15]

On the question of the merger of the North-Eastern Province, however, Mohamed Ashraff clearly sided with the Tamil parties in protesting against the de-merger of the North-East Province:

"The SLMC's consistent position is that neither an unconditional merger nor an unconditional separation of the north and east is a solution to the problem. The solution lies in a conditional merger".[16]

Mohamed Ashraff concluded his interview by reiterating that the fears and sensitivities of the two minorities in the North-East, i.e., the Muslims and the Sinhalese, had to be removed in any terms of settlement, and suggested that a possible basis for reconciliation lay in the demarcation of these areas into "ethnic-orientated cantons". Furthermore, he indicated that there should be a maximum devolution of power to these cantons, including powers relating to "land and security", and that the remaining powers could be given to an "upper tier which could be dominated by the Tamils".

Before addressing more recent debates that have arisen amongst Sri

Lanka's political leaders over the future configuration of the polity of Sri Lanka, this chapter shall examine some of the difficulties that have beset international efforts at relief and potection in Sri Lanka.

In mid-December, 1992, the United Nation's office for refugees, the United Nations High Commissioner for Refugees (UNHCR), attempted to enter into agreements with the government of Sri Lanka and the LTTE, to open a humanitarian relief corridor to the beleaguered Jaffna peninsula through the Pooneryn-Sangupiddy crossing. The UNHCR planned to restore the 500 metre ferry crossing at the mouth of the Jaffna lagoon, which has been closed since the Sri Lankan troops occupied the islands west of Jaffna in October, 1991, for vital food aid and medical evacuations from Jaffna, where one million people had been under siege since 1990. If the lifeline had been successful, the crossing was subsequently to be used by civilians.

On 22nd July, 1993, however, UN officials announced that the negotiations had irrevocably broken down. The LTTE had refused to agree to army checks on those leaving Jaffna, insisting that searches be carried out by UN staff. Such checks, however, can only be carried out by UN guards or "blue helmets", requiring *de facto* UN military intervention. As a result, UN officials declared themselves "saddened and frustrated" by the LTTE's maximalist stance.

Following the publication of details of an impending agreement between the government and the UNHCR in the Colombo newspaper *The Island*, and allegations of government approval for an UNHCR-LTTE pact, SLFP leader, Sirimavo Bandaranaike accused UNHCR of dabbling with political issues and demanded full disclosure. She claimed that the agreement conceded a separate identity for Jaffna, excising the peninsula from the sovereign state of Sri Lanka. Others alleged that the proposed agreement between UNHCR and LTTE would confer the international legal status on the militant group. Perplexed UNHCR officials denied that any agreement had been concluded.

Whilst neither the Sri Lankan government nor the LTTE wish for the UN to intervene, they both have reasons of their own for engaging the UNHCR in the conflict. The government, whilst clearly vetoing UN intervention, maintaining that the conflict is an "internal terrorist" problem, nevertheless wants to show the international community its humanitarian regard for the people of Jaffna. The LTTE, on the other hand, are actively seeking to internationalise the Sri Lankan conflict, to gain support from human rights organisations. However, it has been made clear in the recent Pooneryn debacle, that the Sri Lankan government will not sign any agreement that offers even a tacit recognition to the LTTE *The Island* columnist *Taraki* has maintained that:

"Contrary to the general perception in the south that the LTTE, and it's expatriate lobby are seeking UN intervention to further their separatist cause, the Tiger leadership is taking careful precautions to make sure that western mediation should be strictly limited to facilitating and consolidating a *de facto* sovereignty which they are hopeful of establishing at some point of time".[17]

In the eyes of the LTTE, Western intervention through the UN could seriously hamper the LTTE's military progress, and their consolidation of territory. Thus the LTTE preferred to turn down the UNHCR plan to open the Sanguppidy ferry. According to the LTTE, if the plan had been implemented, it could have represented a "legal" acknowledgement on their part of Sri Lankan sovereignty within the territory which they control. Clearly, the LTTE's lobbying in the West, does not seek intervention, but a gradual recognition of a *de facto* sovereignty, which if accepted in principle, could lead to *de jure* sovereignty.

"Whilst there may be cause for the United States and United Nations to step into civil war for reasons of international security, the goal of intervention must be clearly defined. Only a combination of coherent strategy, sufficient leverage and a keen sense of timing will allow a third party to bring peace. Most civil wars become amenable to settlement only after they have played themselves out with ferocity. A short term emphasis on ceasefires many only prolong conflicts and mitigate against parties perceiving that their survival depends on political settlement. While attempting mediation or urging negotiation, third parties may inadvertently prolong conflicts...Many civil wars may have to be allowed to run an ugly course".[18]

Accepting the above interpretation, in the absence of any third-party intervention, it remains to be asked how much longer the civil war in Sri Lanka must continue, before the parties to the conflict "have played themselves out with ferocity" and become "amenable to settlement". Surely, after ten years of bloody civil war, the question is not, when will the government and the LTTE begin to perceive "that *their* survival depends on political settlement", but rather, when will the international community recognise that the parties to the conflict are content to fight to the bitter end, at the expense of the survival and dignity of tens of thousands of civilians. While the UNHCR initiative has foundered, new international concern must provide a humanitarian corridor for Jaffna's one million war-weary.

After the recent Pooneryn debacle, the last exit to the Jaffna Peninsula remains the treacherous night crossing over the lagoon from Kilali, where Tamil civilians protected by LTTE patrol boats, run the gauntlet of Sri Lankan naval attacks. The military have outlawed the Kilali run in a determined effort to break the LTTE's vital supply corridor that keeps the Jaffna economy an inch away from collapse, proclaiming that those crossing will be shot on sight. During 1993, the strategic coastal Kilali area became the focus for two of the bloodiest skirmishes between the Sri Lankan forces and the LTTE, in the decade-long insurgency. If Kilali was permanently lost to the Tigers, it would represent a substantial defeat for them in civilian and military terms. For the last few years, they have based their military campaign around their perceived ability to defend the Jaffna population and to ensure that hundreds of thousands of Jaffna residents would be able to travel South under their supervision to government-controlled areas. If they can no longer guarantee this, the Tigers' legitimacy will surely diminish. Similarly, the government forces want civilians to cross the lagoon under their supervision, so that they can claim legitimacy in the North for themselves.

On September 30th, 1993, Sri Lankan land, sea and air forces attacked and captured the landing point at Kilali, in what was the largest military offensive in over a year. This military offensive on the Jaffna peninsula, in which several hundred combatants and civilians were killed, has focused attention on the aims and intentions of the Sri Lankan military. Clearly, the new government has not taken heed of the important lesson of the battle for Elephant Pass, in July, 1991, viz. that a military confrontation with the LTTE forces, who now have the military capability to extract a high cost for government victories, is certain to be lengthy, cruel and inconclusive. Furthermore, it is unlikely that future such offensives will radically alter the current military stalemate. Whilst neither party to the conflict is able to achieve their long-term military aims, the politicians on both sides continue to adopt a "bunker mentality", whilst retaining the *status quo*. In the absence of outside, international pressure, political dialogue between the parties will remain non-existent, the only contact being on the battle field.

On 11 November, approximately 700 Sri Lankan soldiers were killed, over 400 wounded, and hundreds went missing after the LTTE overran a key military complex at Pooneryn, in what was one of the guerrilla's greatest successes in the ten-year civil war. After twelve hours of fighting, hundreds of soldiers fled the base into the jungles as the Tigers looted the armoury, capturing Rs.300 million ($7 million) worth of arms and equipment. Another 500 soldiers remained pinned down on the Army camp's perimeter, before the Sri Lankan air and sea reinforcements landed at Kalmunai Point after three days of fighting and the LTTE withdrew.[19]

The military's reputation was badly bruised by the Pooneryn attack and raised questions about the Sri Lankan forces capabilities. Recently recruited troops are extremely poorly trained and the bulk of the front-line fighting is done by the same battalions transferred from one area to another. More than seventeen thousand men have deserted in the last decade, and the army is still seven hundred men short of a full officer corps. In addition, internal disputes within the army are rife and promotion is often reported to have been given to personal favourites over the heads of more talented men. However, it is clear that the Sri Lankan armed forces do not suffer from political constraints. Indeed, with the election of the new President, the military appears to have been given a free hand to show what it can do. With the Presidential elections approaching, it is possible that the advisors of President Wijetunge, who has often been perceived as a weak leader, have decided that a show of military muscle will improve his profile. The government has accordingly approved military demands to increase its numbers.

For the time being, it is clear that the government is determined to pursue a military rather than a political solution to the ethnic conflict. However, it remains highly unlikely that the armed forces can defeat the Tamil Tigers outright, thus it seems that the long-term policy is to weaken them sufficiently for negotiations to be held on the government's terms. It is clear that as long as both the LTTE and the Sri Lankan government remain intransigent, there will be no political negotiations unless there is international pressure. However, despite the increasing controversy over UN involvement in Sri Lanka, the Sri Lankan government has remained adamant that the conflict is an internal terrorist problem and has aborted several international efforts at mediation.

In early August, the Sri Lankan government rejected a new peace plan presented by four Nobel laureates on behalf of the Canada-based World Council for Global Cooperation (WCGC). The peace plan by Ilya Prigogine of Belgium, Mairead Maguire of Britain, Jan Tinbergen of Netherlands and George Weld of the US, called for; a ceasefire verified by the UN, the establishment of buffer zones, the adoption of federalism, and UN-observed elections in the North *and* Eastern Provinces. In a letter to the WCGC, however, the Sri Lankan government reiterated that the conflict was an internal terrorist problem and maintained that peace efforts were continuing through the PSC.[20]

Delegates attending an international conference on "Democracy and Displacement" in Colombo in mid-August, 1993, also urged the Sri Lankan government to resolve the basic problems of the ethnic conflict and seek UN mediation. The government had earlier refused permission for the UN Secretary General's Special Representative on Internally Displaced Persons, Francis Deng, to attend the conference.[21]

The UN saga continued when Sri Lankan diplomats panicked over a hard-hitting resolution planned to be tabled before the UN Sub-Commission on the Prevention of Discrimination and Protection of Minorities, in Geneva in February, 1994, by four Western nations calling upon the Sri Lankan government and other parties to the conflict, to seek a cessation of hostilities and obtain the assistance of the UN Secretary General. After frantic diplomatic effort, the resolution was withdrawn, but not without a great deal of dust having been kicked up over fears of UN intervention.[22]

Such hostility on the part of the Sri Lankan government to UN mediation, on the basis of sovereignty is clearly shortsighted, given the marked lack of internal initiatives that could work towards peace. It remains to be asked, however, whether there is an alternative regional or international body, whose mediation the Sri Lankan government would accept?

Despite Sri Lanka's improved relations with the Indian government, in the face of a common foe, a regional "terrorist" problem in the form of the LTTE, it remains unrealistic to suppose, after the assassination of Rajiv Gandhi, that India will play a part in such a mediation. Whilst it is possible that the central government of New Delhi and the state government of Tamil Nadu could change their composition and leadership, and thus their persuasion in the near future, it remains unlikely that India will get involved in what it has come to regard as a "poisonous place". Therefore, help to arrange an understanding between the two warring parties will have to come from elsewhere.

Such a dialogue should take place outside of South Asia, preferably in Europe or in one of several "sympathetic" countries. Canada, Norway and Australia have offered their "good offices" to Sri Lanka and therefore present a range of possible rendezvous. Given the Sri Lankan government's obvious distaste for UN involvement, it might be preferable, in the event, to encourage a Commonwealth peace-keeping force. Indeed, the Commonwealth might welcome the chance to flex its muscles as the self-proclaimed model of multilateralism in the post-Cold War era.

Despite the lack of political will and the absence of a genuine desire for peace that currently characterises the political leaders on both sides of the ethnic conflict in Sri Lanka, there is evidence that there is war-weariness in the field. It is becoming increasingly apparent that the civilians, especially those who have been displaced during the ten year civil war, those who are living in refugee camps inside Sri Lanka and in South India, or who have sought asylum outside of Sri Lanka, both the Tamils, the Sinhalese and the Muslims, are beginning to demand peace, over and above the demand for either a united Sri Lanka, or a separate state of *Eelam*.[23]

Hopes were raised recently, when in a BBC interview, Prabhakaran, leader of the LTTE, said that the on-going conflict could end if some acceptable solution, perhaps along federal lines, could be found. When asked whether the LTTE would accept a North-East merged federal set up, Prabhakaran replied:

"If a proposal for a federal set up which recognises our geographic homeland is put forward, we are prepared to examine it. Federalism exists in many forms. It has different dimensions. If a federal set up proposal which gives autonomy and satisfies the expectations of the Tamil people is put forward, we are prepared to consider it".[24]

Whether or not Prabhakaran is ready to replace the concept of a separate state of "*Eelam*", with a definition which implies a greater degree of autonomy and devolution of power, as opposed to independence, remains unclear. However, in a recent interview with *The Island*, Tourism and Rural Industrial Development Minister and CWC leader, Savumiamoorthy Thondaman, on his arrival in Sri Lanka from a European tour, claimed that the expatriate LTTE representatives he had met in London and Paris had shown readiness for negotiations and were "now talking in terms of federalism and not Eelam".[25] He stressed that there was now a common ground of federalism which had been accepted by the UNP and the SLFP in response to the "Srinivasan" proposals placed before the PSC, and which had been accepted by the LTTE, although he acknowledged that federalism could take different forms. However, he stressed that: "No one can contribute towards peace except the Government and the LTTE Anything that is not acceptable to these two parties cannot lead us to a solution".[26] When asked whether he thought the government would continue with its military offensives, Thondaman replied that these would probably continue and that the situation would not change until something "tangible" emerged from the negotiations. When asked whether he thought something would happen by the end of 1993, Thondaman replied: "We all hope. Everybody wants peace in this country. If anything is to happen it must take off before the end of this year".[27]

Rather than witnessing the emergence of some "tangible" measures from the negotiations, however, the New Year heralded a shift away from peace initiatives. Instead, Sri Lanka's civil war seemed destined to enter a decisive phase, as the separatist LTTE declared 1994 to be "A year of battles", while the new Army chief Lt. General Gerry de Silva, vowed to bring victory to government forces as he assumed control on the 1st January. Both armies accordingly prepared for major offensives as soon as the North-East monsoon ended in early February, 1994.

In the lull following the Tigers' successful attack on Pooneryn in November 1993, the LTTE propaganda machine prepared Jaffna civilians for a major escalation in the fighting. The Tigers' political wing held a series of workshops on new civil defence directives, whilst buildings were plastered with posters extolling fallen LTTE martyrs and the final battle to come. Over 3,000 Jaffna school boys joined the Tigers in the weeks following the Pooneryn attack.

Five former service chiefs met President Wijetunge in mid-December to table a review of military shortcomings in the aftermath of the battle at Pooneryn. Their memorandum called for; the establishment of a War Council or Cabinet, to include senior ministers and opposition leader, Mrs Bandaranaike, it called for the country to be put on a war footing, the streamlining of supply logistics; a clearly enunciated military objective "to destroy the military capability of the LTTE and its sympathisers"[28], and a more offensive gound strategy.

In a New Year press interview, President Wijetunge offered peace talks with the Tigers but said "we should know in advance what they want to talk about".[29] Furthermore, the President made it clear that there could be no compromise of Sri Lanka's sovereignty or unitary character when there had already been unprecedented devolution through Provincial Councils. Wijetunge's token offer failed to tempt the Tigers, as positions ominously hardened on both sides.

Whilst it is difficult to make a long-term prognosis, it is relatively easy to predict what will happen during the early months of 1994. It is clear that while ground operations will focus on strengthening the government's hold on the Eastern Province, the LTTE's strongholds in the Northern Province will continue to be subject to aerial and artillery bombardment, and heavy troop deployment will continue to consolidate in the strategic coastal Kilali area. The government of Sri Lanka will continue its regional carve-up, by squeezing the Colombo-based Tamils out of the South, and by "flushing" the tigers out of the East, gradually attempting to lay siege to the Jaffna peninsula. The government will continue to rebuff UN peace approaches, claiming that the conflict is an internal terrorist problem, maintaining at the same time, that peace efforts are continuing throu

Moreover, it is clear that the Tamil parties will not be giving up their historic demand for the right to self-determination. Indeed, in response to the PSC's decision to hold a referendum in the East, both Tamil militants and moderates have proclaimed that the Tamil homeland concept is indivisible. All the main Tamil parties have reiterated that they will not accept anything short of the two main preconditions constituting the "Four Point Formula" presented to the PSC on 17th June, 1992, i.e., an unified politico-administrative entity for the permanently merged North-Eastern Province, and substantial devolution of power ensuring meaningful autonomy to the unified unit. Furthermore, it is clear that they will continue to refuse to participate in any parliamentary process that does not recognise and accept these proposals, as a prerequisite for any long-term meaningful solution. Any permanent political solution to the ethnic conflict in Sri Lanka, whether it is brought about by international mediation, or through political negotiation between the Sri Lankan government and the Tamil parties, has to take into consideration the legitimate aspirations of the Tamil-speaking people to determine their political, economic, social and cultural destiny.

Notes

1 "Unifying nation, my first priority", in: *The Island*, Vol.8, No.19, 12th May, (1993), p.1.

2 Ibid., p.3.

3 Ibid.

4 Ibid.

5 On the 24th August, (1993), the Sri Lankan Presidential Secretariat announced the postponement of the referendum on the North-East merger in the Eastern Province until the 18 February, 1994. It was also announced that there will be a referendum in the Northern Province scheduled to be held on the 28th April, 1994. See *Tamil Information*, August (1993), No.25, p.5.

6 World news in brief, "Poll setback for Tamils", in: *The Guardian*, 3rd February, (1994).

7 Richard. A. Dias., "Devolution of power - problems", in: *The Island*, 30th June, (1993), p.9.

8 On 19th June, (1993), the Sri Lankan Aid Group pledged U.S. $840 million (Rs.40.3 billion) to Sri Lanka, an increase of U.S. $15 million since 1992.

9 Ponnambalam. G. G., (Jr.), "Majority community ignores Tamil issue", in: *The Island*, 7th April, (1993), p.7.

10 "Referendum: Tamil perceptions", in: *The Island*, 23rd June, (1993), p.9.

11 Ibid.

12 Ibid.

13 Ibid.

14 Ponnambalam. G. G., (Jr.), p.7.

15 "Muslims should vote only for SLMC", in: *The Island*, 14th April, (1993), p.15.

16 Ibid.

17 "Tiger objective: De facto sovereignty", in: *The Island*, 8th September, (1993), p.6.

18 Stedman. J. S., "New Interventionists", in: US Journal of Foreign Affairs, cited in: *The Island*, ibid.

19 "Tigers pounce on Pooneryn", in: *The Sri Lanka Monitor*, No. 70, November, (1993), p.1.

20 "Sri Lanka rebuffs UN peace approach", in: *The Sri Lanka Monitor*, No.67, August, (1993), p.1.

21 The UN Secretary-General's Special Representative on Internally

Displaced Persons, Francis Deng, was later invited to Sri Lanka in November, 1993.

22 "Sri Lanka rebuffs UN peace approach", in: *The Sri Lanka Monitor*, No.67, August, (1993), p.1.

23 See Rohini Hensman, "Journey without end: Is there a solution for Sri Lankan refugees?", (1993), The British Refugee Council, in which a collection of interviews with refugees from Tamil, Sinhalese and Muslim communities reflect the people's overwhelming desire for peace.

24 "BBC Interview with Tamil leader - Prabhakaran", in: *Tamil Nation*, March, (1993), p.3.

25 "LTTE now wants federalism", in: *The Island*, 8th September, (1993), p.6.

26 Ibid.

27 Ibid.

28 "LTTE declares 1994 A Year of Battles", in: *The Sri Lanka Monitor*, No.71, December, (1993), p.1.

29 Ibid.

Part 3

The "internationalisation" of intra-state ethnic conflicts

The right to self-determination: The Sri Lankan Tamil national question

Inter-state ethnic conflict is increasingly being portrayed as one of the most serious threats facing the international world today. In the early 1990's, efforts to control regional and intra-state ethnic conflicts assumed a place of central importance on the international agenda. The end of the Cold War appeared to open up new opportunities for the United Nations to determine the future of ethnic groups embroiled in domestic conflict situations. It heralded a new attempt by the UN to tackle the problems of international conflict prevention, management and resolution.

Many of the intra-state ethnic conflicts that sprung up in the post-war era, which were conveniantly shelved during the Cold War years and which are now purported to threaten international peace and security, were often the result of denials of the right to self-determination. It was made apparent in Part One of this study, that the principle of self-determination has currently been left in "limbo", because its political implications are such that different states accept markedly varying versions of the principle. Some members of the international community want to apply the principle in the field of domestic politics of a sovereign state, while others hold that the principle functions only as an instrument of decolonisation.

Clearly, the "internal" aspect of the principle of self-determination applies in the field of domestic politics of a sovereign state. However, the traditional domestic jurisdiction doctrine which has tended to shield oppressive state practices and institutions from international scrutiny, has for all practical purposes lost its meaning, and this notwithstanding the fact that non-intervention in the domestic affairs of a state continues to be a basic UN and International Governmental Organisation (IGO) principle. Inhibitions about interference in the "domestic jurisdiction" of states seem to be less compelling than they used to be. In light of the fact that national guarantees of human rights, including the prerequisite of all fundamental human rights, the right to self-determination, are often not sufficient, the principle of non-interference in the affairs of foreign governments is increasingly being reviewed.

Clearly, there is growing opinion that the international community should pay less heed to the traditional principles of sovereignty, territorial integrity and non-intervention and more to the prevention, control and resolution of protracted and violent intra-state ethnic conflicts. The UN and IGOs are increasingly exerting pressure against governments that oppress their own peoples, by denials not only of the external aspect of self-determination, but also of the internal aspect of self-determination. If a denial of the right to self-determination is recognised as a threat to the peace and security of the international arena, the international community may invoke a variety of collective enforcement measures against the concerned government.

Part Three examines the role of the UN in violent and protracted intra-state ethnic conflicts, especially those which arise as a result of the denial of claims to the right to self-determination. A brief empirical case study of the role of the UN in Sri Lanka, clearly illustrates that the UN is currently incapable of dealing with such intra-state ethnic conflicts, because it lacks the mechanisms with which to deal with ethnic groups' claims to the right to self-determination outside of the decolonisation process.

Studies of intra-state ethnic conflicts in the past, have typically been based upon an "introvert approach", i.e., the evolution, intensification and possible resolution of ethnic conflicts have been assumed to be an internal process, independent of the international context in which such a conflict exists. However, intra-state ethnic conflicts invariably have an external dimension, both as an input into the process, and as an overspill from it.

Intra-state ethnic conflicts are rarely confined to the country of their origin. Driven by factors such as; the "ethnic affinity link", i.e., cross-border links between ethnic groups, the "political power link", i.e., the intervention of unrelated non-ethnic actors pursuing their own political interests, the "economic link", i.e., the diverse commercial and financial interests of non-ethnic actors, the "moral or ethical link", i.e., the growing international concern for human rights, by UN bodies, non-governmental organisations (NGOs) and concerned individuals, the quick dissemination of global news, international terrorism, and easy access to the international arms market, intra-state ethnic conflicts are increasingly becoming "internationalised".[1] It is therefore increasingly being recognised that the external links of an intra-state ethnic conflict, tangible or otherwise, play a significant role in these internal processes and demand attention in any empirical case study of so-called "intra-state" ethnic conflicts.

With the escalation of the ethnic conflict between the Sinhalese and the Tamils in Sri Lanka into a fully-fledged civil war after the July 1983 massacre, the Sri Lankan Tamil separatist struggle became "internationalised". Part Three attempts to analyse the external dimension of the inter-ethnic conflict in Sri Lanka.

The "internationalisation" of the Sri Lankan ethnic conflict has not only evoked international concern among "state-actors", such as India, Western donors of aid to Sri Lanka, and "host" countries to tens of thousands of Tamil asylum-seekers, but it has also created links with "non-state" actors, such as the UN Human Rights Commission and its Sub-Commission on Prevention of Discrimination and Protection of Minorities, and with non-governmental organisations concerned with minority and human rights.

Part Three examines the concerns that have been raised before the UN Human Rights Commission and its Sub-Commission on Prevention of Discrimination and Protection of Minorities, with regard to the Sri Lankan Tamil's right to self-determination. It focuses particularly on the forty-ninth UN Commission on Human Rights held in February 1993, at which fifteen NGOs raised the issue of the Tamils' right to self-determination. It examines the recommendations that have been raised before the UN's subsidiary bodies, on ways in which the conflict in Sri Lanka might be resolved. These include *inter alia*, the clear demand for greater UN involvement in Sri Lanka, greater linkage of the Sri Lankan government's human rights records with Western development aid to Sri Lanka, increased linkage of the arms trade with the human rights record of Sri Lanka and tighter arms export controls on weapons flowing into Sri Lanka.

Such analysis is deemed necessary, since in the absence of a formal UN mechanism which could entertain complaints about self-determination as such, from the parties concerned, as well as from sympathetic governments, NGOs and individuals, the UN Human Rights Commission and its Sub-Commission, will continue to function as one of the major lobbies for the international recognition of a group's claim to the right to self-determination outside of the decolonisation process. However, whilst the UN continues to fail to provide an alternative and effective mechanism for such lobbyists, ethnic groups who are denied their claims to the right to self-determination, will continue to have no prospect of achieving their aims by normal political means.

Whilst the vast majority of violent and protracted intra-state ethnic conflicts arise as the result of denials of the claim to self-determination, nowhere is there a procedure of arbitration, no definition of terms, no UN body which will entertain the complaints about self-determination as such. As a result, whilst groups continue to draw on the right to self-determination, claims for the fulfilment of that right all too often lead to violence, human rights abuse and civil war.

Part Three concludes by recommending ways in which the UN could establish a mechanism which could implement a positive, practical and acceptable doctrine of the right to self-determination, which would be applicable internationally and without prejudice.

Notes

[1]Premdas. R., "The internationalisation of ethnic conflict: Some theoretical explorations", in: "Internationalisation of ethnic conflict", K.M. de Silva & May. R. J., (eds.), (1991), pp.10-25.

CHAPTER 15

United Nations involvement in intra-state ethnic conflict: A case study of Sri Lanka

Whilst there has been a tendency amongst students and specialists of international relations to ignore the issue of violent and protracted ethnic conflict, it is increasingly being recognised that ethnic conflict can have a major impact on the inter-state system. The study of ethnic conflict has therefore become central to the study of international relations.

Whilst in the past it has generally been acknowledged that it is a bad policy to "internationalise" a violent ethnic conflict, especially if this means involving a foreign state, it is increasingly being maintained that certain types of third party involvement, such as the intervention of the United Nations (UN) might be constructive. Until recently, an attempt to link together the UN and intra-state ethnic conflict would not have been welcomed, for the UN, despite its name, is an organisation of states and is concerned primarily with relations between these sovereign entities. Furthermore, as many states already feel threatened by ethnic sentiments held by groups within their borders, they have a vested interest in keeping ethnic issues off the UN's agenda.

"The UN is, first and foremost an organisation of states, not of nations, and since most states are, in fact threatened by the claims of nations, it is little wonder that the UN is pro-state and anti-nation."[1]

Moreover, since most, but by no means all ethnic conflicts are fought out within the borders of a single sovereign state, they have generally been characterised as being within the domestic jurisdiction of the state concerned, which effectively inhibits UN involvement under Article 2(7) of its Charter, which provides that nothing in the Charter "shall authorise the United Nations to intervene in matters which are essentially within the domestic jurisdiction of any State".

Nevertheless, it has not been possible either to keep the ethnic issue off the UN agenda entirely, or to keep the UN from intervening in intra-state ethnic conflicts. There are several reasons to explain this overlapping interest. Firstly, as long as the UN remains true in even a minor way, to the ideals enshrined in Article 1 of its Charter, it will have to, on occasions, respond to intra-state ethnic violence. Article 1 clearly states that two of the purposes of the UN are to maintain international peace and security and to promote and encourage respect for human rights and fundamental freedoms for all. Article 1 states:

1. To maintain international peace and security, and to that end: to take effective collective measures for the prevention and removal of threats to the peace, and for the suppression of acts of aggression or other breaches of the peace, and to bring about by peaceful means, and in conformity with the principles of justice and international law, adjustment or settlement of international disputes or situations which might lead to a breach of the peace;

2. To develop relations among nations, based on respect for the principle of equal rights and self-determination of peoples, and to take other appropriate measures to strengthen universal peace;

3. To achieve international co-operation in solving international problems of an economic, social, cultural or humanitarian character, and in promoting and encouraging respect for human rights and for fundamental freedoms for all without distinction as to race, sex, language or religion.

Article 1 of the United Nations Charter, clearly requires that the UN respects the principle of the self-determination of peoples, as one of the "measures to strengthen universal peace". Similarly, in Article 55 of the UN Charter, "the principle of equal rights and self-determination of peoples" is the basis for "the creation of conditions of stability and well-being which are necessary for peaceful and friendly relations among nations."

There is a clearly stated duty on all UN member states to promote the realisation of self-determination in conformity with the principles and purposes of the UN Charter. However, protracted and violent intra-state ethnic conflicts, which are fast becoming the most widely felt internal difficulty of the late twentieth century, are often the outcome of frustrated claims to self-determination. In many parts of the world today, groups are making demands which often draw on the right of people to self-determination, but claims for the fulfilment of that right, all too often meet with instant rejection and lead too quickly to violence, human rights abuse and in some cases to civil war. However, the failure of the UN to promote the realisation of self-determination in the first instance, does not prevent it from legitimately intervening in an independent state, if the denial of self-determination has led to violence, human rights abuse and a potential threat to international peace and security. Clearly, the UN needs to confine itself to the promotion of self-determination, if it is to retain its integrity as an organisation of states whose practise is above the *real-politick* of its individual members.

Moreover, states themselves, when they have been unable to resolve their own internal problems and are unable to keep the peace without outside assistance, have turned on several occasions to the UN to request its involvement. On the other hand, as the empirical case study of the Sri Lankan government's response to third-party mediation revealed, many states will interpret international offers of arbitration as a violation of their sovereignty. It is worth noting at this juncture, that the Liberation Tigers of Tamil Eelam's reluctance to acede to any international intervention, is illustrative of the fact that many ethnic groups will also reject outside interference, often deeming such involvement to be detrimental to their cause.

There are good reasons for believing that the UN and its various organs, ought to be able to play a more constructive role in intra-state ethnic conflicts than the concerned governments or third-party states. It was made apparent in the empirical case study of the ethnic conflict in Sri Lanka in Part Two, that state governments experiencing ethnic conflict, are frequently party to the conflict, and are unable to devise policies to reduce ethnic tensions. Similarly, it was made apparent with reference to the intervention of the Indian Peace Keeping Force in Sri Lanka in 1987, that external involvement by outside states, is more often than not, biased or self-interested, and often leads to the escalation of the conflict.

In the light of such problems, many have looked to the UN as the best conflict preventing, resolving/managing institution. This is mainly because the UN, ostensibly the guardian of international peace and security, and the promotor of human rights and fundamental freedoms for all, including the right to self-determination, is seen to have no particular stake in the outcome of a dispute, apart from a satisfactory reduction in the level of violence. It is assumed therefore, that the UN is less likely than independent states to exploit an ethnic conflict for its own ends, since it does not have a "national interest" of its own to protect and promote.

There were few grounds to substantiate such an assumption during the Cold War era, during which the UN became little more than "a place to house and service diplomatic negotiations" between the superpower blocs, and in which ethnic conflicts, especially in the Third World, became "the unstable front line in the conflict between the global blocs".[2] However, since the improvements in US-Soviet relations, and the apparent attempt on behalf of the superpower blocs to place greater emphasis on international peace and security, rather than on the pursuit of unilateral advantage, it is increasingly being maintained that the UN is at last beginning to fit the role that was assigned to it at its birth, i.e., an independent actor on the world stage, capable of transforming not only the perspective, but also the behaviour of its member states.

Whilst it is certainly true, that in the post-Cold War era the "front-line" has become less volatile, it would clearly be premature to suggest that it has disappeared altogether. Nevertheless, the end of the Cold War appears to have presented a new opportunity to use the UN to deal with violent ethnic conflicts, and during 1992, efforts to control such conflicts assumed a place of central importance on the international agenda.

"As conflicts related to decolonisation and the Cold War have disappeared, the focus has shifted to disputes arising from the collapse of the Soviet Union as well as from ethnic divisions and troubled political, social and economic conditions in many countries. A number of protracted conflicts of national interests, and disputes over borders, territories or resources, add to the list of concerns."[3]

It is necessary therefore to examine to what extent the UN is currently able to deal with protracted and violent intra-state ethnic conflicts, arising from denials of claims to self-determination.

This chapter shall begin by briefly examining the genesis of the UN and its changing role in international politics. It shall look at its early and formative years, when it was regarded as a tool for small and progressive nations during the decolonisation period, its later years, when it became little more than a tool for the self-interested, partisan superpower blocs during the Cold War and the demands that are currently being made upon the UN, which is regarded by many as being capable of dealing with all the unresolved and festering problems of the Cold War, as well as being able to prevent, resolve/manage new disputes which may arise in the future.

It shall analyse the UN Secretary General's *An Agenda for Peace*, 1992, in which the prospect of the UN's new role in intra-state ethnic conflict has been set out most graphically. It is hoped that such an analysis will reveal the extent to which the UN can involve itself constructively in protracted and violent intra-state ethnic conflicts, which are the result of denials of claims to the right to self-determination.

It also analyses those options which have been utilised by the UN to tackle the violent ethnic conflict in Sri Lanka. It is hoped that an analysis of the UN's involvement in the Sri Lankan ethnic conflict will provide a realistic basis upon which to judge the worth of the UN in the sphere of intra-state ethnic conflict prevention, resolution/management. Such an examination will perhaps enable those who are searching for ways in which to prevent, resolve/manage violent intra-state ethnic conflicts, to avoid either the temptation to embrace the UN too enthusiastically or reject it too hastily. As the following chapter will reveal, the record of the UN is mixed, it "is neither a panacea nor a non-entity".[4]

(i) A brief history of the United Nations

In 1945, when the UN emerged as an international organisation to promote peace and human rights, fifty-one states were admitted to membership. Among these, only three came from Africa (Ethiopia, Liberia, and South Africa), seven belonged to the Middle East and among the three from Asia, only China was independent of colonial rule. The vast majority of member states therefore, represented the countries of Europe (including the Soviet Union), the Americas, and the white Commonwealth countries. Within a single decade however, twenty-five new states had joined the UN By the end of 1965, another fifty-one had been taken into the fold, swelling the membership to 117.

The revolutionary emergence of independent states in Africa and Asia in the decolonisation era, virtually transformed the composition, character, tone, language and much of the agenda of the UN The great flood came in 1960 and 1961, after the UN General Assembly signed the Declaration on the Granting of Independence to Colonial Countries and Peoples in 1960. During these two years alone, nineteen African and two Asian countries joined the ranks of the UN Together, they dramatically shifted the organisations' voting strength. By the end of 1961, the Afro-Asian states constituted fifty-three of the UN member states, whilst the other continents combined, constituted only fifty-one. With this achievement, the Afro-Asian countries secured an absolute majority. From this position, the Afro-Asians were able to express themselves on any subject, determine agenda items, and prevent any proposal from obtaining a two-thirds majority in the General Assembly, without the support of at least some of its contingent. This voting power naturally elevated the Afro-Asian countries to a new international status.

From the very inception of the UN, it was clear that all non-colonial powers would use the organisation as a forum and a focal point to express their undying antagonism toward any system of white domination and to promote racial equality. Due to their pressure and that from non-governmental groups, the UN Charter specifically included the provisions supporting the principle of self-determination and the principle of equal rights. The Afro-Asian contingent, continued to use the UN to turn the attention of the international community to concerns of racial equality and fundamental rights.

The first session of the General Assembly not only passed a resolution condemning discrimination on the basis of race, but also directly called upon South Africa to change its policies towards Africans and Asians. It then went on to create the UN Commission on Human Rights, and its Sub-Commission on Prevention of Discrimination and Protection of Minorities, set standards in the Universal Declaration of Human Rights, and write the Convention on the Prevention and Punishment of the Crime of Genocide.

However, despite the solemn pledges of the signatories to the UN Declaration, promising that should they be victorious in the Second World War they would support not only human rights but liberty and independence for peoples as well, by which they implicitly recognised the changing nature of international relations, the Western world demonstrated a marked unreadiness to abandon its colonial empires. The British, French, Dutch, Belgians, Spanish, Portuguese, Italians, and South Africans all resolved to remain imperial powers, to retain their possessions and to conduct post-war colonial policy in their own way and at their own pace, free from any dictation by an international organisation. In the event, however, these tenacious efforts to perpetrate Western domination over the other peoples of the world were doomed to failure.

Onto this backdrop - the promises for self-determination and political independence, the shattering of the myth of white invincibility during World War Two, the weakening position of Europeans and their loss of confidence in the aftermath of the war - there emerged an escalating competition waged between the Americans and the Soviets, for the affections of the emerging nations, which was to ultimately transform the face of the newly active UN

The insurgent wars in both Vietnam and Malaya, had clearly raised the spectre of communism in decolonisation. The open communist involvement in these two struggles and their support for other "wars of national liberation", suddenly cast disengagement from empire in an entirely new light for many in the West, especially the Americans. Mao Tse-Tung's Communist Chinese victory, the resulting "loss" of China, and the outbreak of the Korean War, in 1950, compounded the problem even further. The "Cold War", as the mounting hostilities between the Americans and the Soviets came to be known, thus ominously appeared capable of bursting beyond its European confines, into Asia, with the potential to further flood the entire globe.

The Americans, who under the visionary impetus of US President Woodrow Wilson, had been in the vanguard of the movement which upheld the principle of "national self-determination" during the inter-war years, rapidly found themselves moving away from their immediate post-war support of decolonisation, and moving instead, toward the view that these insurrections were more important as Cold War battlefields, rather than as struggles against European imperialism. Both the Americans and the Soviets recognised the potential gains and losses to be had in the emerging globalisation of the Cold War.

"Here, among colonial or former colonial peoples, the superpowers could demonstrate the appeal of their particular ideological convictions and the strength of their system. Here, they could obtain access, resources, markets, strategic air and naval bases, and political loyalty for themselves and their allies - or deny them to their adversaries. Here, they could help or hinder international peace, security and respect for human rights."[5]

As a result, the advocates of decolonisation watched in dismay as their own struggles for self-determination and political independence became complicated, confused and at times overwhelmed by the rivalry of the global Cold War. They found themselves not only fighting to emancipate themselves from their imperial yokes, but also hedged between the interests of the East and the West, a battle over which they had little or no control. As the globalisation of the Cold War intensified, both the Americans and the Soviets assumed more rigid positions. They, and then their respective allies, increasingly began to regard the contest as the paramount and most critical dimension of post-war international politics.

"Given the power and influence of the protagonists, this global struggle tended to relegate other States and other issues to positions of secondary importance or less. The latter found themselves not simply influenced by, but at times caught up in and virtually dominated by the bitter rivalries of the Cold War."[6]

Whilst it remained possible for some of the colonial peoples to play one superpower bloc off against the other, or even to try to extract aid simultaneously from both sides, and thus exploit the Cold War to their own advantage, this proved to be an extremely dangerous game to play. In the event, a number of nationalist leaders attempted to break free from this entanglement and advance the cause of decolonisation for its own sake, by joining forces, setting their own agenda, and creating a non-aligned Third World. It soon became apparent, however, that the Non-Aligned Movement's (NAM) standards of international conduct, were no "higher" than those of the West, and that in their own interest, they too could be counted on to immobilise the UN.

Only two decades after it was established, it was apparent that the UN represented no more than a collectivity of independent states, unwilling to renounce the illegal use of unilateral force for political or economic gain.

"While during its inceptive years the UN may occasionally have succeeded in applying its principles and procedures, the successes tended to be serendipitous; the failures, fundamental."[7]

There were two principal tasks for which the UN was initially established and on which it must be judged today. First, there was the task of mitigating or resolving disputes, and maintaining peace between states when interests clashed. Second, there was the task of mobilising the international community to act collectively to deter, or if that fails, to resist aggression by one state against another. The optimistic belief, that states had replaced the use of force with the rule of law, that member states' military self-reliance had been made obsolete by the new arrangements for collective security, and that self-interest would be redefined by each state to give priority to the co-operative nurturing of a new, more peaceful and just international system in which everyone would have an equal stake, were proven false during the first two decades of the UN.

Instead, it soon became clear that most states which had the power to expand their territory or spheres of influence chose to advance their national self-interest through such expansion, at the expense of crippling the fledgling UN system. Furthermore, many ex-colonial nations were no better "socialised" in this respect than were the colonial powers of Europe and North America. Indeed, nationalism, with its associate evils of intolerance and exclusivity, entered a new and virulent phase. It soon became apparent, that "force was not only a bad, and resilient habit of a few old 'imperialistic' superpowers, but had also become a feature of the foreign policies of the new nations born in the idealistic glow of postwar decolonisation."[8]

New developments in the technology of war have made redundant many of the new principles and procedures of collective security. Moreover, as major nuclear powers have begun to negotiate arms reduction agreements, the proliferation of weapons of mass destruction are increasing, and conventional arms continue to be amassed in many parts of the world. Indeed, the increasing accessability of "low tech" arms has been the precursor of much violent ethnic conflict in the post-war era. The system of global policing entrusted to the wartime Big Five, quickly gave way to a system of rival power-blocs that sheltered lawbreakers, permitting smaller states to engage in aggressive acts, often against their own peoples, under the sponsorship of a superpower. Thus, it soon became apparent that the UN, initially believed to be a significant, independent arbitrator on the world scene, and not merely a fighting ring in which the superpowers could throw about their weight, was incapable of transforming the perspective, let alone the behaviour of its member states.

(ii) The United Nations in the post-Cold War era: "An Agenda for Peace", 1993

It is increasingly being maintained that in the post-Cold War era, there exists a new opportunity for the UN to transform the motivation behind traditional state conduct from narrow national self-interest to an international perspective.

"The end of the Cold War has brought about a new era of international relations and with it a new beginning in the work of the United Nations for peace. The new era has been marked by a spirit of cooperation among states which are today working within the framework of the United Nations in ways unforeseen just a few years ago. The era of superpower confrontations, which until recently had prevented the United Nations from taking on a greater role in conflict resolution, has come to an end. There now exists an opportunity to begin utilising the machinery of the United Nations for what it was originally intended to do: keep the peace."[9]

In 1992, major armed conflicts were waged in thirty locations around the world.[10] All of these conflicts except one (India-Pakistan) were intra-state.[11] During the early 1990s, efforts to control regional and intra-state conflicts assumed a place of central importance on the international agenda. In September, 1992, Boutros-Boutros Ghali, Secretary General of the UN declared that:

"A widely varying array of resentments, ambitions, rivalries and hatreds masked for decades have come to the fore to threaten international harmony and shared purpose."[12]

The events in the former Yugoslavia, the atrocities in Somalia, and other similar instances of inhumanity elsewhere, have shocked world opinion and the urgency of effective international action to prevent, control or resolve such problems has been widely acknowledged.

At the same time, the end of the Cold War appears to have opened up a new opportunity to use the UN to deal with such critical conflict problems. The convening of the first ever Security Council Summit Meeting in January 1992, heralded a new attempt by the UN to tackle the problems of international conflict prevention, management and resolution. In effect, it symbolised an unprecedented recommitment at the highest political level to the original principles and purposes of the UN Charter, in particular to the provisions for maintaining international peace and security. The Council expressed a renewed commitment to working collectively for improvements in such fields as peace-making and peace-keeping, as well as arms control and disarmament. Participants of the Council asked the newly installed Secretary General, Boutros-Boutros Ghali, to analyse the situation and recommend ways of making the organisation stronger and more efficient in these areas.

Boutros-Boutros Ghali responded to the request of the Security Council in June, 1992, with *An Agenda for Peace*.[13] It stressed the central role that ought to be played by the UN, it reviewed the various methods of preventing, controlling and resolving disputes, and briefly discussed the UN's work in each area. It now constitutes a focal point for international thinking about preventative diplomacy, peace-making, peace-keeping and post-conflict peace building.

Many of the conflicts that sprang up in the post-war era, which were conveniently shelved during the Cold War period and which now portend to threaten international peace and security, were in many cases the result of denials of the right to self-determination. Moreover, contemporary denials of the right to self-determination continue to lead to violent intra-state ethnic conflict, human rights abuse, and civil war. In the light of the UN's recent commitment to tackle regional and intra-state conflicts, and "to address the deepest causes of conflict; economic despair, social injustice and political oppression", it is important to examine to what extent Boutros-Boutros Ghali's *An Agenda for Peace*, recognises the inter-relationship between denials of the right to self-determination and the escalation of violent intra-state ethnic conflict in the post-decolonisation era.

It is evident that two important principles of international law, that of equal rights and self-determination of peoples and that of the territorial integrity of the state, come into conflict when a group wishes to separate territorially from an existing independent state. In the post-Cold War era, the UN has continued to accord priority to the territorial integrity and established boundaries of states. The overwhelming majority of present

UN members, even those who have come from newly born states, the products of colonial self-determination, prefer the *status quo* which ensures their vested interest. Knowing full well that its power base lies in the support of its member states, the UN is therefore extremely discreet so as not to make a decision inimical to its power source. In fact, in this state-based order, "the UN would be in an extremely difficult position if it were to interpret the right of self-determination in such a way as to invite or justify attacks on the territorial integrity of its own members."[14] This explains in part, why the UN is reluctant to support the right to self-determination outside the decolonisation era.

The UN is widely perceived as having been created to address specific historical problems, international peace-keeping, human rights violations, arms control, etc., and is seen to be struggling to adapt to the realities of the post-Cold War era, a struggle which Boutros-Boutros Ghali has compared to "repairing your car while driving at 120 m.p.h."[15] Indeed, the UN is regarded as being:

"...singularly ill-equipped...to resolve the inherent contradictions between the right of minorities to self-determination and the inviolability of international frontiers...Moreover, the existence of political interest groups...which, by virtue of the fact that they do not represent an internationally recognised state, cannot be easily admitted to negotiations, has greatly complicated efforts to resolve these conflicts."[16]

However, in *An Agenda for Peace*, Boutros-Boutros Ghali does attempt to respond to these "inherent contradictions" and outlines the requirements that are necessary for the resolution of such disputes.

"We have entered a time of global transition marked by uniquely contradictory trends. Regional and continental associations of States are evolving ways to deepen cooperation and ease some of the contentious characteristics of sovereign and nationalistic rivalries. National boundaries are blurred by advanced communications and global commerce, and by the decisions of States to yield some sovereign prerogatives to larger, common political associations. At the same time, however, fierce new assertions of nationalism and sovereignty spring up, and the cohesion of States is threatened by brutal ethnic, religious, social, cultural or linguistic strife. Social peace is challenged on the one hand by new assertions of discrimination and exclusion and, on the other, by acts of terrorism seeking to undermine evolution and change through democratic means."[17]

Whilst the Secretary-General emphasises that the foundation-stone of the UN's work in the sphere of conflict resolution and management "is and must remain the State", stressing that, "Respect for its fundamental sovereignty and integrity are crucial to any common international progress", he does recognise that the "time of absolute and exclusive sovereignty" has passed and admits that "its theory was never matched by reality". He therefore calls upon all the leaders of the states today to understand this and "to find a balance between the needs of good internal governance and the requirements of an ever more interdependent world."[18] He goes on to state:

"Commerce, communications and environmental matters transcend administrative borders; but inside those borders is where individuals carry out the first order of their economic, political and social lives. The United Nations has not closed its door. Yet if every ethnic, religious or linguistic group claimed statehood, there would be no limit to fragmentation, and peace, security and economic well-being for all would become ever more difficult to achieve."[19]

Whilst Boutros-Boutros Ghali clearly opposes the seccession of a group from an independent sovereign state on the grounds of the fear of "indefinite indivisibility", he does suggest that "One requirement for solutions to these problems lies in commitment to human rights with a special sensitivity to those of minorities, whether ethnic, religious, social or linguistic."[20]

Whilst the League of Nations provided machinery for the international protection of minorities, its successor, the UN, has retained to this day a policy which has "deliberately de-emphasised" the minority protection issue. As a result, the role of guarantor of minority rights passed from the international community to the state. Non-discrimination and individualism were the pillars of the UN Charter, and it was hoped that a system of individual human rights protection on the basis of non-discrimination would provide adequate protection to minorities. However, the UN General Assembly will soon have before it a declaration on the rights of minorities. "That instrument", declares Boutros-Boutros Ghali, "together with the increasingly effective machinery of the United Nations dealing with human rights, should enhance the situation of minorities as well as the stability of States."[21]

Boutros-Boutros Ghali goes on to add, that: "Globalism and nationalism need not be viewed as opposing trends, doomed to spur each other on to extremes of reaction".[22] He stressed instead, that "solid identities and fundamental freedoms" at the grass-roots level were axiomatic to "the healthy globalisation of contemporary life".[23] With reference to the "inherent contradictions" between the right of peoples to self-determination and the inviolability of international frontiers, Boutros-Boutros Ghali stated:

"The sovereignty, territorial integrity and independence of States within the established international system, and the principle of self-determination for peoples, both of great value and importance, must not be permitted to work against each other in the period ahead. Respect for democratic principles at all levels of social existence is crucial: in communities, within States and within the community of States. Our constant duty should be to maintain the integrity of each while finding a balanced design for all."[24]

In the above passage, Boutros-Boutros Ghali quite clearly accepts that the right to self-determination will continue to be applied "in the period ahead", therefore reaffirming that the right to self-determination is far from becoming obsolete, despite the fact that there are few countries left which could claim the right in the context of traditional decolonisation. Moreover, he states that the principle of self-determination of peoples and the principles of sovereignty, territorial integrity and independence of states, "need not be permitted to work against each other", i.e. he suggests that they are complementary, rather than mutually exclusive principles. Furthermore, he maintains that "respect for democratic principles at all levels of social existence...in communities within States and within the community of States", would harmonise these "opposing trends". In addition he states:

"Democracy within nations requires respect for human rights and fundamental freedoms, as set forth in the Charter. It requires as well a deeper understanding and respect for the rights of minorities and respect for the needs of the more vulnerable groups of society, especially women and children. This is not only a political matter. The social stability needed for productive growth is nurtured by conditions in which people can readily express their will. For this, strong domestic institutions of participation are essential. Promoting such institutions means promoting the empowerment of the unorganised, the poor, the marginalised. To this end, the focus of the United Nations should be on the "field", the locations where economic, social and political decisions take effect."[25]

The above paragraph suggests that in a democratic state, the legitimate rights of the majority population should be exercised in the context of effective participation by members of minorities in the larger society. It therefore implicitly recognises the "internal" right to self-determination, which as a legal concept, means that full guarantees are provided for a democratic process in which every citizen can participate under conditions of full equality. The above paragraph also recognises the two aspects of the internal right to self-determination, the "political" aspect and the "economic, social and cultural" aspect. It also implies, that the internal right to self-determination, can only be fulfilled if "strong institutions of participation" are available, the promotion of which necessarily entails "the empowerment of the unorganised, the poor, the marginalised". To this end, Boutros-Boutros Ghali suggests that the UN should be working in the "field", equipping people with the means to ensure their internal right to self-determination.

The preservation of territorial integrity and political unity of a multi-racial state depends largely upon the degree of racial integration that yields common nationality feeling. The former will endure if the latter is strengthened. The state should allow minorities or sub-groups to retain their identity and value systems, while accommodating them in an inclusive and more comprehensive identification with the state. Reasonable expectations must be created for such groups to believe that it would be more advantageous for them to remain within the present state, rather than separating from it.

"Realisation of 'internal' self-determination in the form of autonomous status to the constituent groups appears to be the viable and stable means of sustaining the territorial integrity and political unity of a multiracial state. Mere promises is not enough. Effective constitutional recognition and enforcement of promises is essential.

Under a constitutional representative regime, the people concerned can exercise more comprehensive control over, and participate in, the internal power structure of the state. An internal constitutional safety-valve could effectively be regulated to minimise the danger of overt secession. Maximisation of internal equal rights and self-determination would obviate or at least minimise the desire to revolt for outright secession in many instances. This in turn would maximise the territorial integrity of a state and reaffirm *prima facie* respect for the existing state-centric order.

An important contribution of *An Agenda for Peace* was the attempt to outline the different types of activity the UN might pursue in conflict prevention, resolution, and management. It is recommended that the range of options available to the UN Security Council as outlined in *An Agenda for Peace*, from preventative diplomacy, to peace-keeping, peace-making, and post-conflict peace-building, should be fully utilised in the prevention, the resolution and the management of intra-state ethnic conflicts which stem from the denial of claims to the internal and external aspect of the right to self-determination.

In *An Agenda for Peace,* preventative diplomacy was described as action to prevent disputes arising between parties, to prevent existing disputes from escalating into conflicts, or to limit the spread of conflicts when they occur. Such action includes measures to build confidence, such as systematic exchanges of military missions; fact-finding, to obtain information and clarify confused situations; early warning, for example of famines or mass movements of populations; preventive deployment of UN and other forces; and the creation of demilitarised zones.

Peace-making was described as action to bring hostile parties to agreement, including such traditional peace-making activities as mediation and negotiation, and the stronger concept of "peace-enforcement". The section on peace-making in *An Agenda for Peace*, also contained discussion of two issues normally considered under the rubric of "collective security", namely, "sanctions and special economic problems" and the "use of military force". These are both measures that can be taken under Article VII of the UN Charter to maintain or restore international peace and security in the face of a threat to peace, breach of the peace or act of aggression.

Peace-keeping was presented as the deployment of UN or similar forces to bring stability to areas of tension, help implement agreements among parties to a dispute and contribute to settlements. Within the ambit of peace-keeping, an increasing number of new responsibilities other than the traditional military aspects of peace-keeping are evolving, and the UN is duly being requested to perform them. UN peace-keepers have been arranging for the return of refugees, overseeing the conduct of elections, maintaining law and order, and assisting with economic reconstruction and rehabilitation. Most recently, United Nations peace-keepers have also become involved in providing protection for the delivery of humanitarian aid in volatile areas.[27]

In *An Agenda for Peace* it was noted that the deployment of a UN peace-keeping force continues to require the consent of all the main parties to a dispute. The basic conditions for the success of such operations include: a clear and practicable mandate; the co-operation of the parties in implementing that mandate; the continuing support of the Security Council; the readiness of member states to contribute the military, police and civilian personnel required; effective UN command at headquarters and in the field; and adequate financial and logistic support.

Post-conflict peace-building was described as action designed to identify and support structures which will consolidate peace, promote confidence, strengthen links among nations formerly at war and help to develop democratic societies. The report also stressed the importance of tackling the "deepest causes of conflict" such as political oppression, social injustice and economic despair.[28]

The report states that the concept of peace-building, as the construction of a new environment, should be viewed as the counterpart of preventative diplomacy, which in turn seeks to avoid the break-down of peaceful conditions.

"When conflict breaks out, mutually enforcing efforts at peace-making and peace-keeping come into play. Once these have achieved their objectives, only sustained, co-operative work to deal with underlying economic, social, cultural and humanitarian problems can place an achieved peace on a durable foundation. Preventative diplomacy is to avoid a crisis; post-conflict peace-building is to prevent a recurrence."[29]

Post-conflict peace-building may involve reducing hostile perceptions through educational exchanges, and curriculum reform may be essential to forestall tensions which could spark renewed hostilities.

An Agenda for Peace reflected that there is a growing awareness of the need to link the work of the UN in the spheres of peace-making and peace-keeping to the spheres of preventative diplomacy and post-conflict peace-building. It is generally recognised that there are two methods to tackle a dispute, on the one hand, there are those who advocate conflict management and on the other, there are those who espouse conflict resolution. The conflict managers, often regarded as "pessimists", look at the "symptoms" of a dispute, whereas the conflict resolvers, often labelled as "optimists", examine the "causes" of the dispute. Whilst there has been a general tendency in the past to see UN peace-keeping as a panacea for all the world's conflicts, it is becoming increasingly clear that UN peace-keeping initiatives can at best, only deal with the "symptoms" of the conflict.

"The expectations are exaggerated. Peace-keeping should be used only in the last resort. Preventative diplomacy and crisis management are more important."[30]

As early as 1987, a report by the then UN Secretary General, with reference to the conflict between the Greek and Turkish Cypriots, included a clear appreciation of the way that peace-making and peace-keeping operations should be supplemented by preventive diplomacy and post-conflict peace-building activities.

"A major cause of the present difficulties is, of course, the deepening distrust between the two sides and the lack of contact, at all levels between the two communities. Continuation of this trend will further undermine the prospects for a negotiated settlement. A climate must be created in which effective negotiations can take place."[31]

The report went on to call on both Greek and Turkish Cypriots to co-operate with UN efforts to promote normal contacts between the two communities. The report reflected the growing recognition that successful conflict resolution required both mediation and initiatives to deal with ethnic stereotyping, false propaganda and in some cases, the lack of understanding of each other's cultures.

(iii) The role of the United Nations in Sri Lanka

A range of the above options have been utilised by the UN to tackle the violent ethnic conflict in Sri Lanka. Whilst there have been no "traditional" UN peace-making or peace-keeping operations in Sri Lanka, the UN has been involved in several innovative operations, and there have been UN preventative diplomacy and peace-building initiatives.

The UN has made increasing use of the fact-finding or "good offices" mission as an instrument of its preventative diplomacy function. In 1992, the UN Working Group on Enforced or Involuntary Disappearances, the UN Special Rapporteur on Torture and Other Cruel, Inhuman or Degrading Treatment or Punishment, and the UN Special Rapporteur on Extrajudicial, Summary or Arbitrary Executions, visited Sri Lanka at the Government's request, and subsequently submitted to the UN Commission on Human Rights their respective reports and findings.

One of the basic requirements for traditional peace-keeping is that all other measures to bring about a lasting solution to the conflict have to have been previously exhausted. In the case of Sri Lanka, only when the UN's present policy of securing greater peace and normalcy through further and tougher human rights measures is recognised to have failed, will the UN consider strategic intervention. Thus, the Sri Lankan Government needs to respond to all of the UN's present recommendations, if it ever decides to seek UN support.

The UN Commission on Human Rights in February 1993, recommended, *inter alia*, that: the Government of Sri Lanka should implement in full the 14 recommendations of the UN Working Group on Enforced or Involuntary Disappearances contained in their 1992 Report (E/CN. 4/1992/18/Add.1), and the 4 recommendations of the Group in their 1993 Report (E/CN.4/1993/25/Add.1); it called upon the Government of Sri Lanka to invite the Special Rapporteurs on Torture and Extrajudicial, Summary or Arbitrary Executions and the Working Group on Disappearances to visit Sri Lanka in 1993; it invited the Government of

Sri Lanka to become a party to Protocols I and II Additional to the Geneva Conventions relating to the laws of war; and it called upon the Government of Sri Lanka to ratify the Convention against Torture and Other Cruel, Inhuman or Degrading Treatment or Punishment including making the necessary declarations under Article 21 and 22 recognising the competence of the Committee set up under the Convention to receive petitions; and invited the Government of Sri Lanka to ratify the Optional Protocol to the International Covenant on Civil and Political Rights.[32]

In the sphere of peace-keeping, the UN has taken various other measures. The most notorious have been undertaken by the United Nation's refugee agency, the UNHCR has been monitoring the "voluntary" repatriation of thousands of Sri Lankan Tamil refugees from the southern state of India to Sri Lanka, as part of a programme established as one of the key provisions of the Indo-Sri Lankan Accord, 1987. Approximately 30,000 Sri Lankan Tamil refugees returned to the Island during 1992, another 50,000 remain in South Indian refugee camps, whilst another 150,000 refugees live outside the camps. UNHCR has also been involved in programmes to re-build the socio-economic infrastructure of those areas to which the returnees will be sent. Such programmes of rehabilitation and resettlement are also expected to benefit the "internal" refugee community.

Doubts have been raised, however, over the "voluntary" nature of India's most recent repatriation programme which the UNHCR is involved in. NGOs and the UNHCR are currently denied access to the state-run refugee camps in Tamil Nadu. The UNHCR can only interview a tiny selection of the returnees whilst on the boats travelling to Sri Lanka. Furthermore, all letters and information leaflets to refugees in India concerning the situation in Sri Lanka are intercepted. Thus, the UNHCR is barred from carrying out its full mandate.

The operational capacity and objectives of the UNHCR in Sri Lanka were further questioned when the UNHCR was forced to temporarily suspend operations in LTTE-controlled areas of northern Sri Lanka, after thousands of Tamils staged violent demonstrations on 30 October, 1993, at Madhu, the Island's largest refugee camp thirty miles west of Vavuniya.[33] UNHCR refused to intervene after the government cut off food aid to 8,000 of the camp's 30,000 population from 1 November, 1993, to force them back to Army-controlled villages around Cheddikulam further south. Despite the relative success of the UNHCR's use of the "safe-haven" concept as a peace-keeping measure in the past, the Madhu crisis has shown how difficult it is for the UNHCR to protect refugees inside a war-zone on a long-term basis. The UNHCR's use of "Open Refugee Centres" (ORCs) in Sri Lanka as a measure of preventative diplomacy, i.e., to prevent the flow of refugees from the Island, has also been discredited by the recent Madhu debacle.

Another of the UNHCR's attempts at peace-keeping in Sri Lanka which has come to be regarded as highly contentious, was its effort to provide relief aid and humanitarian assistance to the Sri Lankan Tamils in the Jaffna peninsula (mentioned in Chapter 14). Despite the LTTE's indication of its willingness to help re-open the Pooneryn-Sangupiddy ferry in late March 1993, to co-operate with the UNHCR and to drop their pre-condition that the army withdraw, it soon became clear that the UNHCR had become deeply embroiled in a battle between the Sri Lankan government and the LTTE, in which both sides to the conflict were exploiting the presence of the UNHCR for its own interests. In late July, the UNHCR had to admit that the negotiations had irrevocably broken down.

Whereas much has been written about the peace-keeping and peace-making functions of the UN, there is very little available information on the UN's record in peace-building, which involves working with ordinary people from all sides to a conflict to reduce mutual antagonism and promote "peace from below" through attitudinal change and socio-economic reconstruction. The different types of peace-building activity include development, education for mutual understanding, the pursuit of superordinate goals and confidence building. Nevertheless, it is possible to find some examples of work by the UN in inter-communal peace-building. The United Nations Economic, Social and Cultural Organisation (UNESCO) has recently started such an initiative in Sri Lanka. This study based at the Marga Institute, involves a study of conditions,

"conducive to the implementation of development projects likely to ensure mutual understanding and cultural consensus through consultation between all the social partners, and through consideration by the decision-makers of the interests and aspirations of those population groups that are most vulnerable to the adverse effects of social change."[34]

The overall aim of the project is to link development with projects for mutual understanding. This project is itself linked to a wider UNESCO project on the "cultural dimension of development".

So to what extent is the UN currently living up to the standards set by *An Agenda for Peace*? Is it able to tackle the underlying "issues" as well as the "symptoms" of violent intra-state ethnic conflicts caused by denials of the right to self-determination? Has the UN been able to transform the motivation behind traditional state conduct, from narrow national self-interest to an international perspective? Has the UN sufficiently adapted its mechanisms to enable it to consider self-determination claims where there is a risk of violations of fundamental human rights or disturbance of the peace? In other words, to what extent has UN rhetoric matched UN reality?

An Agenda for Peace reiterated that one of the basic requirements for traditional peace-keeping, is the co-operation of the parties involved in the conflict. However, whilst the UN Charter specifically forbids any violation of national sovereignty, it is clear that the UN has begun to doubt the absolute need for consent to intervene from the concerned parties.

"The dynamics and priorities of a new era, along with the difficulties in working with local authorities, have raised profound questions about the absolute need for consent from the parties in the first place. In Somalia and former Yugoslavia, the Security Council has taken the view that desperately needed humanitarian intervention should not necessarily be held up indefinitely by the intransigence of local authorities".[35]

This apparent retreat from the long-standing mandate requiring co-operation from the parties concerned, has raised the spectre of "neo-imperialism" in UN peace-keeping initiatives. Indeed, the term "humanitarian intervention" is increasingly being regarded as "merely the latest, preferred euphemism for foreign intervention, with or without the consent of the invaded country".[36]

Whilst *An Agenda for Peace* reiterated another of the basic requirements for traditional peace-keeping, the support of the Security Council, it is clear that the UN's decision to send its peace-keeping troops into conflict areas, continues to rest less with considerations of the urgency of the situation or the conditions and the circumstances of the conflict, but rather with concerns of a more "real-politik" nature. Moreover, it is becoming increasingly apparent that in the present climate, when wages are already being paid to thousands of UN relief workers, logistics may have to come before human rights.

Concern has begun to be raised over the UN's objectivity and fairness. What was once regarded as a tool for small and progressive nations, is now increasingly being recognised as a tool for the rich and powerful. "Today's UN" writes one United Nations sceptic, "is an essentially and intrinsically conservative institution, operating almost solely for the benefit of the advanced capitalist world and what used to be thought of as the

"West"".37

Since the end of the Cold War, radical policy and organisational changes have been taking place at the UN "that have seen the Security Council become an instrument of US power".38 Moreover, "...in these days of Secretary General Boutros-Boutros Ghali, who has allowed the White House to dictate the reorganisation of the world body down to the appointment of its most senior executives, it matters not what the Charter says, but what Augustus in Washington wants".39

Furthermore, whilst the UN Secretary General is predominantly controlled by the United States of America, the UN "is in effect a dangerous and uncontrolled arm of the American government, with no counter-veiling power to balance it. In 1991 it launched the Gulf War; in 1992 it organised sanctions against Libya; in 1993 it permitted the bombing of Mogadishu. All was done in the name of the UN".40 In response to such scepticism, Boutros-Boutros Ghali states:

"The United Nations will have to be mindful of these concerns and allay such fears by adhering to principles and demonstrating impartiality and consistency in its decisions, particularly with regard to the application of Chapter VII provisions. Any perception that the United Nations was being arbitrary or unfair in its decisions to enact enforcement provisions could seriously undermine the credibility and the effectiveness of the United Nations".41

Certainly, in an era of increasing activity, the Security Council, constituting the most of the major industrially-developed Western powers, needs to allay the fear of conflict-ridden states, who believe that UN involvement depends predominantly on the geo-political significance of the country concerned to the members of the Security Council, or more directly to the US. Whilst on the one hand, the benefits of UN intervention in a country torn assunder by violent ethnic conflict appear attractive, on the other hand, "there may be soon no debate of difference between "intervention", whatever its semantic mask, and imperialism; a non-word in today's Orwellian lexicon of control".42

Whilst UN peace initiatives are decided upon in Washington, calls for increased UN involvement in states that are geo-politically insignificant to the US, will no doubt continue to fall on deaf ears.

During the Cold War, the strategic alignments between the states of South Asia and the external powers were relatively static. India's assumed role as regional South Asian super-power, greatly influenced Western foreign policy towards Sri Lanka. Indeed, in 1987, India was effectively relied upon by the Western super powers to solve Sri Lanka's ethnic conflict. In the aftermath of the Gulf War, and the disintegration of the Soviet Union, however, new strategic alignments have begun to emerge. India's old concern about the possible development of a Sri Lanka-Pakistan-China axis, has changed somewhat. Whilst China remains friendly with Pakistan, and Pakistan remains on good terms with Sri Lanka, the US-Pakistani relationship has begun to crumble. The growing US strategic convergence with India, and divergence from Pakistan, has clearly removed much of India's concern over the protection of her southern flanks.

In the marked absence of a firm, clear and systematic stand on the part of the UN towards separatist conflicts, numerous states continue to become directly or indirectly involved in other state's separatist conflicts. Such a disarray of self-interested and partisan involvement is undoubtedly detrimental to the solution of any separatist conflict.

The increasing tangible involvement of states in the Sri Lankan conflict has been clearly discernible. In spite of the continued violation of human rights by the Sri Lankan armed forces, it has been business as usual for many UN member states in regard to transactional involvement in Sri Lanka. Other states are tangibly involved in a humanitarian fashion, supplying relief aid to civilians, and to displaced persons within the Island, whilst other states are actively involved in a non-military fashion, providing foreign development aid without any concern for human rights issues. Whilst direct military confrontation against the centre and full-scale military intervention has not occurred, indirect military involvement or "physical" intervention has taken place. Individual states have been guilty of military involvement outside the secessionist terrain, providing sanctuary, training camps, bases of operations, arms and other military equipment. Whilst Sri Lanka ostensibly "invited" India to intervene militarily, under the aegis of the Indo-Sri Lanka Accord in 1987, since India's expulsion from the Island in 1989, India has systematically been indirectly, militarily involved in Sri Lanka.

An Agenda for Peace clearly recognised that the UN does not create the conditions of its own success, but that these must be provided by the parties to the conflicts themselves.

"The solution to the conflict not only can come, but must come from the parties themselves. It cannot be imposed from outside. The third party plays a vital role in this, but only to the extent that it can facilitate the interaction process."[43]

Third party peace-keeping can only be effective if a desire to avoid violence exists among all the parties to the conflict and that this desire has been expressed, for example, in the form of a cease-fire agreement. The pre-negotiation phase, is an important part of any UN peace-making initiative.

By virtue of the fact that many parties to violent intra-state ethnic conflicts, do not represent an internationally recognised state, and are therefore not easily admitted to negotiations, efforts to resolve such conflicts are greatly complicated and hindered. A lacuna exists between the UN's apparent willingness to prevent, resolve and manage regional and intra-state violent ethnic conflicts, and the ability of the parties to the conflict to present their case to the UN in the first instance.

"The UN is not very well equipped to deal with non-State actors. The Charter was drafted on the assumption that disputes arise between States...there is no provision in the Charter by which the Security Council or General Assembly may relate to non-State agencies, such as liberation movements, communal minorities, or political parties."[44]

In order to transmit their views to the UN, non-dominant ethnic groups have to rely on either sympathetic individuals, international NGOs with UN consultative status, or on the sponsorship of independent states. In the meantime, many violent ethnic conflicts, which are the outcome of frustrated claims to self-determination, are launched by peoples who see no prospect of achieving their aspirations through the existing political process. In the event, many groups in such conflicts, who are deemed to be illegitimate by the existing power structures, take up arms to pursue their goals.

"If claims to self-determination are only to be admitted after they have been successfully asserted by force, then peoples are being encouraged to take up arms immediately, without even bothering to go through the political motions at the UN Thus, the absence of any international tribunal for hearing claims, and acting upon them where they are found to be justified, is a constant threat to peace and security."[45]

In September 1993, the US Ambassador to Sri Lanka stated that the UN was unwilling to intervene in the ethnic conflict in Sri Lanka, until a "deal" had been struck between both parties to the conflict. Clearly, the Sri Lankan government and the LTTE, need to show a willingness to co-operate and a desire to negotiate a political solution to the conflict, before any form of international peace-keeping can be established by the UN, or any other international organisation in Sri Lanka. However, whilst both the Sri Lankan government and the LTTE, remain equally intransigent, the materialisation of this deal remains unlikely in the near future.

Whilst there have been some UN preventative diplomacy and

peace-building initiatives and other less traditional peace-keeping functions in Sri Lanka, the failure of the UN to intervene constructively in the conflict, until after a deal has been achieved, highlights the inadequacies of the UN when it comes to dealing with violent intra-state ethnic conflicts, which are the result of claims to self-determination. Claims to the right to self-determination, are supra-national and supra-regional affairs, i.e., they are international affairs, and therefore ought to be dealt with by the international community, rather than being left to state governments and self-interested outside states. It is becoming increasingly clear, that a group's claim to the right to self-determination has to be heeded by the international community, if an upsurge of ethnic violence is to be avoided in the future.

Notes

1 Pierre van den Burthe., quoted in: Ryan. S., "Ethnic conflict and international relations", (1990), p.98.

2 Gellner. E., (1974), p.24, quoted in Ryan.S., p.98.

3 Roger Hill., in: Stockholm International Peace Research Institute Yearbook 1993: Armaments and Disarmament, p.49, (hereafter referred to as Sipri).

4 Ryan. S., p.122.

5 Lauren. P.G., "Power and prejudice: The politics and diplomacy of racial discrimination", (1988), p.205.

6 Ibid. p.187.

7 Franck. T.M., "Nation against nation: What happened to the UN dream and what the US can do about it?", (1985), p.45.

8 Ibid., p.53.

9 Boutros-Boutros Ghali, "UN peace-keeping in a new era: A new chance for peace", in: The World Today, Vol.49, No.4, (April 1993), pp.66-69, p.69.

10 In: The Sipri Yearbook (Sipri), 1993, a major armed conflict is characterised by protracted combat between the military forces of two or more governments or of one government and at least one organised armed group, and incurring battle-related deaths of at least 1000 persons during the entire conflict (p.81). Sipri, 1993, cites Sri Lanka as one of the thirty major armed conflicts in 1992. The total number of Sri Lankan armed forces in 1992 was 125,000 and the total number of LTTE was 7,000. The total deaths resulting from the conflict since 1983 is 24,000, 4,000 of which died in 1992. There has been an increase in battle-related deaths of 10-50% since 1991. Figures taken from: Appendix 3A, "Major Armed Conflicts, 1992", in: Sipri, 1993.

11 "The relationship between the number of inter-state and intra-state major armed conflicts has not changed appreciably since the mid-1980s. A clear trend towards a greater number of intra-state wars can be observed for the period from 1945 until the late 1980s. The annual number of inter-state wars in this period did not exceed 8, with a peak in 1965-72". Lindgren, K., Varldens Krig (Swedish Institute of International Affairs: Stockholm, 1990), quoted in: Sipri, p.81.

12 United Nations General Assembly, Report of the Secretary General on the Work of the Organisations, September, 1992, UN Document A/47/1 (United Nations: New York, 11 September, 1992), p.43, cited in: Sipri, p.45.

13 United Nations Security Council, "An Agenda for Peace: Preventative

diplomacy, Peace making and Peace-keeping", Report of the Secretary-General pursuant to the statement adopted by the Summit Meeting of the Security Council on 31 January, 1992, UN Document A/47/277 (S/24111) (United Nations: New York, 17 June, 1992), paras 1-15, reproduced in: Sipri, Appendix 2A, (hereafter referred to as "An Agenda for Peace").

14 V. Van Dyke, "Self-determination and minority rights", in: V. Van Dyke, (ed.), "Human rights, the US and world community", p.102, quoted in: Islam, M. R., "Bangladesh liberation movement", (1987), p.267.

15 Boutros-Boutros Ghali, in: *Time*, 8th January, 1993, quoted in: Fuller, E., "Mediators for Transcancasia's conflict", in: The World Today, (May, 1993), Vol.49, No.5, pp.89-92, p.89.

16 Ibid.

17 Boutros-Boutros Ghali, "An Agenda for Peace", Para.11.

18 Ibid., Para.17.

19 Ibid.

20 Ibid., Para.18.

21 Ibid.

22 Ibid., Para.19.

23 Ibid.

24 Ibid.

25 Ibid., Para.81.

26 Islam. M. R., "Bangladesh liberation movement", (1987), p.293.

27 Since 1988, the UN has created as many peace-keeping operations, in four years, as it did in the previous four decades. The number of military personnel involved in peace-keeping operations rose from 15,000 in 1991 to 62,000 in 1992.

28 "An Agenda for Peace", Para.15.

29 Ibid., Para.57.

30 Mr. Rotfeld. A. D., Sipri Director, "UN called on to revise its rules on peace-keeping", in: *The Financial Times*, June 16th, 1993.

31 UN Doc. S/18880, 29 May, 1987, cited in: Ryan. S., p.149.

32 In 1993, Sri Lanka ratified the Convention against Torture and Other Cruel, Inhuman or Degarding Treatment or Punishment.

33 See "Revolt at Madhu", in: *The Sri Lanka Monitor*, October, 1993, p.3.

34 UNESCO Budget Proposal for 1988, UN Doc. 24/C/5, Paris, Project No. 08104, cited in: Ryan. S., p.148.

35 Boutros-Boutros Ghali, in: "UN peace-keeping in a new era: A new chance for peace", p.68.

36 John Pilger, "The US fraud in Africa: Operation Restore Hope is part of a new age imperialism", in: <u>New Statesman Society</u>, 8 January, 1991, p.11.
37 Richard Gott, "Nations divided by a lost vision", in: *The Guardian*, Saturday August 28, 1993.
38 John Pilger, pp.10-11.
39 Ibid.
40 Richard Gott.
41 Boutros-Boutros Ghali., p.66.
42 John Pilger., p.11.
43 Ryan. S., p.104
44 Ibid., p.143.
45 Lord Avebury, "Self-determination: The way forward", a discussion paper, published by International Alert, July, 1992, p.8.

CHAPTER 16

The "internationalisation" of the Sri Lankan Tamils' right to self-determination

One of the ways in which the UN has been forced to consider ethnic issues, is through the work of the UN Human Rights Commission and its Sub-Commission on the Prevention of Discrimination and the Protection of Minorities (hereafter referred to as the Sub-Commission). Whilst the UN Charter does not refer to minority rights or minority protection as such, but relies instead on an approach based on the principle of individual rights and non-discrimination, the UN has not been able to avoid minority protection and group rights altogether. Indeed, the measures adopted by the UN for the protection of ethnic minority and group rights, provide an important mechanism for the prevention of violent intra-state ethnic conflict.

This chapter shall begin with a brief analysis of the genesis and development of the UN Human Rights Commission and its Sub-Commission. In this way it will reveal to what extent the UN Human Rights Commission and its Sub-Commission are simply the political organs of a corporate body consisting of sovereign member states, thereby determining the effectiveness of these UN organs in preventing, managing and resolving protracted and violent intra-state ethnic conflicts.

In the absence of a mechanism which can entertain complaints about self-determination as such, from the parties concerned as well as from sympathetic governments, NGOs and concerned individuals, the UN Human Rights Commission and its Sub-Commission function as one of the major lobbies for the international recognition of an ethnic group's claim to the right to self-determination. An empirical case study of the international lobby for the recognition of the Sri Lankan Tamils' claim to self-determination that has been raised before the UN Human Rights Commission and its Sub-Commission over the last decade will illustrate the effectiveness of the UN organs as mechanisms for addresssing complaints regarding the claims to the right to self-determination from groups within independent states outside of the decolonisation process.

This chapter is separated into two sections. The first section will examine the demands that have been raised over the last decade before the UN Human Rights Commission and its Sub-Commission, for the United Nations to initiate steps to satisfy the aspirations of the Tamil people within the framework of human rights and the right to self-determination. Moreover, it will reveal to what extent the UN, the Sri Lankan government and independent states have complied with such recommendations in an attempt to resolve the conflict. It also examines the recommendations that were raised before the UN Human Rights Commission on ways in which the conflict might be resolved. These recommendation included; the clear demand for greater UN involvement in the ethnic conflict, further linkage of the Sri Lankan government's human right's record with Western development aid, increased linkage of the arms trade with human rights record of Sri Lanka and tighter arms export controls, and enhanced efforts to make economic development initiatives in Sri Lanka reflect ethnic and cultural imperatives. Such an analysis reveals that the Sri Lankan government has failed to respond seriously to the many proposals for cease-fire and peace-talks that have been presented before the UN Commission, by other concerned governments.

It is hoped that such a study will reveal to what extent the Sri Lankan Tamils' claim to self-determination has been and continues to be "trapped, used and abused" by the politics and diplomacy of contemporary "interracial relations". Furthermore, it will reveal the "double standards" that are employed by the majority of UN member states in their relations with Sri Lanka, under the aegis of the UN and its subsidiary bodies. Moreover, it is hoped that such an analysis will reveal that the more a secessionist movement becomes internationalised, the more the inherent weight of the centre comes to bear, as the centre is more often than not able to muster external aid and cut down, one by one, the secessionists' allies. The internationalisation of the Sri Lankan Tamil national question, has ultimately favoured the Sri Lankan government, at the expense of the Tamil-speaking people, i.e., it has favoured Sri Lanka's right to territorial integrity over the right of the Tamil-speaking people to the right to self-determination.

The second section of this chapter shall focus on the forty-ninth sitting of the UN Human Rights Commission, held in Geneva, on 8 February, 1993, at which further concern was raised regarding the Sri Lankan Tamils' right to self-determination. This section shall focus predominantly on the response of the Sri Lankan government to the various issues raised by the fifteen NGOs at this session. An examination of the issues raised before the UN Commission by the various international NGOs, and by the Sri Lankan government, clearly reveals the polarity of views held with regard to the exercise of the right to self-determination in the post-decolonisation era. The majority of the NGOs represented at the sitting, maintained that because the Tamils are a "people", who occupy a contiguous territory, and who suffer from marked discrimination and oppression, they are therefore entitled to the right to self-determination. The Sri Lankan government on the other hand, adopted a state-centred approach, maintaining that the Tamils are a minority group, whose protection and interests should lie within the unified state of Sri Lanka. Moreover, it is clearly revealed in the final recommendations submitted by the UN Human Rights Commission with regards to the Sri Lankan ethnic conflict, that the UN itself remains unwilling to countenance claims to the right to self-determination, made by ethnic groups living within independent states. It is apparent that the UN continues to rely on recommendations for the promotion and protection of individual human rights, for the resolution of intra-state ethnic conflicts, whilst de-emphasising the necessity of international minority rights protection and the integral role that denials of claims to the right to self-determination have in many violent and protracted intra-state ethnic conflicts.

(i) A brief history of the UN Human Rights Commission and its Sub-Commission on the Prevention of Discrimination and the Protection of Minorities

Once the UN General Assembly had drafted the Universal Declaration of Human Rights, proclaimed on December, 10, 1948, which was to become "the moral touchstone for all claims at the international level that justice had not been done at the national level",[1] it turned its attention to providing practical machinery for giving effect to, and monitoring compliance with the proclaimed human rights principles.

This practical machinery was inaugurated in 1946, when the Economic and Social Council (ECOSOC) established a Commission on Human Rights, which one year later created a Sub-Commission on the Prevention of Discrimination and the Protection of Minorities. Following the Declaration of Human Rights, the UN began to receive a steady stream of communications from governments, NGOs, and individuals complaining of serious human rights violations. In response, in 1970, ECOSOC authorised the Sub-Commission to create a working group that would review all such communications, and transmit to the Sub-Commission those that revealed a "consistent pattern of gross...violations".[2] The Sub-Commission would then consider these and report to the Commission on Human Rights, which would then choose from among three courses of action; to do nothing, to undertake a study of the situation, or to establish an investigating committee.

Initially, the Sub-Commission was composed of twelve members who were nominated by governments, but who were supposed to serve as independent experts. Today, (1993) the Sub-Commission is composed of twenty-six members, appointed so as to ensure an acceptable regional distribution; seven Africans, five Asians, six West Europeans (including North Americans), five Latin Americans and three East Europeans.

Whilst the establishment of the Commission on Human Rights and its Sub-Commission appeared to mark a milestone on the road towards racial equality and respect for basic human rights, and "began a process of taking the treatment of citizens out of the exclusive confines of domestic jurisdiction and of transforming individuals from mere objects of international sympathy into subjects of international law",[3] the Commission on Human Rights and its Sub-Commission have not been able to shake off the public impression that they are "probably the most elaborate wastepaper basket ever invented".[4]

During the early years, the Commission on Human Rights and its Sub-Commission remained firmly under the control of the Western powers, who demonstrated a distinct reluctance to discuss or to take any meaningful action on the issue of racial discrimination or minority protection. Moreover, governments commonly refused to let their representatives on the Commission take any action upon individual petitions submitted to it that complained of human rights violations.

This distinct pattern of deliberate inaction was dramatically changed, albeit only temporarily, by the rise of Afro-Asian membership in the UN Collectively, these new states from Africa and Asia exerted enough pressure to begin a radical and turbulent transformation in their favour in the composition and character of the Commission on Human Rights and its Sub-Commission.

However, the UN is eminently a corporate body, consisting of sovereign member states gathered in political organs, such as the General Assembly, the ECOSOC, the Security Council, and in subsidiary bodies such as the Human Rights Commission and its Sub-Commission.

"These political organs, components of the UN system, deliberate and act in accordance with the perceived national self-interest of the Member States. The outcome may be a "UN" resolution, but is, in fact, no more than an expression of the collective political will of a multitude of sovereign States. If there is a UN "double standard", it is the "double standard" of the *member states* that is to blame".[5]

The member states who are guilty of such "double standards", include not only the old imperial powers but also the newly independent Afro-Asian states. The double standards of the UN member states which have led states and individuals to regard international relations as no more than "interracial relations", includes the open and frequent verbal castigation by states of the gross human rights violations of particular countries, whilst they themselves remain unwilling to enforce human rights standards in practice. States continue to refuse to acknowledge for example, that their political and financial support helps to perpetuate racial policies in the receiving state. Similarly, states often argue that the immediate strategic, economic and ideological interests are more important than defending human rights.

It was precisely this use of double standards in the inter-state system, which prompted Jeane Kirkpatrick, US Ambassador before the UN, to deliver a courageous and contentious statement, in which she declared that it was neither fair nor reasonable to judge the human rights violations of some states harshly, while completely ignoring the gross abuse of others. She accused some nations of attempting to "use human rights less as a standard and a goal than as a political weapon; less to expand the domains of freedom and law than to expand the scope of their hegemony".[6]

The application of standards, she continued, "has grown more distorted and more cynical" while human rights have "become a bludgeon to be wielded by the strong against the weak, by the majority against the isolated, by the blocs against the disorganised".[7] Kirkpatrick concluded her speech, by accusing the UN of "moral hypocrisy".

International concern over questions of human rights has frequently been in open conflict with the basic principles of sovereignty and non-intervention, governing the politics and diplomacy of states in their internal and external relations.

"No major power - white, black, or brown; Communist, capitalist, or non-aligned - has committed its resources...purely out of moral conviction. Nations undertake the use of force, military or economic, only when their national interests are threatened or can be greatly enhanced".[8]

However, the maintenance of the territorial integrity of a state is not a goal to be pursued above all others. The cardinal purpose is to create the atmosphere for dignified human existence, and the principle of equal

321

rights and self-determination, being essentially fundamental human rights, must be given priority. There need not be any conflict between the right of a state to territorial integrity and the right of peoples to self-determination. Neither of them is irrefutable, but implies corresponding duties. Both rights ought to be asserted and considered strictly in terms of the responsibilities that accompany them. The situation therefore warrants a balance between them.

The fact remains, however, that the effectiveness of the UN and other international bodies ultimately rests upon the willingness of their sovereign member states to enforce decisions. The following sections of this chapter will clearly illustrate that the absence of political will on behalf of both the Sri Lankan government and the LTTE to achieve a political solution to the ethnic conflict in the Island, is compounded by the absence of political will on behalf of the majority of UN member states. However, the following examination of the various submissions made to the U.N Human Rights Commission, reveals that there does exist a contingent of sympathetic governments and international NGOs, which could be exploited further by both parties to the conflict, if there was a genuine willingness on both sides to establish a political dialogue.

(ii) Sri Lanka's human rights record is scrutinized by the UN Human Rights Commission 1983-1993

Over the last fifteen years, the LTTE have grown from a ragged guerrilla outfit into a fully-fledged military movement, capable of engaging the Sri Lankan security forces in conventional warfare. In this capacity, they have quite clearly become an effective guerrilla movement. However, militarism alone is failing to achieve the goals of the LTTE The movement seems to be afflicted by political impotency, which is proving an obstacle to becoming an internationally recognised liberation movement. The LTTE often seems to lack political vision and seems to be more intent on the suppression of freedoms. Indeed, the fundamental rights of freedom of association and expression, which are essential ingredients in a democratic society, have almost become non-existent in the LTTE-controlled areas of the Northern and Eastern Provinces of Sri Lanka, due to persistent and co-ordinated suppression. As a result, the genuine commitment of the LTTE to international humanitarian standards remains questionable.

This impression is maintained not only by international independent observers, but also by members of the international Tamil diaspora, including members of the LTTE itself. On January 15, 1993, Sathasivam Krishnakumar, otherwise known as "Kittu", the senior international representative of the LTTE, died when a ship returning him to Jaffna, after being intercepted by Indian navy craft, was blown up.[9] A former Jaffna military commander, cousin and confidante of LTTE leader, Prabhakaran, Kittu had kept in close contact with his leader during a four-year spell as the LTTE's senior representative in Europe. Kittu's death was significant, for it appeared that much of his thinking had changed during his years of exile, and that he was returning in order to inform Prabhakaran, how the ruthless inward-looking Tiger movement was perceived by the 250,000 strong Tamil diaspora in Europe. Furthermore, it seemed that Kittu believed that if the Tamil liberation struggle was to be successful in the long term, it must win acceptance from the international community and observe international human rights standards. Whatever the true purpose of Kittu's mission to Sri Lanka, it is clear that his death, following the collapse of the Parliamentary Select Committee negotiations, represented another lost opportunity to break down intransigence, polarisation and escalation on both sides of the conflict.

International lobby for recognition is clearly an important intermediate stage in the development of a separatist movement from a para-military, guerrilla group, to an internationally recognised national liberation movement. Such recognition will usually culminate in a politically negotiated compromise, and/or the devolution of meaningful power, and in the final instance in the acquisition of territory and the attainment of independence.[10] The preoccupation of the LTTE with the control of the community in the Northern and Eastern Provinces, and the lack of credible lobby of its own, has affected the momentum of the international campaign for recognition of the Sri Lankan Tamils' right to self-determination.

However, since 1983, the year in which Sri Lanka was consumed by violent ethnic conflict on an unprecedented scale, the Tamil national struggle has been put firmly on the international agenda, with increasing verbal support for a solution to the conflict coming from various sympathetic governments and NGOs. The international campaign for the resolution of the conflict has been raised primarily before the United Nations Human Rights Commission and its Sub-Commission on Prevention of Discrimination and Protection of Minorities.

The UN Sub-Commission on Prevention of Discrimination and Protection of Minorities, first adopted a resolution on Sri Lanka in 1984, following extensive testimony regarding communal violence against the Tamil-speaking people.[11] The UN Commission on Human Rights has also responded, most notably in Resolution 61/1987.

"The Commission on Human Rights, guided by the Universal Declaration of Human Rights, the International Covenant on Civil and Political Rights and the universally accepted rules of international humanitarian law...noting also that more than a hundred new cases of alleged disappearances in Sri Lanka have been transmitted to the Government by the Working Group on Enforced or Involuntary Disappearances...calls upon all parties and groups to respect fully the universally accepted rules of humanitarian law...appeals to the Government of Sri Lanka to intensify its cooperation with the International Committee of the Red Cross in the fields of dissemination and promotion of international humanitarian law and invites the Government of Sri Lanka to consider favourably the offer of the services of the ICRC to fulfil its functions of protection of human rights standards..."[12]

Whilst there has been no official action by the UN Human Rights Commission on Sri Lanka since its adoption of Resolution 61/1987, international NGOs have consistently exerted pressure on the UN Human Rights Commission to take measures to resolve the ethnic conflict in Sri Lanka over the last decade. At the forty-seventh session of the UN Human Rights Commission held in February, 1991, twenty-two NGOs made a joint statement on Sri Lanka, urging the Commission to pass a resolution which:

(i) recalled Resolution 61/1987 which recognised the necessity of ending the existing armed hostilities to enable the resumption of negotiations;

(ii) expressed serious concern regarding the continuing violations of human rights and fundamental freedoms in Sri Lanka, and;

(iii) conveyed its support for the role that the Centre for Human Rights and its mechanisms can play in the promotion of human rights in Sri Lanka.[13]

Since the forty-second session of the UN Commission on Human Rights in 1986, international NGOs have consistently requested that the UN Commission initiate steps to satisfy the aspirations of the Tamil people within the framework of human rights *and* the right to self-determination. During the forty-second session of the UN Sub-Commission on Human Rights in 1986, the Tamil peoples' right to self-determination was invoked vehemently by a number of NGOs. A joint statement was made by eighteen international NGOs under Agenda item 6, which dealt with violations of human rights, stating:

"It has become a matter of urgent importance to act on the reports of

several Human Rights Organisations on the gross and consistent violations of human rights in Sri Lanka and to initiate steps to satisfy the aspirations of the Tamil people within the framework of Human Rights and
the Right to Self-determination."[14]

A year later, at the forty-third session of the UN Sub-Commission on
Prevention of Discrimination and Protection of Minorities, the
International Educational Development Inc. (IED), under Agenda item 6
stated that they were:

"...convinced that the extreme racist nature of the Sinhala government
justifies invoking the principle of self-determination of peoples and the
application of armed conflict rules governing wars against racist regimes
in the exercise of the right to self-determination. Indeed, the international
community must invoke self-determination due to persistent non-fulfil-
ment of the rights of minorities who have been subsumed into larger
States, because, as a last resort, it is the only means of assuring human
rights".[15]

At the forty-eighth session, of the UN Commission on Human Rights
on 31 January, 1992, the IED once again addressed the principle of
self-determination in application to the Sri Lankan Tamils under Agenda
item 9, which dealt with "The rights of peoples to self-determination and
its application to peoples under colonial or alien domination or foreign
occupation." The IED's statements were clearly made in response to
international events that had taken place during 1991:

"Recently, a number of governments have recognised the right of the
peoples of Croatia and Slovenia to their independence and the full realisation of self-determination. Western Sahara is now finally on the way to its
realization of self-determination. The Baltic states now sit here as independent governments".[16]

With reference to Article 1(2) of the International Covenant on Civil
and Political Rights, and the International Covenant on Social and
Economic Rights, which reads "All peoples have the right to self-determination", the IED stated:

"Our organisation would like to emphasize the word ALL. This word
does not mean that only certain peoples, such as those who are favourites
of one government or another, have the right. This word does not mean
that only white, Eastern Europeans have the right. This word does not
mean that only those who fight for the right or only those that do not fight
for the right have it. The word all means all."[17]

The IED submitted that the right to self-determination is a pre-requisite to the realisation and enjoyment of all other fundamental human

rights, and quoting the words of legal scholar, Professor Chen, it stated that the right to self-determination is "an expression of human dignity and is deeply rooted in the concept of human dignity", maintaining that self-determination has, at its heart, the peoples' wish to be "active agents of their own history".[18] Self-determination, the IED asserted, is simply the other side of the coin of democracy. The IED continued:

"Regardless of the high esteem that the international community has afforded the right to self-determination in international instruments, the same international community has been reluctant to apply the principle or, most appallingly, has applied it in a biased way".[19]

The IED recognised the continuing problem that the international community has in defining the "peoples" to whom the right of self-determination applies, and suggested that dispositive guidance had been provided by the International Court of Justice, in the Western Sahara Case (ICJ Reports, 1975), in which it identified the elements of a "people" as, subjective and objective factors coupled with a relationship to identifiable territory.[20]

The IED stated that the Sri Lankan situation had generated discriminatory reactions and warranted discussion under Agenda item 9, which dealt with "The rights of peoples to self-determination and its application to peoples under colonial or alien domination or foreign occupation." The IED suggested that the Tamil population of the Northern and Eastern parts of Sri Lanka, clearly satisfied the definition of "peoples" as stipulated under international standards, and most importantly, that their relationship to their territory, i.e., the Northern and Eastern Provinces, had already been specifically recognised by the government of Sri Lanka in the Bandaranaike-Chelvanayakam Pact, 1967.[21]

The IED acknowledged that the UN Human Rights Commission had passed resolution 61/1987, but stated that there have been many tragic events in the Tamil-Sinhala conflict since then, and that the Commission, although not its Rapporteur, have remained silent. It contended:

"Now, the Liberation Tigers of Tamil Eelam, the military force defending the rights of the Tamil people, has again called for a ceasefire and a process of negotiation in order to realise the rights of self-determination of both the Tamil and Sinhalese peoples in a peaceful manner. It appears that the Government of Sri Lanka intends to continue to pursue a military victory over the Tamil people and their armed forces...We call upon the Commission to...place the legitimate call of the Tamil people for their self-determination on an equal basis as that of others now recognized by the international community."[22]

Under Agenda item 12, which dealt with violations of human rights, the IED stated that since 1987, when the Commission last took action on the situation in Sri Lanka: "...the Tamil people may have lost any acceptance of Sinhala rule and indeed have a clear case for self-determination based on historical reality and on the persistent refusal of the Sinhala majority to address the aspirations and goals of the Tamil people within the context of national integrity".[23]

At the forty-seventh session of the UN Human Rights Commission, held in February 1991, under Agenda item 9, "Liberation, The Anti-Imperialist, Anti-Racist Organisation" (hereafter referred to as Liberation), stated:

"The systematic violations of human rights by the Sri Lankan Government over a period of four decades are well documented and are clearly no accidental happenings. They constitute evidence of the resolute and determined efforts of alien Sinhala Governments to subjugate and assimilate the people of Tamil Eelam within the framework of a unitary Sinhala Buddhist Sri Lankan State. The people of Tamil Eelam have suffered long enough and have waited long enough for their human rights. Today, they are a people who can no longer be denied their right to self-determination".[24]

"Liberation" urged the Commission to give renewed attention to the views of UN Special Rapporteur, Dr. Hector Gros Espiell, expressed in his report for the United Nations Sub-Commission on Prevention of Discrimination of Minorities in 1980, in which he stated:

"Every people subject to any form or type of colonial or alien domination possess the right to self-determination, and no distinction can be drawn between one people and another for the purpose of recognising the existence of this right if there is evidence of colonial or alien domination of the people or peoples in question".[25]

"Liberation" also urged the Commission to give careful consideration to the comments of Professor Leo Kuper in the Minority Rights Group Report on International Action Against Genocide, 1982, in which he asserted: "...genocide continues to be an odious scourge on mankind...there are also at the present time many immediate issues related to genocide which call for the most urgent action...(such as) the communal massacres in Sri Lanka...some of these genocidal massacres arise out of struggles for greater autonomy, and might be regulated by recognition of the right of self-determination".[26]

Since the forty-third session of the UN Commission on Human Rights, in 1987, various international NGOs have consistently urged the

Commission to take various measures to achieve a peaceful resolution to the conflict in Sri Lanka. One of the main recommendations has been to establish direct linkage between international development assistance to an improvement in the human rights situation in the country.

At its forty-third session, under Agenda item 6, which dealt with questions of violations of human rights, IED called upon all members of the Commission and representatives of all governments who were signatories to the Human Rights Charter, to censure the Sri Lankan government for its record on human and democratic rights, suggesting that all aid channelled through such governments should be made conditional on the restoration of democracy and human rights within Sri Lanka. The IED suggested that the Sri Lankan government was interpreting the failure of every Western state to censure it for its human rights record, and every item of foreign aid, however reluctantly given, as an endorsement of its actions.

A significant number of Sri Lankan professionals continue to receive their higher education, and/or find employment overseas, and there is a long history of emigration from the professional classes, especially amongst Sri Lankan Tamils and other minorities, to western Europe, North America and Australia. The country is highly dependent on foreign aid, and a large number of foreign aid agencies are represented in Colombo. The conditions exist therefore for the creation of a strong civil rights/democracy lobby using foreign aid as its point of leverage.[27] However, these possibilities were not fully exploited in the early 1980's, in large part, because the Sri Lankan government was very pro-Western, and in that era of crusading Reaganism/Thatcherism, this was sufficient protection against any major expression of international concern about domestic politics.[28] However, the international environment has changed considerably over the last few years, and for the present at least, international concerns about civil rights are being brought to bear on the Sri Lankan government directly.

With respect to external checks on the Sri Lankan regime, foreign pressure in relation to the violation of civil rights and the frequency of "disappearances" has been successfully tied in as a condition of future foreign aid, obliging the Sri Lankan government to pay more attention to this issue. A reaction that has been partly symbolic, but also partly substantive.

In late October, 1990, Sri Lanka asked for more aid at the Donors Consortium meeting in Paris, to combat the effects of the UN Security Council's trade embargo on Iraq after its invasion of Kuwait, which resulted not only in the loss of a large market, Iraq being the second largest buyer of tea, but also in the loss of an important military supply. Two days before the meeting took place, the twelve countries of the EC released a statement in Brussels deploring Sri Lanka's human rights record, and warned that future assistance could be made conditional upon improvements in human rights.[29] Rather than undertake a position of not giving aid because of human rights violations, however, the UK stated that only in the future would this play a role in the giving of aid. This was a direct contradiction of a statement made earlier by MP Douglas Hurd, in which he said, "Governments who persist with repressive policies should not expect us to support their folly with scarce aid resources."[30] In the event, the UK's reluctance to forgoe a billion dollar's worth of business, was endorsed by the rest of the EC, resulting in the World Bank pledging Sri Lanka $1 billion in aid for the year 1991.

The increased linkage of foreign aid with human rights, however, has generated a strong negative reaction from the Sri Lankan government, and stimulated both the expulsion of the British High Commissioner in mid-1991 on false charges, and a series of speeches aggressively defending Sri Lanka's sovereignty against attempts to use aid to "interfere in internal affairs".

Britain's senior diplomat in Sri Lanka, High Commissioner, David Gladstone, a keen critic of Sri Lanka's human rights record especially in the South, was declared *persona non grata* and asked to leave the country, after what the government described as "unwarranted interference" in the local elections on 11 May, 1991. Mr Gladstone had reported accusations of electoral intimidation and impersonation by ruling UNP supporters.[31] As a result, Britain froze a thirteen million pound aid package to Sri Lanka, declaring that all Britain's subsequent aid commitments would be linked to Sri Lanka's human rights recor

On 21 December, 1991, addressing a one-day summit of regional heads of government at the South Asian Association for Regional Cooperation (SAARC), in Colombo, President Ranasinghe Premadasa fiercely rejected attempts by Western nations to link development aid to Third World government's human rights' records, saying that it constituted "a new colonialism".[32]

In a BBC interview in late February, 1993, LTTE leader, Velupillai Prabhakaran, condemned Western countries for indirectly funding the Sri Lankan war effort through foreign aid. Prabhakaran stated:

"Indirectly, the west is helping this war of ethnic destruction. The Sri Lankan government is continuing this war with the help of loans it gets from the west. The government cannot continue this war if the west stops giving money and arms. It is only after that the right environment for peace will prevail".[33]

In February, 1992, Sri Lanka's human rights record was put under even greater scrutiny. The UN Human Rights Commission meeting in Geneva, heard a damning report by the UN Working Group on Disappearances, which had collated 12,000 "disappearance" cases since 1983, after a visit to Sri Lanka in October, 1991. Following the resolution passed by EC donor governments, attending the annual World Bank meeting on Sri Lanka in Paris, in October, 1990, linking future aid to Sri Lanka's human rights record, the Sri Lankan government set up a Presidential Commission on Disappearances, a Human Rights Task Force, and accepted 28 of the 32 recommendations made by Amnesty International, after a visit by the organisation in 1991. In his speech to the UN Human Rights Commission, 1992, Sri Lankan International Affairs Advisor, Bradman Weerakoon, suggested that Sri Lanka would make constitutional changes in line with the International Covenant on Civil and Political Rights (ICCPR), 1966,[34] and would set up a permanent Human Rights Commission.[35] However, whilst these measures were welcomed by the European Community, human rights NGOs in Colombo said these measures were "cosmetic", and called for greater "accountability and transparency".[36]

In the same month, at the World Bank meeting on 7 February, 1992, donor countries pledged over $825 million in foreign aid to Sri Lanka for the coming year. However, whilst some European donors, namely, Britain, Holland and Norway, were seen to be significantly cutting back on bilateral aid, until further improvements in Sri Lanka's human rights record were made, other international countries and financial bodies, remained seemingly impervious to human rights concerns. European countries contributed a meagre 10% of Sri Lanka's foreign aid pledges in 1991, whilst Japan contributed a staggering 35%,[37] the Asian Development Bank, 21%, and the World Bank, 22%.[38]

Clearly, international aid-related pressures are not straightforward or unambiguous in effect. On the one hand, the World Bank has responded to pressure from bilateral aid donors, such that concerns about civil rights are written into the documents of the Sri Lanka Aid Group which the World Bank chairs. On the other hand, the World Bank now exercises major influence over Sri Lanka's economic policy and some of the policies on which it is insisting, for example, higher charges for public utilities and services, reductions in public sector employment and reductions in subsidies, make it more difficult in the short run at least, for the government to maintain popularity. Over 10,000 tea plantation workers went on strike in early March, 1993, demanding the restoration of wage levels. The government is reluctant to enforce agreements on work and wages because of World Bank demands to cut costs, which President Premadasa says run to monthly losses of Rs. 4000 million ($10 million).[39] There is, however, yet "another hand". The World Bank agreed to give substantial funding for President Premadasa's "flagship" anti-poverty programme, the *Janasaviya* Programme, despite major concerns about its macro-economic impact and implementability.[40]

Whilst the international community has increasingly put pressure on the Sri Lankan government to curb its human rights abuse, and has begun to link Sri Lanka's human rights standards to the receipt of development aid, in the absence of adequate international monitoring, Sri Lanka continues to channel aid for military purposes. In the week preceding the Aid Group meeting in Paris, 1993, the World Bank's South Asia Director, Paul Isenman, queried the Sri Lankan government's activities concerning the division of foreign aid monies received in 1992, for the purpose of defence expenditure. Senior government officials explained that the understanding between the donor governments and agencies in the Sri Lanka Aid Group and the Sri Lanka government, was that the funds committed annually by the donor community for economic development, would not be diverted for defence purposes. "However," they are reported to have said, "it appears that last year this practice was violated".[41] They pointed out that the government was expected to mobilise funds for defence internally be means of the Defence Levy. In 1992, the levy was raised from one percent to three percent, due to heightened defence expenditure. In 1992, some Rs.16 billion was spent on defence. The initial defence allocation for 1993 was Rs.19.8 billion, but the Defence Ministry has now asked for an additional Rs.8 billion. The World Bank's query, however, did not have any effect on the outcome of the meeting of the Consortium on 19 June, 1993, as the aid was increased by US$15 million from the aid pledge for 1992, to Rs 40.3 billion (US$847 million).[42]

In the light of such "double standards", the initiative for political dialogue must come not only from the LTTE and the Sri Lankan government, but also from an increasingly discredited international community. Increased international monitoring of the use to which the Sri Lankan government puts its imported military arms and increased monitoring of the division of development aid in Sri Lanka, i.e., ensuring that development aid reaches those areas of Sri Lanka, for example the North and

Eastern Provinces, where it is most needed, would potentially put an end to the military impasse, restore the Tamil-speaking peoples' hope in the international community, and demonstrate to the Sri Lankan government that its policies are not acceptable to the international community.

At the forty-eighth session of the UN Commission on Human Rights, in February, 1992, the International Council of Voluntary Agencies (ICVA), made a statement in which it recommended that the Commission "urge governments and arms suppliers to cease supplying arms and military equipment to both protagonists in the conflict".[43]

Unfortunately, however, many countries are increasingly finding themselves in a cycle of dependency on the arms trade. Indeed, whilst the Sri Lankan government continues to increase its expenditure on defence, Western governments will inevitably want to tap as much of this market as possible. There has been a 500% increase in Sri Lanka's defence expenditure since 1983. In 1982, Sri Lanka spent $63 million (Rs.1,117), 1.2 of its Gross National Product (GNP), on defence, whilst in 1991, it spent $357 million (Rs.17,323), 4.8 of its GNP on defence.[44] Similarly, the LTTE's demand for weapons provides a steady market for the arms trade in South East Asia and other Third World states, particularly in "low tech" arms. Moreover, Sri Lanka provides a clear case of the fact that arms acquisitions and their timing are often prompted by developments in the conflict.

Sri Lanka received large consignments of weapons appropriate for anti-guerrilla campaign from China in 1991, including F-7 and F-5 fighters, HY-2 transport planes, Shanghai Class patrol craft, landing ships and 130-mm type 59-1 artillery pieces. The re-supply of the armed forces was directly instrumental in the government's successful operations against the LTTE in 1991. The Sri Lankan armed forces were able to place the Jaffna peninsula under siege, the main stronghold for the LTTE forces. The Sri Lankan government's arms acquistions, were directly responsive to the government's need to deal with the LTTE and the re-supplies aided that struggle. The supplies enabled the army to maintain the upper hand and removed pressures to submit to cease-fires and negotiations.[45]

In 1992, during Britain's junior Foreign Minister, Marx Lennon Boyd's visit to Sri Lanka, in mid-October, Britain conveyed to President Premadasa its decision to normalise bilateral relations with Sri Lanka, announcing that it would lift its ban on arms sales. A decision which was interpreted by Mr B. Weerakoon, Presidential Adviser on Foreign Relations in Sri Lanka, to be a confirmation of Britain's "earlier committment and support to the government in its fight against terrorism."[46] The

U.S.A. and Scandinavian countries, who continue to maintain an embargo on arms sales to Sri Lanka, privately criticised this move.[47] However, Argentina also sold the Sri Lankan government four FMA IA 58A Pucara light ground attack aircraft, worth $1.8, with spares and support pushing the price up to around $2.8 million per unit.[48] Similarly, the Russian government sold Mi-8 helicopters to Sri Lanka's airforce. The Sri Lankan government is also reported to have plans to acquire French built Fast Attack Craft for the navy.[49]

In a press release on February 5, 1992, the Canadian Human Rights Mission to Sri Lanka made the following recommendations:

*Canada should suspend the part of Canadian bilateral assistance that is channelled to Sri Lanka government projects. These funds should be re-allocated to other programs in Sri Lanka.

*Canada should continue to channel aid through Sri Lankan, Canadian, and international Non-Governmental Organisations.

*Canada should intensify its leadership role within the donor community and urge international financial institutions (such as the World Bank) to relate levels of aid to an improvement in the human rights situation.

*At the upcoming February 7th Sri Lanka Donors Consortium meeting in Paris, Canada should urge the following; (1) direct linkage between development assistance and other financial involvements to a timetable for improvements in the human rights situation and (2) mechanisms for monitoring the human rights situation in Sri Lanka by the donor community.[50]

Clearly, governments should suspend bilateral assistance that is channelled to Sri Lankan government projects until such time as it has restored its internal stability. These funds should be re-allocated to other programmes in Sri Lanka. Similarly, governments should continue to channel aid to Sri Lanka through international NGOs. In early 1993, commodity aid worth Rs.265 million (10 million Deutsch Marks) was granted by the German Government, as refugee relief assistance. The aid was to be utilised by NGOs and international relief agencies.[51]

However, despite the admirable intentions behind the recommendations of the Canadian Human Rights Mission, Canada itself has also been known to give lip-service to the linkage of human rights violations with the arms trade to Sri Lanka. In late 1992, Sri Lanka was keen to buy up to one dozen Brazilian EMB-312 Tucano aircraft. However, the Tucano's turboprop engines are built in Montreal by Pratt and Whitney Canada. Under strict application of existing Canadian military expert guidelines, Sri Lanka, as a country involved in hostilities, cannot order the engines directly from Canada. However, because the government views the Tucano's manufacturer as the end user of the engines, the Brazilian company was free to export its aircraft, alongwith the engines, to any country sanctioned by the Brazillain government.

There is evidence, however, that support is increasingly being found for the policy not to supply to combatants or states close to war. Arms transfers to either side of an intra-state ethnic civil war have predominantly negative consequences. Even if one side is clearly favoured, it makes more sense to seek to engage the UN Security Council in peace-making efforts rather than to send weapons unilaterally. In this sense, the handling of the Yugoslav crisis, with all its manifold and tragic conequences, is generally recognised to be an improvement over what is happening in states such as Sri Lanka.[52]

Another major recommendation for the resolution of the conflict which has been placed before the UN Commission, has been to establish an international monitoring framework, in which the parties to the conflict can come to a negotiated settlement. The Canadian Human Rights Mission to Sri Lanka, submitted as one of their recommendations, that:

*The Sri Lankan government and the LTTE must agree to an immediate, internationally monitored cease-fire leading to a negotiated settlement. The international community must apply pressure to achieve these objectives.[53]

Australian Foreign Minister, Gareth Evans, speaking in parliament on 4 November, 1992, renewed Australia's offer to mediate in Sri Lanka's North-East conflict as part of a high level Commonwealth initiative. Since June, 1990, Norway, Sweden, Canada and Switzerland have offered to mediate or to provide the venue for peace talks.[54]

In March, 1993, Sri Lankan Ambassador for Scandinavia, N. Jayaweera, called on State Secretary to the Royal Norwegian Foreign Ministry, Jan Egland, and several other senior offices at the Foreign Development Co-operation Ministries, as part of routine deliberations. The Norwegian Government, while noting the Sri Lankan government's failure to implement all of the UN's and Amnesty International's recommendations on human rights, renewed its offer to assist the government in the peace-building process after a settlement to the North-East conflict is reached. Whilst the Norwegian Government declined to act as "mediators" due to the complex situation of the conflict, Jan Egland stated, "Once a settlement is reached, the Norwegian Government is anxious to help build the peace-process". In the meantime, the Norwegian Government stressed the need to implement all the recommendations of the UN and A.I., and called on the government of Sri Lanka to maintain the present momentum in relation to the human rights situation.[55]

Other recommendations for the resolution of the conflict have been put before the Commission by various NGOs during the last decade. At the forty-eighth session, under Agenda item 10, which dealt with the human rights of all persons subjected to any form of detention or imprisonment, particularly enforced or involuntary disappearances, "Liberation" stated that in order to prevent the recurrence of human rights violations in Sri Lanka, the government should:

(1) repeal the Emergency Regulation and Prevention of Terrorism Act, 1981;

(2) repeal the Indemnity Act that shields the perpetrators from prosecution; and

(3) ratify the Optional Protocol to the International Covenant on Civil and Political Rights and the Convention against torture and other cruel inhuman or degrading treatment and punishment.[56]

Sri Lanka continues to be ruled for the twelfth successive year (1993), under a State of Emergency, under which many of the normal safeguards concerning democratic and human rights and fundamental freedoms have remained suspended. Under the provisions of the Prevention of Terrorism Act, a person can be detained for up to eighteen months without trial and court decisions to transfer suspects to the custody of the judiciary can be reversed by parliament.

"These provisions are quite extraordinarily wide. No legislation conferring even remotely comparable powers is in force in any other free democracy operating under the Rule of Law, however troubled it may be by politically motivated violence. Indeed there is only one known precedent for the power to impose restriction orders under section 11 of the Sri Lankan PTA, and that...is the comparable legislation currently in force in South Africa...such a provision is an ugly blot on the statute book of any civilised country."[57]

The terms and utilisation of the permanent preventive detention legislation and temporary emergency legislation, clearly brings Sri Lanka, a signatory to the International Covenant on Civil and Political Rights and the International Covenant on Economic, Social and Cultural Rights, into conflict with her obligations under international law.

(iii) Sri Lanka's human rights record is scrutinized at the Forty-Ninth Session of the UN Human Rights Commission 1993

The internationalisation of the Tamil-speaking peoples' claim to the right to self-determination gathered momentum in early 1993, at the forty-ninth session of the UN Human Rights Commission. On 8 February, 1993, fifteen international NGOs with UN consultative status,[58] raised the issue of the Tamil national question in Sri Lanka under agenda item 8, which relates to "The rights of peoples to self-determination and its application to peoples under colonial or alien domination or foreign occupation".[59] The joint statement declared:

"...despite the sustained attacks of Sinhala dominated governments over a period of several decades, the territorial integrity of the Tamil "homeland" in the North and East of the Island has remained. The Tamil population in the North and East, who have lived for many centuries within relatively well defined geographical boundaries, share an ancient heritage, a vibrant culture, and a living language which traces its origins to more that 2500 years ago. A social group, which shares objective elements such as a common language and which has acquired a subjective consciousness of togetherness by its life within a relatively well defined territory, and its struggle against alien domination, clearly constitutes a "people" with the right to self-determination. Today, there is an urgent need for the international community to recognise that the Tamil population in the North and East of the Island of Sri Lanka are such a "people" with the right to freely choose their political status. It is our view that such recognition will prepare the ground for the resolution of a conflict which has taken such a heavy toll in human lives and suffering during the past several years."[60]

In the joint statement, the fifteen NGOs accordingly requested the delegates to the forty-ninth session of the Commission on Human Rights to:

(a) accord open recognition to the existence of the Tamil "homeland" in the North and East of the Island; and

(b) recognise that the Tamil population in the North and East of the Island constitute a "people" with the right to self-determination.

Clearly, the joint declaration made by the various NGOs in February, 1993, was a significant step forward in the effort to win international recognition for the Sri Lankan Tamils' right to self-determination.[61]

In response to the joint statement made by the fifteen NGOs, at the UN Commission, the government of Sri Lanka exercised its right to reply, ensuring that, in the words of Ambassador, Bernard A. B. Goonetilleke,

"...the Commission will not be misled by baseless propaganda". It is worth documenting the Sri Lankan Ambassador's response to the NGOs' joint statement, because it documents well, the current ideological and political position of the Sinhalese-dominated Sri Lankan government viv-a-vis the Tamil peoples' right to self-determination.

In response to the justification of the NGOs' joint statement, Ambassador Bernard A. B. Goonetilleke, submitted several points which he suggested the statement failed to include. Firstly, in response to the claim for a Tamil "homeland", he submitted that: "...there is a justification to a claim that Sri Lanka, in its entirety, is the homeland of the Tamil people, just the same way as it is the homeland of the Sinhalese, Moors, Malays, Burghers and the original inhabitants of the Island, the "Veddas"".[62]

Secondly, in response to the claim that the Tamil people are subjected to "alien domination", the Ambassador declared:

"...the fact remains that neither the Sinhalese nor the Tamils nor for that matter, the Moors, Malays and Burghers are aliens to Sri Lanka. They are all citizens of Sri Lanka and have an equal right to live in any part of the Island".[63]

Thirdly, Ambassador Bernard A. B. Goonetilleke reminded the Commission that the group of Tamils known as Sri Lankan Tamils who claim as their "homelands" the Northern and Eastern Provinces of Sri Lanka, comprise 12.7% of the population and that 2.3% of this group live outside the two Provinces along with members of the other communities.

Fourthly, the Ambassador informed the Commission that there is another group of Tamils, approximately 5.5% of the population, the "Indian" or "Plantation" Tamils, who also live outside the Northern and the Eastern Province, and that this group does not support the claim of their cousins for a separate state in the Northern and Eastern Provinces and that furthermore, they are represented in the Sri Lankan government by senior members of the Cabinet. He went on to add, that of the 18.2% of the total Tamil population in the Island, not more than 10.4% live in the Northern and Eastern Provinces, yet the area claimed by them, exceeds 30% of the landmass of the Island and 60% of its coastline (including the strategically valuable port of Trincomalee, the loss of which would jeopardise Sri Lanka's present economy, by blocking external trade routes and communication).

Ambassador Bernard A. B. Goonetilleke, did not deny that the Northern Province is at present inhabited almost entirely by Tamils, but suggested that this situation arose only as a result of the LTTE forcibly evicting tens of thousands of Muslims and a lesser number of Sinhalese from the area. He stated that the concept of "ethnic cleansing" did not originate in former Yugoslavia in 1992, but that "[I]t was practised as a tool of achieving a political objective by the LTTE as early as 1990".[64] Moreover, he added that the Tamils remain a minority in the Eastern Province, despite massacring and forcing thousands of Muslims and Sinhalese out of the Province.

The reply of the Sri Lankan Ambassador, at the UN Commission, contributes nicely to the mass of contradictory reports that already surround the facts of the ethnic conflict in Sri Lanka. Some of the above points shall be briefly examined here, in an attempt to shed light on some of the more obscured facts. Such an analysis reveals the fears that are inherent in much of the rhetoric of the Sinhalese-dominated government and its representatives, with regard to the Tamil-speaking peoples' separatist claims.

One basis of international concern regarding secessionist claims is often the presence of "trapped minorities" within the seceding state, and the willingness of the emerging government of the "latent" state, to accord respect for human and minority rights. The Eastern Province, which constitutes part of the Tamil "homeland" or Eelam, is currently divided among three substantial minorities. The Sri Lankan Tamils and Muslims constitute approximately 40% respectively of the Province, and the Sinhalese constitute the remaining 20%.[65] In the event of Eelam becoming a reality, the Sinhalese and Muslim communities inhabiting the Eastern Province would have to be assured of their safety. Similarly, the Tamils remaining in the South and West would also have to be assured of their safety.[66] So far, despite assurances from both communities, this has not been the case.

Until three years ago, the Muslim community, which predominantly inhabits the Eastern Province, appeared content to be considered part of an independent Tamil state carved out of Sri Lanka's Northern and Eastern Provinces, but since the June, 1990 War began, the LTTE has pursued a two-track policy, forcing 50,000 Muslims out of the Northern districts and attacking Muslim settlements in the East. The Tigers maintain that Muslim village leaders have systematically betrayed LTTE positions to the incoming Sri Lankan army and therefore regard the Tamil-speaking Muslims as traitors.[67] These attacks have reinforced the view that the LTTE are unwilling to acknowledge the legitimate rights of the Muslim and Sinhalese minorities in the North and East. The LTTE continues to pursue such policies, despite repeated assurances by Tamil political party leaders, that minorities in the Northern and Eastern Provinces will be assured of their safety.

The "Four Point Formula", presented by the seven Tamil political parties, to address the Tamil national question at the Parliamentary Select Committee, on the 17th June, 1992, provided assurances that minorities in the Northern and Eastern Provinces would be assured of their safety. However, the last provision, which states that the: "Sinhalese will enjoy all the rights that other minorities have in the rest of the country", is written in such a way, that it seems to imply that in the absence of any real minority protection in the present Sri Lankan Constitution, the Sinhalese can expect to be treated in the Northern and Eastern Provinces, in much the same way as the Tamils have been treated in the rest of the Island over the last four decades.

The Four Point Formula was endorsed by the Ceylon Workers Congress (CWC), the representative of the "Up Country" or "Plantation" Tamils, thereby confirming the support of the "Plantation" Tamils for the establishment of meaningful autonomy in a permanently merged North-Eastern Province. Mr. S. Thondaman, leader of the CWC, has consistently maintained that a solution to the ethnic problem lies in the government's recognition and respect of the multi-ethnic composition of the Island.

The Sri Lankan government has spent large sums of money in the public sector in the Eastern Province, in a desperate attempt to ween support from both Tamils and Muslims away from the LTTE In the run up to the Provincial Council elections held in May, 1993, it was hoped that the six million pounds spent on upgrading the Trincomalee hospital, and the plans to set up a University and Medical faculty in Batticaloa, would not be lost on a population suffering from unemployment and economic hardship.

Addressing a mammoth rally at Akkaraipattu junction in Amparai district in the Eastern Province, after the establishment of two new garment factories in the vicinity, President Premadasa, after declaring that Rs.23,000 million were spent on defence alone in Sri Lanka, stated, "If a lasting solution can be evolved to the North East crisis then the pace of development and progress can be stepped up". Continuing, he said, "All this money is going to waste. If it is possible to solve the North East conflict, I pledge to eradicate poverty and fulfil the needs of the masses in six months". He concluded, "We are prepared to give 'ellam' (everything) but not 'Eelam' (a separate state). After we give 'ellam' there will be no need for 'Eelam'". Moreover, in an attempt to appease all minority communities in the Eastern Province, Premadasa added that Rs.5 lakhs had been donated to renovate Buddhist temples, Mosques, Churches and Hindu Kovils in Akkaraipattu.

Not only is their concern for the status of "trapped minorities", in the event of the emergence of *Eelam*, but there is also wide concern over the future of the international Tamil diaspora, which is predominantly made up of refugees and asylum-seekers. There are over 200,000 Tamil refugees in Europe, and another 25,000 arrive each year.[68] In addition, over 123,000 Tamil refugees currently live in 243 official camps throughout the state of Tamil Nadu, India, whilst another 100,000 are living outside government controlled camps in India.[69] Moreover, more than 250,000 of Jaffna's one million population are now "internal refugees".[70] Foreboding predictions of the situation that is likely to arise if Tamil *Eelam* were to become a reality, which reveal some of the worst fears, are provided by S.J. Tambiah:

"Whether the rest of the Sri Lankan community can accept an influx of a million refugees will not be a matter for debate - it would be a situation impossible to contemplate. At the same time pressure would mount in the rest of the country for the forcible repatriation to Eelam of the half-million Tamil population resident in other parts of Sri Lanka. This exercise which could not be carried out without causing massive hardship and human misery far exceeding in volume any hardship alleged to have been inflicted so far on the Tamil community".[71]

S.J. Tambiah continues with his gloomy presentiments by stating:

"If large scale movements of population do not take place - as indeed they cannot - after the establishment of the mythical State, the country would be faced with minority problems far greater that it has ever faced in its history. Besides the problems of a minority of a half million Tamils living outside the State of Eelam, (accentuated by the fact that the Sinhala community will find it increasingly difficult to live or function within the new State) the Eelam State itself will be faced with a non-Tamil minority consisting of 35% of its population...If the pattern of voting in the 1977 General Election is repeated at a future election in the State of Tamil Eelam it is quite conceivable that the TULF (which secured only 48% of the votes in this region in 1977), may once again find itself in a minority and the State of Eelam could well come under a government which might oppose the idea of a separate State. More terrorism would then be required to save Eelam from its own government".[72]

To return once more to the Ambassador's remarks to the forty-ninth session of the UN Commission on Human Rights, with respect to the temporary merger of the Northern and Eastern Provinces, he stated that the Provinces were merged on the specific and clear understanding that it would be subject to a referendum. This referendum, he declared, was not able to take place, "...as the LTTE does not believe either in democracy or elections." The government, he continued, "under no circumstances, will hand over the Eastern Province to a minority over the interests of other communities or to the LTTE who has a criminal record of oppressing both the Muslims and the Sinhalese living in that Province".[73]

In response to the NGOs' reference in the joint statement to the failure of the Sri Lankan government to share power, the Ambassador stated:

"The power could be shared once the negotiations for devolution are completed and an understanding has been reached. Moreover, the Tamil people themselves should decide as to whom they should hand over power in the Northern and Eastern Provinces. The Government has no intention of handing over the power, for that matter to a group of terrorists, under threat or intimidation".[74]

The Ambassador concluded his right to reply, by warning that:

"If the Commission were to accept the two requests by NGOs, not only will it be interfering in the internal affairs of my country, but also, it will put the future of the Tamil population living outside the Northern and Eastern Provinces in jeopardy. The tragic events that followed the frag-mentation of former Yugoslavia are examples of dividing countries on the basis of race or religion. I do not think that the Commission is ready to take a step in that direction and reap the bitter harvest in the form of *inter alia*, displacing tens of thousands of Sri Lankans and forcing them to seek refugee status in Western Europe and elsewhere."[75]

Clearly, the Sri Lankan Tamil refugee exodus has internationalised the Tamils' claim to the right to self-determination. However, in a climate of increasingly restrictive immigration rules, especially in Europe, host countries are keen not only to prevent a further influx of Sri Lankan Tamil refugees, but also to return Sri Lankan Tamil refugees to Sri Lanka. Since India began her intensive repatriation scheme, repatriating 29,000 Sri Lankan Tamils from South India to Sri Lanka during 1992,[76] various members of the European Community are beginning to follow suit and are planning to repatriate rejected Sri Lankan Tamil asylum seekers in the near future. Switzerland signed a repatriation programme with Sri Lanka in January, 1994. In this context, the Sri Lankan Ambassador's warning at the recent UN Human Rights Commission, will not fall on deaf ears. Moreover, Western governments are strategically ignoring the situation in the North-East of the Island, while emphasising improvements in the

South, because it is imperative under international law, to establish "safe" areas to which the Sri Lankan Tamils can return.[77] Western governments failed to challenge Sri Lanka's human rights record at the recent UN Human Rights Commission, precisely because the wide range of "cosmetic" reforms made by the Government, ostensibly provide "internal flight alternatives" for Sri Lankan Tamil returnees.

Let us consider the Sri Lankan government's recent human rights reforms, in an attempt to determine to what extent they have been "cosmetic", a camouflage to dupe the international community into believing that there are "safe" zones to which Sri Lankan Tamil refugees can be safely returned.

At the forty-ninth session of the UN Commission on Human Rights, the Permanent Mission of Sri Lanka submitted a nine-point Situation Report, which presented the measures initiated by the government to deal with the current human rights situation in Sri Lanka. The Report, stated that on the 11th January, 1991, the government appointed The Independent Commission on the Involuntary Removal of Persons. The Report stated that the five member Commission, headed by a retired Supreme Court Judge and consisting of independent members of the judiciary and the legal profession had a mandate to inquire and report on complaints of involuntary removals alleged to have taken place during the period 11/01/1991 to 10/01/1992. The mandate of the Commission was subsequently extended to cover cases alleged to have occured during the period 11/01/1992 to 10/01/1993.

The Situation Report stated that the general public was free to provide information to the Commission, and that the proceedings of the Commission were open to the public and were freely reported in the press. The Report stated that during the period 11/01/91 to 10/01/92, a total of 541 allegations from all parts of the country, and falling within the Commission's mandate, were received. It stated that forty-nine allegedly disappeared persons were traced, and 460 cases were under investigation. The Situation Report further stated, that during the period 11/01/92 to 21/12/92, ninety-two allegations were recieved by the Commission, of whom 31 persons were traced and that 58 cases were presently under investigation.

Non-governmental human rights agencies, however, have stated that the Presidential Commission of Inquirey into Involuntary Removal of Persons had concluded hearings in only four cases, and that the reports in these four cases were not available to the public. Moreover, human rights agencies have testified to the fact that a number of people who had given evidence before the Commission have been intimidated by police within the premises of the Commission. Furthermore, human rights agencies have stated that legal action has only been taken in one case brought before the Commission. Human rights agencies are convinced that the Commission is merely a cosmetic exercise and suggest that the mechanism is clearly inadequate to deal with the number of cases brought before it.

In the report of MEP Christine Oddy's informal visit to Sri Lanka, during 8-12 November, 1993, it was stated that:

"The Presidential Commission on Disappearances can only investigate cases after January 1991 and has no power to investigate cases prior to that date. Even after that date, it has not successfully brought to trial and sentence any of the perpretators of disappearances post January 1991. This apparent immunity from persecution and punishment is not conducive to confidence in its work. Many of the relatives of disappeared had still not obtained death certificates for their presumed dead relatives. Consequently, there was an urgent need for the proposed relaxation in the law to obtain death certificates to be implemented."[78]

According to human rights organisations, the reduction in disappearances in Sri Lanka in 1992, which the UN Commission on Human Rights was keen to acknowledge at its forty-ninth session, is directly linked to the reduction in the intensity of militarised conflict in certain areas and not to any conscious effort on the part of the state authorities to dismantle the mechanisms that permit disappearances to occur. In the Eastern Province alone, there were over 400 disappearances in 1992 and several persons in the South also disappeared. No action has been taken regarding the 40,000 persons who disappeared in the South in the early 1980's as a result of the governments' major crackdown on the JVP, and over 5,000 who have disappeared in the East.

Another of the new mechanisms which the Sri Lankan government has established to deal with human rights concerns in Sri Lanka, is the Human Rights Task Force (HRTF), set up in August, 1991, to monitor the observance of fundamental rights of detainees taken into custody under Emergency Regulations or the PTA The Situation Report stated that the work of the HRTF includes unrestricted and unannounced visits to all persons in detention. It stated that from the inception of its work on the 10/07/1991 to the 31/12/1992, the HRTF had made 155 visits to detention centres and rehabilitation camps, 370 visits to police stations, 18 visits to army camps, principally in the Eastern Province and Vavuniya District in the Northern Province, and had seen a total of 1225 detainees during visits to army camps and police stations.

The Situation Report stated that the public could obtain a computer data print-out with regard to any person in detention. It stated that members of the armed forces and police are under instructions to inform the HRTF promptly when an arrest is made. The Situation Report stated that the HRTF provides legal services to the detainees by ensuring that lawyers and relatives are allowed scheduled visits. It stated that the detainees could make applications to the Supreme Court to test the legality of the their detention. The Situation Report stated that there have been many occasions where such applications have received favourable rulings by the court.

Concerned human rights agencies, however, have stated that the HRTF has been unable to compile a complete list of either the detainees or the places of detention, and thus has been unable to fulfil the primary function for which it was set up. In its first report of August, 1992, the HRTF admitted to the particular practice of "mobile detention", in which detainees are continually transferred from place to place. This has enabled security forces to prevent detection of large number of Tamils taken into custody, particularly in the North and East, despite the regional offices of the HRTF, set up with the assistance of Western nations. According to the HRTF report for 1992/1993, of the reported 2,351 missing persons, the HRTF has been able to trace only 114.

The report by the Canada-Asia Working Group submitted to the UN Commission on Human Rights at its forty-ninth session, clearly highlighted the inability of the HRTF to provide effective monitoring, stating that: "the efforts of the government human rights bodies have been limited in their efficacy and have failed completely to remedy the root cause of the situation which gives rise to human rights violations".

In MEP Christine Oddy's report to Sri Lanka, it was stated that: "...a number of criticisms need to be made about the new circumstances. In relation to the investigation of the disappeared the Human Rights Task Force was only established for a three year term of office and needs to have its mandate extended beyond 1994. Its powers to locate the whereabouts of disappeared relatives is heavily dependent upon the respect and authority of the Judge leading the Task Force."[79]

Violations of the rights of persons in detention under the PTA and Emergency Regulations have continued unabated since the forty-ninth session of the UN Human Rights Commission. In it's October, 1993, statement, (ASA 37/WU/04/93; 27 October 1993) Amnesty International stated: "Since June, there have been several waves of such arrests forming part of a pattern of human rights violations directed at the Tamil community, in which thousands of people appear to have been arrested solely on the basis of their ethnic origin."

The Permanent Mission of Sri Lanka's Situation Report, also stated what measures the Sri Lankan government have taken to deal with human rights violations by the security forces. A Special Presidential Commission was accordingly set up to investigate into the Kokkaddicholai case. Captain Kudaligama, who was responsible for the massacre of 180 Tamils at Kokkaddicholai in June, 1991, was subsequently found guilty. Human rights agencies were distressed however, when Captain Kudaligama was found guilty only of failure to control his subordinates and of the disposal of dead bodies, and was only dismissed from service. The seventeen soldiers implicated in the massacre, were acquited. Human rights agencies are concerned that such events encourage the security forces to further violate human rights with impunity.

Clearly, these state mechanisms are little more than a camouflage to dupe the international community into believing that the situation in Sri Lanka is improving. Unfortunately, the fiftieth session of the UN Commission on Human Rights, held on February, 1994, was once again manipulated not only by the Sri Lankan government, who anticipating the annual meeting of the Paris Aid Donors Consortium, in the Spring of 1994, was even more keen to be seen as a country conscious of its human rights record, but also by Western governments, some of whom were actively engaged in proposals with the Sri Lankan government to repatriate rejected Tamil asylum-seekers, and who were therefore eager to hear that Sri Lanka was safe for potential returnees.

It is not correct to say at this stage, that the Sri Lankan authorities are able and willing to provide effective protection to all of its citizens. Sri Lanka continues to be ruled under a State of Emergency. The continued intimidation and harassment of members of the opposition political parties, as well as attacks on journalists, media personnel, printers and newspaper distributors, have served as major constraints on freedom of expression and opinion. Draconian provisions of the Prevention of Terrorism Act, investing the executive and security forces with extraordinary powers, including those relating to arrest and detention, also remain in force.[80]

In Part Five of the Situation Report, submitted by the Permanent Mission of Sri Lanka at the forty-ninth UN Commission on Human Rights, the Sri Lankan government outlined its "Prospects for a long term political solution". The report emphasised the Sri Lankan governments' desire for "a negotiated political settlement" and its continued exploration of "all avenues for such a solution".[81] The Situation Report highlighted legislative measures that have already been taken by the government in response to the "legitimate grievances of the Tamils", i.e., the Thirteenth Amendment to the Constitution, which "devolved administrative power to the nine Provincial Councils", and the elevation of Tamil, by the 1978 Constitution, to the status of an "official language", along with Sinhalese. In addition, the report declared, "the Government has expressed its resolve that the LTTE should not be able to by-pass the electoral process and enforce a mono-ethnic one-party State in the North and East, through terror and violence".[82] The Situation Report stated that "The Government has nevertheless clearly stated its readiness to a political solution through negotiations", stressing that in the meantime it has "continued its dialogue with the recognised political parties of Tamil and other communities, initially within the framework of the All Party Conference (APC) and later through the Parliamentary Select Committee (PSC)".[83] The Situation Report was keen to point out that apart from the CWC, the TULF and the ACTC, all other Tamil parties that took part in the PSC, were former militant groups, which during the post-1987 period, had joined the democratic political mainstream. The Situation Report continued:

"On 12 December, [1992] the PSC concluded its deliberations on the basis of which the Government is expected to conduct further negotiations with interested political parties in order to arrive at an acceptable package of devolution of power".[84] It stated, that the LTTE alone, had opted not to join in this process of, "democratic dialogue aimed at a moderate non-violent, democratic and durable solution to the problems involving the North and the East acceptable to all communities in Sri Lanka".[85]

Furthermore, the Situation Report stated that in early October, 1992, the President of Sri Lanka had publicly declared his willingness to recommence the negotiating process unilaterally broken by the LTTE in June 1990, provided that the LTTE were willing to:

(a) stop the use of arms;

(b) agree to join the democratic process; and

(c) recognise the right of other Tamil groups to contest elections.[86]

Part Five of the Situation Report concluded:

"It is therefore clearly seen that the doors are wide open for the LTTE to join the negotiating process once they agree to meet these basic principles".[87]

Clearly, the single most significant reality in 1993, was the failure of both the Sri Lankan government and the LTTE to take the necessary steps to begin a process that would involve an internationally monitored cease-fire and lead to a negotiated political settlement to the conflict. It was made apparent in the empirical case study in Part Two of this study, that while the government of Sri Lanka claimed that the Parliamentary Select Committee was mandated with finding a solution to the ethnic conflict, the ruling UNP and the principal opposition party, the SLFP, failed to put forward proposals which might have begun the process of negotiations. Likewise, it was made apparent that the leadership of the LTTE, whilst claiming to be prepared to negotiate without conditions, has given no indication that it is prepared to compromise on a number of positions unacceptable to the Sri Lankan government, including the merger of the North and East Provinces and the participation of other Tamil parties at the negotiating table.

It is useful at this juncture, to analyse a paper that was submitted by the Canada-Asia Working Group before the forty-ninth session of the UN Human Rights Commission in February, 1993, in which it stated that the Sri Lankan conflict was not an "internal" affair, but an "international" affair.[88] The Canada-Asia Working Group, presented Sri Lanka's ethnic conflict within an international framework, in which UN member states were held responsible, in part at least, for the continuation and escalation of the warfare. It maintained that because it was taking place within the inter-state system, it therefore placed responsibility on the international community to resolve the ethnic conflict. In the light of the international community's responsibility to contribute to the resolution of the ethnic conflict in Sri Lanka, the Canada-Asia Working Group presented recommendations for the roles which the member states of the United Nations could assume. The Canada-Asia Working Group maintained that any resolution of the conflict, must take into consideration, not only civil and political rights, but also social, economic and cultural rights. The Canada-Asia Working Group, also reminded the international community of its responsibility to encourage the development of developing countries, such as Sri Lanka, within a human rights dimension. Lastly, the Working Group, called for the international community to recognise the need to explore all possible interventions, including international peace-keeping and the need for internationally mediated peace talks in Sri Lanka, in order to negotiate a lasting political settlement.

The paper further maintained, that the human rights criticisms of the international community are often too facile, contending that while concern is expressed regarding the most flagrant civil and political human rights concerns, it neither acknowledges the compounding economic and political factors, nor exerts the necessary influence to create the political will to remedy the situation. The Working Group suggested that the support provided to the Sri Lankan government, in the form of pledges by the international community of $825 million, at the February, 1992, Donors Consortium meeting in Paris, has been interpreted by the Sri Lankan government as an indication that its strategy of limiting gross violations of civil and political rights, while pursuing a military victory over the LTTE, is an acceptable response to the conflict. The Canada-Asia Working Group deplored any state that donated aid to Sri Lanka, without a concern for the human rights dimension in the country.

It is worth noting here, the proportion of Sri Lanka's national budget that is required to finance the governments' military actions in Sri Lanka, and the corresponding amount of relief aid that is subsequently required to care for the victims of the war. In 1992, budgeted defence expenditures comprised 18.9% of the national budget, whilst the cost of providing humanitarian relief to internally displaced refugees, was US $100 million in 1991. US $24 million was budgeted in 1992.[89]

The Canada-Asia Working Group suggested that a broader understanding of human rights was necessary, one that would recognise the indivisibility of civil, political, economic, social and cultural rights. It contended, however, that the efforts of the Sri Lankan government have only served to curtail the very severest of violations of civil and political rights, whilst concerns regarding economic, social and cultural rights, which are a vital part of the analysis of the human rights situation in Sri Lanka have been neglected.

"The ongoing armed conflict in the North and East of Sri Lanka, is the principal condition which denies a significant proportion of the population the right to development. The relationship of the civil war to the right to development is cyclical. Not only has the unequal distribution of economic, social and cultural rights given rise to the armed conflict but the continuation of a military response to the conflict further deepens the unequal distribution of economic, social and cultural rights".[90]

Economic development within the country has been severely hindered as a result of the war in the North and East. However, the economic policies pursued by the Sri Lankan government, with the support of the international community also provide an obstacle to the realisation of the right to development in Sri Lanka. Article 8, paragraph 1, of the Declaration on the Right to Development, UN General Assembly Resolution 41/128, 4

December, 1986, states that:

"States should undertake, at the national level, all necessary measures for the realisation of the right to development and shall ensure, *inter alia,* equality of opportunity for all in their access to basic resources, education, health services, food, housing, employment and the fair distribution of income".

A widening of the disparity in income between the rich and poor in Sri Lanka, has started to raise serious doubts about equity and social justice in the design of Sri Lanka's economic programmes.

The Declaration of the Right to Development, clearly indicates the obligations of states to promote international conditions favourable to the realisation of the right to development. Article 3, paragraph 1 states that: "States have the primary responsibility for the creation of national and international conditions favourable to the realisation of the Right to Development", and Article 4, paragraph 1 states that: "States have the duty to take steps, individually and collectively, to formulate international development policies with a view to facilitating the full realisation of the Right to Development". The Canada-Asia Working Group suggested that in this respect, the international community has failed Sri Lanka in a number of ways. For instance, the policy recommendations of the Donors Consortium, have failed to promote economic policies within Sri Lanka which promote a fairer distribution of economic, social and cultural rights. Furthermore, by limiting the conditionality of its development assistance to economic performance, principally related to the ability of the Sri Lankan government to meet its international debt obligations, the international community has not used its influence to end an armed conflict which undermines the economic, social and cultural rights of a significant percentage of the population.[91]

It is worth noting here, that Sri Lanka's per capita foreign debt reached approximately CDN $360 in 1989, as against a per capita income level of CDN $440. The debt service ratio (debt payments as a percentage of exports of goods and services) in 1990, was 14.2 %. In order to meet its debt servicing commitments, Sri Lanka pays out to creditor countries and institutions, almost as much as it obtains in aid from the donor countries. During the period between 1987 and 1989, debt service payments equalled 94% of the Overseas Development Assistance (ODA) received.

The Canada-Asia Working Group, suggested that what is most important amongst human rights concerns in Sri Lanka, is the question of the rights of persons belonging to national, ethnic, religious and linguistic minorities. It regarded the failure of successive Sri Lankan governments, to respect the rights of minorities, as the root of the ethnic conflict. It maintained that the failure to identify a constitutional proposal, which ensured the rights of all minorities, was at the heart of the inability to identify a political resolution to the conflict.

Furthermore, the Canada-Asia Working Group stated that the historic and ongoing refusal of successive Sri Lankan governments to recognise the legitimate right of the Tamil-speaking people in the Northern and Eastern Provinces to the right to self-determination, provided the grounds of support for the armed struggle of the LTTE In order for there to be lasting peace and respect for all basic human rights in Sri Lanka, the Canada-Asia Working Group submitted that it was essential that the following four steps be taken:

1. the lifting of the State of Emergency, the holding of free and fair elections, the repeal of repressive laws and the preservation of the independence and integrity of the judicial system and the observance of Sri Lanka's obligations under international human rights covenants;

2. the evolution of a framework of regional autonomy in which all citizens can fully exercise their democratic rights without being subject to any form of intimidation or coercion and in which all ethnic groups can fully exercise their collective rights;

3. the assurance of freedom of thought and expression, including freedom of the mass media from State control and within a structure that will make them reflective of the plurality of Sri Lankan society; and

4. the development of economic strategies that would support and enhance the values of a democratic society.[92]

Within the above framework, the Canada-Asia Working Group, recommended that the Canadian government, in addition:

*assume a leadership role within the international community to address seriously the profound human rights and humanitarian concerns in Sri Lanka, exploring all possible interventions including international peace-keeping which will lead to a cease-fire, authentic mediation and a negotiated political settlement.

Regarding the victims of the Sri Lankan conflict, it recommended that the Candadian government:

*continue to respond with financial assistance for emergency, relief and rehabilitation needs of internally displaced persons within Sri Lanka.

With respect to multilateral development assistance in which Canada participates, and bilateral aid programmes to the Sri Lankan government and non-governmental organisations of Sri Lanka, it recommended that the Canadian government:

*ensure that development assistance is provided to programmes and initiatives which promote fundamental human rights and people-centred sustainable development; and

*ensure that development assistance and other financial involvements with the government of Sri Lanka be directly linked to a timetable for improvements in the human rights situation and clear progress towards a negotiated political settlement of the ethnic conflict.

In regard to the ongoing conflict in Sri Lanka, the UN Commission on Human Rights at its forty-ninth session, urged the Sri Lankan government "to continue to pursue a negotiated political solution with all parties, based on principles of respect for human rights and fundamental freedoms leading to a durable peace in the north and east of the country". The Commission went on to say, that despite its expression of concern, and its urging and pleadings to the Sri Lankan government, the Sri Lankan government has failed to establish a situation in which there is "full protection of human rights", or full respect for the universally accepted rules of humanitarian law and that the government has failed to take any concrete steps "to pursue a negotiated political solution with all parties".

To sum up, it is clear that Sri Lanka has come under considerable international scrutiny regarding its human rights record over the last decade. The UN Commission on Human Rights, at its forty-ninth session in February, 1993, openely expressed its concern about human rights violations committed by both the government of Sri Lanka and the LTTE The Commission acknowledged that the LTTE was engaged in violent armed conflict with the Sri Lankan forces and that it continued to commit violations of human rights, including arbitrary killings of persons belonging to all communities in areas under their control, mainly in the North and East of the Island.

The Canada-Asia Working Group maintained at the UN Commission on Human Rights in February, 1993, that allegations regarding the failure of the LTTE to respect human rights, have had limited response and that there are no established mechanisms for monitoring human rights in LTTE-controlled areas in Sri Lanka. However, in February, 1992, the LTTE did release a statement renewing its 1988 pledge to abide by the Geneva Convention and its additional protocols.

The UN Commission recommended, *inter alia*, that the government of Sri Lanka should implement in full the 14 recommendations of the UN Working Group on Enforced or Involuntary Disappearances contained in their 1992 Report (E/CN. 4/1992/18/Add.1) and the 4 recommendations of the Group in their 1993 Report (E/CN.4/1993/25/Add.1). In view of the fact that the UN Working Group noted that "few of its recommendations had been implemented as yet" by the Sri Lankan government, the Commission on Human Rights committed itself to following developments closely in this regard from year to year, and for this purpose called upon the government of Sri Lanka to invite the Special Rapporteur on Torture and Other Cruel, Inhuman or Degrading Treatment and the Special Rapporteur on Extrajudicial, Summary or Arbitrary Executions and the Working Group on Disappearances to visit Sri Lanka in 1993, and thereafter yearly, until there has been a substantial improvement of the human rights situation in the country. The UN Commission suggested that the government of Sri Lanka be invited to become a party to Protocols I and II Additional to the Geneva Conventions relating to the Laws of War, and to ratify the Convention against Torture and Other Cruel, Inhuman or Degrading Treatment or Punishment, including making the necessary declarations under Article 21 and 22 recognising the competence of the Committee set up under the Convention to receive petitions. Furthermore, the UN Commission suggested that the government of Sri Lanka be invited to ratify the Optional Protocol to the International Covenant on Civil and Political Rights.

Since the UN Commission on Human Rights, in 1993, Sri Lanka has since become a signatory to the UN Convention on Torture. However, "it is important to ensure that the Convention is properly observed and, in particular, training is given on a systematic basis to the police force on the moral imperative against torture."[93]

Despite the fact that at its last sitting, the UN Commission for Human Rights failed to acknowledge that a peaceful settlement to the conflict in Sri Lanka requires the satisfaction of the aspirations of the Tamil speaking-people, within a framework of human rights *and* the right to self-determination, the UN Commission's recommendations, if fully implemented, would enhance the possibilities for a resolution to the conflict (See Appendix IV). Ultimately, however, the will and responsibility for drafting a political solution to the conflict, remains firmly in the hands of the parties to the conflict, i.e., the Sri Lankan government and the LTTE.

Notes

1 Ruddle. N.S., "The development of UN activities in the field of human rights and the role of NGOs", cited in: Franck. T.M., "Nation against nation", (1985), p.232.

2 ECOSOC Res. 1503 (XL VIII), 27 May 1970, cited in: Franck. T.M., p.232.

3 Lauren. P.G., "Power and prejudice: The politics and diplomacy of racial discrimination", (1988), p.196.

4 Humphrey. J.P., "Human rights and the UN", p.28, quoted in: Lauren. P.G., p.226.

5 Franck. T.M., "Nation against nation: What happened to the UN dream and what the US can do about it?", pp.242-243.

6 Kirkpatrick. J., "Double standards in human rights", in: US Dept. of State Current Policy, No.353, 24 November, (1981), cited in: Lauren. P.G., p.275.

7 Ibid., p276.

8 Lugum. C., "Color and power in the South African situation", in Franklin. J.H., (ed.), "Color and race", p.215, quoted in: Lauren. P.G., p.278.

9 "Kittu dies in mystery ship blast", in *The Sri Lanka Monitor*, No.60, January, (1993), p.1.

10 The agreement signed in Washington on 13 September 1993, between the Palestine Liberation Organisation (PLO) and Israel, is a recent example of a government (Israel), recognising a paramilitary guerrilla group (PLO), which has renounced armed struggle, as a national liberation organisation. For a comprehensive account of this historic agreement, see: "Israel and Palestine: Most unexpected dawn", in *The Independent*, 13 September, (1993) pp.19-22.

11 For a comprehensive account of the 1983 massacre, see: Piyadasa. L., "The holocaust and after", (1984).

12 Resolution 61/1987 of the United Nations Human Rights Commission, co-sponsored by Canada, Norway and Argentina and unanimously adopted on 12 March, (1987).

13 The joint statement made by twenty-two NGOs at the forty-seventh session of the UN Human Rights Commission, 28 February-8 March, (1991), Geneva.

14 A joint statement was made by eighteen NGOs under Agenda item 6, which dealt with violations of human rights, at the forty second session of the UN Commission on Human Rights, (1986).

15 International Education Development (IED) Inc., forty-third session of the UN Sub-Commission on Prevention of Discrimination and Protection of Minorities, under Agenda item 6, (1987).

16 IED Inc., forty-eighth session of the UN Commission on Human Rights, under Agenda item 9, (1992) p.1.

17 Ibid.

18 Ibid.

19 Ibid., p.1-2.

20 Ibid.

21 Ibid.

22 Ibid., p.2-3.

23 Ibid.

24 "Liberation, The Anti-Imperialist, Anti-Racist Organisation", forty-seventh session of the UN Commission on Human Rights, under Agenda item 12, February, (1991).

25 Ibid., p.2.

26 Ibid.

27 Moore. M., "Retreat from democracy in Sri Lanka?", in: Journal of Commonwealth and Comparative Politics, Vol.30, No.1, March, (1992), pp.64-84, p.78.

28 Ibid.

29 "A fistful of dollars", in: *The Sri Lanka Monitor*, No.33, October, (1990), p.2.

30 Quoted in a letter to Carver. R., Research Director of Africa, in: *The Guardian*, 10 July, (1990).

31 "British envoy expelled over lection complaint" in: *The Sri Lanka Monitor*, No.40, May, (1991) p.4.

32 "SAARC pledges poverty offensive", ibid, No.47 (December 1991), p.4.

33 "BBC interview with Tamil leader Prabhakaran", in: *Tamil Nation*, March, (1993), p.3.

34 Sri Lanka acceded to the International Covenant on Civil and Political Rights (ICCPR), (1966), and the International Covenant on Economic, Social and Cultural Rights (ICESCR), (1966), on 11 June (1980).

35 In response to an escalation of national reports on the violation of human rights in India, the Government of India also considered setting up a statutory National Human Rights Commission, namely for the reason that, "[I]n addition to this there was also the question of similar reports getting publicity in the Western press, which in turn influenced the policy-makers in these countries who quite often assume the role of

self-appointed custodians of human rights in the Third World countries and seek to interfere in these countries' affairs under the pretext of defence of human rights. Certainly, the country could not have allowed a situation to continue when an unbalanced picture of human rights record is being presented in the West". Prem Singh, "Human Rights Commission: Need for consensus", in: *Link*, 8 November, (1992), p.20.

36 "Paris blues", in: *The Sri Lanka Monitor*, No.48, February, (1992), p.4.

37 Japan pledged 20,550m yen on March 31 1993, under the 26th Official Development Assiatance (ODA) programme. The aid is intended to finance six high priority development projects designed to enhance the economic infrastructure in Sri Lanka. (Figures taken from: *SWB Weekly Economic Report*, part 3, Far East, 14 April, (1993).

38 Figures taken from : "Damned with faint praise", in: *The Sri Lanka Monitor*, No.48, January, (1992), p.4.

39 Figures taken from: "Broken promises", ibid., No.61, February, (1993), p.3.

40 Moore. M., p.83.

41 Dharmawardhamna. Anoj., "World Bank queries diversion of foreign aid", in: *The Island*, 23 June, (1993), p.10.

42 Figures taken from: "Militarisation in Sri Lanka", in: *Tamil Information*, No.24 July, (1993), p.1.

43 International Council of Voluntary Agencies (ICVA), forty-eighth session of the UN Commission on Human Rights, February, (1992), p.7.

44 Figures taken from SIPRI, 1992.

45 SIPRI, 1992, p.415.

46 *NewsLanka*, (November 14 1992), Issue 51.

47 "Arms trade", in: *The Sri Lanka Monitor*, No.58, November, (1992), p.2.

48 *Jane's Defence Weekly*, 23 January, (1993).

49 *The Island*, Vol.8, No.4, 27 January, (1993), p.4.

50 Canadian Human Rights Mission to Sri Lanka, "Canadian Huamn Rights Mission calls for immmediate internationally monitored ceasefire and negotiations to resolve the conflict in Sri Lanka", 5 February, (1992), p.2.

51 *The Island*, 10 February, (1993), p.2.

52 SIPRI, 1992, p.415.

53 Canadian Human Rights Mission to Sri Lanka, p.2.

54 *The Sri Lanka Monitor*, No.58, November, (1992), p.1.

55 Wijesinghe Sisiva., "Norway renews peace brokering offer", in: *The Island*, Vol.8, No.10, 10 March, (1993), p.2.

56 "Liberation, The Anti-Imperialist, Anti-Racist Organisation", forty-eighth session of the UN Commission on Human Rights, under Agenda item 10, p.2.

57 Sieghart. P., "Sri Lanka: A mounting tragedy of errors - Report of the International Commission of Jurists", (1984).

58 The NGOs who signed the joint statement included amongst others: Pax Christie International, the International League for the Rights and Liberation of Peoples, Centre Europe Tiers Monde, International Educational Development, the International Organisation for the Elimination of All Forms of Racial Discrimination and the World Confederation of Labour.

59 At the fiftieth session of the UN Human Rights Commission in 1994, under Agenda item 9, "The rights peoples to self-determination and its application to peoples under colonial or alien domination or foreign occupation", seventeen NGOs made a joint statement regarding the continuing armed conflict and the violations of humanitarian law in Sri Lanka.

60 The joint statement made by fifteen NGOs on "The situation in Sri Lanka" at the forty-ninth session of the UN Commission on Human Rights, Agenda item 9, 8 February, (1993).

61 "Internationalisation of Tamil struggle for self-determination gathers momentum", in: *Tamil Nation*, 15 February, (1992), at p.3.

62 Right of Reply by Ambassador Bernard A. B. Goonetilleke, on the "Situation in Sri Lanka", at the UN Commission on Human Rights, 8 February, (1993), p.1.

63 Ibid., p.3.

64 Ibid., p.2.

65 Figures taken from Susanne Goldenberg, "Muslim scepticism blocks way for Tamil Homeland", in: *The Guardian*, 14 April, (1993).

66 Over 100,000 Tamils have fled to Colombo from the North-East to join friends or relatives among the 150,000 Tamils who currently live in the capital, see "Crackdown in Colombo", in: *The Sri Lanka Monitor*, No. 58, November, (1992).

67 See "Muslims massacred in the East", in: *The Sri Lanka Monitor*, No. 57, October, (1992), p.1.

68 Figures taken from: "Refugee backlash in Europe", in: *The Sri Lanka Monitor*, No.45, October, (1991), p.4.

69 Figures taken from "Lankans under siege in South India", in: *The Sri Lanka Monitor*, No.38, March, (1991), p.2.

70 See "The battle for Jaffna" in: *The Sri Lanka Monitor*, No.53, June, (1992).

71 Tambiah, S. J., "Sri Lanka: Ethnic fratricide and the dismantling of democracy", (1986), p.180.

72 Ibid., p.180-181.

73 Right of Reply by Ambassador Bernard A. B. Goonetilleke, p.2.

74 Ibid., p.3.

75 Ibid.

76 6,000 Sri Lankan Tamil refugees in South India are reported to have voluntarily registered to return to Sri Lanka from mid-February, 1993. Figures taken from: "Limbo", in: *The Sri Lankan Monitor*, No.61, February, (1993), p.2.

77 "Passport to impunity: Western governments look the other way at UN Human Rights sessions", in: *The Sri Lankan Monitor*, No.61, February, (1993), p.3.

78 Christine Oddy, MEP, Midlands Central, Report of a visit to Sri Lanka, 8-12 November, (1993), pp.1-3, p.2.

79 Ibid., p.1.

80 See "The Human Rights situation of the Tamil-speaking people of Sri Lanka", Memorandum prepared for the fiftieth session of the UN Human Rights Commission, Geneva, February, (1994), Tamil Information Centre, London.

81 Permanent Mission of Sri Lanka, Situation Report, Part Five, "Prospects for a long term political solution", at the Forty-ninth session of the UN Commission on Human Rights, February-March, (1993), p.5.

82 Ibid.

83 Ibid.

84 Ibid., p.6.

85 Ibid.

86 Ibid.

87 Ibid.

88 The Canada-Asia Working Group Submission, prepared for the forty-ninth session of the UN Commission on Human Rights, February, (1993).

89 Figures taken from the Canada-Asia Working Group Submission, p.32. For a detailed account of the economic dimension of the Sri Lankan civil war, see: Samarasinghe and R. Coughan., (ed.) "Economic dimensions of ethnic conflict: International perspectives", Chapter Nine, (1991).

90 The Canada-Asia Working Group Submission, p.32.

91 Figures taken from the Canada-Asia Working Group Submission, p.33.

92 "Forum Statement", World Solidarity Forum on Sri Lanka for Justice and Peace, Chonburi, Thailand, 10 May, (1990), cited in Canada-Asia Working Group Submission, p.34.

93 Christine Oddy, p.2.

CHAPTER 17

Recommendations for the resolution of disputes relating to the right to self-determination

The empirical study of the international dimension of the ethnic conflict in Sri Lanka underscores the urgent need for the establishment of international procedures for the resolution of disputes relating to self-determination upon legal principles rather than on political expedience. These are necessary in order to minimise peoples' suffering, pain and dehumanisation while they are engaged in either pursuing or resisting the right of self-determination. The Human Rights Committee which could well have assumed that role, at least in respect of states parties to the *Optional Protocol*, has been persuaded that since the right of self-determination is a collective right, it may not arbitrate over such claims. The Commission on Human Rights which meets every year to consider *inter alia*, an item entitled "The Right of Peoples to Self-Determination", was revealed in Chapter 16 to be essentially a political institution, where decisions are usually based on political motivations. Similarly, the decisions of the United Nations General Assembly and the Security Council are more often than not, based on the constituent states' self-interest.

Clealry, additional legal and political attention needs to be given to elaborating the substantive content of, and a procedural mechanism for peoples to achieve their right to self-determination. Concepts such as sovereignty, statehood, nationalism, territorial integrity and discovery and settlement, based on the doctrine of *terra nullius* which have evolved in specific historical contexts, have not prevented human rights abuses or wars, and do not respond adequately to the complex and often contradictory requirements of the political, economic, and technological realities of the post-Cold War era. New solutions must be found that go beyond the current, limited domain of international law, so as to address the changing nature of state sovereignty and the implications of an increasingly interdependent and interpenetrative world, in which borders are becoming less relevant.

This chapter shall recommend ways in which the UN could more effectively deal with intra-state ethnic conflicts, which are the result of denials of claims to self-determination. The recommendations are based on the recommendations made at the Martin Ennals Memorial Symposium on Self-Determination in Saskatoon, Canada, in March 1993. The Symposium was originally organised by Martin Ennals himself, who recognised that events in the former Soviet Union, debates in Canada over the rights of Quebecans and demands of groups throughout Asia, Africa and Latin America, all drew on the right of peoples to self-determination, but that claims for the fulfilment of that right too often led to violence, human rights abuses and civil war.

"Nowhere is there a procedure of arbitration, no definition of terms, no UN body which will entertain the complaints about self-determination as such. It is a right which creates expectation without fulfilment. People are dying for that right, which is known to exist, but is nowhere defined."[1]

The following recommendations are seen as the first step in establishing the parameters of the right to self-determination of peoples and creating means of implementing a positive, practical and acceptable doctrine which is applicable internationally and without prejudice.

The UN and its member states should give serious consideration to the progressive development of the concept of self-determination, especially to the increasingly normative internal aspect of the right to self-determination, and to identifying or creating a mechanism which could consider claims to self-determination where there is a risk of disturbance of the peace or violations of fundamental human rights. It was suggested at the Symposium on Self-Determination, that such a mechanism could involve a new UN Commission on Self-determination (equivalent to the existing UN Commission on Human Rights), or it could expand the mandates of existing bodies such as the Trusteeship Council, Committee of 24, Fourth Committee of the General Assembly, or the Security Council. It was also suggested, that pursuant to article 36(3) of the UN Charter, the Security Council should consider referring appropriate situations to the International Court of Justice (ICJ) for an advisory opinion, or where the parties agree, a judgement. In whatever form this mechanism takes, the peoples concerned must be assured of having direct and effective access to any such procedure.

In a discussion paper presented by Lord Avebury, entitled "Self-determination: The way forward", it was tentatively suggested that the UN could appoint a High Commissioner for Self-determination, to whom claims would be referred in the first instance. The High Commissioner would be charged with the duty of examining all the claims, rejecting those which in his or her opinion were manifestly frivolous or ill-founded. The claims would then be analysed by the General Assembly according to special criteria, including, *inter alia*; previous history of statehood or existence as a separate territorial entity, geographical unity, ethnicity, language, religion, culture, existence of separate institutions, and evidence of the will to separation.

The High Commissioner could report on these criteria to the Committee of 24, renamed the Committee on Self-Determination, taking over the remaining cases of European decolonisation still on its agenda. It is worth noting at this juncture, that although it is popularly believed that the era of decolonisation has ended, several "leftovers" of colonialism still exist. Among them, is East Timor, the Portuguese colony which was occupied by Indonesia eighteen years ago, with the tacit approval of the British, Australian and United States governments, and thereby prevented from being decolonised.[2] Another instance is Tibet, which since 1949, has been under the alien occupation and domination of the People's Republic of China. Yet another example is Hong Kong, whose six million inhabitants are also being denied the right to self-determination, not by invasion, but by reason of an agreement between the colonial power and another sovereign state, an agreement by which the people of a free country are being stripped of their citizenship and are being handed over to a "geriatric autocracy".[3] Since that agreement was signed and ratified without consulting the people of Hong Kong, there appears to have been a conspiracy of silence within the international community.

The new Committee would be composed of experts in their own right, like the Sub-Commission on Protection of Minorities. It would have the power to recommend that a referendum be held in the territory concerned, and to make the necessary arrangements with the consent of the state or states concerned. It was suggested that as a corollary of this proposal, the High Commissioner and the Committee should have the right to examine applications for transfer of sovereignty by groups on the boundary of states. The Albanians of Kosovo for instance, the Romanians of Moldova, or the Somalis of Ogaden, might not constitute peoples within the meaning of the Charter and Covenants, but there should be peaceful means of deciding whether they should be reunited with their mother peoples if that is their wish.

The Symposium on Self-Determination maintained that national, ethnic, religious, linguistic and other minorities are entitled to respect and the fullest opportunity to maintain and develop their distinctive characteristics. Moreover, minorities lacking adequate resources to do so, should be accorded a fair share of public funds, sufficient to enable the preservation of their distinctive characteristics. Furthermore, States should, at a minimum, conform to the principles set forth in the Declaration on the Rights of Persons Belonging to National or Ethnic, Religious or Linguistic Minorities, which was adopted by the UN General Assembly, in December, 1992. It concluded that the legitimate rights of the majority in a state should be exercised in the context of effective participation by members of minorities in the larger society.

The Symposium on Self-Determination suggested that the UN should immediately establish a High Commissioner, Working Group or Special Rapporteur with appropriate resources, to monitor implementations of the Declaration on the Rights of Persons Belonging to National or Ethnic, Religious or Linguistic Minorities. It also suggested that similar action should be taken immediately upon adoption of the Declaration on the Rights of Indigenous Peoples, which was then being drafted by a Working Group of the Sub-Commission on Prevention of Discrimination and Protection of Minorities. It concluded that the peoples or minorities affected should have direct and effective access to any such person or body.

Furthermore, the Symposium recommended that the UN member states and the Secretary General should pay particular attention to claims for self-determination in implementing the Secretary General's *An Agenda for Peace*. Where legitimate claims for self-determination are denied, or illegitimate claims are made, there is an obvious potential for breaches of international peace and security. It therefore suggested that the range of options available to the Secretary General, from early warning, to peace-making, peace-keeping, and peace-enforcement, should be fully utilised. It concluded that the UN should consider the adoption of a convention or conventions to protect cultures and languages from destruction.

To assist the UN and to stimulate action by the international community, the Symposium further recommended the establishment of an independent non-governmental Commission on Self-Determination. It was proposed that this international non-governmental Commission could review the implementation of the right to self-determination and attempt to define procedures for making claims to self-determination justiciable.

"Such a move would recognise that for the time being, it would be unlikely that any Member State of the UN would initiate discussion of an idea which could threaten the territorial integrity of a friendly power. The States which might be the targets of claims to self-determination wield a great deal of political and economic power, and others would be loath to antagonise them. If, however, the proposal comes from Non-Governmental Organisation, it may be possible to promote a dispassionate discussion of its objective merits, as a means of solving long-running "domestic" conflicts."[4]

The Symposium recommended that this proposed non-governmental Commission on Self-Determination should be charged with: examining the scope and substance of the right to self-determination; identifying the relevant criteria for determining the legitimacy of a claim to self-determination; recommending particular mechanisms which would have the ability to decide such claims; proposing means of encouraging dialogue in respect of such claims; and suggesting effective ways in which the right to self-determination might be exercised in the face of resistance by those with the power to deny the right.

Furthermore, the Symposium proposed that the Commission on Self-Determination should receive information from all relevant sources and cooperate with existing institutions relevant to the issue of self-determination, including the International Commission on Global Governance. It suggested that members of the proposed Commission should serve in their individual capacity and the Commission's membership should reflect as broad a political and regional representation as possible. It concluded by stating that access to the proposed Commission by all concerned peoples, minorities, groups and individuals should be assured. Obviously, whether even a non-governmental Commission could be persuaded to espouse a people's plight will also depend on that NGOs' own agenda.

Clearly, many of the intra-state ethnic conflicts that currently consume numerous parts of the world, are the outcome of frustrated claims to self-determination. Whether they are well founded or not, the point is, that the conflicts are launched by people who see no prospect of achieving their aims by normal political means. The existence of mechanisms such as those tentatively discussed above, would at least provide the aggrieved groups with an impartial international tribunal at which their claims would be heard. It would provide a formal, quasi-legal structure for the claims, instead of considering each one on its separate merits *ad hoc*. Indeed, in domestic law, it is axiomatic that rights are enforceable, and that they can be tested in courts. To maintain peace and security in the world, international law has to be reinforced by corresponding mechanisms. At a time when many peoples are realising their aims fortuitously, as a result of the weakening of some of the centralised multi-national states, and when others are refusing to accept the status of marginalisation within existing polyethnic superstates, it is essential to create the means of orderly change, giving effect to the democratic will of those still oppressed under colonialism or alien and racist domination "in *all* its various manifestations and forms."

Notes

1 Statement and recommendations arising from the Martin Ennals Memorial Symposium on Self-Determination, Saskatoon, Canada, March, (1993), published by International Alert, (hereafter referred to as Symposium on Self-determination).

2 See: Pilger. J., "Distant Voices", which has been reissued by Vintage with a new section on his reporting from East Timor.

3 Jayawickrama. N., "The right of self-determination", Report of the Martin Ennals Memorial Symposium on Self-Determination, co-sponsored by the University of Saskatchewan and International Alert, p.5.

4 Lord Avebury, "Self-determination: The way forward", a discussion paper, published by International Alert, July, (1988), p.8.

Appendix I

Tamil United Liberation Front
Pannakam (Vaddukoddai Constituency) 14 May, 1976
Presided over by the late Mr. S.J.V. Chelvanayakam, QC, MP

The following Political Resolution was unanimously adopted.

Whereas throughout the centuries from the dawn of history the Sinhalese and Tamil nations have divided between them the possession of Ceylon, the Sinhalese inhabiting the interior of the country in its southern and western parts from the river Walawe to that of Chilaw and the Tamils possessing the Northern and Eastern districts.

And whereas the Tamil kingdom was overthrown in war and conquered by the Portuguese in 1619 and from them by the Dutch and the British in turn independent of the Sinhalese kingdoms.

And whereas the British Imperialists who ruled the territories of the Sinhalese and Tamil kingdoms separately joined under compulsion the territories of the Tamil kingdom to the territories of the Sinhalese kingdom for purposes of administrative conveniance on the recommendation of the Colebrooke Commission in 1833.

And whereas the Tamil leaders were in the forefront of the Freedom movement to rid Ceylon of colonial bondage which ultimately led to the grant of independence to Ceylon in 1948.

And whereas the foregoing facts of history were completely over-looked and power was transferred to the Sinhalese nation over the entire country on the basis of a numerical majority thereby reducing the Tamil nation to the position of a subject people.

And whereas successive Sinhalese governments since independence have always encouraged and fostered the aggressive nationalism of the Sinhalese people and have used their political power to the detriment of the Tamils by:

(a) Depriving one half of the Tamil people of their citizenship and franchise rights thereby reducing Tamil representation in Parliament,

(b) Making serious inroads into the territories of the former Tamil kingdom by a system of planned and state-aided Sinhalese colonisation and large scale regularisation of recently encouraged Sinhalese encroachments calculated to make the Tamils a minority in their own homeland,

(c) Making Sinhala the only official language throughout Ceylon thereby placing the stamp of inferiority on the Tamils and the Tamil language,

(d) Giving the foremost place to Buddhism under the Republican Constitution thereby reducing the Hindus, Christians and Muslims to second class status in this country,

(e) Denying to the Tamils equality of opportunity in the spheres of employment, education, land alienation and economic life in general and starving Tamil areas of large scale industries and development schemes thereby seriously endangering their very existence in Ceylon,

(f) Systematically cutting them off from the mainstream of Tamil cultures in South India while denying them opportunities of developing their language and culture in Ceylon thereby working inexorably towards the cultural genocide of the Tamils,

(g) Permitting and unleashing communal violence and intimidation against the Tamil-speaking people, as happened in Amparai and Colombo in 1956; all over the country in 1958; army reign of terror in the Northern and Eastern provinces in 1961; police violence at the International Tamil Research Conference in 1974 resulting in the death of nine persons in Jaffna: police and communal violence against Tamil-speaking Muslims at Puttalam and various other parts of Ceylon in 1976 - all these calculated to instil terror in the minds of the Tamil-speaking people thereby breaking their spirit and the will to resist the injustices heaped on them,

(h) By terrorising, torturing and imprisoning Tamil youths without trial for long periods on the flimsiest grounds,

(i) Capping it all by imposing on the Tamil nation a *constitution* drafted under conditions of Emergency without opportunities for free discussion by a constituent assembly elected on the basis of the Soulbury Constitution distorted by the Citizenship Laws resulting in weightage in representation to the Sinhalese majority thereby depriving the Tamils of even the remnants of safeguards they had under the earlier constitution.

And whereas all attempts by the various Tamil political paties to win their rights by co-operation with the governments, by parliamentary and extra-parliamentary agitations, by entering into pacts and understandings with successive Prime Ministers in order to achieve the bare minimum of political rights consistent with the self-respect of the Tamil people have proved to be futile;

And whereas the efforts of the All Ceylon Tamil Congress to ensure non-domination of the minorities by the adoption of a scheme of balanced representation in a Unitary Constitution have failed and even the meagre safeguards provided in article 29 of the Soulbury Constitution against discriminatory legislation have been removed by the Republican Constitution;

And whereas the proposals submitted to the Constituent Assembly by the Ilankai Thamil Arasu Kadchi for maintaining the unity of the country while preserving the integrity of the Tamil people by the establishment of an autonomous Tamil state within the framework of a Federal Republic of Ceylon were summarily and totally rejected without even the courtesy of a consideration of its merits;

And whereas the amendments to the basic resolutions intended to ensure the minimum of safeguards to the Tamil people moved on the basis of the nine point demands formulated at the conference of all Tamil political parties at Valvettithurai on 7th February, 1971 and by individual parties and Tamil members of Parliament including those now in the government party were rejected in toto by the government and Constituent Assembly;

And whereas even amendments to the draft proposals relating to language, religion and fundamental rights including one calculated to ensure that at least the provision of the Tamil Language (Special Provisions) Regulations of 1966 be included in the Constitution were defeated resulting in the boycott of the Constituent Assembly by a large majority of the Tamil members of Parliament;

And whereas the Tamil Liberation Front, after rejecting the Republic Constitution adopted on the 22nd of May, 1972 presented a six point demand to the Prime Minister and the Government on 25th June, 1972 and gave three months time within which the government was called upon to take meaningful steps to amend the Constitution so as to meet the aspirations of the Tamil nation on the basis of the six points and informed the government that it failed to do so the Tamil Liberation Front would launch non-violent direct action against the government in order to win the freedom and the rights of the Tamil nation on the basis of the right of self-determination;

And whereras this last attempt by the Tamil Liberation Front to win Constitutional recognition of the rights of the Tamil nation without jeopardising the unity of the country was callously ignored by the Prime Minister and the Government;

And wheras the opportunity provided by the Tamil Liberation leader to vindicate the Government's contention that their consitution had the backing of the Tamil people, by resigning fro his membership of the National State Assembly and creating a by-election was deliberately put off for over two years in utter disregard of the democratic right of the Tamil voters of Kankesanthurai; and

Whereas in the by-election held on the 6th February, 1975 the voters of Kankesanthurai by a preponderant majority not only rejected the Republican Constitution imposed on them by the Sinhalese Government but also gave a mandate to Mr S.J.V. Chelvanayakam, QC and through him to the Tamil Liberation Front for the restoration and reconstitution of the Free, Sovereign, Secular, Socialist State of TAMIL EELAM.

The first National Convention of the Tamil United Liberation Front meeting at Pannakam (Vaddukoddai Constituency) on the 14th day of May 1976, hereby declares that the Tamils of Ceylon, by virtue of their great language, their religions, their separate culture and heritage, their history of independent existence as a separate state over a distinct territory for several centuries till they were conquered by the armed might of the European invaders, and above all by their will to exist as a separate entity ruling themselves in their own territory, are a nation distinct and apart from the Sinhalese and their constitution announces to the world that the Republican Constitution of 1972 has made the Tamils a slave nation ruled by the new colonial masters, the Sinhalese, who are using the power they have wrongly usurped to deprive the Tamil nation of its territory, language, citizenship, economic life, opportunities of employment and education, thereby destroying all attributes of nationhood of the Tamil people.

And therefore, while taking note of the reservations in relation to its committment to the setting up of a separate state of TAMIL EELAM expressed by the Ceylon Workers Congress as a Trade Union of the Plantation Workers, the majority of whom live and work outside the Northern and Eastern areas,

This convention resolves that the restoration and reconstitution of the Free, Sovereign, Secular, Socialist State of TAMIL EELAM based on the right of self-determination inherent to every nation has become inevitable in order to safeguard the very existence of the Tamil nation in this country.

Appendix II

The Sixth Amendment to the Constitution, 8th August, 1983.

WHEREAS Sri Lanka is a Free, Sovereign, Independent and Unitary State and it is the duty of the State to safeguard the independence, sovereignty, unity and the territorial integrity of Sri Lanka:

AND WHEREAS the independence, sovereignty, unity and the territorial integrity of Sri Lanka has been threatened by activities of certain persons, political parties and other associations and organisations:

AND WHEREAS it has become necessary to prohibit such activities and to provide punishments therefor:

3. The following Article is hereby inserted after Article 157, and shall have effect as Article 157A, of the Constitution:-

157A. (1) No person shall, directly or indirectly, in or outside Sri Lanka, support, espouse, promote, finance, encourage or advocate the establishment of a separate State within the territory of Sri Lanka.

(2) No political party or other association or organisation shall have as one of its aims or objects the establishment of a separate State within the territory of Sri Lanka.

(3) Any person who acts in contravention of the provisions of paragraph (1) shall, on conviction by the Court of Appeal, after trial on indictment and according to such procedure as may be prescribed by law, -

(a) be subject to civic disability for such period not exceeding seven years as may be determined by such Court;

(b) forfeit his movable and immovable property other than such property as is determined by an order of such Court as being necessary for the sustenance of such person and his family;

(c) not be entitled to civic rights for such period not exceeding seven years as may be determined by such Court; and

(d) if he is a Member of Parliament or a person in such service or holding such office as is referred to in paragraph (1) of Article 165, cease to be such Member or to be in such service or to hold such office.

Appendix III

The Indo-Sri Lanka Accord, 1987

The President of Sri Lanka and the Prime Minister of India, having met on July 29, 1987:

"Attaching utmost importance to nurturing and strengthening the traditional friendship of Sri Lanka and India, and acknowledging the imperative need of resolving the ethnic problem of Sri Lanka, and the consequent violence, and for the safety, well-being and prosperity of people belonging to all communities in Sri Lanka,

Have this day entered into the following Agreement to fulfil this objective.

In this context,

1.1 *desiring* to preserve the unity, sovereignty and territorial integrity of Sri Lanka;

1.2 *acknowledging* that Sri Lanka is multi-ethnic and a multi-lingual plural society consisting, inter alia, of Sinhalese, Tamils, Muslims (Moors), and Burghers;

1.3 *recognising* that each ethnic group has a distinct cultural and linguistic identity which has to be carefully nurtured;

1.4 *also recognising* that the Northern and Eastern Provinces have been areas of historical habitation of Sri Lankan Tamil speaking peoples, who have at all times hitherto lived together in this territory with other ethnic groups;

1.5 *conscious* of the necessity of strengthening the forces contributing to the unity, sovereignty and territorial integrity of Sri Lanka, and preserving its character as a multi-ethnic, multi-lingual and multi-religious plural society, in which all citizens can live in equality, safety and harmony, and prosper and fulfil their aspirations;"

2. Resolve that:

2.1 Since the Government of Sri Lanka proposes to permit adjoining Provinces to join to form one administrative unit and also be a Referendum to separate as may be permitted to the Northern and Eastern Provinces as outlined below:

2.2 During the period, which shall be considered an interim period, (i.e. from the date of the elections to the Provincial Council, as specified in para 2.8, to the date of the referendum as specified in para 2.3,) the Northern and Eastern Provinces as now constituted, will form one administrative unit, having one elected Provincial Council. Such a unit will have one Governor, one Chief Minister and one Board of Ministers.

2.3 There will be a referendum on or before 31st December, 1988 to enable the people of the Eastern Province to decide whether:

(a) The Eastern Province should remain linked with the Northern Province as one administrative unit, and continue to be governed together with the Northern Province as specified in para 2.2, or

(b) The Eastern Province should constitute a separate administrative unit having its own distinct Provincial Council with a separate Governor, Chief Minister and Board of Ministers.

The President may, at his discretion, decide to postpone such a referendum.

2.8 Elections to Provincial Councils, will be held within the next three months, in any event before 31st December 1987. Indian observers will be invited for elections to the Provincial Council of the North and East.

2.9 The Emergency will be lifted in the Eastern and Northern Provinces by August 15, 1987. A cessation of hostilities will come into effect all over the Island within 48 hours of the signing of this Agreement. All arms presently held by militant groups will be surrendered...

Consequent to the cessation of hostilities and the surrender of arms by militant groups, the Army and other security personnel will be confined to barracks in camps as on 25th May 1987. The process of surrendering of arms and the confining of security personnel moving back to barracks shall be completed within 72 hours of the cessation of hostilities coming into effect.

2.14 The Government of India will underwrite and guarantee the resolutions, and co-operate in the implementation of these proposals.

2.16 These proposals are also conditional to the Government of India taking the following actions if any militant groups operating in Sri Lanka do not accept this framework of proposals for a settlement, namely,

(c) In the event that the Government of Sri Lanka requests the Government of India to afford military assistance to implement these proposals the Government of India will co-operate by giving to the Government of Sri Lanka such military assistance as and when requested."

Appendix IV

UN Commission on Human Rights
Forty-Ninth Session

<u>Agenda Item 12: Question on the violation of human rights and Fundamental freedoms in any part of the world, with particular reference to colonial and other dependent countries and territories</u>

<u>Situation of Human Rights in Sri Lanka</u>

The Commission on Human Rights

<u>Guided</u> by the principles embodied in the Charter of the United Nations, the Universal Declaration of Human Rights and the International Covenant on Human Rights,

<u>Reaffirming</u> that all Member States have an obligation to promote and protect human rights and fundamental freedoms to fulfill the obligations they have undertaken under the various international instruments in this field,

<u>Recalling</u> its resolution 1987/61 regarding the situation in Sri Lanka,

<u>Recalling also</u> the Chairman's Statement (E/CN.4/1992/84, para. 476) adopted unanimously at the 48th session of the Commission,

<u>Taking Note</u> of the contents of the Reports of the Working Group on Enforced or Involuntary Disappearances (E/CN.4/1993/25 and E/CN.4/1993/25/Add.1) the Report of the Special Rapporteur on Torture and Other Cruel, Inhuman or Degrading Treatment or Punishment (E/CN.4/1993/26) and the Report of the Special Rapporteur on Extrajudicial, Summary or Arbitrary Executions,

<u>Concerned</u> that, despite a reduction in disappearances in 1992, the Working Group has observed that,

(a) "disappearances persist in Sri Lanka at a level that should be of serious concern to the Commission on Human Rights" (E/CN.4/1993/25/Add.1 para 128), and that "the situation regarding disappearances in Sri Lanka continues to be serious" (para. 147),

(b) "the single most important factor contributing to the phenomenon of disappearances is that of impunity" (para. 87),

(c) "there is no official mechanism in place in Sri Lanka with the principal task of clarifying the fate of more than 12,000 outstanding cases of disappearances reported to the Working Group" (para. 133), and

(d) only a few of the recommendations of the Working Group had been implemented by the Government of Sri Lanka (para. 131),

<u>Noting</u> that the Working Group on Disappearances has recommended that the "Commission on Human Rights may wish to follow developments in this regard from year to year" (E/CN.4/1993/25/Add.1, para. 131),

<u>Deeply Concerned</u> about the level of other violations of human rights notably arbitrary detention, torture, summary or arbitrary execution and the infringement of rights such as freedom of the press and freedom of association,

<u>Deeply Regretting</u> the continuation of the armed conflict in the north and east of Sri Lanka resulting in considerable loss of life and property and the displacement of tens of thousands of people,

<u>Deeply Concerned</u> by the non-observance by the parties to the conflict of internationally accepted norms of humanitarian law as set down in Common Article 3 of the Geneva Conventions of 1949,

1.<u>Expresses</u> grave concern at the level of gross violations of human rights in Sri Lanka,

2.<u>Urges</u> the Government of Sri Lanka to ensure full respect for human rights and fundamental freedoms,

3.Calls upon the Government of Sri Lanka to appoint appropriate independent judicial commissions or tribunals to investigate all cases of
enforced or involuntary disappearances, summary or arbitrary executions
and cases of torture that have already occurred,

4.Urges the Government of Sri Lanka to cooperate with the Commission
on Human Rights and, in particular, to help clarify the pending cases of
enforced or involuntary disappearances noted in the reports on the
Working Group on Enforced or Involuntary Disappearances, and to com-
municate to the Commission new measures the government of Sri Lanka
may take in the field of human rights,

5.Calls upon the Government of Sri Lanka and all other parties to the
conflict to strictly adhere to the obligations under Common Article 3 of
the Geneva Convention,

6.Condemns the Liberation Tigers of Tamil Eelam (LTTE) which is
engaged in summary or arbitrary executions of non-combatant civilians,
the practice of torture, abductions and arbitrary detention of persons,

7.Urges the government of Sri Lanka and other parties to the conflict to
seek a cessation of hostilities with a view to achieving a political solution
to the conflict through negotiations among all concerned parties and to
obtain the assistance of the Secretary General of the United Nations in
any mediation that may become necessary,

9.Decides to continue its consideration of the situation of human rights in
Sri Lanka under the present agenda item at its fiftieth session.

Table 1

Population - Ethnic composition

Ethnic Communities Sri Lanka

	Numbers	%
Total	14,850,000	100.0
Sinhalese	10,989,000	74.0
Tamils	1,871,000	12.6
"Up Country" Tamils	817,000	5.5
Muslims (Malays & Moors)	1,054,000	7.1
Others (inc. Burghers)	119,000	0.8

Figures taken from the Department of Census and Statistics, Census of Population and Housing, Sri Lanka, 1981.

Table 2

Population - Eastern Province

Year	Sinhalese	%	Tamils	%	Muslims	%
1921	8744	4.5	103251	53.5	75992	39.4
1946	23456	8.4	146059	52.3	109024	39.1
1953	46470	13.1	167898	47.3	135322	38.1
1963	109690	20.1	246120	45.1	185750	34.0
1971	148572	20.7	315560	43.9	248567	34.6
1981	243358	24.9	409451	41.9	315201	32.2

Figures taken from the Department of Census and Statistics, Census of Population and Housing, Sri Lanka, 1981

380

MAP 1

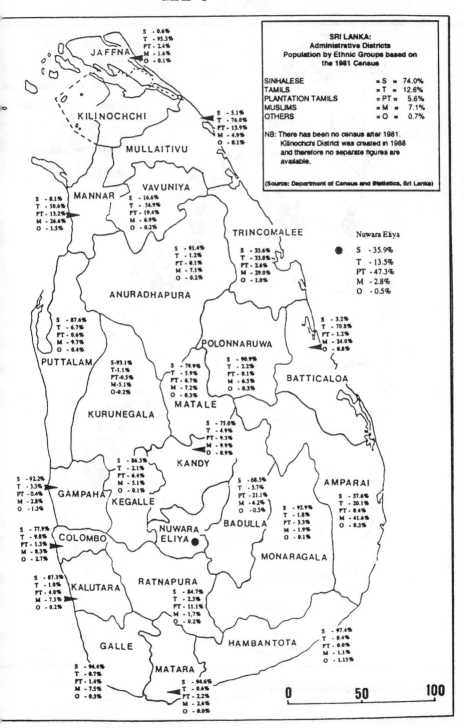

MAP 11

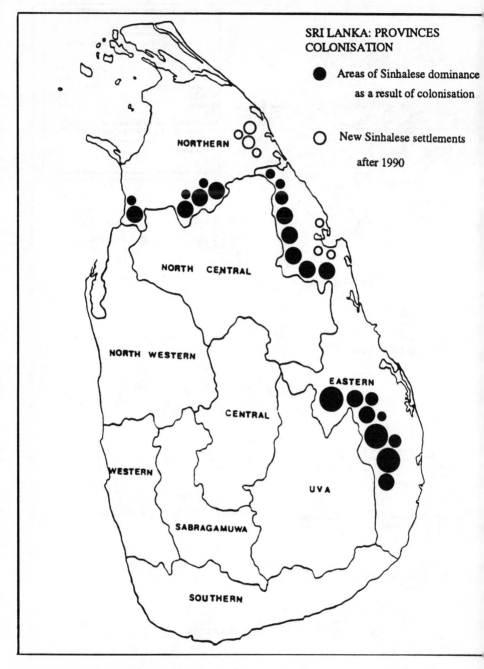

SRI LANKA: PROVINCES
COLONISATION

● Areas of Sinhalese dominance
as a result of colonisation

○ New Sinhalese settlements
after 1990

NORTHERN

NORTH CENTRAL

NORTH WESTERN

CENTRAL

EASTERN

WESTERN

UVA

SABRAGAMUWA

SOUTHERN

Source: Tamil Information Centre   0   50   100 km

Select Bibliography

Alexander & Freidlander., (eds.), "Self-determination: National, regional and global dimensions", (1980), Westview Press, Boulder, Colorado.

Anderson. B., "Imagined communities", (1983), Verso.

Brownlie. I., "Principles of public international law", (1979), Clarendon Press, Oxford.

Buchheit. L.C., "Secession: The legitimacy of self-determination", (1978), Yale University Press, New Haven/London.

Cassese. A., "International law in a divided world", (1990), Clarendon Press, Oxford.

Chandra. S., (ed.), "Minorities in national and international laws", (1985), Deep & Deep Publications, New Delhi.

Cristescu. A., Special Rapporteur of the UN Sub-Commission on Prevention of Discrimination and Protection of Minorities, "The right to self-determination: Historical and current development on the basis of United Nations instruments", United Nations Department of Public Information, (1978).

De Silva. K.M., "A history of Sri Lanka", (1982), C. Hurst & Company, London.

De Silva. K.M., "Managing ethnic tensions in multi-ethnic societies: Sri Lanka 1880-1985", (1986), University Press of America, Inc.

De Silva. K.M., "Sri Lanka, a survey", (1977), University of Hawaii Press, Honolulu.

383

Emerson. R., "From empire to nation: The rise to self-determination of Asian and African peoples", (1960), Harvard, Harvard University Press.

Emerson. R., "Self-determination revisited in the era of decolonisation", (1964), Center for International Affairs, Harvard University.

Franck. T., "Nation against nation: What happened to the U.N. dream and what the U.S. can do about it", (1985), Oxford University Press.

Furedi. F., "The new ideology of imperialism: Renewing the moral imperative.", (1994), Pluto Press.

Gellner. E., "Nations and nationalism", (1983), Blackwell.

Goldmann. R.B., & Wilson. A.J., (eds.), "From independence to statehood: Managing ethnic conflict in five African and Asian states", (1984), Pinter Publishers, London.

Gurr. T.R., "Minorities at risk: A global view of ethnopolitical conflicts", (1993), United States Institute of Peace.

Hall. R.L., (ed.), "Ethnic autonomy-comparative dynamics: The Americas, Europe and the developing world", (1979), Pergamon, New York.

Hannum. H., "Autonomy, sovereignty, and self-determination: The accommodation of conflicting rights", (1990), University of Pennsylvania Press, Philadelphia.

Helgesen. J., & Rosas. A., "The strength of diversity: Human rights and pluralist democracy", (1992), International Studies in human rights, Martinus Nijhoff Publishers, Netherlands.

Heraclides, A., "The self-determination of minorities in international politics", (1991), Frank Cass and Company Limited, England.

Higgins. R., "The development of international law through the political organs of the United Nations", (1963), Oxford University Press, London.

Hobsbawm. E., "Nations and nationalism since 1870", (1992), Harvard.

Ignatieff. M., "Blood and belonging: Journeys into the new nationalism", (1993), BBC Books, Chatto and Windus.

Islam. M.R., "Bangladesh liberation movement", (1987), University Press Ltd.

Jayawickrama. N., "The right to self-determination", Report of the Martin Ennals Memorial Symposium on Self-Determination, Saskatoon, Canada, March 3-6, (1993), International Alert, London.

Jupp. J., "Sri Lanka: Third world democracy", (1978), Franck Cass, London.

Lauren. P.G., "Power and prejudice: The politics and diplomacy of racial discrimination", (1988), Westview Press Inc., Boulder & London.

Lenin. V., "Collected Works", (1930), New York.

Liberation Tigers of Tamil Eelam, "An autopsy on autonomy: A provisional assessment of the Thirteenth Amendment to the Constitution of Sri Lanka", (1988), Political Committee, London.

Liberation Tigers of Tamil Eelam, "Indictment against Sri Lanka", (1993) Legal & Human Rights Division, International Secretariat, London.

Liberation Tigers of Tamil Eelam, "The Indo-Sri Lanka Accord and the Thirteenth Amendment to the Sri Lankan Constitution", London.

Lutz., Hannum., Burke., (eds.), "New directions in human rights", (1989), University of Pennsylvania Press, Philadelphia.

Macartney, W.J. Allan., (ed.), "Self-determination in the Commonwealth", (1988), Aberdeen University Press.

Manogaran. C., "Ethnic conflict and reconciliation in Sri Lanka", (1987), University of Hawaii Press, Honolulu.

Manor. J., (ed.), "Rethinking third world politics", (1991), Longman.

Manor. J., (ed.), "Sri Lanka: In change and crisis", (1984), Croom Helm, London.

Mayall. J., "Nationalism and international society", (1990), Cambridge University Press.

Nanda., Scarritt., & Shepherd., (eds.), "Global human rights: Public policies, comparative measures, and NGO strategies", (1985), Westview Press, Boulder, Colorado.

Nevitte. N., & Kennedy. C. H., (eds.), "Ethnic preferences and public policy in developing states", (1986), Lynne Reinner Publishers Inc., Boulder, Colorado.

Parker. K., "Self-determination of peoples and the Tamil national struggle", International Federation of Tamils, London.

Piyadasa. L., "Sri Lanka: The holocaust and after", (1984), Marram, London.

Ponnambalam. S., "Sri Lanka: The national question and the Tamil liberation struggle", (1983), Zed Press, London.

Premdas. R., Samarasinghe. S.W.R.de A., & Anderson. A., (eds.), "Secessionist movements in comparative perspective", (1990), Pinter Publishers, London.

Ragupathy. P., "Tamil social formation in Sri Lanka: A historical outline", (1986), Institute of Research & Development.

Rajanayagam. P., "Arrest, detention, and torture", (1987), Tamil Information Centre and Human Rights Council.

Renteln. A. D., "International human rights: Universalism versus relativism", (1990), Sage, Newbury Park, California.

Rupesinghe. K., (ed.), "Ethnic conflict and human rights", (1988), The United Nations University and the Norwegian University Press.

Roberts. M., (ed.), "Collective identities, nationalisms and protest in modern Sri Lanka", (1979), Colombo Catholic Press, Marga Institute, Colombo, Sri Lanka.

Ronen. D., "The quest for self-determination", (1979), Yale Unversity Press, New Haven/London.

Rousseau. J., "The Social Contract", (1968), Penguin Books Ltd., London.

Ryan. S., "Ethnic conflict and international relations", (1990), Dartmouth Publishing Company Ltd, England.

Said. E.W., "The question of Palestine", (1992), Vintage, London.

Samarasinghe. S.W.R.de A., & Coughlan. R., "Economic dimensions of ethnic conflict: International perspectives", (1991), Pinters Publishers, London.

Sarayanarayan. P.S., "The peace trap: An Indo-Sri Lankan political crisis", (1988), Affiliated East-West Press Pulbications Ltd.

Satyendra. N., "Thirteenth Amendment to Sri Lankan Constitution", (1988), London Tamil Forum, London.

Saxena. J. N., "Self-determiriation: From Biafra to Bangla Desh", (1978), Konarks Publishing Pvt. Ltd.

Seevaratnam. N., (ed.), "The Tamil national question and the Indo-Sri Lanka Accord", (1989), Konarak Publishers, Delhi.

Shepherd. G.W., Nanda. V. P., (ed.), "Human rights and third world development", (1985), Greenwood Press, Westport, Connecticut/London.

Shiels. F.L., (ed.), "Ethnic separatism and world politics", (1984), University Press of America, Lanham, New York.

Silva. K.M. de., (ed.), "Sri Lanka: A survey", (1977), C. Hurst & Co., London.

Silva de K.M. & May. R.J. (eds.), "Internationalisation of ethnic conflict", (1991), Pinter Publishers, London.

Smith. A., "National identity", (1991), Penguin, London.

Steinberg. J., "Locke, Rousseau and the idea of consent: An enquirey into the liberal democratic theory of political obligation", (1978), Greenwood Press, Westport, Connecticut/London.

Tambiah. S.J., "Sri Lanka: Ethnic franticide and the dismantling of democracy", (1986), I.B. Tauris & Co. Ltd., London.

Twining. W., (ed.), "Issues of self-determination", (1991), Aberdeen University Press.

Vije. M., "Sri Lanka: Economic blockade", (1993), Tamil Information Centre, London.

Wilson. A.J., "The break-up of Sri Lanka: The Sinhalese-Tamil conflict", (1988), C. Hurst & Company, London.

Wirsing. R.G., (ed.), "Protection of ethnic minorities: comparative perspectives", (1987), Pergamon Press, New York.

Journals

Beran. H., "A liberal theory of secession", in: Political Studies, Vol.18, (1984), pp.25-32.

Boutros-Boutros Ghali., "U.N. peace-keeping in a new era: A new chance for peace", in: The World Today, Vol.49, No.4, pp.66-69.

Brillmayer. L., "Secession and self-determination: A territorial interpretation", in: Yale Journal of International Law, Vol.16, (1991), pp.177-202.

Burger. A.S., "Policing a communal society", in: Asian Survey, Vol.27, No.7, (1987), p.822-833.

Codrington. H.W., "The decline of the medieval Sinhalese kingdom", in: Journal of Royal Asiatic (Ceylon), Vol.VII, (1959), pp.93-103.

Connor. W., "Nation building or nation destroying?", in: World Politics, Vol.24, (1971-72), pp.319-355.

Connor. W., "Self-determination: The new phase", in: World Politics, Vol.20, (1967), pp.30-53.

Denis. A., & Fernando. N., "Peninsula Jaffna from ancient to medieval times", in: Journal of Royal Asiatic Society of Sri Lanka, Vol.XXXII, (1987/88), pp.63-90.

De Silva. C.R., "Weightage in university admissions: Standardisation and district quotas in Sri Lanka", in: Modern Ceylon Studies, Vol.5, No.2, July, (1974).

Donnelly. J., "Human dignity, human rights, and political regimes", in: American Political Science Review, Vol.80, No.3, (1986), pp.801-817.

Donnelly. J., "Human rights and human dignity: An analytic critique of non-western conceptions of human rights", in: The American Political Science Review, Vol.76, (1982), pp.303-316.

Dyke. V.V., "The individual, the state, and ethnic communities in political theory", in: World Politics, Vol.29, (1976-77), pp.343-369.

Emerson. R., "Self-determination", in: American Journal of International Law, 65, (1971), pp.459-475.

Franck. T.M., "The emerging right to democratic governance", in: American Journal of International Law, 86, (1992), pp.46-91.

Fuller. E., "Mediators for Transcaucasia's conflict", in: The World Today, Vol.49, No.5, May, (1993), pp.89-92.

Giddens. A., "Dare to care, conserve and repair", in: NewStatesman Society, 29th October, (1993), pp.18-20.

Greenwood. C., "Is there a right of humanitarian intervention?", in: The World Today, Vol.49, No.2, (1993), pp.34-40.

Hellmann. D., "The concept of a "Tamil Homeland" in Sri Lanka - its meaning and development", in: South Asia, Vol.XIII, No.2, (1990), pp.79-110.

Hennayake. S.K., "The peace accord and the Tamils in Sri Lanka", in: Asian Survey, Vol.29, No.4, (1989), pp.401-415.

Higgins. R., "Self-determination", (1991), Hague lecture, (unpublished paper), pp.1-25.

Higgins. R., "The evolution of the right of self-determination: Commentary on Professor Franck's paper", pp.1-6.

Indrapala. K., "Early Tamil settlements in Ceylon" in: Journal of the Royal Asiatic Society (Ceylon), Vol.XIII, (1969), pp.43-63.

Kamanu, O.S., "Secession and the right of self-determination: an OAU dilemma", in: Journal of Modern African Studies, (1974), pp.355-370.

Kearney. R.N., "Language and the rise of separatism", in: Asian Survey, Vol.18, (1978), pp.521-534.

Kiwanuka. R.N., "The meaning of "people" in the African Charter on Human and Peoples Rights", in: The American Journal of International Law, Vol.82, (1988), pp.80-101.

Mathews. B., "District Development Councils in Sri Lanka", in: Asian Survey, Vol.22, No.5, (1982), pp.1117-1134.

Mathews. B., "Sri Lanka in 1989: Peril and good luck", in: Asian Survey, Vol. 30, No.2, (1990), pp.144-149.

Meadwell. H., "The politics of nationalism in Quebec", in: World Politics, 45 January, (1993), pp.203-41.

Mendis. G.C., "The evolution of a Ceylonese nation", in: Journal of Royal Asiatic Society (Ceylon), Vol.XI, (1967), pp.1-22.

Moore. M., "Retreat from democracy in Sri Lanka?", In: <u>Journal of Commonwealth & Comparative Politics</u>, Vol.30, No.1, March, (1992), pp.64-84.

Nanda, V.P., "Self-determination in international law: The tragic tale of two cities - Islamabad (West Pakistan) and Dacca (East Pakistan)", in: <u>American Journal of International Law,</u> (1972), pp.321-336.

Nixon. C.R., "Self-determination: The Nigeria/Biafra case", in: <u>World Politics,</u> Vol.24, (1971-72), pp.473-497.

Palley. C., "The international protection of minorities", in: <u>Minority Rights Group Report</u>, No.41.

Paranavitna. S., "The Arya kingdom in North Ceylon" in: <u>Journal of the Royal Asiatic Society (Ceylon)</u>, Vol.VII, Part 2, (1961), pp.175-224.

Peebles. P., "Colonisation and ethnic conflict in the Dry Zone of Sri Lanka", in: <u>The Journal of Asian Studies</u>, 49, No.1, February, (1990), pp.30-55.

Peiris. G.L., "Provincial autonomy within a unitary constitutional frame-work: The Sri Lankan crisis", in: <u>CILSA</u> , XXII, (1989), pp.165-189.

Perumal. C.A., & Thandavan. R., "Ethnic violence in Sri Lanka: Causes and consequences", in: <u>The Indian Journal of Political Science</u>, Vol.50, No.1, (1989), pp.1-17.

Pfaffenberger. B., "The political construction of defensive nationalism: The 1968 temple-entry crisis in northern Sri Lanka", in: <u>The Journal of Asian Studies</u>, 49, No.1, February, (1990), pp.78-96.

Phadnis. U., "Keeping the Tamils internal", in: <u>Far Eastern Economic Review</u>, March 25, (1972), pp.21-22.

Pilger. J., "The US fraud in Africa: Operation Restore Hope is part of a new age of imperialism", in: <u>NewStatesman Society</u>, 8 January (1993), pp.10-11.

Rao. M.K., "Right of self-determination in the post-colonial era: A survey of juristic opinion and state practice", in: Indian Journal of International Law, Vol.28, No.1, (1988), pp.58-71.

Reisman. W.M., "Sovereignty and human rights in contemporary international law", in: The American Journal of International Law, Vol. 84, (1990), pp.866-876.

Roberts. M., "Ethnic conflict in Sri Lanka and Sinhalese perspectives: Barriers to accommodation", in: Modern Asian Studies, Vol.12, No.3, (1978), pp.353-376.

Roberts. M., "Nationalism, the past and the present: The case of Sri Lanka", in: Ethnic and Racial Studies, Vol.16, No.1, January, (1993).

Sabaratnam. L., "Intra-ethnic stratification and ethno-nationalism", in: Journal of Developing Societies, Vol.5, (1989), pp.15-29.

Schwarz. W., "The Tamils of Sri Lanka", in: Minority Rights Group Report, No.25.

Shastri. A., "The material basis for separatism: The Tamil Eelam movement in Sri Lanka", in: The Journal of Asian Studies, 49, No.1, (February, 1990), pp.56-77.

Spencer. J., "Problems in the analysis of communal violence", in: Contributions to Indian Sociology, 26, 2, (1992), pp.261-279.

Stockholm International Peace Research Institute (Sipri) Yearbook 1993: World armaments and disarmament.

Thornberry. P., "Minorities and human rights law", in: Minority Rights Group Report, No.73.

Thornberry. P., "Self-determination, minorities, human rights: A review of international instruments", in: International and Comparative Law Quarterly, Vol.38, (1989), pp.867-889.

Viswanathan. V.N., "Indo-Sri Lankan relations -towards confidence building", in: India Quarterly, 46, (1990), pp.90-95.

Warnapala. W.A., "The All Party Conference in Sri Lanka", in: India Quarterly, 47, (1991), pp.39-62.

Newspapers and periodicals

The Economist, London.

The Financial Times, London.

Frontline, Madras, India.

The Guardian, London.

The Independent, London.

India Today, India.

The Island, Colombo, Sri Lanka.

Link, India.

Newslanka, London.

The Sri Lanka Monitor, produced by the British Refugee Council, London.

Tamil Information, News Bulletin of the Tamil Information Centre, London.

Tamil Nation, London.

Index